Napier

Napier

The first to wear the green

David Venables

Foreword by Bill Boddy, MBE

First published 1998

British Library Cataloguing-in-Publication Data:
A catalogue record for this book is
available from the British Library

ISBN 0 85429 989 0

Library of Congress catalog card number 97-76835

Haynes North America Inc,
861 Lawrence Drive, Newbury Park,
California 91320, USA

G.T. Foulis & Company is an imprint of
Haynes Publishing, Sparkford, Nr Yeovil, Somerset BA22 7JJ

Tel: 01963 440635 Fax: 01963 440001
Int. tel: +44 1963 440635 Fax: +44 1963 440001

E-mail: sales@haynes-manuals.co.uk
Web site: http://www.haynes.com

Designed & typeset by G&M, Raunds, Northamptonshire
Printed and bound in Italy by G. Canale & C. S.p.A. – Borgaro Torinese (Turin)

Frontispiece: Selwyn Edge using the L48, fitted with headlights, to practise at Brooklands prior to the 24-hour record run in June 1907. Dario Resta is in the passenger seat. (John Maitland Collection)

Contents

Foreword

WE have waited a long time for the full story of the part played by Napier in establishing British prestige in the early days of motor racing. Who better to unravel it than David Venables? For it is a complex dose of motoring history. The late Anthony Heal first drew attention to it many years ago with an article in *Motor Sport* entitled 'The First to Wear the Green', which title David has retained for this book.

Although Napier green became the official British racing colour during motor sport's pioneering years, until now the story of S.F. Edge's Napier team-cars has been largely ignored. In this important contribution to motoring history, David expounds the marque's performance and successes, an awesome task, in the execution of which he ackowledges the help received from people who still hold original Napier documents or who had worked at Acton – Guy Griffiths, for instance, who knows so many of the people behind the cars and the stories associated with them.

Although, in Napier days, Herbert Austin raced Wolseley Beetles, Napier was the top British marque, both on the track and on the road, until – in the luxury road-car field – Rolls-Royce came up with the 40–50hp 'Silver Ghost'. But this book is about Napier's career in *racing*, and about how its wonderful Lion aero engine enabled Sir Malcolm Campbell, Sir Henry Segrave and John Cobb to win the land speed record for Britain between 1927 and 1947, and secured for Cobb the all-time Brooklands lap record and more besides.

The book opens with a valuable account of the early races, incidentally making the little-known point that it was not entirely the accidents in the 1903 Paris–Madrid event that resulted in the ban on open-road racing in France. The Napier racing story is a complicated one, because Edge used various drivers and a number of different cars at Brooklands, the swapping about of which has, up till now, never been properly sorted out. The author, however, has succeeded in this, and has tackled other Napier mysteries too, such as the weight of the 50hp racer; how Edge's Napier was able to win the Gordon Bennett accolade in 1902 without getting further than Innsbruck in the race to Vienna; and why the two contests were combined. Indeed, all students of motor racing evolution will benefit from reading the opening chapters.

Later, other Napier posers are tackled – had a car actually been built by the time of the 1908 French GP, when it was known that Napier's entry with detachable wheels would be refused? And what exactly was the cause of the dismal retirement of Newton's Napier in the much-publicised match race with Nazzaro's Fiat at Brooklands in 1908, over which there was drawn an Edged veil? The author tells us that it really *was* the crankshaft of 'Samson' which broke . . .

Although Napier did not race officially at Brooklands after World War One, David has included the Napier hybrids which did appear, like the Wolseley Viper and the Sunbeam-Napier, the origins of which I had the good fortune to discover when writing my Brooklands history. The great 24-hour drive by Edge and his Napier team (defying media-hype that they would either be unable to breathe at such prodigious speed or else would be driven mad by the monotony), which actually opened the new Brooklands Motor Course in 1907, also gets full coverage.

The Napier influence on speed, on land, water and in the air is skilfully presented as a mix of early Brooklands history, accounts of the land and water speed record attempts, and the story of the Napier company itself, together with a detailed discourse on the career of John Cobb's Thomson & Taylor-built, Lion-powered Napier-Railton, and his twin-Lion-engined Railton LSR car. With its insight into Napier's achievements in the sphere of high speed competition, this well-researched and fascinating book is long-overdue. Warm congratulations to David Venables, who has achieved something that few, if any others, would have cared to attempt.

Bill Boddy MBE
Founder Editor of *Motor Sport*

Preface

THE events which led to the writing of this book began over 50 years ago, when Anthony Heal, who had a great admiration for Napier motor cars, began collecting material about the firm's racing achievements. At that time many of the key figures in the story, such as Frank Newton and Henry Tryon, were still alive, so Anthony was able not only to meet them and hear their own accounts first-hand, but also had access to their notes and records.

In 1950–51, Anthony published a series of articles in *Motor Sport* about Napier's racing history between 1900 and 1908 – the first time that a proper account of those years had appeared in print. These articles were called 'The First to Wear the Green', and this was such a splendid title that I have appropriated it as the sub-title for this book. Later in the 1950s, Anthony published further articles in *Veteran & Vintage* magazine. It had been his intention to write a full account of Napier racing history, as a companion to his superb account of the racing Sunbeams. Unfortunately, however, his health began to fail, and he realised that he would not be able to write it. He therefore passed his collection of papers and photographs to Guy Griffiths, suggesting that Guy should either write the story himself or find someone else to do it.

Guy shares all Anthony's enthusiasm for Napier. He worked in the Napier research department between 1939 and 1946, alongside many of the men who feature in this story, and while he was there he gained a full appreciation of the ethos of the firm, its engineering integrity, and the desire always to obtain the highest performance with reliability. His experiences at Napier stimulated Guy to collect Napier papers and photographs himself.

Since my retirement in 1993, I have spent countless hours with Guy, talking about a mutual passion for motor racing and motor racing history. During the winter of 1993–94, Guy kept saying, 'Someone must write the Napier story'. To my discredit, I did not at first evince a very positive reaction. But one day Guy opened a filing cabinet in his study and handed me a large number of files. 'Here you are, you're going to write the Napier story. Take these away and think about it.'

I did as I was bidden and began to read. As soon as I started, I too became fired with the same enthusiasm as Anthony and Guy. I realised it was a noble story which had to be told, not only as a memorial to the men responsible, but also as a very important piece of British motoring history. I also began to appreciate that it was not just the story of early racing cars – that was only half the tale: I would also have to include the heroic exploits of the men who used the Napier Lion aero engine. I agreed to take the task on, and was able to meet Anthony Heal and tell him that the story which he had nurtured for so long would at last be written.

It is a matter of much sadness to me that Anthony died on 25 March 1995, and will not see this book published. It could not have been written at all but for the initial work that he did, and I referred to his material continuously while writing the first half. Indeed, without Anthony much of the story of Napier's early racing era would have been lost for ever.

Nor could the story have been written without Guy Griffiths. He, too, had invaluable papers and photographs, together with an intimate knowledge of the Napier company and the personalities who worked in it. Even more important, throughout the gestation of the book he has been a constant source of advice, information, and encouragement. He has read and re-read the manuscript as it developed and grew, and has listened to me for hours as I agonised about the accuracy of the contents and the elucidation of obscure points. The pictures have been almost entirely Guy's responsibility. He has copied and enlarged innumerable photographs, often transforming seemingly hopeless originals into gems. I cannot stress too much what an important part he has played in the completion of this book.

Soon after I started writing, Guy introduced me to Derek Grossmark. Derek, a past president of the Veteran Car Club, is another who shares a passion for Napier. When Rolls-Royce took over the Napier works at Acton in 1958, Derek, on his own initiative, saved as much of the Napier archives as he could. He has given me free access to these, and his help and advice – particularly on the identification of individual cars – has been invaluable. He has also read and made most helpful comments on that part of the manuscript which takes the story up to 1914. Without the access which Derek gave me to both the original chassis number book and the record book of the racing and experimental department, the authority of the first half of the text would have been greatly diminished.

Others who deserve a special mention include Ronald 'Steady' Barker, who has maintained a long-standing interest in Napier cars – he restored and ran the ex-Bird car which features in these pages. 'Steady' has been a most helpful source of information and material and has supplied some remarkable photographs. He too read the manuscript in its early stages and gave much advice and help. John Maitland has, over many years, built up a large motoring library, and at my frequently impatient request has spent many hours ferreting out obscure points of history for me, often from long-forgotten magazines of the Edwardian era. He has also been able to let me have a number of photographs. David Thirlby, an ex-Napier employee, read the manuscript in its final form and was able to point out some silly errors, as well as making many valuable suggestions and contributions.

There are many other people from whom I have received enthusiastic and unstinting help. I am most grateful to the Librarian, Bentley Drivers' Club; William Boddy; Angela Coleman, Society of British Aerospace Constructors; Barry Clarke; Julian Collins; Mike Evans, Rolls-Royce Heritage Trust; Paul Foulkes-Halbard; Geoffrey Goddard; Philip Hall and Peter Baynes, Sir Henry Royce Memorial Foundation; Tony Hutchings, Brooklands Society; Malcolm Jeal and Margaret Golding, Veteran Car Club; Jo Lintott; Lord Montagu of Beaulieu, and the librarians of the National Motor Museum; Roger Newstead, BP–Mobil Ltd; Alec Pine, Midland Automobile Club; Angela Pugh; John Pulford, Brooklands Museum; Duncan Rabagliati; Shell International Petroleum Co; Vanna Skelley, Burmah–Castrol Ltd; Simon Taylor, Haymarket Press; Thomas Ulrich; Baron von Veyler-Malberg; Alan Vessey, Napier Power Heritage Trust; David Watson; Dr Neville Whitehurst; and Joan Williamson, Royal Automobile Club Librarian.

I fear that some who have helped me may have been overlooked, and I offer them my apologies – the oversight was unintentional, and their help has been nonetheless invaluable.

I am also very grateful to all those who found pictures for me and gave permission for their publication. The sources of individual photographs are acknowledged in the captions.

I decided that, in order to set down as complete a record as possible, I should include details of not only the racing and speed events, but also the more important road trials and observed runs. There are nevertheless places in the narrative where some of the technical detail may not be entirely reliable – the result of too much original material having been destroyed. Even the early Brooklands records are incomplete.

Writing this book has given me the most enormous pleasure. I have been slightly awed by the responsibility of the task, but I hope it will be considered that I have done it justice, and that I will be forgiven for any errors which may be found.

David Venables
July 1997

The Players Make their Entrance

IN 1805, the year of the Battle of Trafalgar, a 23-year-old Scot left his native land and, journeying by ship, came to London. His name was David Napier, the son of Robert Napier of Inverary, blacksmith to the Duke of Argyll. David Napier was an engineer and had already received some technical training in Scotland. On arriving in London, he went to work for Henry Maudslay, who must be regarded as one of the founding fathers of the Industrial Revolution and, indeed, of modern technology. Maudslay had invented the original lathe with a slide rest and then the screw-cutting lathe, from which all modern engineering technology has subsequently evolved. For a young engineer who wanted to be at the forefront of technical developments, Maudslay's workshop in Lambeth on the south bank of the Thames was the only place to be.

Napier went to Maudslay for education as much as employment. After about a year, he left Maudslay and opened a small workshop of his own at Lloyd Court, St Giles High Street, between New Oxford Street and Charing Cross Road. At first he did general engineering, but he had an inventive mind and designed a tracing instrument for draughtsmen which he called a Universal Perspectigraph.

Among the industries which had benefited from the surge of new technology was printing. The rotary press had come into general use about the time that David Napier had arrived in London. In 1820 he built a small treadle-operated printing press for an American, Daniel Treadwell, and then built a small rotary press for another customer. He began work on a design of his own and after a false start perfected a printing machine which was a considerable technical advance. Using two rollers, it printed on both sides of the sheet in a continuous process. It attracted the attention of Thomas Hansard, who had succeeded his father as printer of the daily reports of Parliament's proceedings. In 1824 Hansard commissioned several of these printing machines from Napier, who called his new press the 'Nay-peer'. The reputation of Napier grew rapidly, and his printing presses found a ready market. He developed improved designs which were bought by several newspapers, mostly in the provinces.

The firm had now outgrown the St Giles workshop, and between 1830 and 1835 Napier moved back to the south bank. He bought a house in York Road (which now runs along the side of Waterloo Station) and built a factory behind the house, in Vine Street. The firm grew, and by 1840 there were about 200 employees, including David Napier's younger son James (born 1823), who had joined the business in 1837. Napier ensured that his company always had the best machine tools available and he gained the reputation of tackling precision work that other London engineering firms were unable to do.

At about this time Napier began to diversify. He had invented a machine which could produce 25,000 bullets a day, and the Board of Ordnance soon made an approach to him, seeking to buy both the machine and its design. Napier was not keen to hand over his design, and instead had it patented before selling the complete bullet-making machinery to the Board and installing it at Woolwich Arsenal. Orders for additional machines included sales to the French and Egyptian governments. There were also further orders from Woolwich Arsenal, such as one for a ten-ton steam crane and many machine tools, while the export market expanded to include Spain and Russia.

For some time the Bank of England had been seeking ways of sorting gold coins by weight to find those which were below the legal limit. William Cotton, the Bank's deputy governor, devised a mechanical method of weighing the coins accurately, and on being introduced to David Napier they jointly invented and developed a suitable weighing machine. The final development was produced at Vine Street and several examples were sold to the Bank. The experience and knowledge gained from this exercise now led the Napier firm into a new field, that of precision weighing equipment, while the heavy engineering side of the business was supplying cranes and steam presses to the Great Western Railway.

In 1847 David Napier took James into partnership and the firm became D. Napier & Son. Once more, the nature of the business was changing. There had been a another revolution in printing methods. Newspapers were now printed on a rotary press and the old roller machines developed by Napier were obsolete. The firm had the opportunity to go into rotary press manufacture but the size of the new machines was greater than the small factory could handle. David Napier was gradually relaxing his control and James became the dominant partner. He strengthened the links with the Bank of England and at the Bank's request devised a new method of printing bank notes. This was the platen machine, which James patented in 1853. This brought new success to the firm, as the platen presses were not only adopted by the Bank of England but also by other firms printing stamps, foreign banknotes, and similar fine work.

The company's technical success in producing equipment to make paper money led to an approach from the Royal Mint for the development of machinery for testing coins by weight and thence to the making of machines for coin manufacture. Napier coin-making machinery found a large export market and big orders came from Russia and Spain. The stamp presses led to the invention of machinery for the perforation of stamps. In their book *Men & Machines*, which narrates the history of the Napier company, Charles Wilson and William Reader say that by 1866

> it would have been possible, theoretically at any rate, to read at breakfast time, an out-of-date copy of a New York newspaper printed on a Napier machine, receive a letter bearing an Italian stamp (perforated, and perhaps printed also, by Napiers' apparatus) and containing a note (printed from electrotypes supplied by Napier) of the Bank of Buenos Aires, which one could change at the Bank of England for gold and silver coin weighed at the Mint and at the Bank on balances made at Napiers' works at Lambeth.

David Napier retired from the firm in 1866, and James now became the sole proprietor. Unfortunately he did not have his father's strong commercial acumen and he was becoming an eccentric and difficult man to deal with. He had a quarrel with the Hon Charles Freemantle, who was appointed as deputy Master of the Royal Mint in 1868, and orders from the Royal Mint stopped forthwith. The business began to contract sharply during the 1870s. James Napier had nevertheless inherited his father's inventive mind, and there was a steady stream of patent applications relating to such varied subjects as boot-cleaning devices, the exact measurement of portions of mustard from a pot, and speedometers for railway locomotives. Some of these inventions would have had a commercial future, but James did not have either the urge or the apparent ability to develop them successfully.

David Napier died in 1873 and the decline of the firm accelerated. By 1885 the work-force had fallen from its peak strength of 300 men to a mere seven. Coin weighing machin-

Montague Napier. (Guy Griffiths Collection)

ery and small engineering piece-work kept the firm alive but it was doing no more than providing James Napier with an income and paying the wages of the skeleton staff. The firm limped along for another ten years and then, in March 1895, James Napier died.

James had four sons: one, Walter, had worked in the firm, but on James's death it was the youngest son who took control. Montague Stanley Napier was 25 years old when his father died. He was not working in the business. It is believed that he had done an engineering apprenticeship but almost nothing is known of his early life and it is possible that his engineering skills were gained by working at Vine Street. D. Napier & Son was now worth very little but Montague Napier purchased what was left from his father's executors and took stock of what he now controlled. For the first three years he consolidated the existing firm and continued to manufacture coin-classifying machinery and printing equipment. Montague Napier was a keen cyclist and had gained some competition successes riding an 'ordinary' – what is today popularly known as a 'penny-farthing' or 'high-wheeler' – and his hobby led him to make machinery for the bicycle industry. A further move into the area of wheeled transport came when he started to manufacture the Ritter road-skate, a form of skate with very large wheels which in appearance was the precursor of the modern roller-blade or in-line skate. (Ritter was the works foreman at Vine Street, so it is likely that he was the originator of the skate.) Montague Napier wanted to expand into other new fields, and the motor car now excited his interest.

Meanwhile, as Napier was starting to restore the fortunes of his family firm, another young man was starting to make his own mark in the world. Selwyn Francis Edge was born at Concord, New South Wales, Australia, in 1868. His parents Alexander and Annie were British, and in 1871 they had returned to England and settled in Upper Norwood, a South London suburb. His father had wanted Edge to enter the Army, and it is not clear if he failed the entrance examinations or, with an evident engineering and mechanical aptitude, decided instead to seek his fortune in the rapidly expanding field of technical commerce.

Selwyn Edge. (Guy Griffiths Collection)

Edge became a keen cyclist from the age of 16, joining the local Anerley Bicycle Club, with which he started racing. It is now hard to appreciate the impact that the invention and development of the bicycle in its modern form – the 'safety' bicycle – had in the last two decades

The Napier works at Vine Street, Lambeth, about 1900. (Guy Griffiths Collection)

of the 19th century. It gave a freedom and a mobility to all social classes, and especially to the young, which had never been available before. Great numbers were drawn to take part in this new and exhilarating pastime. Edge gained many successes racing bicycles and tricycles and set a number of records. In 1888, he set a new record for the ride from London to Brighton and back, covering the 108 miles (173km) in 7hr 2min, one of the official observers of the run being Montague Napier. For this record Edge used a Marriott & Cooper bicycle, manufactured by Rudge. In the same year he set world records over distances between 21 and 25 miles and also won the North Road Open 100-mile race and the Bath Road 50-mile handicap.

By 1891 he was a travelling sales representative for Marriott & Cooper and competed in the Paris–Bordeaux road race. In June 1891 he made another attempt on the London–Brighton and back record, seeking to beat 6hr 52min, and Montague Napier was again among the official observers. For this successful attempt he used a geared 'ordinary', reducing the record by 1min 3sec. After a short time with the New Howe cycle company in Glasgow, Edge moved back to London and in 1896 was the manager of the Dunlop Tyre Company in Regent Street. A year earlier, he had visited Paris and had been given his first ride in a motor car, a Panhard-Levassor, by the French pioneer Fernand Charron. This short ride made Edge realise the unlimited possibilities of the motor car and he decided that his future lay in the new and developing motor industry.

A natural progression for Edge was to move from racing bicycles to motor tricycles. A number of races were being held for these machines on short quarter-mile (400m) tracks, and he became a successful exponent of the sport, using Ariels and De Dions.

Montague Napier and Selwyn Edge were both now travelling along the same road. Shortly their paths were to cross.

Chapter 1: 1896–9

The First Napier Evolves

THE first motor race took place between Paris and Bordeaux on 11, 12 and 13 June 1895. There had been an earlier event – the Paris–Rouen Trial on 22 July 1894 – but speed alone had not been the arbiter of success in this first motoring competition. In the Paris–Bordeaux–Paris event a year later, however, it was the competitor who completed the run in the fastest time who was adjudged the winner; and thus motor racing began.

This first race was declared to be such a success that the organising committee became the nucleus of the Automobile Club de France, which was formed in the autumn of 1895. The new club decided to run a more ambitious event in 1896: the race was to be held in October, and was to be in ten daily stages, from Paris to Marseilles and back. The overnight stops would be at Auxerre, Dijon, Lyons, Avignon, and Marseilles. The competitors would return to Paris by the same route, but would stop at Sens instead of Dijon on the last stage before Paris. The total distance would be 1,062 miles (1,709km). There were classes for cars and motor cycles, and the cars running in Class A were divided into two groups, the first seating up to four people, and the second seating more than four. Repairs were to be carried out in 'running time', and competitors were only allowed to work on their car for 15 minutes in the *parc ferme* when arriving at night, and for an hour before departure the following morning. Although it was not evident at the time, this event was to mark the beginning of the Napier car and its racing exploits.

Initially the entries were disappointing, but the ACF then realised that the date clashed with a state visit of the Czar of Russia, and competitors were reluctant to miss the fun. The date was therefore brought forward to 24 September, and the entry list grew accordingly. The non-starter, or entrant that failed to make it to the starting point, had already become an established feature of motor-racing, but on Thursday 24 September, 32 vehicles assembled in the Place de l'Etoile by the Arc de Triomphe, from whence they proceeded in single file to the Place d'Armes, in front of the Palace of Versailles.

The Comte de la Valette, the official starter of the ACF, released them at one minute intervals. Despite accidents and the inevitable mechanical disasters, 27 competitors reached Auxerre that night, but the next day the weather intervened and torrential storms and gales swept France. Another nine cars fell by the wayside. Some were victims of the adverse conditions, but even at this early stage of motor racing evolution it seems that the Darwinian theory of natural selection was making itself felt, thinning the field so that only the fittest and hardiest were left to go on to Marseilles. Only two more dropped out during the next three stages, and 15 vehicles set off from Marseilles for Paris on the return leg. Fourteen reached the finish at the Porte Maillot at about 11 o'clock on Saturday 4 October.

When the results were announced, it was evident that Panhard had made a clean sweep of the places in the car class. The winner was Mayade, driving car No 6; in second place was Merkel, driving car No 8; and d'Hostingue was third, driving car No 5. The No 5 Panhard had started out being driven by Emil Levassor, the patron of the Panhard et Levassor firm, who had led the race until the Lyons–Avignon stage, when the car had overturned after hitting a dog. Levassor had been too badly shaken to continue, so the tiller had been taken over by d'Hostingue. Levassor's injuries, although apparently slight, may have been a contributory factor in his sudden death while working at his drawing board about six months later.

The identity of the driver of the second Panhard, No 8, gives rise to what must be the first controversy of motor racing history. According to the records the car was driven by Merkel, who seems to have been an employee of Panhard et Levassor, a works driver in fact. However, the race was followed by H.O. Duncan, an English journalist who was living in Paris, and in his account of the race he states that the second Panhard was driven by Count René De Knyff, who was soon to become one of the heroic figures of early motor racing. A study of photographs of the flower-bedecked car at the finish shows a small, anxious-looking man at the wheel, doubtless the worthy Merkel, but beside him is the clearly recognisable Count De Knyff. It seems likely that De Knyff was merely the co-driver, but that 19th century social prejudice dictated that credit for the car's success had to go to the aristocrat.

The early history of the British motor industry is inextricably linked with the activities of Harry John Lawson. Lawson, who had earlier been involved with bicycle manufacture, realised that once the statutory shackles strangling the nascent British motor industry were removed, there was the possibility of making a fortune in the boom which would inevitably follow. Ingeniously, Lawson decided that the best way to enrich himself would be to buy up all the British patents affecting the motor car, and to obtain the British patent rights to all the major European motor car makers.

Lawson had begun to acquire and register these patents as early as 1880, when, on 27 June, patent No 2591 was taken out by him for 'the first British motor car', under the title; 'Improvements in Velocipedes and the application of Motive Power thereto, such improvements also being applicable to Tram Cars, Traction Engines and other Road Locomotives'. The complete patent was granted to Lawson on 27 September. It would probably be an exaggeration to call Lawson a visionary, as he was too commercially-orientated for that, but he was certainly far-sighted, as Otto Benz did not make his first car work for another four years.

4 October 1896: At the end of the Paris–Marseilles–Paris, Merkel sits at the wheel of Panhard No 8 with the Count De Knyff beside him. (Guy Griffiths Collection)

By 1895 Lawson had formed the British Motor Syndicate Limited as a holding company for the patents, and in the autumn of the following year he was in Paris to watch the Paris–Marseilles–Paris race in the company of H.O. Duncan, who was one of the very first motoring journalists. Lawson had concluded that to assist him in his patenting and licensing operations, he needed to have 'state of the art' examples of the leading French marques, so a few days before the race, accompanied by Duncan, he visited the Panhard et Levassor works at 19 Avenue d'Ivry and, after some hard bargaining, bought the 1895 Paris–Bordeaux winner on behalf of his company. In his book *World on Wheels*, Duncan recounts that Levassor was apparently a reluctant seller, but eventually agreed to part with the car for 30,000 francs, or about £1,200, which was a very high price – about £60,000 in the values of the 1990s. Probably Levassor chuckled quietly to himself after Lawson had departed with the car, because, with the rapid technological advances that were being made, it was already obsolescent.

It was in the 1895 Panhard that Lawson and Duncan followed the Paris–Marseilles–Paris race, and afterwards Duncan – who was the Paris agent for the British Motor Syndicate – made arrangements to have the car sent back to England. Before the event, Lawson had said to Duncan, 'If the Panhards win the race, I will buy the winning cars, at any price, for England.' A few weeks later, early in October, Duncan received a telegram from Lawson, instructing him to negotiate with Panhard et Levassor for the purchase of the three winning cars. Once again there was a fierce haggle and a deal was struck for the sale of the three cars at 30,000 francs each. Lawson concluded the carriage arrangements and the cars were dispatched to London on 20 October.

The autumn of 1896 was a memorable time for the small band of British motorists. From the very beginning of motoring in Britain their activities had been curtailed, almost to the point of extinction, by legislation that was intended to protect and safeguard horse-drawn transport. The statutory cornerstone was the Locomotive Act 1865. Section 3 of this Act, as amended by Section 29 of the Highways and Locomotives (Amendment) Act 1878, provided that every locomotive propelled by steam or any motive force other than animal power, on any turnpike road or public highway, should be worked according to certain rules and regulations specified in the Act. This required that at least three persons should be employed to drive or conduct such a locomotive; that every such locomotive should be instantly stopped, on any person with a horse or carriage signalling for the locomotive to be stopped; that each locomotive should be preceded by some person on foot at least 20yd (18m) ahead, who, in case of need, should assist horses in passing; and that the locomotive should not proceed at a speed greater than 4mph. The Acts also empowered county authorities to grant licences for the use of locomotives, which meant that a separate licence was required for each county. When Parliament enacted these statutes it had the use of steam traction engines in mind, and the legislation had failed to keep up with the subsequent appearance and rapid evolution of the motor car. By 1896 the pressure for change had become irresistible, and even the most reactionary elements in Parliament could not stop the passing of the Light Locomotives and Highways Act, which repealed the repressive sections of the earlier Acts and established the speed limit at 12mph (19kmh).

The new Act came into force on 14 November 1896 and this 'emancipation' of the British motorist was celebrated by the London to Brighton Emancipation Run, held the same day. Lawson had been in the vanguard of the pressure groups seeking a change in the law, and had also founded the Motor Car Club as a focal point for British motorists. The club was the organising body for the Emancipation Run, which some hoped would be the British equivalent of the Paris–Marseilles event. Charles Turrell, who was Secretary of the British Motor Syndicate and probably the first motor racing correspondent of *The Autocar*, was certainly of this view. When Lawson bought the successful team of Panhards, he had done so with the Emancipation Run in mind. All three were entered. No 6 (the Paris–Marseilles winner) was again to be driven by Mayade, and No 8 was also to be driven by a works driver, provided by Emil Levassor. The suspicion has to be that it was Merkel once again, but also riding in No 8 was the Earl of Winchilsea and two companions, and all contemporary accounts refer only to the Earl and his party, so social prejudice may have denied Merkel his claim to fame for a second time. Turrell rode in the third car, No 5, which had its chains tightened by the driver of No 8 before the start. Unfortunately they were over-tightened and the countershaft bearings over-heated, so that Turrell's anger may be an additional reason for the subsequent anonymity of the No 8 driver! Thirty-three starters left the Hotel Metropole in Northumberland Avenue, and ten of these survived to reach the Hotel Metropole in Brighton.

It had been a typical November day with fog and dampness, but this did little to repress the Bollee brothers, who had brought their racing Bollee tricycles over from Le Mans and treated the event as a British equivalent of the Paris–Marseilles. The Bollees finished first and second, but the third car into Brighton was Panhard No 8, while No 6 was the fifth arrival. The over-tightened No 5 was the last car to finish, much to Turrell's disgust, as he had written that it was 'then reputed to be the fastest car in the World'.

After the Emancipation Run, it was reported that Lawson had the three Panhards stripped down by his engineers, so that a full technical assessment could be made, and the lessons learned could be applied to the manufacture of cars by the British Motor Syndicate and its subsidiaries. In reality it seems unlikely that this happened, but in any event the Panhards, and No 8 in particular, were used to gain much publicity for Lawson and his enterprises.

At the beginning of 1898, Selwyn Edge was still the London manager of the Dunlop Pneumatic Tyre Company and the favoured protégé of the Dunlop Chairman, Harvey du Cros senior, but there was friction with du Cros's sons, who were also in the company. Edge was now more certain than ever that his future lay with the rapidly growing motor industry, and he believed there was an opening for a British-built car on the lines of the Panhard. He agreed with Lawson to buy Panhard No 8, which he had admired since he first saw it when it was imported in October 1896. The price is not recorded, but Edge said 'it was high'. The negotiations between two such tough entrepreneurs must have been memorable!

Edge intended to drive No 8 for long distances to find out its strengths and weaknesses and eliminate the weaknesses as these appeared. The first modification was to remove the wagonette body and replace it with a two-seater. The next modification became the turning point in the whole Napier story. The tiller steering system was tiring to use and gave the driver very poor control – indeed, in some circumstances its effects could be lethal. He realised that wheel steering was the only answer and pondered upon who would carry out the conversion for him. During his cycle racing days, Edge had been a keen member of the Bath Road Cycle Club and had become acquainted with Montague Napier, who was a fellow member. After abandoning cycle racing for the more sophisticated delights of the motor tricycle, Edge had lost touch with Napier. A mutual friend, Walter Munn, suggested to Edge that D. Napier & Son would have the skills to undertake the steering modification, as Montague Napier's interest in motoring was growing and he was now contemplating the design of his own car. Edge wrote to Napier and received a reply, inviting him to visit the Napier works at Vine Street.

Vine Street and the first Napier factory disappeared when the area was cleared for the Festival of Britain in 1951, and the Royal Festival Hall now stands on or near the site. In his memoirs (*My Motoring Reminiscences*), Edge says: 'The works were quite small and the sort that one would imagine to be suitable for the manufacture of such delicate machines as were made there, but I failed to see what possibilities there were for anything like the making of motor cars'.

Napier proudly showed Edge his prototype car, which was being assembled in one of the workshops. From Edge's own account, Napier must have been left in little doubt about the manner of man with whom he was to deal:

> It was a crude-looking machine when compared with my own Panhard-Levassor, with a twin-cylinder water cooled horizontal engine. The most unorthodox feature about it, even in those early days, was the system of transmission. It had four speeds, and all the gears were constantly in mesh. The change of gear was effected by a system of fibre clutches, and it did not take me long to make up my mind that Napier was working on the wrong design. I did not hesitate to tell him so; in fact, I told him frankly if he continued working on this type of car, he would soon be in the bankruptcy court.

However, despite this unpromising start, the high quality of the engineering that Edge had seen in the Napier works had made such a good impression that he asked Montague Napier to design a wheel steering system to fit to No 8. Edge returned a few days later and was impressed when Napier showed him the drawings. He had devised a worm and nut system, with the steering arm attached to the frame on a centre bracket. The work was carried out and Edge found that it transformed the Panhard. So pleased was he with the result that it inspired him to write to *The Autocar*, extolling the virtues of the system and commending Napier to all tiller-steering motorists. No doubt Edge expected and received a commission from Napier for each satisfied customer! The next modification was to fit $3^1/2$ in (89mm) Dunlop pneumatic tyres, which must have greatly improved the comfort of the occupants and, probably more importantly, considerably enhanced the performance, as had also happened when pneumatic tyres were fitted to bicycles.

Having taken Edge's comments to heart, Montague Napier had abandoned his original engine design, and he now suggested that he should develop a new design which could be fitted to Edge's Panhard. Edge agreed, as this very much accorded with his plans; meanwhile he continued with his own programme of modifications. The lubricators were centralised on the dashboard and modified, making it possible to turn off the oil supply, which prevented the car leaving a series of oil puddles when parked, and – of much greater importance – a radiator was fitted. Of this, Edge observed: 'I find there is no need to renew the water in the tank all day. In fact, none is used up in a day's run and the cooler is an unqualified success.'

Charles Jarrott at the wheel of No 8 – now fitted with Dunlop pneumatic tyres – with Mrs Kennard in the passenger seat. St John Nixon sits on the step. (Guy Griffiths Collection)

Edge's experiments and his modifications to No 8 had a remarkable similarity to the activities of Tony Vandervell over 50 years later. Vandervell too bought the best Formula 1 racing car available at the time – the 4.5 litre Ferrari – took it to bits, modified it, and decided that he could do better. The Vanwall was the outcome. Vandervell and Edge probably had a lot in common, with their tough, inflexible tenacity of purpose, and their determination that only the best would do.

While the engine development continued, Edge's other business affairs had not prospered as well as he had probably hoped. At the beginning of 1899, he had parted company with du Cros in their only remaining mutual business interest, the John Griffiths Cycle Corporation, as he felt that there was now little future in bicycles, but he seemed unable to persuade du Cros to take the future of the motor car seriously.

Apart from his link with Napier, for a short time Edge had no active part in the motor industry, and busied himself in the activities of the Incandescent Gas Mantle Company. Meanwhile, Napier had finished the new engine. Edge regarded it as a great advance on the Panhard. It was a water-cooled vertical twin with one automatic inlet valve per cylinder, opened by the suction of the piston on its down stroke. The cylinders fired one after the other, but the crankpins were on the same plane, so there were two firing strokes followed by two non-firing strokes. Napier had rejected the still fashionable hot-tube ignition and had shown foresight in using an electrical system. The cylinder block was made of cast-iron with an aluminium sump. The engine, with a bore and stroke of 101.6mm x 152.4mm, had a capacity of 2,471cc, and developed about 10bhp. Edge fitted it to No 8 immediately. He found it pulled better than the Panhard unit, was quieter, and started more easily. It also needed less maintenance and was much easier to work on.

The first Napier engine. (Napier Power Heritage Trust)

If Edge had been harshly critical of Napier's designs before, he was now fulsome in his praise. 'I was convinced that in Napier I had the good fortune to alight on a motor engineer of outstanding ability. I saw no reason why he should not design and produce a British car which would be second to none in the world'. Edge went back to du Cros again, expressed his views about Napier's abilities, and emphasised that this was an opportunity that du Cros could not afford to miss. Edge's powers of persuasion succeeded this time, and du Cros agreed to finance a partnership with him, forming the Motor Power Company, with premises at 14 Regent Street in the West End of London. There was a staff of seven, including Edge. The firm would have the English agency for Gladiator and Clement-Panhard, but its main business would be the sale of Napier cars and there would be a contract with Napier to take all the cars he could make.

The initial agreement provided for the supply of six Napiers: three would have the twin-cylinder engine, and three would be fitted with a new four-cylinder engine, which was, in effect, a double twin, although the cylinders were cast in one block. The cars were to be bodied by Arthur Mulliner Ltd at Northampton, and all six were to be delivered by 31 March 1900 – a condition which, as will soon be seen, cannot have been met. The agreement provided for the delivery of 396 cars by the end of 1904. The partnership was paying Napier £400 for each twin-cylinder car and selling them for £500 each. Montague Napier must have been satisfied that he had made a good deal for himself and his small firm. There was no need to establish any sales or publicity organisation – the partnership would take care of these matters – and there was also a guaranteed market for all the cars which were made. As subsequent events were to show, Napier's technical skill and Edge's commercial flair were to be a most successful combination

Chapter 2: 1900–1

The Frustrations of Horsepower

WHILE waiting for the delivery of the first Napiers, Edge was not idle. In November 1899 he entered No 8 for a 100 mile (160km) trial between London and Oxford, organised by the Automobile Club of Great Britain and Ireland (the 'Royal' accolade had yet to come), and received a certificate of commendation. This trial, though, was only a foretaste of what was to come in the spring of 1900.

In many parts of Great Britain the motor car had still not been seen at all, and to many people it seemed unlikely that it would ever become a practical commercial proposition. The Automobile Club decided that in order to make the British public aware of the potential of the motor car, it would organise a 1,000 mile (1,600km) trial. The event would start in London on 23 April and the route would run to Bristol, Birmingham, Manchester, Kendal, Carlisle, Edinburgh, Newcastle, Leeds, Sheffield, and Nottingham before finishing in London on 12 May. The participating cars would be exhibited for at least one day in each of these towns and for two days in some. During the Trial there were to be hill-climbing tests, some of which would be compulsory, and an optional speed trial. Edge realised it was essential that a Napier should be entered in the Trial, as the chance of gaining such valuable publicity for the new marque would not be offered again. When the decision was taken to enter a car none of the first batch of six had yet been built; and there was an additional problem – the only car likely to be finished by 23 April had already been sold 'off the drawing board'.

Leaving Napier and his staff at the Vine Street works to deal with the problems of finishing the car in time, Edge ascertained that it had been purchased by Arthur Mulliner Ltd, who were to build a body for a customer, Edward Kennard, a landowner at Market Harborough. Kennard was a sporting man, who was a keen huntsman, while his wife, a novelist, was an emancipated woman for those times, being a motoring enthusiast who already owned a Benz car and a De Dion motor cycle, on which she did all the repairs and maintenance. Edge visited the Kennards at Market Harborough and told them of the problem. To his delight, Edge found that Kennard was most enthusiastic about the whole project. He made only one stipulation: that he should accompany Edge in the car on the Trial.

Meanwhile the construction and preparation of the new car continued at a frantic pace. The chassis had much in common with the Panhard, but Napier and Edge agreed that where the French design was considered as needing improvement, this would be done, even though it meant that the car would start the Trial with a number of untried features. One particular change was the replacement of plain bearings by roller bearings on the countershaft. The radiator was mounted behind the engine, and there was an all-metal chassis frame and engine subframe. The car was given the type number G 20. It had a wheelbase of 7ft 3¾in (215cm), a track of 4ft 1½in (126cm), and weighed 2,520lb (1,145kg). There was no time for it to be sent to Mulliners for the fitting of its proper body, and a stark, rough, two-seater, painted with grey undercoat, was the best that could be managed in the time. The front wings were merely two crude bent planks, while there were none at the rear. With five days to spare the car was finished. Edge and Napier then tested it as hard as they could in the time that was left. To their satisfaction, nothing broke and there were no unforeseen snags. In addition to Kennard, Edge decided to take with him St John Nixon, a 14-year-old working at the Motor Power Company, who would ride on the step in proper racing mechanic fashion.

During the week prior to the event the participating cars were exhibited at the Royal Agricultural Society Hall, Islington, but the Napier was not among them – it was still being assembled at Vine Street – and Edge only exhibited an Ariel quadricycle on the Motor Power Company stand. However, it was at the Hall on

Sunday 22 April, bearing the competition number A10, when the cars were scrutinised and the stamping of major components took place. The start was at Hyde Park Corner the following morning.

Edge had a comparatively uneventful Trial. Outside Reading he stopped to replace a burnt inlet valve, having what *The Autocar* described as 'a fit of the slows'. Between Birmingham and Manchester, the governor hammer broke; this was a device which acted as a primitive throttle, moving the exhaust valve tappets away from the valve stems, and so limiting the engine speed. Edge wired this up and Nixon thenceforth worked it manually, on Edge's command.

On arriving at Manchester, it was found that the float chamber had broken away from the carburettor. Edge sent a telegram to Napier seeking help. The next day the cars were exhibited to the public so there was an opportunity to make repairs. Napier arrived in Manchester and bound the carburettor together with copper wire, sealing it with plaster of Paris. This repair was so effective it lasted until the end of the Trial without further trouble. On the Kendal–Carlisle leg there was a hill-climb at Dunmail Raise. Shortly after this, the Napier's clutch began to slip and it began to run backwards down the hill. The brakes would not hold it and Edge shouted at Nixon to jump off and let down the sprag, a mechanical device which dug into the road surface and stopped the car running back. Nixon could not reach the device in time and the car began to gather momentum. Kennard jumped clear, but Edge, as befitted a good captain, stayed at the wheel and steered the car backwards down the hill until it eventually stopped. Meanwhile the engine had been over-revving, as the manual 'governor' was standing by the roadside, unable to help. Edge adjusted the clutch after this and there were no further problems with it.

During the Sheffield–Nottingham leg, on 11 May, a speed trial was held in Welbeck Park over a flying mile (1.6km) course, the cars being released at half-minute intervals. The Napier recorded the equal second best time with a mean average speed of 29.60mph (47.62kmh). In terms of British motor racing history, the test in Welbeck Park was of some significance as it was the first proper British speed trial.

It was on the last leg of the Trial, with the end in sight, that the most serious mechanical problem arose. The competitors had stopped at St Albans for tea, before going on to the finish in London, and when Edge

The end of the 1,000-mile Trial on 12 May 1900. The second car is the Napier, with Edward Kennard in the driving seat and St John Nixon beside him. A bearded and hatted Montague Napier stands behind the car. (Derek Grossmark)

attempted to restart he found that the Napier's gear lever was jammed in neutral. Nixon borrowed a crowbar from a nearby blacksmith, and with much brute force Edge managed to free the jammed sliding sleeve on the countershaft. After this the Napier went on to the finish in Whitehall with no more problems. The cars were then driven to the Crystal Palace, where they were displayed until 19 May. The results were announced during the exhibition: the Napier had not only won its class, but also received the silver-gilt medal of the Automobile Club de France for taking second place overall, and a bronze medal from the Automobile Club of Great Britain.

Since he was driving the new car, Edge had offered old No 8 to Charles Jarrott for the Trial. Jarrott found what many racing drivers were to discover in later years – that the offer of a factory 'hack' may not be quite the bonus it seems, particularly when the factory is busy with its own entry. When Jarrott appeared at the start, accompanied by Harvey du Cros junior, he found that No 8 seemed most unwilling to run on two cylinders. He told Edge and Napier of the problem. Napier told him there was a short in a high tension lead, while Edge airily suggested that he 'joggle the wires', offering no more help or advice. By now du Cros junior must have felt that his previous impressions of Edge had been fully confirmed! No 8 managed to stagger as far as Reading, consuming enormous quantities of fuel and at Reading the tank was found to be empty. During the run du Cros received such a shock 'joggling the wires' that he was thrown over the bonnet. The next time 'joggling' was required, du Cros said, Jarrott could do it himself. He did, and he too received a massive shock. When, between Reading and Bristol, some retaining bolts in the gearbox sheared, Jarrott decided that as far as he was concerned the Trial was over. The car had expired outside a house where a garden party was taking place, so Jarrott and du Cros joined the party, which they felt offered better prospects than No 8, which was abandoned. It was towed by horse to the nearby station and returned to London by train. Nothing is known of its fate after that, so it was probably broken up – a sad end for such an historic car.

Work at Vine Street had been proceeding on the first of the 16hp four-cylinder cars, and Edge decided that the most effective way of testing the new machine would be to run it in one of the long-distance French open road races. Edge already had his eye on an entry in the Gordon-Bennett Race for 1901, and felt that a preliminary run could gain valuable experience from which a lot could be learned. The first 16hp car was selected, though what the customer thought about this is not recorded. He was probably told either that there were production delays, or, perhaps, that he was particularly lucky, since his car was to be given an extended road test at the hands of Edge himself, to ensure that all was well before delivery.

The event selected for the Napier's racing debut was the Paris–Toulouse–Paris, which was being run between 25 and 28 July 1900. The car, which was given the type number H 70, was tested extensively in chassis form and Edge found that it produced more problems than the two-cylinder machine – doubling the number of cylinders seemed to double the number of problems, though these seemed to be centred mainly in the ignition. Napier was using British-made coils, but the British manufacturers had very little experience of making these components, so the coils were less reliable than the French ones which had previously been used. The car had a leather lined double cone clutch, a four-speed gearbox, and the chassis frame was steel channel section. The wheelbase was 7ft 8in (234cm) and the track 4ft 1½in (126cm). The 16hp engine had the same dimensions as the two-cylinder model, so the capacity was 4,940cc.

While he was testing the H 70, Edge entered into a £50 wager with Roger Fuller, a stockbroker who had ordered a four-cylinder model. The challenge was for Edge to take his machine up Porlock Hill, which at this time had never been climbed by a car. Edge took the precaution of fitting smaller sprockets on the countershaft, to lower the gearing. On the day of the wager, he was accompanied in the car by a friend, F.T. Bidlake, and a mechanic. A big crowd assembled and saw the Napier romp up Porlock without any problem, leaving Edge £50 better off, and a horse – which was to be ridden up the hill with the car – a long way behind. Apart from the wager at Porlock, Edge was testing the 16hp car in much more serious events. On 30 June, the Catford Cycle Club held a hill climb at Westerham, for which the Napier did a practice run before being withdrawn with unspecified problems. A week later, the English Motor Club, which was Lawson's old Motor Car Club in a new guise, ran a hill-climb at Tilburstowe Hill, near Godstone in Surrey. Eight cars ran, and Edge's 16hp Napier was the fastest car (18.39mph/29.58kmh average), though well behind Jarrott's De Dion tricycle (25.80mph/41.51kmh average). The Napier won its class, but was demoted to third place on handicap.

After Tilburstowe, final preparations were made to the car before its departure to France for the race on 25 July. Edge had asked the Hon Charles Rolls to be his riding mechanic in the event, and received strict instructions from Lady Llangattock, Rolls's mother, that he was to ensure no harm befell her son! The start of the race was at Mongeron, on the outskirts of Paris, at 3.30am, as day was breaking. On their way to the start, Edge and Rolls found that one of the pipes joining the water jackets had cracked. A cycle black-

The first British racing car. This is the 16hp H70 Napier which Edge drove in the Paris–Toulouse–Paris on 25 July 1900. (Guy Griffiths Collection)

smith was knocked up and put to work. At first, he brazed the wrong end of the broken pipe; then, as it was too short, he decided to cut it and join the ends with a piece of rubber piping. He then cut the wrong piece. However, the repair was eventually effected and the Napier went to the start, though it was 45 minutes late. The venture was not to be crowned with success. At the start, the Napier had a collision with a Belgian-built Bolide driven by Jenatzy, which caused the Bolide's retirement, though the Napier was unharmed; and almost immediately after the start the engine began to misfire – first one trembler stuck, and then another, and the car would not run on four cylinders. With the time lost in the collision with Jenatzy, and now the ignition problems, Edge realised that there was little point in continuing, so he abandoned the race at Nemours after about 50 miles (80km) and returned to Paris.

During his brief run, Edge had reached two conclusions: that British coil manufacturers needed to do some more work on their products, and that to compete successfully in French open road races he needed a car with much more power. On his return to England, he went to Vine Street and spoke to Montague Napier on the subject. No doubt Edge addressed him in his usual forceful style, to which Napier by now must have become accustomed. However, Napier appreciated the need for the quickest possible car to run in the 1901 Gordon Bennett, and he set to work on a new design at once.

The Napier's unsuccessful participation in the Paris–Toulouse–Paris event was the first time a British car had competed in a Continental motor race, the forerunner of a noble band of competitors. It has been suggested in the past that this distinction belongs to the Hon John Montagu (later the second Lord Montagu of Beaulieu), who drove a British Daimler in the Tourist class of the 1899 Paris–Ostend. However, the Tourist class did not compete in the race itself, but merely followed it in a touring itinerary. The true honour therefore lies with Edge and his Napier.

As Montague Napier worked with his draftsmen in the drawing office at Vine Street in the late summer and early autumn of 1900, he must have reflected that if Edge wanted a big, fast racing car, then he should have one, with no half-measures. The end product has not been called 'The Monster' without reason. A four-cylinder of very similar design to the 16hp, the new engine was over three times as large; with a bore and stroke of 165.1mm x 190.5mm, the swept volume was 16,315cc. Like the smaller engine, it had triple automatic inlet valves, cast iron cylinder blocks, cast in pairs, an aluminium crankcase, and it was cooled with a pump and tubular radiator. It was probably the biggest car engine that had then been built, and it has been suggested that it developed 103hp at 800rpm. It had one curious and almost eccentric feature: there was no throttle, engine speed being controlled by advancing and retarding the ignition. High tension ignition was fitted. The commutator was on the dashboard in front of the driver and mechanic; it was driven from the half-time shaft by a bicycle chain, tensioned by a jockey pulley and spring, each cylinder having its own trembler coil. This massive piece of machinery, known as the 50hp, which never had a factory type number, was installed under a bonnet which itself was 5ft 2in (157cm) long and 2ft 11in (89cm) wide. The chassis was again very similar to that of the 16hp, with a wheelbase of 8ft 9in (267cm) and a track of 4ft 9in (145cm). There was a metal-to-metal clutch which took the power to a four-speed gearbox, thence through left and right hand bevel boxes to a chain-driven rear axle. The fuel tank contained 50 gallons (227.3 litres) which it consumed at the rate of 4mpg, while the cooling system had a capacity of 14 gallons (63.6 litres).

The 1901 Gordon Bennett Trophy was to be combined with the Paris–Bordeaux race and was to be held on 29 May, the distance being 327 miles (526km). The award for this event has been described both as a trophy and a cup, but since it would be very difficult to consume liquid from the object in question, in this story it is called a trophy. The event was limited to national teams of three cars, to be entered by each national motor club, and – an important restriction – every component of the competing cars had to be made in the country of their manufacture. Napier had intended to put forward four 50hp cars for selection for the British Gordon Bennett team. It was intended that these four cars should be driven by Edge, Count Zborowski, the Hon Charles Rolls, and Mark Mayhew. All the other British contenders for selection faded away, and only one Napier was built in time, and even that was not ready until 25 May. It had originally been ordered by Rolls, but when he realised that it might not be finished in time for the race, he cancelled the order, which appears to have been taken over by Mayhew, a rich 31-year-old London flour miller, living at Roehampton. Certainly it seems that the car was in the nominal ownership of Mayhew when it was finished.

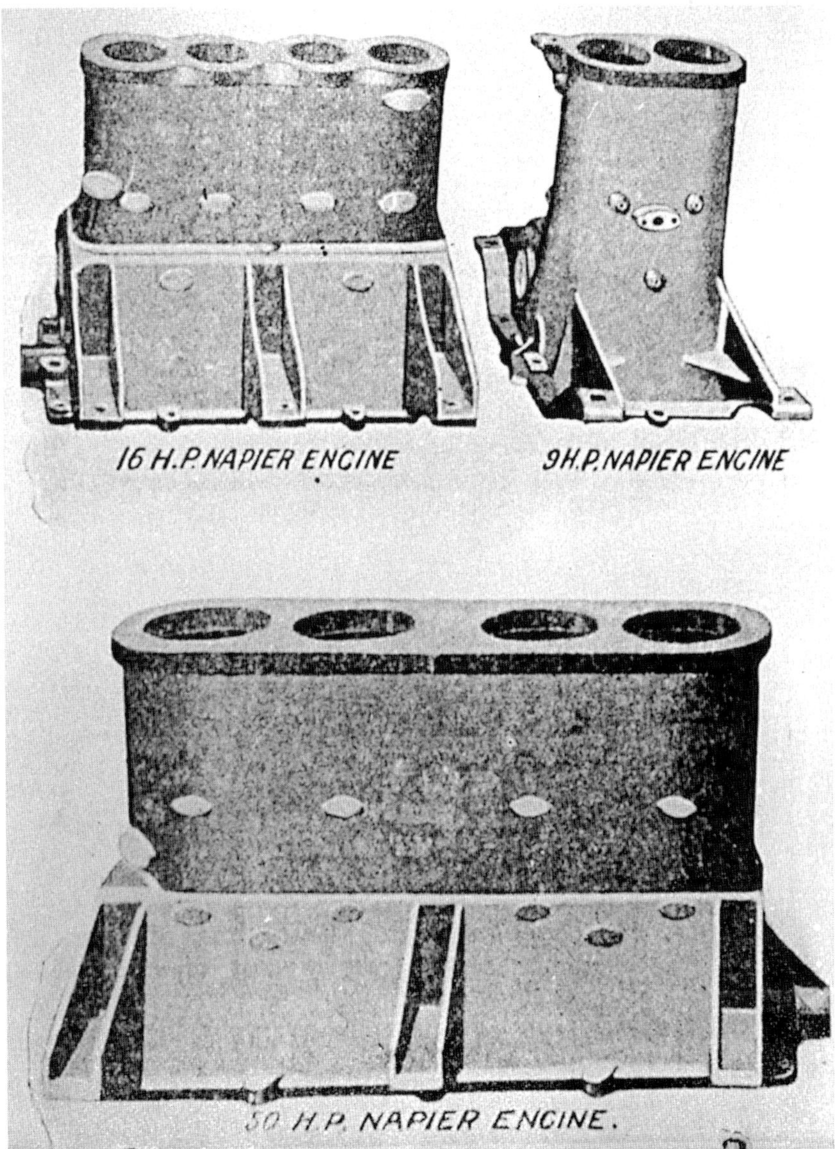

A press photograph of 1901 shows the comparative sizes of the cylinder blocks of the 8hp G20, the 16hp H70 – the first four-cylinder Napier – and the enormous block of the 50hp 'Monster'. The design similarities are apparent. (Derek Grossmark)

With the little time that was left to them, Edge and Napier conducted what tests they could. The main problem was to find a venue where the performance could be evaluated. The legal speed limit was 12mph (19.3kmh) and Edge estimated that the maximum speed of the car was 85mph (135kmh). Napier and Edge rose early in the morning and conducted a test, accompanied by St John Nixon, at Frensham in Surrey,

The 50hp 'Monster'. Mark Mayhew is at the wheel, with Cecil Edge beside him. This is the 'production' car sold to Mayhew. (Derek Grossmark)

on the Hindhead road alongside Frensham Pond. The roads were deserted, and the police were still abed. Edge's comments about the car are illuminating.

> I had to admit I had never handled anything approaching it in point of speed. After all the other cars I had then driven, this one seemed like a thing possessed; there seemed to be no limit to its capabilities, but I had early evidence that speed, although desirable and necessary, was not everything. Tyres began to give trouble very early in our trials.

Edge was to be accompanied in the race by Napier himself, as riding mechanic, much as W.O. Bentley was to do in the Tourist Trophy nearly 30 years later. They set off for France with high hopes, but even while travelling to Folkestone for the Channel ferry the tyres began to raise doubts. As soon as any sustained speed was attempted the treads were thrown and the tyres came off the rims. Between Boulogne and Paris, the problem became worse, and Edge realised he had an insoluble problem. For a car to be eligible to take part in the Gordon Bennett race, the tyres had to be made in the country of the car's manufacture. Running on the defective Dunlops, the car would make no showing at all, so when Edge and Napier arrived in Paris, at midnight on the Sunday before the race, they had already decided to cut their losses and fit French tyres. This would mean that the car would no longer be eligible for the Gordon Bennett Trophy, but could still compete in the Paris–Bordeaux. To the French motor racing world, British efforts in the sport so far had been of no consequence whatever, so when the Napier arrived at the headquarters of the Automobile Club de France in the Place de la Concorde for scrutinising, it aroused considerable interest and no little admiration. It looked bigger and heavier than any of the French competitors and the formidable looks were accentuated by its red paint; green was still a year away.

Edge, however, had another problem. To declare to the world that the car had been scratched from the Gordon Bennett because its Dunlop tyres were not up to the job would be the worst possible publicity for Dunlop. This, in itself, probably would not have worried Edge, but the Chairman of Dunlop was Harvey du Cros senior; du Cros was Edge's partner in the Motor Power Company. Any public criticism of Dunlop would certainly not have gone down well with du Cros, and could have initiated a dispute between the partners. This in turn could have lost money for both and, equally seriously, it could have dealt a severe blow to the commercial prospects of Napier, just as the new marque was getting into its stride and the sale of cars was beginning to flourish.

Edge and Napier undoubtedly discussed the problem when they

arrived in Paris, and although nothing has ever been recorded on the matter, it seems likely that the sharp commercial acumen of Edge came up with an answer which solved the problem, and achieved a most happy result for all concerned. At the scrutinising, the cars had to be weighed. The official weight recorded for the Napier has never been disclosed, but after the inspection was over, Edge declared to the world that the Napier had been weighed at three and a half tons (3,563kg). This was an astonishing figure, but anyone looking at the giant Napier would not have disputed it. The tyre difficulty, however, was thereby solved, as Dunlop could not have reasonably been expected to make a tyre to match the demands of such a heavy car; and as far as Napier was concerned, the contemporary public had the view that weight equalled strength. If the Napier was that heavy, it meant it was rugged and therefore well-made. Nothing would be likely to break; light cars were flimsy cars. It is most significant that when the Napier was weighed for the Paris–Berlin, just four weeks later, the official weight was recorded as 1,800kg. The Paris–Berlin weights were only recorded to the nearest 50kg, but even so, this meant the Napier was only recorded at one and three-quarter tons, which was a much more realistic figure for a car of its size and construction.

The true story of the Napier's weight discrepancy will probably never be known, but it has puzzled motoring historians since 1901, and the hypothesis proposed here may be as close to the truth as we are likely to get. At Napiers – a firm that made its name with the construction of accurate weighing equipment – the factory records show that the weighing of individual items and complete products became almost a fetish, so it is strange that the weight of the car was not recorded. Although Edge may have decided to spare Dunlop's blushes, the English press was not so kind. The *Automotor Journal* referred to 'productions which Mr Harvey du Cros is pleased to call tyres'.

The Paris–Bordeaux race was to start at Versailles at 4am on 29 May. It had become the talk of all Paris, and a huge crowd gathered to watch the greatest motor race yet. As the cars lined up in the dawn, the Prefect of Police raised a bureaucratic point of law that seemed likely to prevent the event taking place: he demanded the production by each driver of a *certificat de reception et capacité*. These documents showed that the car was suitable to be driven on the public road and that the driver was capable of taking charge of it. Most drivers could produce a driving licence, but the *certificat de reception* was a different matter. There was much telephoning to the Prefecture in Paris and a dispensation was granted at the last moment. In the half-light at 4am, M. Huet, the ACF starter, began flagging the cars away at two minute intervals. Charron (Panhard) was the first to go, followed by Levegh's Mors and Giradot with the second Panhard. Edge thundered away at 4.15, the apprehensive Napier at his side. The crowd at Versailles then awaited reports on the progress of the race.

At Chartres, Levegh was in the lead, in front of Giradot, Voigt's Panhard, and Fournier's Mors. Edge was in fifth place in the Napier. At Châteaudun, Levegh and Fournier were still in front, but Fournier was closing up on them, while Edge had fallen back to seventh, as he had been forced to stop several times to adjust the clutch, thereby losing nearly 30 minutes. Edge found that with the lack of a throttle he was forced to reduce speed on corners by declutching, which cannot have helped this component. When he declutched on one corner he found that an oil-can was jammed under the clutch pedal, so the Napier continued round the corner at unabated speed, on two wheels. Despite the clutch problem, however, the Napier had been timed over a measured kilometre between Paris and Chartres at 110kmh (68.3mph). Fournier was timed at 100kmh (62.1mph).

A large British contingent, including Edge's cousin Cecil, Charles Jarrott, and Harvey du Cros junior, had assembled at Tours to replenish the Napier. It arrived at 8.16am, still in seventh place, though 46 minutes behind Levegh. The cars were flagged down on the outskirts of Tours and were then given a bicycle escort to the departure control on the southern exit of the city. The cars were allowed to spend 25 minutes in the 'neutral zone' of the city while they were replenished, this not being added to their running time. The amateur pit crew went into action and huge quantities of Stelline fuel were poured into the tank from 20-litre cans. Napier went round the car, lubricating the vital points, and Edge was fed by his cousin with champagne and sponge cake.

Once the car and crew were revictualled there was a slight drama, as the engine was reluctant to start again. This was because 'The Monster' required a complicated starting ritual: the float chamber – known by the car's crew as the 'Ladies only', had to be filled, then an enormous crow bar, several feet long, was attached to a dog at the front of the crankshaft. The engine was pulled over on compression, so each cylinder was filled; the ignition was fully retarded, so it would not fire in the wrong rotation; then the coils were switched on and the resultant spark fired the engine. Napier found he did not have the strength to do it, and the task fell to Jarrott, who pulled at it for several minutes before the engine burst into life. Napier leapt on board and the car went down the hill and through Tours, to be released from the official time control with the prospect ahead of some 215 miles (345km) of open, indifferently surfaced roads between there and Bordeaux.

It was calculated that there would be no need to refuel again before the finish. The Napier lasted another 85 miles (140km) and then at Couhé, south of Poitiers, the clutch cried 'enough' and the fuel tank sprang a large leak. Later in the morning, Jarrott came upon Edge and Napier. Edge was still sitting in the driving seat, while Napier was lying on the verge in a state of total exhaustion. Not a strong man, Napier's reserves must finally have been sapped, not just by the rigours of the road, but also, no doubt, by Edge's terse comments about the design of the car. Edge said afterwards:

> I remember telling Napier, as we sat there on the car stranded at the side of the road, that it was hopeless going to the great expense of producing a huge car capable of immense speed, if it was impossible to utilize that speed . . . it had begun to dawn on me that it would not be safe to leave Napier in future to design racing cars.

Victory in the race went to Fournier, whose Mors averaged 53mph (85kmh) over the 327 miles (526km) to Bordeaux, an average speed which a modern motorist, eschewing the autoroutes, would be hard pressed to achieve. With the technical limitations and the road conditions of the time, such speeds are almost beyond belief.

Presumably 'The Monster's clutch and fuel tank were repaired in France, so that the 50hp car could return to England by road, and within two weeks it was ready for action again, as Edge had entered it for the Tilburstowe hill-climb on Saturday 15 June. The sheer power of the car carried the day and Edge was easily the fastest, climbing the hill in 67.8 seconds, well ahead of Mark Mayhew's Panhard. Edge and the car did not rest on their laurels, as they were on their way back to France almost as soon as the Tilburstowe event was over. The destination was Paris, where the car was to run in the next heroic road race, the Paris–Berlin on 27 June. The ACF had decided that as a gesture, to improve Franco–German relations, and to continue the healing of the wounds caused by the Franco-Prussian War of 1870, a motor race should be held between Paris and Berlin. This would be run in three stages over three days: the first would be from Paris to Aachen, the second from Aachen to Hanover, and the final stage would be from Hanover to Berlin. In the light of what was to ensue a decade later, the motive behind the race was sadly ironic. Edge arrived in Paris several days before the start, to give himself time to make final preparations to the car and to reconnoitre the first leg of the route. He was accompanied by Montague Napier again, but this time Napier had decided that he would only be a spectator.

Before the race, Edge carried out speed tests on the Paris–Chartres road, between the 75th and 83rd kilometre stones. The car was timed over a kilometre at 69mph (110kmh) and over the 8km distance the speed was 67mph (107kmh). The cars were scrutinised again at the ACF in the Place de la Concorde, where the competitors found that the regulations for these open road races were being more strictly defined. One of the problems of the Paris–Bordeaux had been the clouds of dust raised by the competitors, and in an attempt to overcome this it was stipulated that no car would be allowed to start for Berlin unless it was fitted with a proper exhaust box, arranged so that it did not discharge onto the ground and raise dust. Great attempts had been made to ensure that the course would be as safe as possible. There were 53 time controls, flag-men and soldiers guarded the road, and M. Serpollet drove over the whole course, at the request of the ACF, and reported that the surface was generally good, but that dust would be a problem as ever.

The race was divided into two main classes: the racing class, which had 40 large racing cars, 48 light cars, 12 small cars, and 10 motor cycles; and a touring car class, which followed an easier route, over eight stages, which was intended to arrive in Berlin at the same time as the racers. Forty-five cars started in the touring class, which left on the day when the racers were being scrutineered. As had happened with the Paris–Bordeaux, the race captured the imagination of the Parisians, and the night before the event huge crowds made their way out to Champigny, just east of the Bois de Vincennes, where the race was to start. Amidst the throng were thousands of cyclists with Chinese lanterns hung on their machines, which added to the picturesque scene. So great were the crowds that many of the competitors had difficulty in getting to the start in time, and the police found they were almost unable to keep the road clear.

At 3.30am, Giraud's Panhard was the first car to be flagged away by the Comte de Chasseloup-Laubat, and the rest of the field of 110 followed at two minute intervals. Edge set off at a most impressive pace, despite the poor surface at the beginning of the first leg. There were two other British competitors in the race: Rolls was driving a Mors and Jarrott had a factory-prepared Panhard, entered by Harvey du Cros senior. This bore the race number '13', but it was painted dark green, which was a good luck colour in France, and intended to ward off the malevolent effects of the number! Jarrott had trouble with the ignition, and had to stop for repairs. He got going again but was dismayed to find, as he approached Viels-Maisons about 75km (46½ miles) after the start, that he had been caught by Edge, who had left the start much later. For some distance the two British drivers battled together, with Jarrott just keeping ahead, but as they breasted a rise Jarrott found a right-angle corner ahead. He was approaching it much too fast, and his problems

The 50hp is worked on at the Clement works in Paris before the start of the Paris–Berlin in June 1901. (Guy Griffiths Collection)

were compounded by the wreckage of Loysel's Panhard, which had already demolished itself against a stone wall on the outside of the bend. Jarrott just scraped round, well over the limit, but his unfortunate mechanic, Smits, was flung off the step of the Panhard, narrowly missing the wall. He staggered to his feet, shaken but unhurt, and while Jarrott stopped to recover him Edge swept past and roared into the distance.

Shortly after this, Edge ran into trouble. While going down a hill he was passed by a tyre which, he realised, had very recently been attached to the near-side back wheel of the Napier. The tyre struck a tree and, with its inner tube, bounced into the air and lodged on a branch. The mechanic was directed to climb the tree and recover the tyre and tube, but the rim had been badly battered and it took Edge and his mechanic 34 minutes to straighten it sufficiently to refit the tyre. After this, he had four separate punctures in the same tyre, but despite these delays the Napier was still in eighth place when it arrived at the Rheims time control. The run into Rheims itself was dramatic and dangerous, as the crowd blocking the road only separated as the cars approached at 70mph (112kmh). In Edge's own words, 'It was really quite "off"!' While the mechanic refuelled and lubricated the car, Edge gave a graphic and dramatic account of the morning's incidents to H.O. Duncan, who was standing at the control and preparing his report for *The Autocar*. As the identity of the intrepid mechanic was not recorded in any of the contemporary accounts, it has to be supposed that he was a press-ganged Napier employee, not deemed worthy of notice!

Edge set off from Rheims with hopes of picking up several places, but just outside Sedan, about 60 miles (95km) further on, he pulled over to pass another competitor while crossing a bridge. In the cloud of dust, Edge made a slight error and the Napier struck the parapet; a rear spring was broken and the car's race was over. Edge wrote a letter to Montague Napier from Sedan, explaining the reason for the failure, but he was concerned that the reputation of the Napier should be preserved, so he also wrote to *The Automotor Journal*, giving an account of what had happened, and his letter was published in the issue of July 1901. The race continued to Berlin and it gave a second victory, in a month, to Fournier and his Mors. Jarrott and the long-suffering Smits finished in tenth place, which was a good result for his first road race.

The problems that Edge had encountered with the crowd outside Rheims had serious consequences. At Monchenot, a small village near the city, Brasier, driving a Mors, had knocked down and killed a small boy who was standing in the middle of the road, watching another competitor disappearing into the distance. This accident became the focus of public opposition to open road races, and a few days later M. Waldeck-Rousseau, the French Minister of the Interior, announced that there would be an absolute ban on any further racing in France. This was to be a ban of short duration, but the days of open road racing were numbered.

Edge made repairs to the Napier at Sedan and then returned to England without delay. It seems certain that the damage was limited to the broken spring, the rugged construction of the car preventing any further harm, since only eight days later, on Saturday 6 July, Edge ran it at the hill-climb at Dashwood Hill, outside High Wycombe in Buckinghamshire. This was an ACGBI meeting on the public highway (the London–Oxford road), subject to all the might of the law, and although the Napier was the winner its average speed was reported as just 12 mph (19kmh) – the legal limit! Edge went back to France again for the Gaillon hill-climb on 17 November. The Gaillon course was in the Seine valley, near Vernon. It was a straight kilometre on the N15 with a gradient of 1 in 10, climbing out of Gaillon village to the north-west on the Rouen side. He was joined at Gaillon by another 50hp car, which the factory had now built for Mark Mayhew – presumably he had decided to have a new car and not the rebuilt racer, which had been his original purchase. This had been fitted with a rudimentary tonneau body, which qualified it for the touring car class. The situation had a parallel in the attempts by Ferrari to sell some of his fiercest sports racers to rich amateurs in the 1950s. Gaillon attracted 79 entrants, who tackled the course on a damp foggy day. Edge won the racing car class with a time of 63.6 seconds over the flying start kilometre course, despite missing a gear change during his run, and Mayhew took second place in the large touring class. Mayhew's run was spoiled slightly when he was baulked by a spectator's car as he left the start.

This was almost the end of the road for the 50hp 'Monster'. It appeared a few times in 1902, but shortly after that the car was broken up and the engine was installed in Edge's racing motor boat, where the lack of a throttle would have been less of a handicap. Edge had already decided that Napier was not to have a free hand in future, but Napier had been noting carefully what the French manufacturers were producing, and the design taking shape on his drawing board, with Edge looking over his shoulder, showed that he had learned his lesson well.

Chapter 3: 1902

A Famous Victory

AT the beginning of 1902, motor racing was still a banned sport in France. The Automobile Club de Nice nevertheless decided to hold a race from Nice to Abbazzia (now Opatija, Slovenia) on 8, 9 and 10 April. It was proposed to overcome the difficulties presented by the fact that the French and Austrian governments would not permit racing within their frontiers, by making the sections of the course within these countries 'neutral' zones, where no racing would be permitted; the cars would simply proceed in single file, at a limited speed. This left Italy as the only place where actual racing would take place. However, just before the race, alarmed by the furious driving of competitors practising over the course, the Italian Government followed the example of its neighbours and insisted that Italy, too, should be a neutral zone. The Automobile Club de Nice had no alternative but to cancel the event.

For a few weeks it seemed as if motor racing had run its course. But then the infinite wiles of politics began to play a part. As has happened in France in more recent times, there was a wine surplus, which had been converted to industrial alcohol. The Minister of Agriculture, M. Jean Dupuy, decided that this could be used as an alternative motor spirit. The French motoring public, however, seemed to have little enthusiasm for alcohol except when used in the conventional manner, so, with an eye to attracting the agricultural vote in the forthcoming elections, the Minister set up a commission to advise him on the best way of persuading the public to use the new motor spirit. The secretary of the commission, M. Famechon, informed the Minister almost immediately that a motor race, in which the competitors would be restricted to using alcohol fuel, would be an ideal mode of publicity. M. Dupuy was delighted by this idea and went to see his ministerial colleague, the Minister of the Interior, M. Waldeck-Rousseau. Waldeck-Rousseau was probably surprised, if not irked, by the proposal, as he had only imposed the ban a few months earlier. Votes were in it though, and the ban was lifted, but only for the one race, the alcoholic Circuit du Nord, which was to be a two-day event, starting and finishing in Paris and running through such towns as Arras, Abbeville, and Dieppe. It was organised by the Government itself and became known as the Concours de Ministre, and there was much publicity about the exclusive use of alcohol fuel.

As soon as the 1901 Paris–Berlin race was over, the Automobile Club de France had announced its plan for an ambitious race from Paris to Vienna. Though the ban had already been imposed, the ACF was confident that it could probably be raised or circumvented for the Paris–Vienna, so the race's regulations were published in January 1902. It was accepted that some sort of curb needed to be put on the monster racers, such as the 50hp Napier, which were now appearing, so in its wisdom the ACF concluded that if car weights were restricted, speed would also be controlled – a delusion that has bedevilled the devisors of motor racing formulae at irregular intervals ever since. It was decreed that for the Paris–Vienna, no car should exceed 1,000kg (2,205lb), though an extra 7kg (15.4lb) would be allowed for cars with magneto ignition. There would be two subsidiary classes, for light cars which did not exceed 650kg (1,433lb), and for voiturettes, which were limited to 400kg (881.8lb).

Having announced the rules, the ACF now waited, hoping that its patience would be rewarded. The alcohol-fuelled Circuit du Nord took place on 15 and 16 May and was declared to be a great success, especially as there were no serious accidents, so the ACF now sought permission for the Paris–Vienna. There was a need to obtain governmental approval not only in France, but also in Switzerland and Austria. There had been a dramatic change of heart in Austria since the Nice–Abbazzia fiasco in April, and the city fathers of Vienna were putting together a prize fund. Things were very different in Switzerland, though, where a ban was still being maintained and was unlikely to be lifted. The ACF considered taking the race through Bavaria instead, but the Bavarian government indicated that the ACF and its racers would be most unwelcome.

The French government now relented and gave permission for the Paris–Vienna event, but stipulated that it would be the only race that the ACF would be permitted to run during 1902; there was no prospect of the ACF also being allowed to run the Paris–Bordeaux. Having received authority to run the Paris–Vienna through France and Austria the ACF declared that Switzerland would be a neutral zone, with no racing taking place on Swiss soil. The route was now settled: Paris–Belfort, the neutral zone across Switzerland from Belfort to Bregenz, then racing again on the final two stages, Bregenz–Salzburg and Salzburg–Vienna.

At the end of each stage the cars would be taken to a *parc ferme*, where each would have an assigned place. All the driver and mechanic would be permitted to do, before leaving the car for the night, would be to switch off the electric current and inject fuel into the cylinders to help in starting the following day. Next morning, the crew would only be permitted to enter the park and start work on the car at their appointed starting time, so all work had to be done in running time. Perhaps it was as an additional political sop that the ACF put up an award, the Arenberg Cup, to go to the first car to finish the Paris–Belfort stage using alcohol fuel.

As there would be no possibility of getting permission for a separate race, the ACF incorporated the Gordon Bennett Trophy into the Paris–Vienna. The Gordon Bennett competitors, being governed by the separate rules of that competition, had only to cover 610km (379.1 miles), so their race would finish at Innsbruck, which was in the middle of the Bregenz–Salzburg stage. The Gordon Bennett competitors would still be able to race on to Vienna in the main competition, so it would be possible for one competitor to win both races.

Montague Napier and Selwyn Edge decided that they would compete in the race as soon as it was announced, and while the political tussle continued across the Channel, Napier worked steadily. During 1901 a 25-year old-engineer, Arthur Rowledge, had joined the firm as a designer, and it seems certain that Napier delegated much of the detail design to him. Rowledge's book of calculations still exists and shows weight tables and comparisons with competitors. Napier had looked very carefully at the Paris–Berlin competitors while attending the 1901 race, as there was very little opportunity to study contemporary developments in England, where to some extent he was working in an isolated backwater. Napier – as Edge reminded him at every opportunity – had made the 50hp car much too heavy. Not only was there a need to make a lighter car to save the tyres, but he now had to build it within the new weight limits.

The technical innovation which impressed Napier most was the transmission of the victorious Renault. He decided to follow Louis Renault's example, and the new Napier was designed with a propeller shaft and live axle, abandoning the countershaft sprockets and chains of the 50hp. Edge had some doubts:

While realising the advantages of a live axle, I could not help feeling somewhat

The Paris–Vienna and Gordon Bennett races, 1902. The Gordon Bennett competition finished at Innsbruck. The total racing distance was 615 miles (989km), the Gordon Bennett course being 351 miles (564km). There was a neutral zone between Belfort and Bregenz where no racing was permitted.

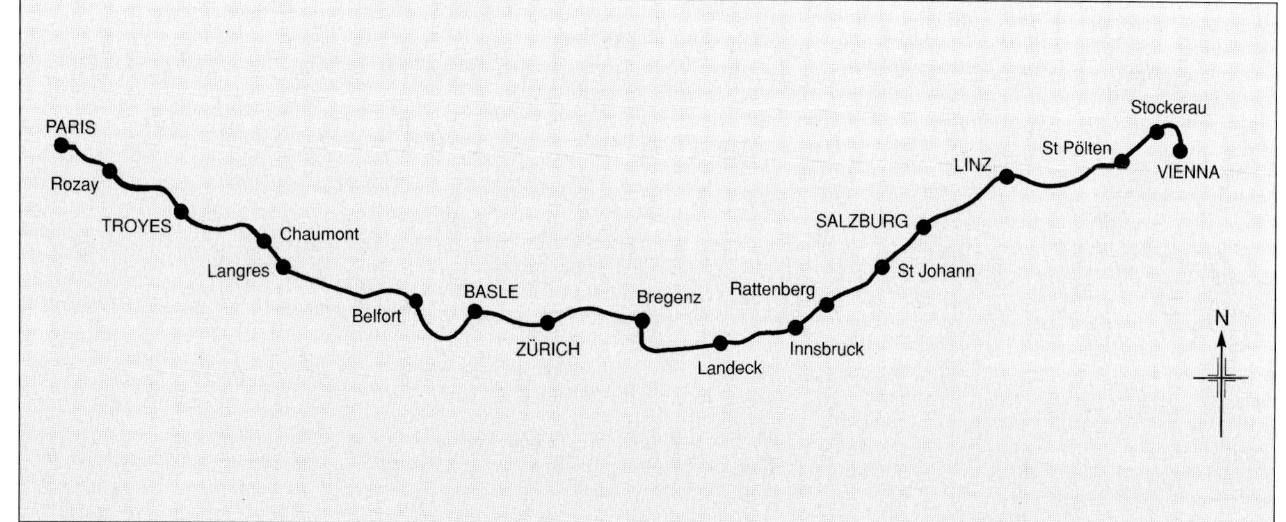

doubtful whether the method would stand up to the strains imposed. Napier's mind, however, was centred on the abolition of chains and sprockets, and as I had to admit the success which had attended the Renault cars in competitions, I did not raise any objection.

The live axle design effected a considerable saving in weight, but Napier went much further. The new car had a 'square' engine, with an equal bore and stroke of 127mm (5in), giving a swept volume of 6,436cc. As before, the design relied on automatic inlet valves, but this time there were four per cylinder. The ignition was by coil and battery. To make a comparatively light engine, the upper crankcase and cylinder block were cast in one piece in aluminium, and cast iron cylinder liners were pressed into the block. The engine was pump-cooled, and a particularly inelegant radiator – made by Clarksons, who also made steam omnibuses – was mounted in front of the engine. There was an 11 gallon water tank.

This new engine was put in a wooden frame, reinforced with metal flitch plates in the stressed areas. Power was taken from the engine through a metal to metal clutch, which incorporated a cooling fan, to a three-speed gearbox – as the car was lighter, Edge felt that four speeds would be unnecessary. The car had 34in (86cm) wooden wheels fitted with 920 x 120 tyres. The front wheels had ten spokes, but the rear had twelve to take the 44.5hp that the engine developed. A 40-gallon (180 litre) fuel tank was shaped to make a base for the two seats. The large tank was essential, as the Napier team would not be setting up fuel depots during the race and there would be little prospect of finding other sources on the road. The wheelbase was 7ft 8in (244cm), the track was 4ft 8$^{1}/_{2}$in (143.5cm), and Napier had been so determined that weight should not be an issue that the car only scaled 933kg even with a full fuel tank. Finally – no doubt to Edge's great relief – engine speed was now governed by a throttle.

The car was known within the Napier works as the D50 model, and factory records show that it had the chassis number 239 and the engine number 111. It is difficult to be certain, but it seems likely that the firm had built at least that number of cars by the spring of 1902.

Perhaps persuaded by Charles Jarrott that it was a lucky colour, the car was painted in a shade of olive green, and so a great tradition was begun. It is not known how the exact shade was decided in 1902, but two years later, when Napiers moved to Acton, the doors and window-frames of the works were painted with a shade of olive green supplied by Carsons, a London paint manufacturer. Many years later Charlie Childs, who worked on the racing cars, said that when a car was ready for painting, a boy was sent to the stores to obtain a supply of the standard green factory paint, so the same paint sufficed for both factory buildings and racing cars. Some authorities have suggested that Napiers were not painted green until 1903, but Lord Montagu, in his book *The Gordon Bennett Races*, says that an eyewitness, Henry Knox, recalled the olive green colour of the 1902 car.

While Napier was working on the D50, Edge was keeping his hand in by competing in hill-climbs and speed trials. On 8 February the Automobile Club of Great Britain and Ireland held a hill-climb at Petersham Hill (now the Star and Garter Hill) on the outskirts of Richmond, with another course in Richmond Park. Edge entered a 16hp Tourer only to be beaten by a steam-powered 4$^{1}/_{2}$ hp Locomobile. It seems unlikely that Edge used this event in Napier publicity. During the Easter holiday, the ACGBI ran a tour to Cromer, in Norfolk, which included a speed trial in Gunton Park, the estate of Lord Cromer. Edge brought out the 50hp car again and defeated the field of 19, averaging 44mph (70kmh) over the flying kilometre course, which was uphill and tortuous with a soft, sticky surface.

The 50hp racer had its swan-song at Bexhill on 19 May. Impressed by the success of the speed trials held on the Promenade des Anglais at Nice the previous year, the ACGBI, not to be outdone, decided to hold a similar event along the promenade at Bexhill. The course started on the top of Galley Hill at the eastern end of the front, and ran westwards onto De La Warr Parade, named after the owner of the course, Earl De La Warr. It incorporated a flying kilometre, and to aid initial acceleration a ramp was constructed on the start line, down which the cars were launched. The slower cars were to run in pairs and the contest was held in heats, though, with commendable prudence, it was decided that the faster machines would run singly. The course was too short to enable the fastest cars to reach their maximum speed, but at the finish there was a right-hand curve, with an adverse camber round which the quicker cars scrabbled, trying to avoid ending up on the beach below. The event attracted a large crowd, and special trains brought spectators from London. There were a number of French entrants including De Knyff, Giradot, and Gabriel. The organisers had included a class for over-1,000kg cars, which provided Edge with an opportunity to give the 50hp car its last outing. The class winner was Rolls with a 1901 28hp Mors, recording a speed of 48.61mph (78kmh), but Edge was second at 47.57mph (76kmh). Edge then made haste to fit vestigial touring equipment, and ran the 50hp again in the Touring class, where he won the category for the largest cars.

While Edge was gaining minor glory at the seaside, work was continuing apace at Vine Street. The Paris–Vienna race was to begin on 26 June, but the new car was not finished until Thursday 19 June. Perhaps there was a conflict between the need to maintain the production of cars to meet customers' orders and the demands on the time of skilled men to prepare the racing car. The pressure on the resources of the small works must have been considerable. With only seven days in hand, the car was tested around the South London suburbs. This showed up the usual small problems and the car was still being worked on in the factory throughout the night of 23/24 June by Edge, his cousin Cecil, who was to be the riding mechanic, Montague Napier himself, and a small team of mechanics.

Before dawn, the team set off for Folkestone. Edge drove, with Napier beside him, while Cecil sat on the step, as the car – loaded with tyres, spare tools, and equipment – rumbled across southern England towards Folkestone and the 11.30am ferry. Edge commented, 'We had a splendid run to Folkestone, and our spirits rose as we felt the general liveliness of the car.' The rising spirits heralded a false dawn as far as the hopes of the team were concerned, though. As the car entered Folkestone, Edge felt that the engine had lost its tune. He pulled up and, on lifting the bonnet, he found that one of the cylinder heads had cracked. Napier said that nothing could be done, as there were no spare heads at Vine Street. He was a man of limited physical stamina, and, leaving the Edges with the car, he went to a nearby hotel and booked a room. Edge was unwilling to admit defeat before the venture had even started, and thought it was unlikely that no spares existed. Leaving Cecil with the car, he found a telephone and contacted the works at Vine Street. He spoke to Ritter, the works foreman, who had just arrived at the factory, and to his relief and delight Ritter said there was a spare head. Edge instructed Ritter to send two of his best mechanics to Folkestone with it by train.

While awaiting their arrival, Edge decided that he and Cecil would remove the damaged head, so the new one could be fitted during the crossing to Boulogne. Napier was roused from his hotel room with the encouraging news and joined the Edges in stripping the engine and preparing the car for hoisting on to the ferry. At Vine Street, Ritter consulted the South East & Chatham Railway timetables, and the two mechanics were sent hot-foot to Charing Cross Station with their tool-bags and the precious head. Catching the Folkestone Boat Train, they were met at the dockside station by Edge.

The new head was fitted during the cross-channel voyage, and the car was ready for the road by the time the ferry docked at Boulogne. Edge sent one of the mechanics back on the ferry, but decided that the other should go with the car to Paris, perhaps suspecting that there could be more trouble. The car, now with the extra mechanic perched on the back among the tyres and impedimenta, motored along well for about 50 miles. Then, going up a hill near Abbeville in second gear, a very nasty noise came from the gearbox. They stopped, and on taking the top off the box they found that the second gear pinion was badly damaged. In his account, Edge says that the teeth were bent right over, but Napier said later that the teeth were only badly burred. The cause was evident, though: the pinion had not been case-hardened before it was fitted to the box. Edge now wished he had stipulated four speeds, since though he could have driven to Innsbruck with three, it would be impossible with only two. Napier said that if the facilities could be found, he could case-harden the pinion with the help of the mechanic.

The car limped into Paris, using first and top gear. After a hasty meal, the car was put in a stable, and Napier and the mechanic, assisted by Cecil, began removing the gearbox. Edge, meanwhile, went to see an old acquaintance, Adolphe Clement, at his factory at Levallois-Perret, near the Bois de Boulogne. He explained that he needed to make some adjustments to the gearbox and asked Clement for the use of his works for a few hours. Edge was concerned that if it became known that any major work had been done on the car in Paris, this could disqualify it from competing for the Gordon Bennett Trophy. Clement agreed to give any help that was needed, so Napier and the mechanic took the second gear pinion to the Clement works where they either cleaned up the teeth or straightened them, depending on which report is to be believed.

The predicament of Montague Napier deserves sympathy. Edge's scathing comments about the condition of the gear pinion can be imagined. Napier and the mechanic now had to work in a strange workshop, with unfamiliar equipment, knowing that if advice or help was sought, the car could be disqualified. The case-hardening itself would have presented few problems. It was a process with which Napier would have been familiar. The gear pinion would have been heated to white heat and then plunged into a mixture of 90 per cent charcoal and 10 per cent common salt. It would then have been reheated and quenched in oil or water and then heated again to temper it. While the gearbox was dismantled, Napier probably looked for high spots on the gears and stoned these off to improve the gear mating. When the job was completed, Napier and the mechanic took the gear pinion back to the stable where the Edges waited.

The team worked all night reassembling the gearbox, working with a constant eye on the clock, as the car had to be presented for scrutineering at the Ministry of Mines in the morning. When the gearbox was assembled and installed, Edge found another problem. The car jumped out of reverse as soon as this gear was engaged. This was serious, as an effective reverse gear was stipulated in the regulations, and this would be tested at the Ministry. There was no time to investigate the problem and Edge set off for the scrutineering. While going along the Champs Elysées, Edge was stopped by a gendarme who demanded to see his driving licence. Edge feared that the licence would be impounded, which would prevent him starting in the race. He prevaricated and produced every paper he had except the licence. He then showed the gendarme his pocket watch, with his name engraved on the back, as further proof of his identity. There was a dramatic change in the atmosphere; the gendarme smiled and shook Edge's hand – they had been fellow-competitors in the 1891 Paris–Bordeaux cycle race! He was waved on accompanied by the best wishes of the Paris constabulary.

Edge had not resolved the problem when he was asked to demonstrate the reversible qualities of the car. He engaged reverse and let the clutch in at maximum revs. The car jumped out of gear as it shot back, but it had gone backwards far enough to satisfy the scrutineer and Edge received the equivalent of a 'passed by scrutineer' ticket. All that now remained was the weighing-in, and while this was being done a very agitated Napier appeared. He explained that when the gearbox had been reassembled a spacer had been left out, and there was nothing to prevent the simultaneous engagement of two gears. The satisfaction that the car had only weighed 933kg was forgotten in the realisation that the gearbox would have to be stripped again, with the race on the morrow.

Edge drove the car carefully back to the stable. The gearbox had to come out again, and the car had to be ready to be presented at the start at 3am. The small team worked in sullen silence, and by the time the gearbox was reassembled with the vital spacer replaced, and installed in the car, the Edges only had time to go to the hotel, where rooms had been booked, to collect some food which they would eat during the first leg of the race. There was no time to wash, shave, or change their clothes. As the car left the stable the engine was misfiring, but Edge, who by then was almost past caring, did not bother to investigate. To his astonishment, when the engine was started again outside the hotel the misfire had disappeared.

It was a fine night, and there were the usual scenes which accompanied the start of the great open road races. A stream of cars, carriages, and cyclists, the latter carrying the customary paper lanterns, made its way to the start at the Fourche de Champigny about two kilometres from the Bois des Vincennes, on the eastern outskirts of Paris. The crowd was singing, blowing horns and whistles, and ringing bells. Through this cheerful assembly, the competitors made their way to the start-line, where the road was lined with carts and wagons supplying petrol, oil, and alcohol fuel, together with countless stalls purveying food and drink for the crowd. Some spectators were driving their own cars along the first leg of the course, to have a view of the competitors at speed. Just as dawn was breaking at 3.30am, the first competitor – Giradot on his CGV – was flagged away.

The ACF had entered a team of three cars to represent France in the Gordon Bennett Trophy – Giradot's CGV, Fournier's Mors, and De Knyff's Panhard. But, while the Edges and Montague Napier toiled away repairing the gearbox in the stable, they still did not know if they would be representing Britain in the Trophy event, or merely competing for the prestige of Napier in the Paris–Vienna. The ACGBI had the responsibility of selecting the British team and had already indicated that its preference lay with Wolseley. The Birmingham company had been building three cars for the event, designed by Herbert Austin. There was a 45hp car, with a horizontal

Champigny before dawn, 26 June 1902. Selwyn Edge sits at the wheel of the D50 Napier waiting for the start of the Paris–Vienna and Gordon Bennett. Cecil Edge stands beside him. (Derek Grossmark)

three-cylinder engine, and two 30hp cars with horizontally opposed four-cylinder engines. Perhaps uncertain if the race would actually take place, Wolseleys had not hurried in the construction and the cars were not well-prepared. In his autobiography *At the Wheel Ashore and Afloat*, Montague Graham-White, one of the Wolseley drivers, wrote that the 45 only arrived in Paris 12 hours before the race was due to start. It had major lubrication problems and was unfit to race, so the Wolseley team was able to present only the two 30hp cars. One was to be driven by Graham-White, accompanied by Herbert Austin himself, and the other was in the hands of a driver named Callan, who had the august figure of Claude Johnson, the ACGBI secretary, as his companion. Johnson's presence in the Wolseley team seemed a clear indication of the preferences of the ACGBI regarding the British team. With the withdrawal of the Wolseley 45, however, the ACGBI now had no alternative but to include the Napier if a full British team was to run. With only hours to go, Edge realised that he had achieved at least one of his aims and was competing in the Gordon Bennett.

If the Wolseley 45 was unfit, the two 30s were in little better state. The car driven by Graham-White broke its crankshaft while being driven out of Paris to the start. Graham-White and Austin immediately started to strip down the engine by the roadside, but their car was effectively eliminated before it ever came to the line, only starting the race – with a new crankshaft – nearly 12 hours later. The other 30, driven by Callan, left the start with magnificent elan, and 200 yards down the road the whole rear of the body fell off, depositing tyres, spares, and equipment on the road. After repairs were effected the car ran as far as the first time control, and then retired with run bearings. French spectators and competitors alike, watching the Wolseley farce, must have thought that the Gordon Bennett Trophy was already won for France. Sadly, a more depressing tradition of British motor racing was being established, that would still be in full flower with the BRM team 50 years later.

Events had conspired to leave Edge as the sole British representative, and while he had 136 competitors to beat in the Paris–Vienna, he now only had three Gordon Bennett rivals. As they waited their turn at the start, he commented to Cecil that the disappearance of the misfire indicated that their luck had turned. The competitors were started at two minute intervals: after Giradot came Fournier's Mors, then Edge, followed by De Knyff's Panhard, which bore the letters 'AL', denoting that it was alcohol-fuelled.

The Napier left the start and set off on the first leg of 267 miles, running as well as it had done when it left Vine Street, though the crew were already physically drained, not only from lack of sleep, but also from the sheer physical effort of the work on the car. A special train had been arranged for spectators, who joined it at Nogent-Le Perreux, near the start, and would be carried through to Belfort to see the finish. In the early stages the cars and the train matched each other for speed, and where the track ran alongside the road, the rail travellers could watch the progress of the race. Fournier led to the first time control at Provins, having averaged 71mph (114kmh) despite a poor road surface. He still held the lead at Troyes, 100 miles from Paris, followed by De Knyff, with Edge in a creditable third place. Giradot had meanwhile fallen out with a split fuel tank. Between Chaumont and Langres, after nearly 200 miles, disaster struck Fournier's Mors when the clutch-shaft broke. Fournier went the rest of the way to Belfort on the spectators' train.

Edge, too, had his problems when a rear tyre punctured. The inevitability of a puncture for the early racer, and equally for the early motorist, was not due solely to inadequate tyre technology. Almost all road traffic was horse-drawn. The horses lost their shoes frequently, and the large, square nails which secured them had a natural attraction to motor tyres. When the Edges changed the tube, though, they found that the tyre pump would not work; they still had a flat tyre and no means of inflating it. Frantically they dismantled the pump and tried to repair it, but despite all their efforts it could not be made to work. As the pair were cursing the return of their ill-fortune, a Mercedes appeared in a cloud of dust. Edge waved at the driver, who pulled up. It was Count Eliot Zborowski; Edge explained his predicament, and without any preamble the Count threw his tyre pump to Edge and raced away, not waiting for its return.

With the tyre inflated, the Napier set off again for Belfort. However, it was gradually slipping down the order as the faster cars, which had started behind it, steadily caught up. Sheer fatigue had probably taken its toll on Edge, and he later admitted that he also had considerable doubts about the newly-hardened gear pinion. He was driving on first and top only, which was a handicap in the hilly country beyond Chaumont. A problem which had beset Edge two years earlier was also slowing the Napier: the British motor industry still had not mastered the art of making completely reliable ignition coils. The electrical problems could have been worse, but Edge had realised, just in time, that the strap holding the battery box had broken and the battery was about to fall out onto the road.

Dust, as ever, had made difficulties for all the competitors, and it was a dust-covered Napier whose arrival at Belfort was heralded by a bugler. It passed through the triumphal arch, which welcomed the competitors, in eleventh place, in a time of 6hr 6min 18.6sec. At the finish, the Edges were fed with champagne and sponge cake by the Panhard pit crew, perhaps as a goodwill gesture to a former owner. The only other Gordon Bennett competitor still running was De Knyff, who had finished the stage in the overall lead of the Paris–Vienna event, as well as the Gordon Bennett. Furthermore, he was one hour and 48 minutes in front of Edge, a seemingly impregnable lead. His drive had also gained him the alcohol prize. However, though Edge did not know it, all was not well with De Knyff's Panhard. During the evening De Knyff confided in Charles Jarrott, a fellow-member of the Panhard team, that the differential casing of his car had cracked. He had doubts about its chances of reaching Innsbruck, let alone Vienna.

The victorious D50 Napier enters Innsbruck on 26 June 1902. Knowing they have won the Gordon Bennett Trophy, Selwyn and Cecil Edge wave to bystanders. (Derek Grossmark)

Amid the dramas and tribulations of getting the Napier ready for the race, no thought had been given to booking accommodation for the night, so now the dusty and exhausted Edges trudged the streets of Belfort looking for a bed. The need for a good night's sleep was essential after the privations of the previous 48 hours. All the hotel rooms had been taken by the French teams, but they were helped in their search by Jarrott and eventually a bed was found in an attic, above a provisions merchant's shop. The attic was used for storing smoked hams, but the aroma of the meat did not prevent the Edges from sleeping soundly. They had to report at the start at 3.00am, so before settling down for the night Cecil Edge had arranged with a policeman, encouraged by the prospect of a large tip, to wake them by throwing stones at their window. Before going to the start, Edge had arranged to meet the Dunlop representative at Belfort station to collect a supply of new tyres. The train was due to arrive at 2.30am, but if it was late his start time would be hazarded. Fortunately it came into the station on time, but the station authorities said he could not remove the box containing the tyres from the train, as it was booked through to Innsbruck. While the Dunlop representative argued, Edge opened the box and removed the tyres, leaving the representative and the empty box to go on to Innsbruck.

The cars had been impounded for the night in a large riding-school. They were to be flagged away for the next stage in the order of their arrival and the driver and mechanic of each car were admitted through the gate of the school two minutes before their starting time. After the two minutes elapsed, the flag fell and the clock started to run. There were scenes of drama and panic as each team sprinted to their car only to find leaks, flat tyres and other mechanical disasters. There were fights for the water buckets and around the water taps. When the Edges dashed to the Napier at 3.22am they were confronted by a car sitting on four flat tyres. All four tubes had to be changed, so time had been lost even before they set off on the 'neutral' stage of the course through Switzerland.

The cars ran through Switzerland in an extended convoy and in a continuous cloud of dust. The official speed limit was set at 15mph, and between Basle and Bregenz each competitor was halted to receive a lecture on the Swiss rules. To avoid any problems, the neutral zone was extended seven kilometres into Austria. The day's run had few problems for the Napier, but there was a nagging worry for Edge: the brakes were deteriorating, and on the morrow the Arlberg Pass had to be crossed. He could not rely on the gearbox to assist the braking, as his doubts about second gear were still unassuaged; furthermore, second was going to be essential in the mountains. The principal desire of the Edges when they arrived at Bregenz was to find a bath to remove the caked dust of the day. They joined forces with Jarrott, but their rudimentary German led them to seek a

Bahnhof (railway station) and not a *Badhaus*, so it was some time before the grime was removed.

The morning start was again at 3.00am, and there was the same frenzied dash to the cars from the gates of the barracks, where they had been impounded for the night. Edge intended to adjust the brakes, but found that the Napier was once more sitting on flat tyres. All four tubes were changed and then he looked at the brakes. The linings, which appeared to be leather on the externally contracting bands, had almost gone. Edge tightened them as best he could and was comforted that the engine started immediately, and was still running as well as it had at the start two days earlier. He knew now that the Gordon Bennett Trophy lay between him and De Knyff, although apparently he did not know about De Knyff's problems. The only Panhard disaster of which Edge was aware was the broken frame on Jarrott's car, and even as he was changing the Napier's inner tubes, Jarrott – as he recounted in *Ten Years of Motors and Motor Racing* – was surreptitiously tearing his hotel bedroom to pieces, assisted by George du Cros, to find suitable wood to lash the frame together.

What happened to Edge and the Napier on the last stage of the Gordon Bennett, has been the subject of much controversy. The bare facts are that the car went over the Arlberg Pass in conditions which were graphically described by Gerald Rose in *A Record of Motor Racing*:

> The pass was nearly 6,000ft above sea-level, and shortly before the competitors were due the roads were almost impassable from snow. And such roads! Hardly more than tracks in some cases, winding along precipices with nothing but boundary stones between the road and the drop beyond, crossing torrents on improvised bridges made of a few planks, climbing hills of extraordinary steepness with descents on the other side of equally terrifying appearance, with the constant fear of the precipice before the eyes of the driver should he miss his corner at the bottom. Small wonder that the competitors imagined at times that they had mistaken the road, and were only reassured by the constantly-recurring flagmen. Up the drivers went, climbing to the clouds through the snow-covered passes, with nerves strained to the utmost by the unknown peril behind every bend in the road.

The Napier brakes lost their effectiveness early on, and Edge had to rely on the gearbox for retardation. He did not use second gear, instead going from top to first. On the descent, the road had been cut into steps to help horse drawn vehicles and the cars crashed down each step. Edge recorded that he passed a blue Panhard broken-down by the roadside, but did not realise the significance until about ten kilometres later, when, pulled up at a level crossing, he was caught up by Jarrott, who said that the Panhard had been De Knyff's. So now Edge had only to reach Innsbruck and the Trophy was his. Jarrott counselled him to drive the rest of the way to Innsbruck with caution, but says that he shot away from the level crossing and round the next corner so fast that inversion seemed inevitable. Despite this, however, the Napier reached Innsbruck without any mishap and was duly feted as the winner of the Gordon Bennett Trophy.

The controversy comes with the various accounts of the day's events, as given by Edge and in various reports published in the motoring journals. According to *The Autocar* the Napier went off the road about 20 miles (32km) after the start at Bregenz, when a man waved a blue flag at the car. Edge braked so hard that the Napier spun and shot off the road, landing on soft ground about 15ft (5m) below the level of the road. The Edges were able to regain the road without outside help. If the brakes were as bad as Edge described, it is surprising that they could be locked to spin the car, and the flag-waving man was fortunate! *The Automotor Journal* reported that the incident happened near Innsbruck, when Edge left the road while trying to pass another car in a dust cloud and struck a bridge. Memories of the Paris–Berlin are evoked here! Edge himself said of the run into Innsbruck: 'We improved our pace and were going rather fast when we came to a curve. We thought we were going to finish up against a wall. Somehow the wheels struck the bottom of the wall and the car escaped injury.' The Automobile Club de France protested at the Napier victory, on the grounds that when the car went off the road in one of these incidents it was manhandled back on to it by 30 Austrian soldiers. Another account stated that the manhandling was done by 30 Austrian peasants, who Edge could not stop because he could not speak the local dialect.

The story of the tyres has also been a puzzle ever since. According to Edge, during the descent of the Arlberg the battering the car received caused the rear of the body to break away and the bottom dropped out of the tool box. All the tools and the spare inner tubes fell out on the road and were lost. After he had been told the news of De Knyff's breakdown, Edge decided to change the covers. He had no more inner tubes, and if he received another puncture the race would be lost. New covers would reduce the chance of such a mishap. According to Edge, since they had no tools he and his cousin removed the worn covers and replaced the new ones with their bare hands. This was truly a Herculean feat of strength and effort. On reflection it would have been almost physically impossible, and one must wonder if Edge felt that the victory might sound rather hollow and wanted to boost the heroic element. In the light of the foregoing it is more puzzling that after the race, Edge claimed in *The Automotor Journal* that the Napier had run through the whole Gordon Bennett race on the same set of tyres. The set was later exhibited in the Dunlop showroom in Regent Street.

It is a pity that Edge's affinity with hyperbole and his desire for publicity slightly tarnished the glory of what was a famous victory. He and the Napier had won against the odds and had overcome some formidable problems. Even without the legend of the tyres, his courage and tenacity cannot be doubted. Although it could be said that they had won by default, they had reached Innsbruck, which was more than any of the French team had managed. H.O. Duncan was in Salzburg, waiting for the Paris–Vienna cars to arrive at the end of the day's stage, when the news of the Napier victory was received. André Michelin, the tyre manufacturer, turned to him and, in a few words, summed up the French attitude. 'This is a bad business. It will mean a lot of trade for English makers.'

Although the Napier had won the Gordon Bennett Trophy, the Paris–Vienna was still going on. Edge, to his credit, decided not to rest on his well-deserved laurels, but to carry on from Innsbruck to Salzburg, to finish the stage, with the aim of reaching Vienna and being classified in the main event. He was relieved of one burden: in the Paris–Vienna, he was not required to rely solely on British-made parts and accessories. Immediately, he pulled up at a French tyre manufacturer's depot and requested tyres, hoping the Napier would be mistaken for a Panhard. At the first depot he was recognised and shooed away, but at the second the ruse worked. The tyres were changed and the driver and mechanic were also refuelled with champagne. At Innsbruck the Napier had been in 15th place, but, perhaps inspired by the champagne, Edge had worked up to tenth place at Salzburg. The town was dressed with bunting, flowers, and flags, and the sole topic of conversation was the defeat of the French Gordon Bennett team. The nature of the defeat seemed to register more with the motor racing world than the British victory. The French, who until then were inclined to be slightly dismissive of the Trophy, suddenly realised the importance of what they had lost.

It must be suspected that much more champagne was consumed by Selwyn and Cecil Edge that afternoon and evening. It was probably a relief to them that the following morning's start was slightly later, at 5.00am. There was the usual dash at the start as the cars set off on the final leg to Vienna. History does not relate if the French tyres, on which the Napier now stood, had also flattened overnight. The roads on the final leg were probably the worst the competitors had yet encountered, being laid in continuous steps, the effect of which was probably similar to modern 'traffic-calming' humps.

Selwyn Edge and Montague Napier pose in the victorious 1902 Gordon Bennett car. (Derek Grossmark)

Any attempt to maintain speed resulted in shattering shocks to the cars. The competitors may have hated it, but the crowd loved it. *L'Auto* commented that the crowd was thickest on the worst sections.

The finish of the race was on the Prater trotting track just outside Vienna. The special train which had been following the race arrived in Vienna at about five o'clock in the morning and the occupants then had to wait. The first car was expected at about 3.00pm, but just after two o'clock a car appeared going the wrong way round the track and pulled up at the finish. It was Marcel Renault in his light car, who had beaten all the heavy car class. The outraged officials told Renault to go away and make his entrance from the proper direction, but despite this he still won. About an hour and a half after Renault had crossed the line in the proper direction, Edge finished with the Napier, taking eighth place in the heavy car class and 15th place overall. His average for the whole course had been 31.9mph (51kmh), compared to Renault's 38.9mph (62.2kmh) and the 38.4mph (61.4kmh) average of Henri Farman, whose Panhard had won the heavy class. Count Zborowski, whose sporting gesture had helped Edge in his hour of need, had not apparently suffered from this and was second among the heavies. The cars were then taken to the Rotunda in the centre of Vienna where they were exhibited, and that evening there was a celebration banquet. Next day, the delegates from the national clubs considered the ACF protest that Edge had received outside assistance, but after deliberation the protest was dismissed. To his credit, De Knyff refused to be associated with the club's objection.

The Napier and the Edges returned to England by train and the car was put on show in the Regent Street showroom of the Motor Power Company, where there was also a special display of the tyres. On Wednesday 23 July, Edge was feted at a banquet given by the ACGBI at the Hotel Metropole, and during the evening Giradot handed him the Trophy. The day before, at a celebratory luncheon, Edge was presented with the first gold medal of the Society of Motor Manufacturers and Traders. Another medal was to have been presented to Montague Napier, but he had been called to the War Office to discuss a contract, so Edge received it on his behalf. For Montague Napier and the Motor Power Company, the victory had brought substantial commercial benefits. If before now the Napier marque had not been of much significance in the British motoring world, that was no longer the case. Orders flowed in, not only for cars, but for commercial vehicles too. Edge was determined to get the maximum publicity for the Trophy and it appears that he had an exact replica made by a London silversmith so that he was able to display it in his showrooms long after the original had gone elsewhere.

With the rapid expansion of business, the company was outgrowing the Vine Street works. A 3¾ acre (1.5 hectare) site was bought at Acton Vale, on the south side of the

Two views of the replica Gordon Bennett Trophy which was commissioned by Edge for display in the New Burlington Street showroom. It is now owned by the Veteran Car Club of Great Britain. (Veteran Car Club of Great Britain)

A primeval sports car, 1902. J.A. Holder sits in his new 16hp H70, with which he had some hill-climb successes. The size of the driving sprocket shows that the car was intended for competition use. The rear section of the body could be removed for competitions. (Derek Grossmark)

Uxbridge Road on the western outskirts of London, where there were still green fields in 1902. Work began at once on the building of a new stone-faced brick factory that would have the capacity to meet the demand for Napiers. Edge did not race again in 1902, probably being fully occupied in pressing home the commercial advantages of the Gordon Bennett victory and basking in his well-earned glory. Besides, opportunities to race were limited. The organisers of speed trials and hill-climbs were having great difficulty in running events on public roads without police prosecution, and in the latter half of 1902 the number was greatly reduced. The Midland Automobile Club held a hill-climb at Gorcot on 11 October. To avoid the attentions of the local constabulary, neither speeds nor distances were published, but J.A. Holder gained a second place in his class in a touring 16hp Napier.

During the autumn S.F. Edge Ltd was formed and took over the business of the Motor Power Company, at the same time moving from Regent Street to 14 New Burlington Street. The new organisation exhibited at the Paris Show at the end of the year and received a gold medal from the ACF for the Napier exhibit.

The Gordon Bennett car was sold to Arthur Brown of Luton in September 1902, for £1,200 (£60,000 in the values of the 1990s). He did not keep it long, however, and Edge then negotiated its sale to the Marquess of Anglesey. It later went to the United States, and in the 1980s many of its components were found in the Harrah Collection at Reno, Nevada. These were brought back to Britain and built up into the car which now competes honourably in veteran and vintage events.

Edge calculated that the total expenditure of competing in the Gordon Bennett was £1,418, so that after the sale of the car, the finest publicity that Napier and the British motor industry could hope to receive had cost just £218.

Chapter 4: 1903

Frustrations and Setbacks

CRITICS have often belittled Edge's victory in the 1902 Gordon Bennett Trophy, pointing out that it was a hollow triumph, that went almost unnoticed in its day. Events at the end of 1902 seem to belie this contention. France suddenly woke up to the realisation that a Trophy regarded as exclusive French property was no longer in the country. The win had been recognised in other countries too: there was a general acceptance that the Gordon Bennett Trophy was something worth winning, and it soon became evident that the 1903 event was likely to be much more keenly contested.

As Edge had won the Trophy for Great Britain, the onus was now on the ACGBI to organise the 1903 event. The first problem which confronted the club was the complete ban on any kind of competitive motoring event on British roads. It was suggested that the race should be held in France again, but the ACGBI was determined to stage the event and had resolved to do so as early as August 1902. A number of proposals were investigated, but there was little prospect of the race taking place on the British mainland, as there was too much opposition to overcome. Ireland was another matter. The population was more sparse and there was the inherent Irish enthusiasm for sporting events. It was also suggested that the race would give a useful boost to the Irish economy. The ban on motor racing on public roads nevertheless affected Ireland as well as Great Britain, so legislation would be needed for the race to take place. However, the chances of getting a Bill through Parliament for a race in Ireland were good. While preparations were made to draft a Bill, the ACGBI sent an inspection team to Ireland to find a suitable course.

A date had already been chosen – Thursday 2 July 1903. The decision to avoid a Sunday event, in order not to offend the influential ecclesiastical lobby, immediately earned the race the strong support of the Bishop of Kildare and Loughlin. According to Edge, Claude Johnson spent nearly three months in Ireland looking at possible courses, assisted by Count Zborowski and Edge among others. After much deliberation a figure-of-eight course was chosen in County Kildare, comprising a shorter loop of 40 miles (64km) and a longer loop of nearly 52 miles (83km). The move from a linear race to a circuit followed a trend started the previous year by the Circuit des Ardennes in Belgium, although in reality the ACGBI had little alternative, as an open road race with all its inherent problems would not have had any support in Parliament.

The proposal that the Gordon Bennett would be run over a closed circuit was received with some scorn in France, where the ACF was making plans for the greatest open road race yet. With hindsight it is possible to wonder if the French club was in the throes of *folie de grandeur*. To talk of a Greek tragedy is perhaps a cliché, but the elements were falling into place. The major race of 1903 was to be from Paris to Madrid. Once again, the French government was reluctant to grant permission. It had already refused to sanction a speed week at Pau in February and a race from Nice to Salon and back again. However, the ACF, encouraged by the experience of the previous year, carried on with the organisation of its mammoth event, anticipating that permission would be forthcoming, and then received support from an unexpected source. The youthful King Alfonso of Spain, who had assumed full monarchical powers on his 16th birthday in 1902 and was a great enthusiast for motor cars and motor racing, signed a decree permitting the race to run through Spain, from the frontier at Irun to Madrid. This left the French government in a quandary: if it continued to refuse permission for the race, Spain could be offended and there could be diplomatic problems. Eventually the Government caved in and organisation of the race went ahead. It was to start at Versailles on Sunday 24 May.

The motor manufacturers now had two races to aim for. The Paris–Madrid would be a free-for-all, while the Gordon Bennett would be for the usual national teams of three cars, for which selection would be eagerly sought. In Britain the selection of the team was already under way. As the winning marque in 1902, two Napiers were selected automatically, but the third place was to be filled by an eliminating trial. The entries had to be with the ACGBI by noon on 8 December 1902 along with a cheque for £500 as a guarantee of the bona fides of the entrant. This was no trifling sum and it probably had the desired effect of keeping faint-hearted and opportunist firms away.

Edge realised that a combination of luck and reliability had been responsible for his 1902 victory; speed had not been a winning factor. He now urged Napier to build a faster car, but knew that, once again, the governing factor would be the tyres. The team would have to run on Dunlops, and although this firm was learning, its technology was still behind the better continental firms, and Michelin in particular.

The decision was made to build new cars. Three would be improved D50 models, and there would also be a new design with a larger engine, a car which Edge believed should lie between the D50 and the 1901 'Monster'. Little was done to the D50 design apart from enlarging the bore to 139.7mm, which increased the swept volume to 7,708cc. The engine was set further back in the frame, and the wheelbase was increased to 7ft 10in (239cm). A honeycomb radiator with a brass header tank replaced the ugly Clarkson, but in all other main respects the cars were similar to the 1902 racer, but were known by their factory order number, E61. The chassis numbers of the new cars were 400, 401, and 402, and the respective engine numbers were 141, 172, and 173, which seems to indicate that number 141 was built and tested before the decision was made to build two more engines. The E61s would perhaps not be fast enough even with the larger engine, but it was hoped they would be reliable, a quality which had already paid off for Napier. Frank Newton, who was then a factory test driver, entered in his notes that one of the E61 engines developed 58bhp at 1,495rpm on the bench, and was timed on its first road run at 66.2mph (106.5kmh).

The new racer was known as the K5 and there was one fundamental change of design as it had a pressed steel chassis frame. The four-cylinder engine had a bore of 165.1mm and a stroke of 152.4mm, so it was well over-square; the capacity was 13,726cc. Napier was still using the quadruple automatic inlet valves and it was claimed to develop 80bhp at 1,200rpm. As before, the engine drove through a metal-to-metal clutch to a three-speed gearbox, which had a separate lever to engage reverse. The rear axle was stiffened by tie-rods and located by radius arms. The new radiator had the unusual feature of six cooling tubes passing through the header tank. The driver's seat was mounted on the frame, so he was sitting much lower, and the steering column was steeply raked. There was a large bolster fuel tank behind him. The appearance was a great improvement on the earlier racers, as the radiator was set behind the front axle line.

The body, as with the E61s, was built by H.J. Mulliner. The wheelbase was 9ft (274cm) and the track was 4ft 8ins (142cm). The car weighed 987kg, which was a small increase on the weight of the D50 and comparable with the E61, which was surprising considering the much greater size of the car. The chassis number of the K5 was 405, and its engine number was 174. The company built another competition car at the same time, the L1 model, which was, in many respects, an interim design. The new, longer chassis of the E61 was used, with the earlier D50 engine of 1902. Two L1s were built, with the chassis numbers 403 and 404, and the engine numbers 174 and 187, thus joining the number sequence of the E61s and the K5, so clearly a batch of chassis and engine numbers may have been allocated to the 1903 racers. It must have been a testing time for Montague Napier. The order book was filling up, the company was about to move to Acton, and he had Edge pressing him, as forcefully as usual, about the new car.

Edge would be driving one of the Napiers selected for the British team, and the second car would be driven by Charles Jarrott. Jarrott and Edge were now regarded as the leading British drivers, and Jarrott had been most successful in 1902, driving for Panhard. As well as bringing his sick car through to finish 12th in the Paris–Vienna, he had taken second place in the Circuit du Nord and had then scored an excellent win in the Circuit des Ardennes, again with a Panhard.

The ACGBI's eliminating trial, to select the car and driver for the third place in the British team, was to be held in two stages. The first, on Saturday 25 April, would be a timed trial over a flying kilometre and a standing mile on the Duke of Portland's estate at Welbeck. The second would be a timed hill-climb at a venue and time which would not be announced, in order to avoid the unwelcome presence of the local constabulary.

There were many rumours about the cars and drivers entering the trial, but when the dust had settled the field comprised a mere four. Montague Napier and Edge wanted to see an all-Napier team, so the Hon Charles Rolls and J.W. Stocks had been entered in E61s, while Mark Mayhew had been put in with an L1. The only opposition to the Napiers came from an 80hp Star. Similar, in many respects, to a Panhard, this was built by the Star Engineering Company of Wolverhampton and was to be driven by Edward Lisle,

The Napier team has lunch during the Gordon Bennett Eliminating Trials in Welbeck Park on 25 April 1903. Left to right: Stocks, Fuller, Mayhew, Jarrott, Edge (in cap, seated), and Earp (leaning against wheel). (Guy Griffiths Collection)

the son of the firm's proprietor. Dennis Brothers of Guildford were also reported to have built a car, but it was not entered. Wolseley, on the other hand, had built a car, which was to be driven by Lieutenant Mansfield Smith-Cumming. It was a development of the disastrous 1902 cars, having a horizontal four-cylinder engine, and was reputed to develop 70bhp at 900rpm. Unfortunately, Wolseleys made the elementary mistake of failing to send their entry in before the closing date. Edge sportingly pressed the ACGBI to accept a late entry, but although the Club were sympathetic, Lisle, on behalf of Star, opposed it most strongly, so the Wolseley remained untrialled.

The hopeful entrants gathered at Welbeck Abbey on the morning of 25 April. The course was a straight run, on a gradient in the park. The flying kilometre and standing mile distances had to be covered three times by each contender, first downhill and then uphill. Over the downhill flying kilometre, Rolls and Stocks tied with a time of 31 seconds, an average speed of 71mph (113kmh). On his third run, Rolls had valve trouble and was much slower. Mayhew was third fastest at 60.4mph (96.6kmh), ahead of Lisle's Star. On the uphill kilometre, Stocks was fastest at 58.8mph (94kmh), over Rolls's 57mph (91.2kmh) and Mayhew's 52.9mph (84.6kmh), with the Star again trailing behind. On the standing mile, the results were much the same, though skill in making a good getaway must have counted. Downhill, Stocks did 55.4mph (88.6kmh), Rolls did 54mph (86.4kmh), while Mayhew was closer with 51.6mph (82.5kmh). Uphill, the order was the same, with 49.3mph (78.8kmh), 47.8mph (76.4kmh) and 45.3mph (72.4kmh) respectively. On all the runs, Lisle's Star was well behind Mayhew.

The contenders were then told, in the strictest secrecy, to assemble at Banbury just before midnight the following day, Sunday. On arriving at Banbury, each was given a sealed envelope, containing final instructions, and sent to a rendezvous where the envelope was opened. The contenders were directed to Dashwood Hill, just outside West Wycombe, where a 1,184-yard (1.08km) course had been marked out. The hill was reached just as dawn was breaking; it was raining hard and the road was in a poor condition. The thunder of the racing cars passing through the Oxfordshire and Buckinghamshire towns should have woken even the heaviest-sleeping constable, but none appeared on the scene, and the second stage of the trial proceeded without official hindrance. To avoid creating incriminating evidence, no times were given for the climb. The fastest car was given a zero time and only the deficit times of the other cars were announced. Rolls was the only Napier driver to make three clean starts. Stocks stalled on his third run and Mayhew stalled on his first. On aggregate times, Rolls came out ahead of the others, but it was notable that on his unstalled runs Mayhew was in second place, one second behind Stocks on his second run and 1.4 seconds behind Napier on his third. One is left to speculate that in terms of driving skill, perhaps Mayhew was the best of the Napier trio, and merely handicapped by the smaller engine of his L1. Once again, the Star did not distinguish itself. As Edge commented, 'The tests were completed by 4.30am and we were all back in town by 8am feeling very hungry and rather sleepy.'

Having studied the results of the eliminating trials, the ACGBI selected Stocks to fill the vacant place in the British team, thereby guaranteeing an all-Napier line-up. Jack Stocks, the London manager of De Dion-Bouton, was an old friend of Edge. He was 31 years old, had competed against Edge in the cycle races of the 1890s, and had competition successes on an Ariel motor tricycle. To the world at large, the Napier team for the Gordon Bennett would be driving E61s. The K5 was being built in some secrecy, and Edge had agreed with Montague Napier that he would not make a decision about racing the car until he had been able to compare the performance with the E61 on the Irish circuit.

While work proceeded on the K5 in the Napier works, across the English Channel the finishing touches were being made to the arrangements for the Paris–Madrid. For Napiers, there was a double interest in the race: Charles Jarrott, now a Napier works driver, was to drive a De Dietrich, while Mark Mayhew had entered his L1, which the works had prepared for the race. As was to become a motor-racing custom in later years, Mayhew, as a rich private entrant, was being given favoured treatment. Edge had wanted to enter the Paris–Madrid himself, but with the preparation of cars for the Gordon Bennett being paramount, he had to accept that none could be made ready in the time available. He instead decided to follow the race in 'a Napier racing car', to give help to Jarrott if needed. It is rather surprising that in his memoirs he makes no mention of being available to provide a similar service for Mayhew. What car he was using, must remain a matter of speculation, but it is possible that he was using the other L1.

The Paris–Madrid was to start in Paris on Sunday 24 May, when the first stage would be run to Bordeaux. The next day the race would run from Bordeaux into Spain, stopping at Vitoria, and on the final day it would continue from Vitoria to Madrid, completing a total distance of approximately 1,380km (860 miles). The decision had been made to run the first stage on a Sunday so that the greatest number of spectators could enjoy the spectacle. If entries were made before 16 February, the entrants could ballot for starting places, though the list did not close until 16 May. After cancellations, there were 275 confirmed entries. The list comprised 112 heavy cars, 64 light cars, 40 voiturettes, and 59 motor cycles.

The Nice speed week had gone ahead at the beginning of April, although permission for the Nice–Salon–Nice race had been withheld. The principal event was the La Turbie hill-climb, where sadly there was a fatal accident in which Count Eliot Zborowski was killed when his new 60hp Mercedes crashed. A naturalised British citizen, the Count lived the life of an English country gentleman on his estate at Melton Mowbray. With a second place in the Paris–Vienna and a fourth in the Circuit des Ardennes, it was likely that he would have been invited to take part in the Gordon Bennett elimination trials. His death was felt very keenly among the British racing community. There were fears that this accident could alter the attitude of the French Government to the Paris–Madrid, but authority for the race was not withdrawn and the preparations continued, accompanied by the mounting excitement of the French public.

Gerald Rose sets the scene of the night of 23/24 May in his book *A Record of Motor Racing*:

> Early on the Saturday evening the spectators began making their way out to the start at Versailles, and it was a fitting end to the great races which have started from that point, that the exodus

May 1903: Mark Mayhew drives his L1 Napier away from the official verification point before the Paris–Madrid. (Guy Griffiths Collection)

on the night before that Paris–Madrid, should have been far greater than ever before. It was the last of those great steadily-moving processions – a countless mass of cyclists, with their gay Chinese lanterns dancing in the semi-darkness, inextricably mixed with the endless stream of wagonettes, omnibuses, carriages, cars, with here and there a racing car forcing its way through the press, all helping with shout and song, whistle and horn, siren and open exhaust, to swell the pandemonium. As the night drew on the stream became denser and denser; all Paris seemed to be moving out along the Versailles road. So great was the crush that at last the cyclists rode at a foot's pace, shoulder to shoulder.

It was said that a hundred thousand persons passed along the road that night to line the course on either side of the long string of cars waiting to be sent on their race south. Up and down the mile-long row passed the photographers dazzling all with their flashlights.

The drivers, tense with the anticipation of the greatest road race yet, probably slept little, and those who did manage to had to drag themselves from their beds soon after midnight to be ready for the start. The first car, Jarrott's De Dietrich, was to be flagged away at 3.30am, but the drivers asked the organisers to postpone the start for 15 minutes as the dawn had not yet broken. At 3.45am, Jarrott was flagged away followed at one minute intervals by the seemingly endless stream of competitors behind him. As he waited, tensely peering through his goggles in the half-light, Jarrott saw that the road in front was completely blocked with spectators. He asked how the road would be cleared and was told, with a shrug of the shoulder, that the spectators would clear as soon as he started and drove towards them. As he started he found that a wedge shaped space opened out in front of him. He slowed down, but as he did so found that the space ahead became smaller and opened up more slowly, so he resigned himself to the inevitable and carried on at racing speed.

Once again, Gerald Rose sets the scene:

The start of Paris–Madrid – It is a wonderful picture. Up at the line, the busy officials sending off the cars one after the other, the general hubbub cut by the level voice of the timekeeper counting off the remaining seconds to the driver, who leans over to catch the words. Behind him engines running, cutting in and out with a penetrating stutter, covering the surroundings with blue smoke, more felt than seen in the half-light of the dawn. Mechanics look over their cars hurriedly, seeing that everything is in its proper place; drivers nervous and preoccupied, exchanging a few words with friends or fellow-competitors, wondering what the road is going to be like, what the crowds are going to be like, how their cars are going to run, how their rivals' cars are going to run and so on, until it is time to move on again a few yards. Back the long row stretches, amongst the scurrying spectators harried by the over-strained police, the drivers on their cars waiting – waiting as the moment comes nearer and nearer for them to shoot away on their long journey. The line is always on the move up to the front, advancing in jerks, stopping for a few moments and moving on again, while slowly the grey dawn brightens into the clear sunlight of a May morning. Everywhere else the world is awaking; windows are opening in the towns, people are rising for a Sunday of rest, a calm and peaceful day after the toil of the week. But this will be no day of rest on the old high-road from Paris to Bordeaux. From the palaces of Versailles to the spires of Chartres, from the grey roofs of Tours to the winding roads of Libourne, all is tension, excitement, strain. From end to end the dusty highway is lined with crowds, unmanageable, heedless reckless folk who pay but scant attention to the half-hearted attempt to guard the road. There is no thought of danger – nothing except a wild desire to get closer and yet closer to the hurtling cars.

In the midst of this momentous scene was Mayhew's Napier. He was number 138, so he had the nominal starting time of 6.02am. He had the advantage of the sun being well up, but the spectators had been joined by late arrivals, making the crowds even thicker. Ahead of him on the road was a stream of cars over 100 miles long and achieving speeds as yet unknown in road racing. A large number of cars failed to reach the first control at Rambouillet, many broken by the pace being set at the front. At this control, De Knyff (Panhard) led, having passed Jarrott, who was followed closely by Louis Renault. The average speed of the leaders was over 60mph (96kmh) and Renault was reported to have covered a measured distance between Bonneval and Chartres at nearly 90mph (144kmh). There had been some furious and hazardous passing in the thick clouds of dust – Jenatzy's Mercedes had passed 16 cars and Gabriel's Mors 26 by the time they reached Chartres. Mayhew was keeping up with the pace and at this point had only lost seven minutes on the leader.

At Tours, Louis Renault still led, pursued by Werner's Mercedes which had passed Jarrott; but then the Mercedes's rear axle broke and Werner was out. At Poitiers, Renault was 20 minutes ahead of Jarrott, but now the other Renault brother, Marcel, started to come into the reckoning. At Couhé-Verac, though, Marcel hit a drain while trying to pass Thery's Decauville: the car overturned and Renault died of his injures soon afterwards. His brother Louis, unaware of the disaster, raced on to Bordeaux, where a huge crowd awaited the cars at the Quatre Pavillons, about four kilometres from the town. To their astonishment, Fernand Gabriel (Mors), who had a starting number of 168, was the third car home and the race leader, having set the almost unbelievable average of 65.3mph (104.5kmh), passing at least 100 cars en route.

As the drivers finished they were

Mark Mayhew corners his L1 at Petignac, 50 miles (80km) from the finish of the Paris–Madrid. He crashed soon afterwards when the steering broke. (Guy Griffiths Collection)

directed into the town, across the Pont de Pierre, over the River Gironde, and along the quayside to the Esplanade des Quinconces, where the cars were to be held for the night. Jarrott finished fourth, as rumours began to spread about terrible carnage on the road. Sadly, unlike most rumours, these were true. Barrow and his mechanic had been killed when their De Dietrich hit a tree, while his team-mate Stead was not expected to live after another crash. The Ulster driver Leslie Porter, with a Wolseley, had crashed into a level crossing, and his mechanic, Nixon, had been burned to death. A woman crossing the road at Rambouillet had been killed. While trying to avoid a child Tourand, driving a Brouhout, had crashed into the spectators outside Angoulême, killing a soldier as well as his own mechanic; the child was killed as well. There had been countless other accidents where both spectators and competitors had been injured.

Mayhew had gone well in the L1 Napier and was well placed at Angoulême. However, just outside Libourne, with only 25km to go to Bordeaux, he had the terrifying experience that all racing drivers dread – the steering broke, and the car hit a tree. Fortunately the Napier was not going quickly when it happened, and although the radiator and a wheel were smashed, Mayhew and Mosses, his mechanic, were unhurt. C.L. Freeston, the correspondent of *The Car*, who was covering

Mayhew's wrecked L1 Napier after the crash at Libourne. (Guy Griffiths Collection)

the race, sent a terse telegram to London which told the story: 'Mayhew – Steering went wrong. He struck tree and hurt ribs but not seriously. Mechanic turned several somersaults but not hurt.'

As the drivers parked their cars at the Esplanade des Quinconces, they gathered in small sad groups and discussed the news, which seemed to become worse as each report was received. The consensus among the drivers was that they should race no further, but before the drivers could convey this view to the ACF or the Club could make a decision, the French government intervened, decreeing that all racing was banned on French territory. There was some suggestion that the cars could go to the Spanish frontier and race on from there, but the Spanish government immediately followed the French lead and imposed its own ban. Such was the French government's concern that there should be no more accidents that the following morning the drivers were not permitted to start their engines, and the cars had to be towed by horses back across the Pont de Pierre to Bordeaux station, to return to Paris by rail. In his memoirs, Edge says that he followed the race by driving along the course, leaving the start soon after Jarrott. In a passage which must score maximum points for one-upmanship, and also for hyperbole, he says, 'I had passed Jarrott and was very pleased to see him arrive at Bordeaux'.

That was the end of the heroic races from city to city on unclosed roads. The tradition was revived in later years with races such as the Mille Miglia and the Targa Florio, but for these the roads were closed. Nearly a century later, it is hard to comprehend what those early races were like for the drivers. On the open and unmarshalled roads, there were the constant hazards of horse-drawn carts, dogs, farm animals, and country people still unfamiliar with the ways of the motor car. These potential dangers had to be encountered with brakes which were wholly inadequate for the velocities being achieved. Racing at speed on dusty, unmetalled road surfaces, with the ever present fear of mechanical or tyre failure, set these early drivers and their mechanics

Paris–Madrid 1903. The race was stopped at Bordeaux after 342 miles (549km).

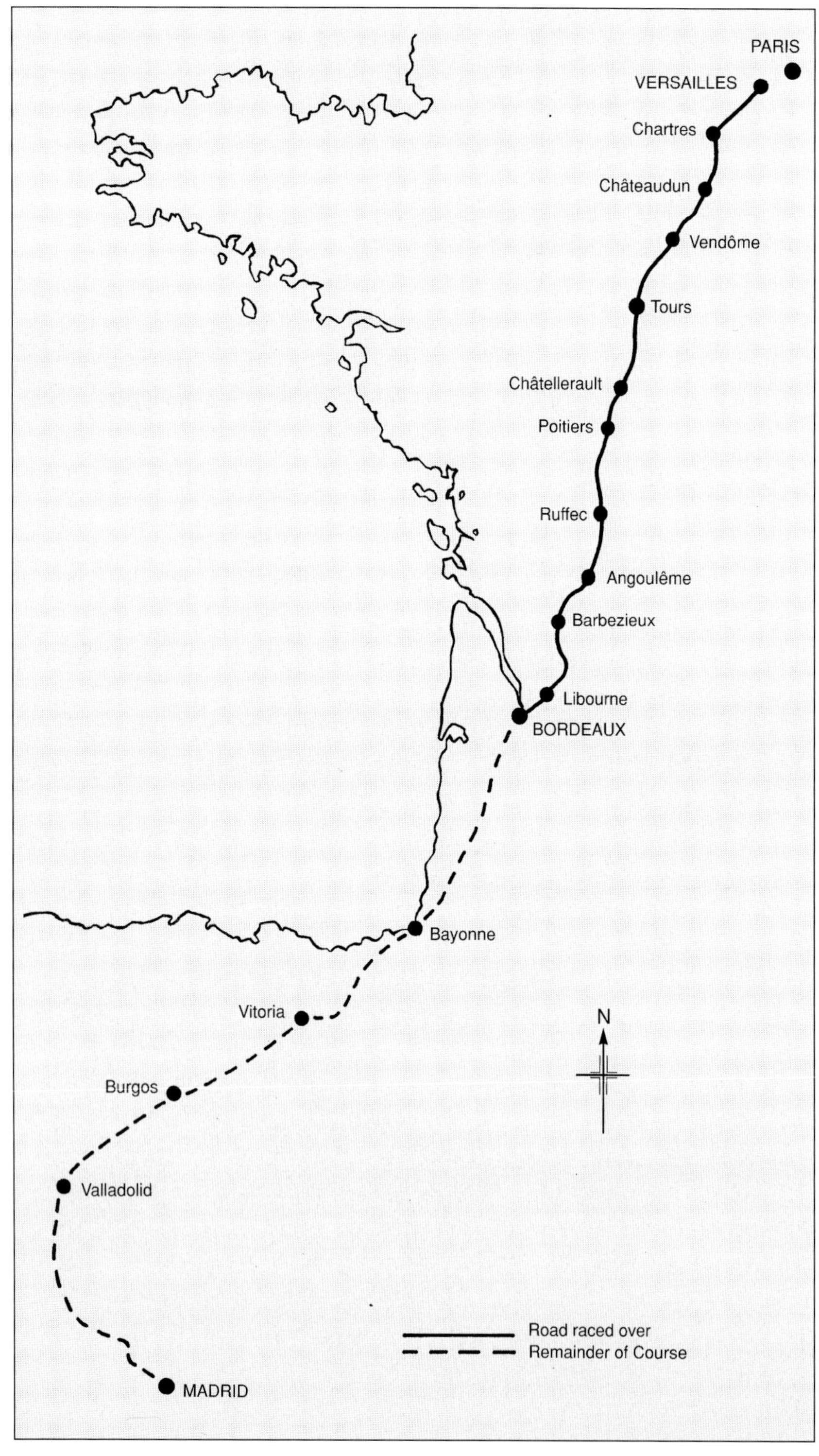

apart as a unique breed of men. With the increasing speed of the cars and the ever-growing public interest in racing the eventual demise of road-racing had been inevitable. Nevertheless, the sight of these cars, thundering through the dust down the tree-lined roads of France, at speeds which even today would seem impressive, must have been an unforgettable spectacle to those who witnessed it. But the future of motor racing now lay in events held on closed circuits, and the Circuit des Ardennes had established the pattern the previous autumn. French criticism of the ACGBI for running the Gordon Bennett Trophy on the Athy circuit would be heard no more.

The Paris–Madrid was soon called the 'Race to Death' by the sensational elements of the British press, and there were some suggestions that the Gordon Bennett should be banned, but these came to nothing. The ACGBI was able to point out that the race would be held on a closed circuit guarded by 7,000 policemen, and great care would be taken to improve the roads. Bumps and ruts would be ironed out and the course would be chemically treated to prevent the usual dust clouds.

The ACGBI had worked hard and well. A Bill was published on 25 February 1903, the Light Locomotives (Ireland) Bill, and this was presented in the House of Commons by the Hon John Scott Montagu MP, father of the present Lord Montagu of Beaulieu, the founder of the National Motor Museum. It had its first reading in the House of Commons on 20 March, was unopposed, and received support from Irish MPs on all sides of the House. Sir Edward Carson commented, 'We see a wonderful blending of the Orange and the Green. There is about this matter an unanimity of which some people considered Irishmen to be incapable.' It passed through the House of Lords without opposition and received the Royal Assent on 27 March. The Act was short and provided that the competing cars would be exempt from observing the speed limit on the day of the race and the local authorities would be absolved from the responsibility for the expense of carrying out any road works and improvements required by the ACGBI for the purpose of the race.

A race supplement was produced by *The Automotor Journal*, which gives a description of the course:

> The Course will be three times round the complete figure '8' = 275 miles 1,073 yards plus once round the Western Circuit (51 miles 1,540 yards) giving a total distance for the Cup race of 327 miles 844 yards, from which the distance occupied in traversing the controls must be deducted to arrive at the net time taken in covering the racing portion of the Course.
>
> The cars will start from the Club Enclosure at Ballyshannon. They will first traverse the eastern section via Castledermot and Carlow to Athy, then up the middle of the figure '8', past the Club Enclosure again, continuing to Kilcullen and round the Western circuit, past Kildare and Stradbally to Athy, and back again to the Club Enclosure at Ballyshannon. The same course will then be repeated round both circuits, the total Course comprising in this manner three circuits of the Eastern circuit and four circuits of the Western. After the last car has passed the Club Enclosure for the last circuit, motor vehicles will follow up, notifying that the race is finished.
>
> There are seven controls, viz: – Kildare, Monasterevin, Stradbally, Athy (two), Carlow and Castledermot. At Kilcullen corner the cars will also stop for one minute.

Work was in hand to improve the course and the steam-rollers were hard at work repairing the road surface. The magazine *Car Illustrated* started a fund to pay for the road repairs and over £800 was collected. There was much local enthusiasm about the road repairs and the farmers, whose land adjoined the course, did their bit, cutting back tree branches and trimming hedges. It was suggested that the usual dust hazard would not be a problem as the damp Irish climate would produce its own solution, but as an additional safeguard the road was to be sprayed before the race with a substance called 'Westrumite'. This was made up of petrol and ammonia and was expected to bind the surface.

The economic benefits of the race were soon appreciated. The City of Dublin Steam Packet Company advertised a nine hour service from London to Dublin. Special fares were quoted on the Liverpool–Dublin steamers: 'Deck 6s 3d return, cabin 21s, motor cars conveyed for 36s return' (a pre-decimal shilling is 5p). French railways, too, laid on special excursions. A Gordon Bennett information office was opened in Lower Sackville Street in the West End of London. The prices of hotel rooms soared in Dublin and were even higher near the course – £6 was asked for a room in a cottage near Athy, the equivalent of £300 in the values of the late 1990s.

Practice was allowed on the course, but entrants were only permitted to use cars with a maximum speed of less than 40mph. The Napier team arrived at the course about three weeks before the race and Jarrott noted that while practice continued, the course was being improved all the time. He was stopped by a policeman and told he had been timed at 15mph (24kmh) in an area where the maximum permitted was 14mph (22.5kmh). On identifying himself, he was waved on with the comment, 'Go as fast as you like, as long as you beat them furriners!' All the drivers found to their cost that the highway was used as a chicken yard by the adjoining farms. At first they paid up cheerfully for any chicken that was killed, but soon realised that there seemed to be more chickens than ever on the road! The increased number of feathered

June 1903: Selwyn Edge poses with one of the Gordon Bennett E61s in front of his showroom at 14 New Burlington Street in the West End of London. Cecil Edge stands behind the bonnet in one picture and alongside his cousin in the other. Henry Tryon sits in the passenger seat. (Guy Griffiths Collection)

pedestrians seemed to be balanced by a rapidly improving road sense on the part of the survivors. The local rook population also suffered heavy losses initially, but soon realised that racing cars were faster than the farm carts to which they were accustomed.

The Napier team were staying at Castle Rheban, near Athy. The castle was owned by Henry Large, who had been a cycle-racing rival of Edge and Stocks. He had raced for the Dunlop team and made his offer to Napiers through Sir Arthur du Cros. Rheban was an ideal base for the team. It had a mile-long avenue which could be used for private testing, a garage was built for the team in the dungeons under the ruins of the old castle, and the team were accommodated in the mansion house, which had such modern facilities as a flush lavatory, a rarity in Ireland in 1903. Despite the modern facilities, Montague Napier preferred to have his morning cold bath in a granite trough in the farmyard, where cold water was pumped over him. Practice soon showed that the E61s might not be fast enough. Jarrott commented that he would have liked another 20bhp, and the car did not compare in speed with his Circuit des Ardennes Panhard, or his Paris–Madrid De Dietrich. Edge told Montague Napier that the new K5 was needed, so this was sent for, with extra mechanics to tend it. Although it was certainly fast enough to give the team a chance of victory, Edge was worried, as he suspected that the car was going to be too hard on its tyres. It was fitted with 34in x 3$^1/_2$in on the advice of Dunlop; Edge would have preferred 36in x 5in, but had been assured that the smaller size would be adequate.

If the Napier team was worried about the performance of the cars, this was as nothing compared with the problems besetting Mercedes, which was representing Germany. A team of three 90s, has been built, similar to the car which had battled with Jarrott in the Paris–Madrid, but early in the morning on 10 June a fire had swept through the Mercedes works at Canstatt, destroying not only the team cars but also the facilities for building replacements in time for the race. To present a team, Mercedes were forced to take three '60' models from the stock of the Paris agent so that these could be stripped and prepared for the race as rather slower substitutes. Not only were Mercedes having trouble with their cars, but drivers were proving equally problematic. Emil Jellinek, the Daimler director who was responsible for the team, had chosen a Belgian, Camille Jenatzy, and two Germans, Werner and Hieronymus, who worked in the Mercedes works. While Jenatzy was acceptable to the German Club, the two Germans were persona non grata, as they were 'factory workers' rather than amateurs with the social position which was felt to be desirable. The row between Jellinek and the Club rumbled on, until eventually it was settled that the drives should go to Jenatzy, Baron De Caters, another Belgian, and James Foxhall-Keene, an American. Not a German in the team!

The ACF had selected two Panhards, to be driven by De Knyff and Henri Farman, which had 13,672cc engines as in 1902, but Panhard had also moved on, and the cars had mechanical inlet valves and pressed steel frames. The third French entry was a 11,559cc Mors, which had overhead mechanical inlet valves, operated by pushrods and rockers, a technical advance which was also being used by Mercedes in the 60 engine. The Mors was to be driven by Henri Fournier, but he fell out with the ACF, and a week before the race it was announced that the car would be driven by Gabriel, who had driven so impressively in the Paris–Madrid. The French team had eschewed the Irish hotels and was housed (or perhaps berthed) in the *Ferdinand de Lesseps*, a 3,500-ton ship moored in Dublin Harbour, with large workshops and a team reported to be 100 strong.

The remaining team to offer a Gordon Bennett challenge had been entered by the Automobile Club of America, a move which would certainly have commended itself to the instigator of the event, James Gordon Bennett. The team comprised two Wintons and a Peerless. The Wintons had in-line engines laid horizontally in the frame. The first car, to be driven by Percy Owen, had a four-cylinder engine of 8,498cc, developing 40bhp at 800rpm, driving through a two-speed gearbox and shaft final drive. The other Winton, to be driven by its constructor, Alexander Winton, had an eight-cylinder engine made up by placing two fours in line. This gave it a capacity of 16,998cc, but it was not a powerful unit and an output of just 80bhp at 1,000rpm was claimed. The Peerless was a conventional four of 11,082cc, with separate blocks and a T-head; the output was also 80bhp, at 1,300rpm. Its chassis also followed current conventions. The driver was the car's designer, Louis Mooers. The American team trials had given rise to much acrimony, particularly as the larger Winton had been selected without appearing.

The teams were to race in their national colours – blue for France, white for Germany, red for America, and, once more, green for Great Britain. As the race was being held in

The Athy circuit, Gordon Bennett Trophy 1903. The eastern loop was 40 miles (64.3km), the western loop was 51.8 miles (83.4km), and total race distance was 327.5 miles (526.6km).

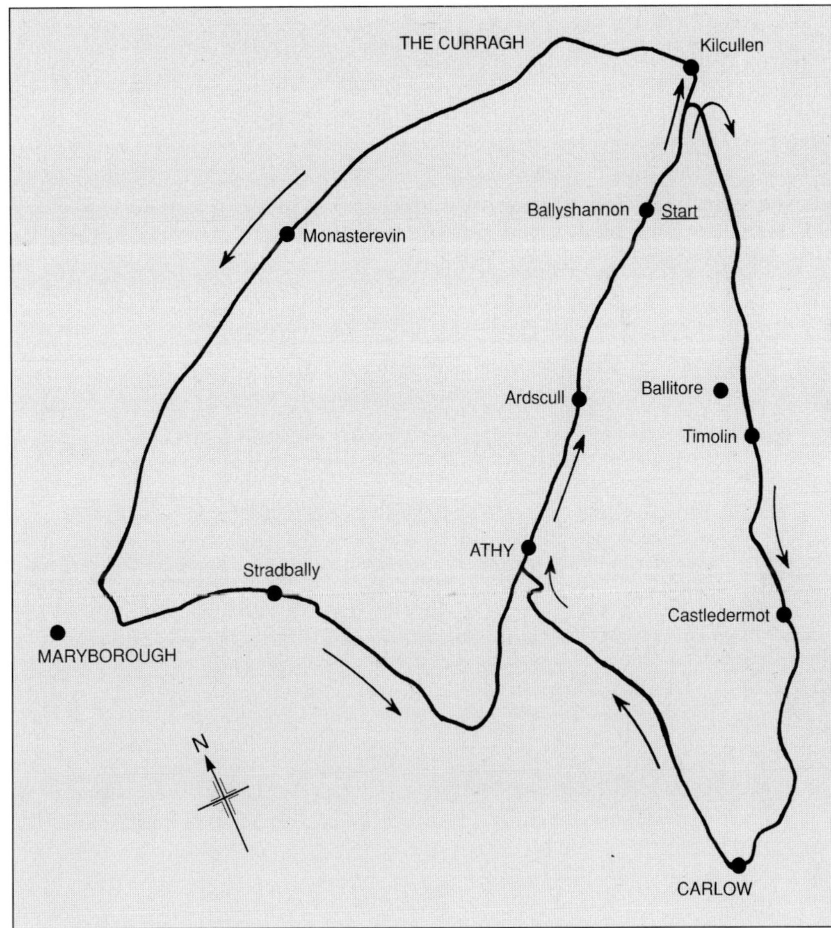

Ireland, the Napiers were painted in an emerald shade in honour of the venue, adopting a suggestion made by Count Zborowski before his death. This decision has added to the confusion apparent in later years as to what constituted 'Napier Green' and 'British Racing Green'. As mentioned earlier, 'Napier Green' seems to have been the colour used around the factory at Acton. The 1903 colour was only used for that one race and the factory colour was resumed thereafter. Green was the British racing colour, and until commercial sponsorship banished national colours, British cars raced in every shade from pale lime to a colour so dark it was almost black. All of these could claim to be 'British Racing Green'.

The morning of Wednesday 1 July was hot, with the sun shining from a clear sky. The town of Naas was packed with race officials, drivers, mechanics, team members, and huge crowds of spectators, who thronged about trying to look at the cars which were being presented to be weighed and scrutineered; one over-eager spectator fell from the balcony of a bank overlooking the weighing scales, as he sought a better view-point. The Napier team passed the scrutineering test, since much attention had been given to this at the factory before leaving for Ireland. For Jarrott's E61, however, it was a fairly close thing, as it registered 999.7kg. Stocks's E61 was lighter, though, at 978kg, while the K5 turned the scales at 987kg. For other teams, the weighing-in posed problems. The Panhard team had to remove all superfluous bits from De Knyff's car, including the seat cushion, to get inside the limit, and De Knyff himself queried the accuracy of the scales until these were checked with the 'standard' weights produced by the local council. Similarly, 14kg worth of various bits had to be taken away from Farman's Panhard, while the silencer, oil caps, battery, and tool box were sacrificed to make the Peerless acceptable. The Mercedes team had another problem, as the scrutineers found the tyres were not of wholly German manufacture. Although the Michelin covers had been made in a factory in Germany, the fabric was Belgian, and the valves had come from France. With some haste, the three 60s were fitted with Continental tyres and tubes of impeccable Germanic origin.

Edge says that the Napier team returned to Castle Rheban, where they spent 'a very lazy afternoon and evening'. Jarrott tells a different tale, saying that Edge and the factory mechanics were still working hard on the details of the K5, though his own E61 was ready for the race, as was Stocks's car. During their stay at Rheban, the Napier drivers had been

A rope is raised so that Selwyn Edge can move the new K5 following weighing-in at Naas, 1 July 1903. Dorothy Levitt stands on the right. (Geoffrey Goddard Collection)

keeping fit. Jarrott and Stocks played cricket, while Edge was doing exercises prescribed by Sandow, an eminent Edwardian body-builder and strong man. The fine day turned into a beautiful evening, and Jarrott was moved to comment about the sunset in his memoirs *Ten Years of Motors and Motor Racing*: 'It was awe-inspiring in its grandeur and beauty, a sky of gold changing into a sea of blood, with heavy ominous clouds rolling up in the distance, causing weird rays of light to strike on the horizon.'

Edge, too, commented about the beauty of the sunset and this, with the tensions of the race to come, gave both Jarrott and Edge uneasy thoughts of mortality that night. Jarrott even went so far as to write a letter 'to be opened in the event . . .' – a custom which would sadly become all too common just over ten years later.

While some of the drivers had a fitful and uneasy sleep, most of Ireland was not abed, but was making its way to the Athy circuit during the night. The roads were jammed with cars, cycles, and horse-drawn vehicles. The Great Western Railway Company of Ireland had laid on special trains which were over-laden with passengers. All were determined to reach the course before it was closed officially at 6.00am. At 6.30am two pilot cars set out from the race headquarters at Ballyshannon. One was to cover the Eastern circuit and the other to cover the Western circuit. The honour of this duty was given to two of the failed British triallists. One was to have been Mark Mayhew, with his L1 Napier, but the car had not yet been repaired after the Paris–Madrid crash, so Lisle with his Star went west, while Smith-Cumming took the easterly course with the rejected Wolseley.

The Star broke down, but the start was not delayed, even though some corners had to be sanded to counteract the over-enthusiastic spreading of 'Westrumite'. The clouds which Jarrott had seen the previous evening had rolled in, and it was grey as the 12 competing cars were lined up at 6.30am. At the time-controls around the course, the officials checked their official watches, each control having a separate watch for each car. On the start-line the drivers were surrounded by their teams, officials, and well-wishers. In honour of the occasion, the Napier team were wearing emerald green ties. National feelings had been running high, and De Knyff had received anonymous, threatening letters from people who believed themselves to be Edge's supporters. Jarrott, embarrassed by this, sought out De Knyff as the cars were lined up, to reassure him. The ever-alert Edge noticed that the seat cushions

Ballyshannon, 2 July 1903. Selwyn Edge awaits the start of the Gordon Bennett in the K5 Napier. Captain Lindsay Lloyd counts down the final seconds, while Charles Jarrott, in a white coat, looks apprehensive. (Guy Griffiths Collection)

had been replaced in De Knyff's car, which presumably took it over the weight limit again. As the holder of the Trophy, Edge, wearing a long white coat and a green cap, was to be the first to start, and a loud cheer rose as he and Cecil Edge climbed up into the K5. At 6.58am the engine was started, and, with one minute to go, Captain Lindsay Lloyd began his countdown. He shouted the final five seconds to Edge, 'Five, four, three, two, one!' then fired a pistol and dropped the flag, to signify the start. Edge was away, to the deafening cheers of the huge crowd.

Behind Edge, the field was started at seven minute intervals; De Knyff was the next to go, followed by Owen's Winton. Farman stalled his Panhard when getting away, while Stocks, who started ninth at 7.56am, also stalled. Jarrott, wearing similar garb to Edge, left the start at 7.28am with a smooth getaway that prompted favourable comments. Winton, with his own machine, who should have left the start at 7.42am, was still there, struggling with a blocked fuel line, when Foxhall-Keene, the last to go, set forth with his Mercedes, at 8.17am. He, too, managed to stall.

Edge had set off on the first lap over the Eastern circuit with a speed that impressed the crowd. The K5 was running as well as he had hoped. In his own words, 'Great Gods, how that car did go!' Edge thundered past the start, where the wretched Winton was still toiling, having done his first lap of the Eastern loop in 46min 23sec, and the crowd realised that the Napier was showing winning form. This time was only bettered by Foxhall-Keene, whose opening lap was the fastest of the race on the Eastern loop, albeit a mere 20 seconds quicker than Edge. Jarrott had also been going well, and half-way round the Eastern loop he caught up with Jenatzy as the cars entered Carlow, having gained almost seven minutes on the Mercedes. The sight of the Napier behind him made the Belgian put on a fierce spurt, but as they passed the line Jarrott was in fourth place, 44 seconds in front of Jenatzy. For Stocks, though, the Eastern loop had been disastrous. De Knyff had run wide when taking the corner at Ballymoon Cross, about four miles from Carlow, and had hit a wire and pole barrier. The Panhard continued after a short stop, but Stocks hit a bump and also ran wide on the same corner. The damaged barrier was now partly obstructing the escape road and the Napier's wheels caught in the wire. A pole was pulled into the wheels breaking the spokes, and Stocks and his mechanic, Arthur Macdonald, were thrown from the car. Fortunately they were only shaken, but they had no means of repairing the wheels, so the Napier was out of the race.

Charles Jarrott about to set off in his ill-fated E61 Napier, with mechanic Cecil Bianchi in the passenger seat. (Guy Griffiths Collection)

Edge had been slightly slower over the Western loop, as he had lost two minutes stopping to replace the radiator cap, which had fallen off. At the end of the first full lap he was in third place. The leader now was Jenatzy, who, with the stimulus of Jarrott, had speeded up, Edge was 3min 9sec behind Jenatzy, but was only 68 seconds behind De Knyff, who had moved up to second place. Jarrott was still fourth when he reached the Kildare control, ten miles (16km) onto the Western loop. About two miles (3.2km) beyond Kildare, the Napier began to misfire, and Jarrott lost about a minute while he and his mechanic, Bianchi, replaced a loose plug lead.

With the end of the Western loop in sight, Jarrott was going along the straight between Maryborough and Stradbally at about 60mph (95kmh) when the steering broke. The car swerved into the side of the road, just missing a telegraph pole, and mounted a high grass bank, then overturned onto the road. Jarrott was thrown clear, but Bianchi, who had been strapped to his seat at Jarrott's suggestion – perhaps with memories of the unfortunate Smits

The Napier pit crew wait on the road by the start-line at Ballyshannon. Dorothy Levitt is the woman on the left. (Guy Griffiths Collection)

in mind – was pinned under the car as it landed upside down on the road. He was screaming for help, as he was being burned by the exhaust pipe, and with extraordinary, adrenalin-induced strength Jarrott managed to lift a corner of the car. Then spectators who had run up lifted up the other corners and, freeing the seat belt, managed to pull Bianchi out. Jarrott then fainted. Shortly afterwards he recovered consciousness while lying under a white sheet in a nearby farmyard, apparently having been assumed dead. Bianchi too was under a sheet, but was also conscious. Jarrott asked Bianchi if he was alive and Bianchi replied that he thought he probably was, but felt rather unwell!

Miraculously, their injuries were comparatively minor: Jarrott had a dislocated collar bone, and both men were badly bruised and shaken. When Jarrott staggered back to the wrecked Napier to inspect the steering, Baron Pierre De Caters stopped his Mercedes to ascertain the gravity of the accident and offer help. Jarrott asked him to stop at Ballyshannon and inform the Napier team that he and Bianchi were alive. Although this lost him nearly two minutes, the Baron considerately did this, which was a great relief to Montague Napier and his team, as they had already received a message that the pair had been killed. Another disaster was narrowly avoided when a doctor, summoned to help the Napier crew, drove his car onto the course in the wrong direction, and nearly collided with Jenatzy.

Misfortune continued to pile up on the Napier team. On the second lap, the K5 lost a rear tyre, and before Edge could pull up the rim had been damaged. The Edges replaced the tyre, but, just as Edge had feared, the tyres now began to fail and the Napier fell steadily behind. His second lap of the Eastern loop was 40 minutes slower than his first lap. The Napier team had sited tyre depots round the course, but this was little help to the frustrated Edge and the K5 limped round the course losing more and more time as the pair made seven stops to replace missing or burst tyres. At one stop, buckets of water were thrown over the rims, but it made no difference. To add to their troubles, the car was also overheating; and from midday, rain had been falling heavily.

The K5 completed the course, but it was over two and a half hours behind the winning Mercedes of Jenatzy. The French team finished in the next three places in the order De Knyff, Farman, and Gabriel. Although the K5 was in fifth place, and the only other car still running, it was then disqualified for receiving outside help: when stopping at Monasterevin on the second lap for a tyre replacement, the Napier had been reluctant to restart and had been push-started by bystanders. Edge's determination to finish despite the odds had won him the admiration of the crowd and it was also perhaps a slight consolation to Edge and to Montague Napier that the K5 had finished the course in good mechanical health. Furthermore, over a measured mile past the grandstands it had been timed at 64mph (102kmh), a speed that was competitive with the 66mph (105kmh) recorded by the Mercedes of Jenatzy and De Caters, and the 65mph (104kmh) of the two Panhards.

Over 90 years later, speculation is vain, but it must be wondered if Selwyn Edge made an error of judgement in racing the untried K5. Although Jarrott was probably a faster driver than Edge, he had shown, in his pursuit of Jenatzy before the crash, that the E61 was fully competitive with the Mercedes. There had been no suggestion before the race that the Dunlops on the E61 were troublesome. In Edge's experienced hands the E61 would surely have acquitted itself well. That night, as a tired and dejected team nursed its wounds at Castle Rheban, Edge and Montague Napier realised that once more, Dunlop tyres had prevented the Napier racing car giving of its best.

For Montague Napier too, there was a further worry: twice in six weeks, the steering of a Napier had failed in a race. On his return to England, he would look carefully at the design and manufacture of the steering components. Metallurgy was still in its infancy, and when the gear problems in the 1902 race are recalled, it seems likely that perhaps Napier had not yet appreciated all the complex problems of metal fatigue.

As the cream of the motor racing world was in Ireland, either competing in the Gordon Bennett Trophy, or watching it, the Trophy race became the high point of an Irish Automobile Fortnight and additional speed events were organised. There was to be a speed trial at Phoenix Park in Dublin on Saturday 4 July, and there were also to be speed trials at Cork and Castlewellan, and hill-climbs at Killarney and Ballybannon. Phoenix Park has been compared with the Bois de Boulogne in Paris, and one of its features is a long, straight road, nearly two miles (3.2 km) in length, running through the middle. This was a natural choice as the venue for the speed trials, and a 2,853-yard (2,607m) course was marked out, which comprised a standing mile, followed by a flying kilometre. There was one hazard, as the Phoenix Park Memorial stood in the middle of the road half-way along the course. Once again, Westrumite was spread, to lay the inevitable dust of a glorious sunny day.

Late in the race, Edge approaches Ballyshannon in the K5, which has a rag stuffed in its radiator to replace the missing cap. Passing would have been difficult on such a narrow road. (Geoffrey Goddard Collection)

The trials were not only a great public attraction, but also a big occasion for Dublin society. The crowds gathered early, to watch the motor cycles which were competing in the morning, and the first runs began at 8.45am. The main attraction would be the cars, which were to run in the afternoon. Edge had entered the third E61 Napier, which had been prepared for him to drive in the Gordon Bennett, but discarded in favour of the K5. In the *Daily Mail* Challenge Cup, for the fastest car over the flying kilometre, in which the cars ran singly, the pace was set by some of the Paris–Madrid competitors, and the cup was won by De Forest, who recorded 27.2 seconds for the distance in his Mors (82.2mph/131.5kmh). This caused great excitement, as the time was approaching the world land speed record time for the distance, 26.8 seconds, (83.4mph/133.4kmh). The competitors ran again for the *Autocar* Challenge Cup, and this time Edge came out with the E61, recording 30.8 seconds (72.6mph/ 116.1kmh), only to be overshadowed by the duel between the Mors of Gabriel and De Forest. Gabriel recorded 26.8 seconds, equalling the world record, but De Forest went even quicker, and was timed at 26.6 seconds (84.1mph/134.5kmh), breaking the land speed record. However, this was not officially recognised as a new record, as the course was not level and there was no return run, but the Dubliners went home feeling they had seen a good day's sport.

The racing entourage now moved north to County Down, where, on

Tuesday 7 July, a hill-climb was being held at Ballybannon, followed by a speed trial between Clough and Castlewellan. Once again, the weather was superb and large crowds came from Belfast to watch the racers in action. At Ballybannon, on a beautiful timbered parkland course, with the Mourne Mountains to the south, Stocks had been entered in the spare E61. He was running in the racing car class and he recorded 37.6 seconds, which equalled the time of Rigolly's Paris–Madrid Gobron-Brillie, but they were both bettered by Werner who, rejected as a Gordon Bennett driver, now achieved 36.0 seconds in Jenatzy's winning car. They were all outpaced by Campbell Muir, who was driving the Mercedes 60 owned by Alfred (later Lord) Harmsworth, the newspaper magnate. There was some consolation for Napier, as the touring class was won by John Hargreaves in his 16hp in 59.4 seconds.

There was an entry of 22 cars for the speed trial, which was over a two and a half mile course, from Clough to the top of Ballybannon hill. It was agreed that the organisation of this event was rather haphazard, and fell short of the standards set in the south. This time, Stocks beat Campbell Muir with a time of 2min 12.6sec, but the longer course suited the Gobron-Brillie, and Rigolly managed 2min 5.4sec, which left Stocks in a rather distant second place.

The following Saturday, 11 July, the next event of the Automobile Fortnight was held at Cork, but the Napier team, along with a growing number of competitors, had decided to return home, though Edge competed successfully in the Harmsworth Trophy for motor boats, held in Cork harbour, using a Napier-engined boat. The Irish venture had not been crowned with the success that Edge and Montague Napier had anticipated. They had discovered that it was tough at the top, and competing at an international level was going to become harder still as more manufacturers realised the value of racing success in marketing their cars. The Gordon Bennett Trophy had now become the most important motor race of the year and already, within weeks of the end of the 1903 event, plans were advanced for the 1904 race. If they were to represent Great Britain again, Edge and Montague Napier realised that they had work to do.

There were no more international races in 1903, but the round of English sprints and hill-climbs continued. It was becoming increasingly difficult to run speed events on public roads without police intervention and the likelihood of subsequent prosecution. On 25 July, the Midland Automobile Club ran its first hill-climb on Sun Rising Hill between Banbury and Stratford-on-Avon, thus beginning an association which the club has maintained with this branch of motor sport to the present day. Sun Rising was a steep and winding hill, with a gradient, in places, of 1 in 6. A 1,000-yard (914m) course was marked out, with a standing start and a stop-and-restart. Cecil Edge ran a 20hp Napier and dominated the event, recording a time of 1min 55.8sec, while his nearest rival could only do 2min 21.8sec. It was rumoured that the touring-bodied Napier had been fitted with a D50 engine, which may explain its impressive performance. There was a protest that the more powerful engine had not been declared and the Midland Automobile Club did not release the full results for several weeks, while the protest was considered and eventually dismissed.

On 2 and 3 October there was a much more ambitious event at Southport. The Lancashire seaside resort decided to follow the example of Bexhill and run a speed trial on the promenade. The meeting was organised by the ACGBI in collaboration with the Liverpool Self-Propelled Traffic Association, and Southport Borough Council gave enthusiastic support. An entry of 188 was received, which would compete on a timed course over a flying kilometre after a run from a standing start. There were touring and racing classes, the tourers being divided by price and the racers by weight. The cars ran in pairs and there were eliminating heats and a final in each class. Selwyn Edge ran what was apparently an E61 in the 1,000kg class, and made the fastest time of the meeting. Press photographs show Edge at the start in an E61, but there are also photographs of him on the course in what looks suspiciously like the K5, though this car is not mentioned in contemporary reports. It is possible that the K5 gave a demonstration run. In the final, Edge ran against J.E. Hutton's 70hp Panhard and recorded a time of 33.2 seconds, an average of 67.33mph (107.72kmh), driving into a strong headwind. However, in a subsequent scratch race Hutton got the better of Edge, but could not improve on the Napier's earlier time. Edge had also entered a 20hp Napier for Arthur Macdonald in the over £1,000 touring class, which was victorious, but with the result at Sun Rising in mind, perhaps the D50 engine had been given another outing!

Edge finished his season, on 24 October, driving in a hill-climb organised by the Nottingham Automobile Club at Kettleby. He again drove an E61, while Stocks's Gordon Bennett E61 also appeared, driven by someone named Lloyd, who may have been Captain Lindsay Lloyd, the Gordon Bennett starter. Fear of prosecution prevented the club publishing any results or times, but press reports gave impressive accounts of the spectacular Napiers. The 1903 season had ended on a happier note than might have been expected after the Paris–Madrid tragedy. Hopes were high for 1904, and already Arthur Rowledge was at his drawing board, with Montague Napier and Edge looking over his shoulder.

Chapter 5: 1904

Enter the Six-Cylinder

THE failure at Athy in the Gordon Bennett Trophy had been a hard blow for Montague Napier and Edge. Edge wrote that 'Napier and I had several serious talks about our racing programme'. Understandably, there must have been some desire to cut their losses and abandon racing. The firm had now moved to Acton, orders were coming in well, there was no difficulty in selling touring Napiers, and the market for commercial vehicles was building up. It would have been easy to sit back and rest on the still-fresh laurels of the 1902 victory. In the end, it seems that patriotism was the deciding factor, though this may have been tempered by commercial considerations. The Gordon Bennett Trophy was now the main event of the motor racing year and substantial benefits accrued to the motor industry of the victorious nation. Napier and Edge had little faith in the other British firms which might seek to represent Britain, and probably feared that a poor showing could have an adverse effect on Napiers, even if they were not taking part.

The prototype six-cylinder Napier engine, autumn 1903. (Guy Griffiths Collection)

For some time Edge had been concerned about the comparative roughness of the Napiers. He believed that some of the tyre problems he had encountered while racing were caused by the 'big bangs' of the large four-cylinder engines. He was fascinated by the apparent advantages of a six-cylinder engine. This concept had been discussed in technical circles and experimental designs had appeared, but no firm had been sufficiently daring to take the plunge and put a six-cylinder engine into production. As early as the beginning of 1903, Edge had suggested to Montague Napier that they should consider the development of a six. At first Napier was unimpressed with Edge's idea, believing that an engine should have the minimum number of working parts. A six would merely compound the problems of a four. Edge continued to argue his case, and gradually Napier began to concede that there was some merit in the concept. A six would be a smoother and more flexible engine, which would be a considerable asset in a superior touring car.

Although he was heavily committed to the responsibilities of moving the firm to the new factory at Acton, Napier set Rowledge and his drawing office team to work, and by the middle of 1903 they had completed the design of a prototype six-cylinder engine. This was a 'square' design with a bore and stroke of

101.8mm and a capacity of 4,942cc. In a radical technical innovation for Napier, the overhead inlet valves were mechanically operated. The engine was installed in a chassis and Edge began the road-testing. On his first outing, accompanied by Arthur Macdonald, who had been Stocks's mechanic in Ireland, he took the car to Tilburstowe Hill where, in confirmation of his arguments, the car climbed the hill smoothly in top gear. Montague Napier was now persuaded that the six had a commercial future, so on 16 October 1903 a dinner was held at the Trocadero Restaurant in Shaftesbury Avenue, in the West End of London, to announce the Napier Six to the world.

To Edge it was important that, having nailed Napier's colours to the six-cylinder mast, this confidence in the design should be seen in competition. Under Montague Napier's supervision, Rowledge started work on the design of a racing six, but time was against him and it was soon evident that the car would not be ready for the Gordon Bennett Eliminating Trials, which the ACGBI had announced would be held on 10, 11 and 12 May. If Napier and Edge had hoped for a place in the British team, as of right, this hope had already been dashed: the glory of 1902 was forgotten and the disasters of 1903 had precluded any chance of an automatic place. It was made clear that the three places in the team would be selected by a competitive eliminating trial and that competition would probably be keen.

The ACGBI had decided that the selection of the British team should be much more rigorous than in 1903. To choose a team to compete in a 300-mile (480km) race from the results of a one mile speed test in a ducal park and a clandestine hill-climb now seemed ludicrous. If the British team was to have credibility, not only amongst its competitors but also with the British motoring public at large, more exacting tests were necessary. The club discussed the possibility of taking the Trials to the Ardennes circuit in Belgium, before it was realised that there was a suitable venue within the British Isles. The authorities in the Isle of Man were willing to permit the Trial to be held on Manx roads – furthermore, there was no need for legislation from Westminster. The House of Keys, the Manx parliament, was autonomous and had the power to enact legislation for the highways of the island. A Bill was introduced and passed through the House within hours, so becoming law, and the way was clear for an exhaustive test to be held. The same legislation paved the way for the motor-cycle Tourist Trophy races, which have been held in the island since 1906.

A 52-mile (83km) circuit was chosen. This started at Quarter Bridge on the outskirts of Douglas, then ran south to Castletown. From here it ran north through the centre of the island, and at Ballacraine it joined what is now the TT circuit. Leaving this at Ballaugh, the course detoured through Sandygate and entered Ramsey from the north. After Ramsey it anticipated the TT circuit, rising to 1,300ft (400m) over the Snaefell Mountain section, then descending, passing by Douglas, to the start at Quarter Bridge.

The candidates would cover five laps of this circuit, which was divided into four sections. A set time was allowed for each section and the competitors were expected to keep as closely to this time as possible. Four miles (6.4km) of the course were designated as controls, and 11 minutes were allowed for these sections, whereas the remaining 48 miles (77km) had to be covered in 65 minutes. During each lap the cars would be timed and marked on the following points: speed over a three-mile stretch; speed over a flying half-mile; speed on the two-mile uphill section out of Ramsey; accuracy of stopping at controls; acceleration out of the controls; the time spent in refuelling, making repairs, and changing tyres; starting skill; time variations over the sections and time spent in passing through the controls – a schedule which would seem familiar, in part, to a modern rally driver. The circuit test would be held on 10 May, there would be a hill-climb at Port Vuillen, on the Ramsey–Laxey road, on the 11th, and the Trials would finish with a speed trial on the Douglas Promenade on the 12th.

Plans were made at Acton for the team which would seek selection. The building and racing of the 1903 team had been expensive – in Edge's words, 'many thousands of pounds had been spent'. The building of an entirely new team could not be justified; as far as new cars were concerned, the six-cylinder, known as the L48, would have to suffice. The three E61s had been retained by the firm and were brought out again. These were to be driven by Stocks, John Hargreaves (who had already competed with a touring 16hp in 1903), and W.T. Clifford Earp, a factory test driver who had begun his career with Napier working in the drawing office at Lambeth. Edge states that Hargreaves had bought his E61, and intended to make an entry for the Eliminating Trials as an independent, but his status was probably similar to the customers of Maserati, nearly 50 years later, who bought their cars on favourable terms and then received full works support. Hargreaves lived in Somerset, and as Master of the Blackmore Vale Foxhounds had a formidable reputation in the hunting field. There was another independent entry of which much was expected. Colonel Mark Mayhew had ordered a K5 from Napiers during the summer of 1903. The delivery date is not known, but he had received the car by the end of the year. Montague Napier had made some significant improvements to the original K5 design. The principal change was the use of mechanically operated inlet

Mark Mayhew sits in his new K5 on the Promenade des Anglais at Nice during the Rothschild Cup speed trials in March 1904. He drove the car from London and back again accompanied by his wife. (Guy Griffiths Collection)

valves, using the experience gained with the new Six, and wherever possible roller bearings replaced the plain bearings of the prototype. The radiator was changed and the wheelbase was 2in (5cm) shorter, at 8ft 10in (269cm). Although it had a redesigned engine, the car was entered in the factory records as a K5, and given the chassis number 405a (the first K5 was 405), while the new engine was numbered 187. As the new L48 would not be ready the original K5 was prepared for Edge, but rather surprisingly it was not fitted with the new, upgraded engine, though Edge reported that 'as the result of certain alterations, [it] was appreciably faster than it was in Ireland'.

In March, Mayhew set off from London, crossed the Channel, and drove the new K5 all the way to Nice for the annual Speed Week. In this venture he was accompanied by his wife. Nice provided the French manufacturers with the chance to give their new cars a test before the French Eliminating Trials, so the K5 faced some impressive opponents. Edge had also entered his K5, but illness prevented him from making the journey. The Rothschild Cup speed trials were held on the Promenade des Anglais and Mayhew ran in the flying mile and flying kilometre events. The star of the meeting was Rigolly's Gobron-Brillie and in the mile, Rigolly won from Duray's Gobron-Brillie and Werner's Mercedes 90, with the K5 back in fourth place. When it came to the kilometre, though, the K5 went much better, and although unable to match the speed of Rigolly's Gobron-Brillie – which achieved a remarkable 23.6 seconds (94.78mph/152.50kmh) – it gained third place with 27.2 seconds (82.26mph/132.35kmh) and beat the Mercedes by nearly a second. In a competition over a short course up La Turbie Hill, the K5 took fifth place. Having achieved some success, Mayhew and his wife drove all the way back to England again. The K5 had shown its performance capabilities against formidable opposition, as the following July, Rigolly broke the land speed record with his Gobron-Brillie at Ostend, at a speed of 103.55mph (166.61kmh), the first to exceed 100mph.

On Saturday 16 April the cars entered for the ACGBI Eliminating Trials had to be presented for scrutiny at the club garage in Down Street, London, behind its headquarters at 119 Piccadilly. The five Napiers appeared, together with three Wolseleys to be driven by Jarrott, Campbell Muir, and Girling. There were also three Darracqs. Although a French marque, these cars had been assembled at the Weir factory in Glasgow from components made in Great Britain, to the designs of the

French factory at Suresnes. The Darracqs were still unfinished and mechanics were working on them; when their unsilenced engines were started, the tranquillity and elegance of the West End were marred not

The engine of Mayhew's K5. The curvature of the pushrods is puzzling. (Derek Grossmark)

The L48 is assembled at Acton, spring 1904. Henry Tryon stands by the radiator, the box behind the radiator contains temporary coils. A second engine is on a test bench in front of the car. (Sir Henry Royce Memorial Foundation)

only by the noise, but also by thick clouds of black smoke.

The Napiers were taken to Douglas well before the Trials, so that the drivers could learn the circuit and final preparations could be made to the cars. Unhappily, misfortune struck Mayhew on one of his final test runs. On Sunday 8 May, while running his K5 on the course near Ramsey, he left the road and ran up a bank and over a stone wall. The front axle was bent and, according to some reports, the flywheel and rear of the crankshaft were damaged when the car grounded on the wall. This was a severe blow to the Napier team, and the factory mechanics worked round the clock to have the car ready for the beginning of the Trials on the Tuesday. The axle was straightened, but then it was mistakenly fitted to the car the wrong way round. Examination of the crankshaft in recent times has shown evidence of hurried machining to the flywheel flange, so if the engine had to be stripped and rebuilt in the short time available, perhaps the axle error was understandable. With much greater angle the front axle would have provided very heavy steering and considerable understeer, and Mayhew found the car did not handle properly.

The cars were weighed on the Monday afternoon in a coal yard on the North Quay of Douglas harbour. The Napiers had no trouble in getting below the 1,000kg limit, but Campbell Muir's Wolseley had to lose its front wings to qualify. The Darracq team was in more serious trouble though, two cars only weighing-in after the removal of their bonnets, battery boxes, silencers, and floor boards, while Rawlinson's was still overweight that evening, it being alleged that even the brake shoes were removed overnight in a search for eligibility!

At 9.00am the following morning the five-lap circuit test began. The Darracqs and Mayhew's Napier were late in coming to the start. Hemery, as he arrived at the line late, assumed that he had already lost time and set off at racing speed in his Darracq, without waiting for the start signal. For Rawlinson's Darracq the Trial was ended just 100 yards after leaving the line, when the propeller shaft broke. On Edmonds's Darracq, a cloth protecting the batteries wound itself around the clutch shaft and then tore away an oil pipe. Mayhew's problems, meanwhile, continued when the floorboards of the K5 broke as he drove up to the line and oil was flung over the coils. By the time the K5 had reached Castletown it was running on three cylinders, and retired when a road spring broke. Perhaps it was a small consolation to Mayhew that during the flying three mile test, shortly before he retired, he was second fastest with a speed of 55.8mph (89.3kmh), behind Edge,

Gordon Bennett Eliminating trials, Isle of Man, 10 May 1904. Selwyn Edge sits in the K5 at Quarter Bridge awaiting the signal to start on the five-lap circuit trial. (Guy Griffiths Collection)

Clifford Earp and his brother wait for the start of the speed trial on Douglas Promenade on 12 May 1904. Behind their E61 are Muir (Wolseley, No 7), Edge (Napier K5, No 9), Girling (Wolseley, No 10), and Jarrott (Wolseley). (Royal Automobile Club)

who recorded 60.1mph (96.1kmh), showing that on speed, the K5s had the legs of the opposition. Edge's K5 was also fastest, by a margin of 8mph, in the flying mile test, doing 73mph (116.8kmh), its nearest rival – Girling's Wolseley – managing only 65.6mph (104.9kmh). Edge had a good five laps, but he had a problem with the exhaust, which was removed at Ramsey during the test. There were the inevitable punctures, and then he had to extinguish a fire on the fourth lap, which started when the carburettor float punctured and the fuel overflowed.

On the Ramsey hill-climb, Edge led the field at 32.5mph (52kmh), Jarrott's Wolseley being second fastest, but by the narrowest margin over Earp's E61, which was going much quicker than forecast. Earp also had an uneventful five laps, the only adjustments that the E61 needed were to the clutch spring, to replace a cap on a king pin, and to remove the nail catcher from a wheel. As the factory tester he may have been more sympathetic to the car. Stocks and Hargreaves, with the other E61s, were slower than Jarrott and Girling on most of the speed tests. With the racing tactics which were to emerge in the future, the 'pit stop' times for refuelling and lubricating were significant. Jarrott took the least time at 4min 15sec, while Edge was only two seconds longer. Earp took 5min 10sec, and Stocks managed the tasks in 6min 34sec, but the rest were rather tardy, Girling being stationary for 19 minutes.

At the end of the five-lap test, when the times and the merit marks were checked, Edge was on top by virtue of his times, but Earp had an equal total of merit marks. Jarrott and Girling were next, so it was a reasonably contented Napier team which took their cars to the official garage, to be locked away for the night and checked by the Club judges. The following morning, a convoy of competitors drove north to Ramsey for the Port Vuillen hill-climb. Here, the triallists had three runs up the hill over a half-mile course, with an average gradient of 1 in 17. It was emphasised that the gear ratios were to remain unchanged from the previous day. The cars were flagged off at three minute intervals and, once again, Edge's K5 was well ahead of the rest. He did his fastest climb in 38.4 seconds; Earp was in second place at 42.8 seconds, ahead of Girling at 43.6 seconds. Among the spectators was Lord Raglan, Lieutenant-Governor of the Isle of Man. The cars returned to Douglas to be locked away by the ACGBI, to await the final speed trial in the morning.

The speed trial was held on the Promenade at Douglas, unfortunately the weather had changed for the worse and there was a sea mist with occasional showers. Despite this a large crowd turned out, and the course was packed with spectators along its length. The cars were timed over a flying kilometre, and each had three runs. The Promenade was an unhappy choice of venue, as raised tram lines ran along it and the cars would cross these when at full speed. At the end of the second series of runs there was an incident which could have been disastrous. The cars had been returning along the course to the start, at a speed which had already been a matter of comment, when Earp, crossing the starting line, realised to his dismay that 60 yards beyond it there was a barrier with the crowd packed in behind. He applied the handbrake and the rear wheels locked; he attempted to release the brake, but the ratchet had broken, jamming the lever. The car skidded towards the barrier, then struck a wall, and a spectator standing in front of it was slightly injured. Earp and his brother Arthur, who was the riding mechanic, were thrown out on to the pavement and also slightly hurt, while the radiator, front wheels, and the frame of the E61 were damaged. This was the second major accident involving this car, as it had been Jarrott's mount in Ireland the previous year. Despite all these vicissitudes, the car has survived to a ripe old age and is now in the National Motor Museum, Beaulieu. After this incident the speed trial was abandoned. Edge had been fastest with 57.3mph (91.7kmh), while Earp had been second, recording 53.2mph (85.1kmh). Once again, Girling and Jarrott had been in the next two places.

Earp's E61 after the crash on 12 May 1904. Earp, in white coat and goggles, looks disconsolately at the wreckage. (Royal Automobile Club)

While the crowds went home and the wreck of the E61 was cleared up, the judges of the ACGBI withdrew into the Peveril Hotel on the Douglas Promenade to consider the results. Previously, it had been declared that the British Gordon Bennett team would be decided after the judges had returned to London, so when, after a short delay, the team was announced that evening, there was some surprise. This turned to astonishment when the team was declared to be Edge driving the K5, Girling with the 72hp Wolseley, and Jarrott with the 96hp Wolseley. The Club added a rider that Earp would have been selected but for his accident, but that it was felt that neither the car nor the driver would be fit to race in the time available.

The decision brought forth much protest, and probably the loudest and strongest came from Edge. He wrote to the ACGBI, pointing out that Earp had finished in an undisputed second place overall in the trials, that the E61 would be repaired within a few days and that Earp had already recovered from his injuries. The correspondence became more heated and Edge invited the Club to withdraw him from the team, a request which was ignored. The press weighed in too, and in an editorial *The Autocar* regretted that the fastest cars had not been selected. To prove the point, Edge and Mayhew with the K5s, and Earp with the repaired E61, ran in the Nottingham Automobile Club Kettleby hill-climb on 28 May. Running in the open class, Edge was fastest at 1min 35sec, Mayhew was second in 1min 37.4sec, and Earp managed 1min 39.8sec to take third place.

All this left the ACGBI unmoved.

At a General Committee meeting of the Club on 30 May, Mark Mayhew, the vice-chairman, moved that the minutes should not be confirmed and that the team selection should be referred back to the Race Committee for further consideration. He pointed out that the Committee had decided to pick Earp before the speed trials and had gone back on its decision after the accident. He had no support from the other members of the Committee and Major Lindsay, the chairman, said he regretted that it had been announced that Earp would have been picked but for the accident. This had been said as a gesture of kindness to Earp and the Club's kindness had been misconstrued. It would not happen again. At the meeting the Committee also had before it a formal protest from Edge. This was rejected as being out of time, and also because it was not accompanied by the requisite fee of ten shillings.

While it was not mentioned at the time, there may have been another reason for the omission of Earp. In January 1904 the International Sporting Commission, mindful of the German team selection problems in 1903, had decided by a majority vote that henceforth, the Gordon Bennett Trophy should be open to all drivers, and not only to amateurs. The two dissenting nations were Belgium and Britain. In Britain the hope was expressed that the competition would again become an event for amateur drivers. To select Earp, a factory test driver, would have destroyed the British case at a stroke, so when Earp skidded into the wall, the Club judges probably breathed a collective sigh of relief, as he had presented them with the solution to their dilemma. Soon after the trials were over, the new Napier six-cylinder L48 was finished. It was suggested that Edge should be permitted to substitute the L48 – a much more powerful car – for the K5, but the ACGBI, standing by the letter of its selection rules, would not sanction any change to the team. The amateurism and rigid attitudes that were to bedevil British motor racing administration for 50 years were already flourishing.

Jenatzy's victory for Mercedes in 1903 meant that the onus of organising the 1904 Gordon Bennett race had fallen on the Automobilclub von Deutschland (AvD). The views of the AvD on how the race should be organised were soon overridden at the highest level. His Imperial Majesty Kaiser Wilhelm II considered that the prestige of the German Empire was at stake and the publicity value of the race presented an opportunity that could not be missed. His approach was a foretaste of that adopted by Hitler in the Berlin Olympic Games 30 years later. The Kaiser, who was a keen motoring enthusiast, decided to take an active part in the organisation of the race. It had been suggested that the race should be run on a remote rural course similar to the Athy circuit and several venues were suggested. All this was forgotten, though, when the royal edict came forth that the race would be run in the Taunus Mountains, and based on the fashionable spa resort of Homburg, about ten miles (16km) north of Frankfurt.

The course chosen was formid-

June 1904: The English Gordon Bennett team. Edge's Napier leads the Wolseleys of Girling and Jarrott. (Guy Griffiths Collection)

able, with a lap of 87 miles (139km), winding through the hills and forests. There were a number of towns and villages to be negotiated, mostly with narrow streets, and these were declared to be control zones, where the speed would be limited; the total control distance was seven and a half miles (12km). In these zones the road was fenced off with netting, and to prevent any repetition of the Paris–Madrid accidents, the entire course was guarded by police and soldiers. This circuit had to be covered four times, making a total race distance of 317.8 miles (511km), ten miles shorter than the Irish race. To deal with the dust hazard, the ubiquitous Westrumite would be used.

The start and finish would be in Saalburg, beside a restored Roman fort, and in keeping with this, grandiose, castellated grandstands and a royal box were built at the especial wish of the Kaiser. The stand was about 300ft (91.5m) long on each side of the track and was linked by an ornate bridge. Even the inscriptions at the race telegraph office were in Latin. The race was to be the centrepiece of a week of events including a ballet festival, opera (surprisingly, works by Wagner were not in the programme), military band concerts, a motoring *concours d'élégance*, an alcohol race, and speed trials in Frankfurt. To set the official seal of approval on the event, the Kaiser would be attending.

The growing importance of the Gordon Bennett Trophy was emphasised by the entry of seven national teams. The United States had been unable to muster a team after unsatisfactory trials, but joining Great Britain, France, and Germany there were now teams from Austria, Belgium, Italy, and Switzerland. The French had taken greater pains than any other nation to select a team. The ban on racing imposed after the Paris–Madrid was still in force at the beginning of 1904 and it seemed likely that the ACF would be forced to go to the Ardennes circuit in Belgium to hold the eliminating race. At the last minute the French government relented and agreed that a six-lap race could be held over a 55-mile (88km) circuit in the Argonne, a remote forested region near the Belgian frontier. Great care was taken over the security of the circuit when the trial was held on 20 May. The disasters of the previous year had done nothing to dampen French enthusiasm and there were 29 entries, even including three steam-powered Serpollets. The much-fancied Panhards had overheating problems and fell back, so victory went to Leon Thery driving a Richard-Brasier, Salleron was second with a Mors, and Rougier was third with a Turcat-Mery. The Turcat-Mery was a De Dietrich built under another radiator badge, which was one method of doubling a marque's chances of selection. The first three home were selected as the French team. Le Blon was fifth with a Serpollet; it is interesting to speculate if he would have been selected if he had been two places higher in the order. One of the De Dietrichs was driven in the French trial by Charles Jarrott. The ACGBI must have been relieved when he finished well down the field. If he had done well, all kinds of problems could have arisen.

The AvD decided not to hold a trial. It was feared that an accident during a trial race could have jeopardised the running of the Gordon Bennett, so the Belgian pair, Jenatzy and De Caters, were chosen again with Mercedes 90s and the third place was taken by Fritz von Opel with an Opel-Darracq. The Darracq firm had also arranged to have contenders built in Germany, but these were rather better propositions than the British versions, and the diligence of Alexandre Darracq in spreading his machinery around had finally paid a solitary dividend for him. The De Dietrich firm also had a factory in Germany at Niederbronn, in Alsace-Lorraine, where the chief designer was a youthful Ettore Bugatti. It was reported that an Alsatian De Dietrich was being prepared for consideration by the AvD, and would be driven by Bugatti, but nothing came of this project.

The Austrian team gave Mercedes three extra chances of success, as the team were using 90s, built in the factory at Weiner-Neustadt. Apart from sprocket details, these were identical to the two German cars, but were painted in the Austrian colours of black and yellow. The drivers were Braun, the American Warden, and Werner – who, unlike 1903, was now considered acceptable as a driver, albeit driving for Austria. Belgium was represented by a team of three Pipes, racing in the Belgian colour of yellow. This marque was built in Brussels and although the chassis and chain-drive were conventional, the magnetic clutch was not; neither was the 13$^{1}/_{2}$ litre engine, which had two camshafts, operating overhead valves by pushrods and rockers, with a hemispherical combustion chamber – the Riley Nine principle, 25 years early. The Pipe drivers were De Crawhez, Augieres, and Hautvast. From Italy came three 65hp Fiats, rudely described by some as Mercedes copies. There were similarities, but already Fiat was showing individualistic design trends. The drivers were Lancia, Storero, and Cagno, the chauffeur to the Queen Mother of Italy. Red had not yet become the legendary racing colour of Italy, so the Fiats were painted in a sombre black. Last of all, the Automobile Club de Suisse had entered a solitary Dufaux, driven by its constructor.

Edge was going to take the youthful St John Nixon as his riding mechanic, but parental disapproval intervened, and Arthur Macdonald went instead. The K5 was driven to Harwich and put on board the ferry to Rotterdam. It was still using the 34 x 3$^{1}/_{2}$ tyres but Edge was satisfied that Dunlop had improved the design and manufacture. The car was driven to Homburg via Cologne but was held up for 12 hours at the Dutch frontier by an argument about its documents. It had run well and Edge was feeling confident about his prospects in the race. The British drivers were staying at the Ritters Park Hotel in Homburg and the cars were kept at a garage at Usingen about five miles away.

Edge did several practice laps, and on Thursday 9 June he took H.J. Swindley of *The Autocar* as his passenger for a lap. It was not a happy outing: at Gravenweisbach, about ten miles after the start, they stopped to change a tyre. They restarted and about another ten miles on, going up a hill into Weilburg, they heard a loud crack come from the engine. Macdonald, who had been riding on the step, thought a piston had gone, but Edge feared a worse problem, and after the rear cylinder head was removed his fears were confirmed. When the engine was turned on the handle the rear pistons did not move. The crankshaft had broken. With admirable restraint, he commented to Swindley, 'That's very annoying'. A horse was found to tow the car as far as Weilmunster, about three miles on, and Edge then attempted to telephone Homburg for help. He was unable to make the call and a rumour soon spread at Saalburg that the Napier had crashed. Jarrott set out in his Wolseley to find Edge, accompanied by Browning, the Dunlop agent, but roared past without seeing Edge who, by then, was sitting in a local post office cart. Edge and Macdonald were eventually towed back to Homburg by the Wolseley tender car, arriving at 10pm. By then telegrams had been sent to Acton requesting a new crankshaft, mechanics to fit it, and two spare cars.

As soon as the telegram reached Montague Napier, he went into action. Three fitters with a new crankshaft were sent off to Harwich from Liverpool Street Station, and Earp left for Harwich by road, driving the L48. On Friday morning, Edge and Macdonald stripped the engine down in the Usingen garage. To Edge's relief, the two-inch hollow crankshaft had broken cleanly, just inside the front end of the centre main bearing. No damage had been done to the bearing itself and there was no other damage to the engine. The fitters bearing the crankshaft arrived in Homburg on Sunday evening and immediately set to work with Macdonald, rebuilding the engine. Meanwhile, Edge had been attempting to get more practice with borrowed cars. On Friday he tried to do a lap with Jarrott in the Wolseley, but this came to a premature end when the water-pump spindle seized. The next day Browning's Adler was pressed into service, but this fell by the wayside with a broken clutch-shaft, and on Sunday a borrowed Fiat expired at Saalburg after covering only five miles. On Tuesday 14 June, the engine had been rebuilt and installed in the K5. Edge did several practice laps and found it was running well. Meanwhile, Clifford Earp had arrived

The completed L48 stands in front of the Acton factory, June 1904. The conventional radiator would soon be replaced by cooling tubes, and Rudge-Whitworth wire wheels would be fitted in 1905. (David Watson)

with the L48 and Edge tried this over the course, but there was no suggestion of substituting it for the K5. Perhaps Edge had learned from his experience of racing a relatively untried car at Athy.

On Thursday, the day before the race, the competing cars were weighed and scrutineered. The official scales were set up in the Elizabethstrasse in Homburg and the cars were lined up in the street for the formalities. The car queuing behind the Napier was the Opel-Darracq. To ensure that his car was within the limit, Fritz von Opel drained off the dregs of petrol from the tank, just as Edge was about to push the Napier onto the scales. A bystander lit a cigarette and threw down the match, which ignited the petrol, and for a moment it seemed that the Napier and the Opel would both catch fire. However, Edge and his team acted quickly and pushed the K5 forward, away from the flames, while Opel pushed back the Darracq, and the petrol burned out harmlessly. When the drama was over and the K5 was put on the scales, it was found to be the lightest car in the field, weighing 988kg. Apart from the fire risks, weighing-in was a hazardous process; the Swiss Dufaux fell off the weighbridge and a front wheel was broken. As there was no spare, it was posted as a non-starter.

The race began at 7.00am on Friday 17 June. The warmth of the early morning gave an indication of the sweltering day to come. The crowds began to gather soon after dawn, although the grandstand was not full. The Kaiser arrived with his entourage and they took their seats at 6.30am. The start line was at least 200 yards from the Imperial box so that the royal party would see the cars pass at a fair speed after leaving the line. The organisation at the start was somewhat chaotic, but the 18 remaining cars lined up and the drivers waited nervously. Jenatzy was the first to go, climbing into his Mercedes at 6.55am; a minute later his mechanic swung the engine into life. Edge had arrived about ten minutes earlier, taking his place behind the Mercedes, as the K5 would be the second car to start. At 7.00 sharp, Jenatzy was flagged away amid much smoke and steam, followed by Edge and the rest of the field at seven minute intervals. The K5 showed its pace on the first lap. At the Limburg control, half-way round the lap, the Dunlop fitters threw water on to the tyres, which were heating up as the sun rose. At the end of the lap, Thery's Brasier led Jenatzy's Mercedes by the narrow margin of one second. Edge was third, four minutes behind, having lapped in 1hr 31min 44sec, followed by the Wolseleys of Girling and Jarrott. British prospects looked favourable.

On the second lap Edge had to stop for a puncture, then lost 19 minutes when the chain which drove the distributor broke. There were more problems: the new crankshaft was tightening up, and water was leaking into the crankcase. His time for the second lap was 2hr 36min 8sec, the slowest in the field, and he had dropped back to 15th place, so all

Selwyn Edge enters one of the controls on the Homburg circuit with the K5 during the Gordon Bennett Trophy, 17 June 1904. To reduce the likelihood of punctures, nail deflectors are fitted to the rear wheels. (Geoffrey Goddard Collection)

hope of success had gone. Thery was still in the lead and now nearly two minutes ahead of Jenatzy, which cannot have pleased His Imperial Majesty. A military band was playing in the Royal enclosure, which broke off from its medleys to sound a fanfare of trumpets as each car approached. As a Royal chauffeur, Cagno knew his place and saluted the Kaiser each time he passed the stands. Edge had a less-troubled run on lap three, and went round in 1hr 37min 41sec, which was five seconds quicker than Jenatzy's time for the lap, and he moved up to 13th place. But at Idstein, with only about 20 miles (32km) to go to the finish, disaster struck. An oil dipper broke away from a big end cap and lodged in the timing gears, seizing the engine, which was by then running very hot. Edge's race was over. At the finish there were great scenes of excitement. Thery held his lead and won, leading Jenatzy home by 10½ minutes. The French were jubilant, as the Gordon Bennett Trophy was back in what they regarded as its rightful home.

It had not been a good day for Great Britain. Edge was marooned by the roadside. Girling, who had risen as high as third on lap two, fell back with a blocked carburettor and came ninth. Jarrott had kept going despite losing third gear, breaking a driving chain, mending a burst radiator, and driving with a continuous misfire, to finish 12th and last. In 1931 Nuvolari was asked if he was happy to have won the Targa Florio. 'Well', he said, 'I'm glad I beat Varzi.' In a similar spirit, Jarrott observed that although he was last, he had beaten Edge.

The Gordon Bennett had been particularly disappointing for Edge, who had hoped for more in what he had decided would be his last international road race. He mentioned various reasons for his retirement, including dissatisfaction with the administration of the ACGBI – especially the omission of Earp from the team – and the increasing predominance of professional drivers, but the demands on his time made by the Motor Power Company and his other business commitments were a more likely cause. Nevertheless, he intended to continue with hill-climbs and sprints and further glory was still to come. Jarrott, too, had decided to give up racing. Probably faster than Edge, he can perhaps be compared with drivers of a later generation such as Whitney Straight and Count Trossi, amateurs of the highest standard, who in their day were a match for the best professionals. Once again, the Gordon Bennett had been a setback for Napier. It must be wondered if the broken crankshaft and oil dipper were the 1903 originals; the appreciation of stress fatigue was still in its infancy.

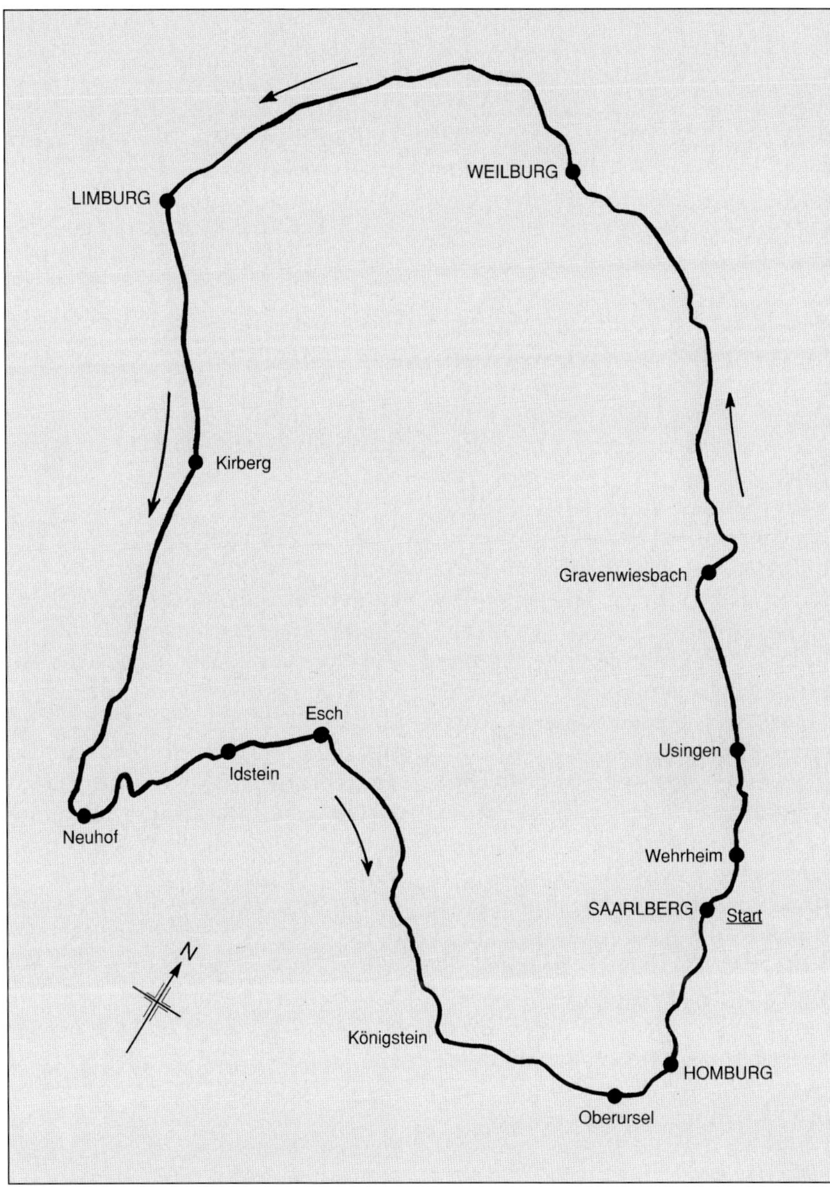

Gordon Bennett race 1904. The Homburg circuit was 87.04 miles (139.9km), and the race distance was 317.8 miles (511km).

On 23 July the Midland Automobile Club returned to Sun Rising, where a hill-climb was held again over a 1,000-yard (914m) course, with a stop and restart test. It was a wet day and the course was slippery. The meeting was for fully-equipped touring cars and Selwyn Edge appeared with what he declared to be a 20hp Napier. His opponents had rather different views about the car, which they perceived to be a 1903 Gordon Bennett E61, fitted with a touring body. Not surprisingly, Edge carried the day with a time of 2min 48.2sec. Encouraged by this success, he next took the 'touring' E61 to Bexhill for the ACGBI speed trial meeting, which was being held over the August Bank Holiday weekend. The course had been changed, the cars now starting their runs at the Sackville Hotel and finishing at Galley Hill, after being timed over a flying kilometre. The classes were run with eliminating heats and in his heat on the first day, Edge, who was running in the under £1,000 class, beat Cordingley's Mercedes 60 with a time of 52 seconds. Cordingley protested that the Napier was not eligible for the class, but the ACGBI dismissed the protest when Edge gave a written guarantee that similar chassis would be available for sale at £850. On the second day, amid more protests, Edge continued to work his way through the heats, improving his time to 50.6 seconds. In the semi-final, though, the protestors probably felt that justice had been done when the E61 was beaten decisively by Algernon Lee-Guinness's Mercedes 60.

While Edge was upsetting his fellow-competitors at Sun Rising, Mark Mayhew was tackling a much more demanding event. He was at Bastogne in Belgium, where he was a 'works' entry with his K5 in the Circuit des Ardennes. For 1904 the circuit had been extended to a lap of 73.5 miles (118km) and the race was over five laps, a total of 367 miles (591km). It had attracted an entry of 40, and three Napiers had been entered by the Acton factory for Mayhew, Edge, and an unnamed driver. Edge had already declared his intention of turning his back on road racing, and as well as driving at Sun Rising he was also reported to have been engaged in motor boat racing at Portsmouth that weekend. The third car also did not materialise, so Mayhew found himself alone, facing a formidable field. The Ardennes race had originally been intended for amateur drivers, but by 1904 all the major factories were there and so were all the leading aces. Although he was a factory entry Mayhew seems to have had little support, though the K5 was prepared at Acton and the damage it had received in the Isle of Man had been made good. He drove the car from his Roehampton home to Bastogne, where the race was to take place on 25 July, which was, unusually for a racing event, a Monday.

It was raining at 4.30am as the cars lined up in the main street of Bastogne, which was then a small village. The first car – Heath's Panhard – was flagged away at five o'clock, followed by the field at one minute intervals. Mayhew's starting number was 37 and he had to watch the rest of the field depart, only one car – Burton's Mors – being behind him when he set off at 6.04am on his first lap, by which time the rain had stopped. The course wound through the Ardennes forests on gritty and stony roads, and there were long straights interspersed with difficult winding sections. At the end of the first lap Duray led with his Darracq, having been round in 1hr 12min 53sec, 42 seconds in front of Tart's Panhard. Mayhew was back in 16th place. He had done a consistent lap in 1hr 25min 42sec but was not going quickly enough to make any serious challenge, though he was one place in front of Bianchi's Wolseley. On the next lap Mayhew lost time for reasons which are not recorded, but since, as *The Motor* reported, he was 'one of the few leading owners whom the puncture demon did not successfully attack', he began to profit from the misfortunes of those ahead of him. His fourth lap was his fastest at 1hr 23min 58sec and he was up to tenth place by the start of the fifth and final lap. Leger's Mors was the car in front of the K5, but it stopped twice while Mayhew did another consistent lap, to finish ninth. Although he was 57 minutes behind the winning car, which was Heath's Panhard, he had the satisfaction of knowing that the cars in front of him were driven by leading drivers. It was a creditable performance by an amateur without much support, who was also, perhaps, a bit out of practice, having raced little during 1904.

The L48 had returned to Acton after the Gordon Bennett, still untried, but the Irish Automobile Club announced that it would hold a speed trial on the Velvet Strand at Portmarnock in August, which would coincide with the Dublin Horse Show. The Velvet Strand was a stretch of smooth sand, two miles long and 200 yards wide, on the coast about ten miles north of Dublin. This presented an opportunity for the L48 to show its paces and Edge made an entry. A study of the tides showed that the meeting could not be held on the original date, so it was postponed until 7 and 8 September. Edge decided not to attend on the rearranged dates, perhaps because it was a mid-week fixture and business interests came first, so the car was entrusted to Arthur Macdonald. Starting as an office junior at Vine Street, he had progressed to riding mechanic and test driver, and was now promoted to the full responsibility of being a competition driver.

When the L48 appeared at Portmarnock the crowd were able to inspect an impressive machine. The six-cylinder engine had a bore of 159mm and a stroke of 127mm, giving a capacity of 15,131cc. The steel cylinders were bolted onto the one-piece aluminium crankcase. The separate copper water jacket round each cylinder was formed by an electrolytic deposit over a wax mould.

The wax was covered with graphite as a conducting element, and when the jacket had formed the wax was melted out, in a variation of the well known 'lost wax' process. The electrolytic process took about three weeks. The overhead inlet valves were operated by pushrods and rockers and were sited over the side exhaust valves. A single up-draught carburettor supplied the mixture through long serpentine induction pipes, and there was HT coil ignition. A metal-to-metal clutch took the power through a two-speed gearbox to a live axle. The chassis was conventional with a pressed steel frame, and the radiator was set back behind the front axle. There were quick-action filler caps on the radiator and fuel tanks. The car weighed 996.5kg, and initially it was fitted with wooden wheels. When the L48 made its first appearance at the Gordon Bennett meeting it had a normal brass radiator with the 'water tower' filler which was becoming a Napier trade mark. At Portmarnock, though, its appearance had changed; the radiator had been abandoned and cooling was effected by a series of copper tubes, which ran along the bonnet sides from a pointed nose. The car looked distinctive and striking, and the aerodynamics must have benefited, though the tubes reduced access to the engine.

The Portmarnock Speed Trials were held in two-car eliminating heats over a standing start measured mile. The racing cars ran on the second day and attracted a crowd of 10,000 spectators. The beach conditions were not quite perfect, as the tide had left slight ripples in the sand. Macdonald brought out the L48 for the 1,000kg racing class. It won its heats easily and in the final it defeated the Hon Charles Rolls's 100hp Mors to win, in a time of 57.4 seconds. The following Saturday, 10 September, Edge was back in action with the '20hp' E61, running at the Hertfordshire Car Club hill-climb at Aston Clinton, near Tring, the inaugural event at this famous venue. The course ran through part of Lord Rothschild's estate and the competitors and officials received lavish hospitality. The course was about 1,100 yards, or just over a kilometre, in length, with a chalk surface, and once again Edge walked away with the touring class in a time of 1min 27.6sec, easily defeating A.J. Dew's Leon Bollee.

The ACGBI rounded off the English sprint season with the biggest event of the year. The club had gone back to the Lancashire coast, but this time the venue was Blackpool. The Council had widened and resurfaced the southern end of the Promenade, between the South and Central Piers, to make what was generally acclaimed as the best sprint course in England. There was a two-day meeting on Friday and Saturday 14–15 October. The premier class was for the 1,000kg racing cars. The standing mile events were held on the Friday, but the following day the highest speeds were expected in the kilometre event, where the competitors had a run of nearly 700 yards (640m) before entering the measured distance. The Gordon Bennett K5 had been rebuilt after its failure in June, and was driven up to Blackpool by Clifford Earp. Earp was matched against Rolls's Mors and Rawlinson's Gordon Bennett Darracq, which after the Isle of Man debacle had been 'sorted' properly, and was now a formidable sprint car. The three cars finished in that order, Earp's winning speed being 84.68mph (136.25kmh), a British record for the distance.

At the end of October, Macdonald took the L48 across the Channel via the Newhaven–Dieppe ferry, and drove to Gaillon for the annual hill-climb on Sunday 30 October. Many of the best French drivers had turned out for the last important event of the French season. Macdonald showed that the L48 was a car to be reckoned with, as he did a time of 29.4 seconds (76.09mph/122.42kmh), which was only 0.4 seconds slower than the joint winners, Rigolly's 110hp Gobron-Brillie and Baras's 100hp Darracq. The driving of the 'works' cars was becoming very much the province of Napier employees. Edge was now selective about his drives, Charles Jarrott had retired, and, at the end of the season, Mark Mayhew had made the same decision. As an amateur he had given valuable support to Napiers and his skill as a driver was probably underestimated. He, too, found that the professional drivers were becoming predominant. He also had other interests which engaged his attention. He had been appointed as the commanding officer of the Motor Volunteer Corps, a part-time military unit of motorists affiliated to the Volunteers, predecessors of the Territorial Army. His K5 was apparently sold back to Napiers to become a 'works' car, a transaction which had its parallel in the arrangements of the Maserati firm with its customers and their 250Fs in the 1950s.

The ownership and financing of Napier racing activities has never been resolved satisfactorily. Edge wanted the world to believe that he owned the cars and met all the racing bills. In his autobiography he states several times that the racing of Napiers cost him 'thousands of pounds'. On the other hand, the building and development of such cars as the L48 seems to have been done at the expense of Montague Napier. The sale and repurchase of Napier racing cars was done at Acton, and not by S.F. Edge Ltd. It is also significant, perhaps, that from 1904 onwards factory employees did most of the competition driving. If an assessment can be made, it seems most likely that Edge met the expenses of running the cars in the Gordon Bennett races and also the other races in which he competed, while such activities as the sprinting and hill-climbing of the L48 were probably paid for by the firm.

Chapter 6: 1905

More Horsepower, More Disappointments

THE 1905 competition season began for Napiers in the autumn of 1904. Soon after the L48 had returned from Gaillon it was being made ready at Acton for a visit to the United States. It was to compete in the Florida Speed Week, organised by the American Automobile Association, which was being held between 23 and 28 January 1905 on the beach which linked the towns of Ormond and Daytona. The L48 was shipped to New York accompanied by Arthur Macdonald and a small team of mechanics. After disembarking, the car and its crew travelled on to Daytona by train.

The Speed Week had attracted 275 entries and the cars and drivers began to gather for practice a week before the event. The course had smooth, hard sand and was usable for eight hours between the tides. There was a tragedy on Sunday 22 January when Frank Croker, driving a Simplex, swerved into the sea to avoid a motor cycle which had strayed on to the course. Croker and his mechanic, Raoul, were both killed. Despite this accident, Macdonald practised with the L48 the same day, causing a sensation when he recorded a speed of 105.88mph (170.36kmh) over a measured mile, which was an unofficial world record.

The meeting had an ambitious programme and the longest event was the 100-mile (160km) Vanderbilt Cup. Macdonald was entered for the sprint events and he soon found that his strongest rival was the ultra-low, streamlined Stanley Steamer driven by Ross, which had the appearance of a car many years in advance of its time. In the Dewar Cup, over a standing start mile, the Stanley achieved 42.0 seconds, beating the L48 by 0.6 seconds. In other events the advantage lay with the L48. Macdonald won the Bowden Cup for the flying start kilometre with an impressive time of 27.4 seconds. He then went on to win the flying start five-mile race at 91.37mph (147.01kmh), the flying start ten-mile race at 96.25mph (154.86kmh) – for which he also won the Miller Trophy – and the flying start 20-mile race at 78.20mph (125.82kmh), collecting the Thomas Trophy. The speed was slower in this event because it involved rounding a pylon at the end of the beach and making a return run.

It was in the flying mile event on Tuesday 24 January that Macdonald achieved his greatest feat. To the acclaim of the crowd, the L48 covered the distance at 104.65mph (168.38kmh), bettering the existing world land speed record of 104.52mph (168.17kmh) established by Baras's Gordon Bennett Darracq at Ostend the previous October. However, as Cyril Posthumus and David Tremayne pointed out in their book *World Land Speed Record*, the L48 'either didn't hold the record at all, it held it for less than an hour, or it held it for twelve months'. The International Commission, which was French-dominated, did not accept the timing methods of the American Automobile Association, so in European eyes Macdonald's record was not valid. In any event, about an hour after the L48's run an American driver, Herbert Bowden, driving a Mercedes with an extended chassis and two '60' engines in tandem, went through the distance at 109.75mph (176.58kmh). Just to make things more complicated, the American Automobile Association would not accept Bowden's speed as a new record, as the Mercedes weighed more than 1,000kg, which was the limit for cars running in the Speed Week. Twelve months later, Hemery covered the distance at 109.65mph (176.42kmh) in another Darracq, so whatever interpretation was placed on the rules, the Napier was by then no longer the fastest.

The results in Florida must have given great satisfaction to Edge and Montague Napier, as they now had one of the fastest cars in the world. When Macdonald returned to London a celebration dinner was held in his honour, where the trophies, described in *The Automotor Journal* as 'artistic', were displayed. Edge now announced that L48s would be built to order, thus giving customers a chance to become record holders. There were no takers for L48s, but there was a sale of another K5, which was bought by John Hargreaves and was delivered to him early in 1905. It was very similar to the Mayhew car delivered a year earlier, and had the same engine capacity. The main differences were the radiator, which reverted to the form of the original K5, and the tyre sizes, which were 870mm x 90mm at the front and 850 x 120 at the rear. It had the chassis number 830 and the engine number 706; the registration number was Y 19. Hargreaves had his eye on the British Gordon Bennett Eliminating Trial, which was to be held in May.

By the end of 1904 the plans for the 1905 Gordon Bennett Trophy were already well under way, and it was announced that the race would be held on 6 July. Thery's victory had dropped the ball at the feet of the ACF, but there were problems. The French motor industry was expanding at a prodigious speed and almost every manufacturer realised that to represent France in the Gordon Bennett team gave large and tangible commercial advantages. Equally, it was realised that only three cars would receive this honour and the rest would merely be regarded as also-rans in the French Eliminating Trials. The ACF was under great pressure from the manufacturers to provide an alternative competition which would give the rejects a chance of glory. A plan was devised which brought forth acclaim in France and scorn from all the other competing nations. It was proposed that a Grand Prix de l'Automobile Club de France should be held concurrently with the Gordon Bennett, in which all the competitors would have an equal chance. The first 15 cars to finish in the French Eliminating Trials would run in the race, and the first three cars in the Trial would be the French Gordon Bennett team. For the foreign opposition, six places each would be allocated to Great Britain and Germany and three places each would go to Austria, Italy, Switzerland, the United States, and Belgium.

Such was the adverse reception to the French proposals that in February 1905 the International Sporting Commission met in Paris to discuss the matter. The ACF realised that the opposition was too strong and agreed to run the Gordon Bennett Trophy as a separate race, with the Grand Prix de l'ACF being run on the following day. Shortly after the meeting of the Commission, the ACF announced that it would not hold the Grand Prix in 1905 and the Gordon Bennnett Trophy would stand alone, but the ACF added that in future years it would not support the Gordon Bennett and French cars would not compete in it. Henceforth, the Grand Prix would be the only race supported by France.

At least the doubts were now removed for 1905, and the ACGBI went ahead with the organisation of the British Eliminating Trial, which were once again to be held on the Isle of Man on Tuesday 30 May. The course would be unchanged from that of 1904, but there was one major difference – in 1905 the Trial would be a proper race over six laps of the circuit, a total of 289 miles (465km). As well as being assessed for their speed over the whole race distance, during each lap the competitors would be timed over a measured two and a half mile section at Fox-

Florida Speed Week, January 1905: Arthur Macdonald with the L48, now with the tubing radiator. At this event he established a world land speed record of 104.65mph (168.38kmh). (Guy Griffiths Collection)

dale, between Castletown and Ballacraine, a half-mile section at Ballaugh, and on the two-mile uphill section out of Ramsey. The entry fee was set at £100 per car and would be forfeited if the car did not start. To prevent the weighbridge comedies of 1904, a car would only be allowed three attempts to weigh-in under the 1,000kg limit, and would be disqualified if any vital part was removed in an effort to squeeze under the limit. In addition all drivers now had to be British subjects and also had to be members of the ACGBI.

When the entry list closed the Napier team found it was facing opposition from Wolseley, Siddeley, Star, and Weir. The Wolseleys were the 1904 96hp cars, brought out again with minor changes, and driven by Cecil Bianchi and the Hon Charles Rolls. The Siddeley, a newcomer, was built in the Wolseley factory but had been designed by J.D. Siddeley to the order of Lionel de Rothschild. It was a massive car, with a 15 litre four-cylinder engine, and had a conventional chassis and transmission. In the Trial it was to be driven by Sidney Girling. Star of Wolverhampton produced two cars, which were Mercedes copies with 10 litre engines. Joseph Lisle, the son of the proprietor was to have driven one car, but he had been suspended by the ACGBI after an incident on the road, so the drivers were to be the brothers F.R. and H.G. Goodwin, who had no motor racing experience but had pedalled well in the cycle world. The Weir was one of the 1904 Darracqs presented under a new name. This had been bought by Algernon Lee-Guinness and had been rebuilt and revised.

There were four Napier contenders. Selwyn Edge had kept to his word and was not competing, so the veteran 1903 K5 was in the hands of Cecil Edge. Clifford Earp was driving the ex-Mayhew K5, and John Hargreaves was giving his new K5 its first outing. Once again, Arthur Macdonald was to drive the L48, the appearance of which had been changed by the fitting of wire-spoked wheels manufactured by Rudge-Whitworth Ltd. The spokes were tangential and the wheels were not detachable. This was the first time that wire-spoked wheels had been fitted to a car of the size and power of the Napier. It was setting a racing design trend which would last for over 50 years.

The regulations required the cars to be properly silenced and registered for road use. The compulsory registration of cars had been imposed by the Motor Car Act 1903, which had come into force on 1 January 1904. Edge's K5 was A 1013 and the L48 was A 9845, so it was a fully-legal team of Napiers which arrived in Douglas some time before the race, to practice over the circuit. This was permitted between 4.00am and 7.00am, and large crowds of Manxmen turned out to watch. The major excitement was provided by Cecil Edge, who bounced his K5 off a wall at Hilberry, on the outskirts of Douglas. The car had to return to Acton, by ferry and train, for chassis repairs, but these were completed well before race-day. On Monday 29 May the cars were weighed on the corporation weighbridge in Douglas. This was temperamental in operation, but when it was persuaded to work properly the Napiers all passed the 1,000kg test without too much trouble. Edge's K5 recorded 993kg, Hargreaves's car was 992kg, and, despite its size, the L48 was the lightest of the team at 980kg. Earp's K5 was overweight at the first attempt, but the removal of minor bits reduced it to 993kg. After the weigh-in, the dignitaries of the Isle, led by the Lieutenant-Governor, accompanied by the drivers and officials, attended a service in St John's Chapel, Douglas, conducted by the Bishop of Sodor & Man. When the service was ended, the Manx Attorney-General read the enabling Act to the congregation.

Early next morning the ten cars were lined up on the course at Quarter Bridge. The three K5s were starting fifth, sixth and seventh, and the L48 would be the last car to go. At 9.00am H.G. Goodwin's Star was flagged away, followed by the field at five minute intervals. It was not a good day for Napier. The four cars were the fastest in the Trial in terms of performance, but they were beset by all kinds of problems. Cecil Edge set off at a spanking pace, doing the fastest time on the first lap in 57min 00sec; on lap two he went even better, producing the fastest lap of the day at 51min 45sec – an average speed of 56.00mph (90.1kmh) – and was leading the race, despite braking problems. Then it all went awry on the third lap, Edge stopping for 20 minutes on Snaefell while he struggled with a lack of ignition. By now the brakes had disappeared completely and he was coasting round. His time on lap four was 1hr 25min 15sec and he did not complete the last two laps, so he was excluded from the results, being over the time limit. Hargreaves had a jammed clutch and did a slow first lap, and was in ninth place when he stopped at Quarter Bridge. The defect was cured by the hands of Selwyn Edge himself and the next lap was done in 57min 00sec. Hargreaves, too, had braking problems, and punctures as well, so only completed four laps.

Macdonald, of whom so much was expected, had an even more disastrous race. He lost 14 minutes on the first lap with a defect described as a 'broken pump chain'. He took 2hr 43min 30sec to cover the second lap, a small chip from a gear tooth had jammed in the selectors, obliging him to drive holding the car in gear with one hand. On the third lap, probably hampered by the gear problem, the L48 skidded into a wall beyond Ramsey, buckling a front wheel; as it was not detachable, the car could not continue, so its race was over. As a small consolation, the L48 had shown it was in another class in terms of sheer performance.

The Gordon Bennett Eliminating Trials on the Isle of Man, 30 May 1905. Clifford Earp (K5 Napier, No 7) is about to pass the Wolseleys of Bianchi (No 4) and Rolls (No 11) at Ramsey. (Guy Griffiths Collection)

Over the two and a half mile timed section it had recorded 81.8mph (131.61kmh), nearly 12mph quicker than the next car, Hargreaves's K5; over the half-mile section, the speed had been 88.2mph (141.9kmh), nearly nine miles an hour quicker than Girling's Siddeley, and on the Ramsey hill section it had a six second advantage over its nearest rival, the Siddeley.

While his team-mates had been battling with adversity on all sides, Clifford Earp had been driving on steadily with his K5. Only on his third lap did his time exceed one hour, and at the beginning of the fourth lap he took the lead and came home to win the race, 14min 30sec ahead of Bianchi, who had also had a consistent and uneventful drive with his Wolseley. Rolls was placed third with the other Wolseley, though he did not complete the sixth lap, and Cecil Edge was adjudged to have finished fourth. Earp had taken 5hr 57min 30sec on his winning drive, and it was mid-afternoon as the tired drivers and mechanics arrived back in Douglas to await the selection of the team. The ACGBI selectors had withdrawn to the Peveril Hotel to consider their findings, and later that evening it was announced that the Gordon Bennett team would be Earp, Bianchi, and Rolls, with Cecil Edge and Hargreaves as reserves. There was immediately concern about the constitution of the team. Earp thoroughly deserved his selection, but doubts were expressed about the wisdom of entering him in the K5, when the L48 had shown that it was in a different class, and one of the fastest racing cars in the world. Pressure was put on the ACGBI by the motoring press and by influential figures, led by Selwyn Edge, to nominate Earp in the L48.

While the ACGBI dignitaries returned to London and pondered on the selection problem, the English sprint season had begun. On Monday 12 June, the Yorkshire Automobile Club held the first sand sprint on the British mainland. This was on the beach at Filey and the course was a flying mile with a half-mile at each end for acceleration and braking. Although crowd control was minimal, and the spectators wandered across the course at will, there were fortunately no accidents. Cecil Edge entered the K5, now recovered from its Manx bothers, and running in the open class against slight opposition he won easily with a speed of 71.42mph (114.91kmh). Leaving Filey, Cecil Edge drove south to Bexhill, where two days later, on 14 June, the ACGBI was holding its speed trials again. Prudently, as cars were getting faster, the course had been shortened to half a mile, and the event attracted a much smaller crowd. The K5 was running in the 1,000kg class, where it was matched against the Weir-Darracq, which was driven once more by Lee-Guinness. The Darracq came out on top, recording 30.2 seconds, to which Edge could only reply with 32.0 seconds to take second place.

The Gordon Bennett Trophy was to be contested over four laps of an 85 mile (136km) circuit in the Auvergne. This bleak and inhospitable area had been chosen as the population was sparse, and the circuit would be free of the neutralised zones which had characterised the courses in 1903 and 1904. The race would be based on Clermont-Ferrand, the only sizeable town in the area, which was about three miles (5km) from the circuit and about ten miles (16km) from the start, at Laschamps. The start itself was overlooked by the Puy-de-Dome, a volcanic mountain which rises to 5,000ft (1,500m). The circuit was hard work for the drivers, as the longest straight was only two and a half miles. At Rochefort, about ten miles after the start, the road rounded a hairpin, so sharp that some drivers contemplated using reverse to get round it. Near Sauvagnat, 40 miles further on and almost half way round the lap, the road ran beside a 500ft (150m) drop. The Continental tyre concern claimed that there were 700 corners per lap. Three long wooden bridges took the road over railway level crossings and the course was protected from wandering spectators by wooden palisades where it passed through the few small towns and villages. A speed limit was imposed over the wooden bridges, which was universally ignored by the drivers. A tented township was erected at the start, with the competitors' garage and the weighbridge opposite the 4,000-seat main grandstands. As overtaking would be difficult, three spacing controls were established on the course. When a car arrived at a control, it would be sent on at once, a clock would then be started which would run for five minutes, if another car arrived, it would be held until the five minutes had elapsed, before being released. The time that the car was held would be subtracted from its running time.

By April drivers were trying the circuit, dodging the three steamrollers engaged by the ACF to improve the road surface, and the local sheep which wandered on to the road. Among the drivers was Selwyn Edge, but it is not recorded which car he was using for his reconnaissance. The French Eliminating Trial was held on 16 June, and early in the month drivers from other nations were mingling with the French hopefuls practising on the circuit. Earp, Rolls, and Bianchi turned up to watch the French race, which was won by Thery, repeating his performance of the previous year in his Richard-Brasier. Another Richard-Brasier was second, driven by Callois, and Duray's De Dietrich was third, so the French team was settled. After the French Trial it was announced that there would be no further practice on the circuit until the Gordon Bennett race day. This decision brought forth a storm of protest from the other competitors, who pointed out that the French had

Gordon Bennett race 1905. The Auvergne circuit was 85.35 miles (137.2km); race distance was 341.4 miles (549km).

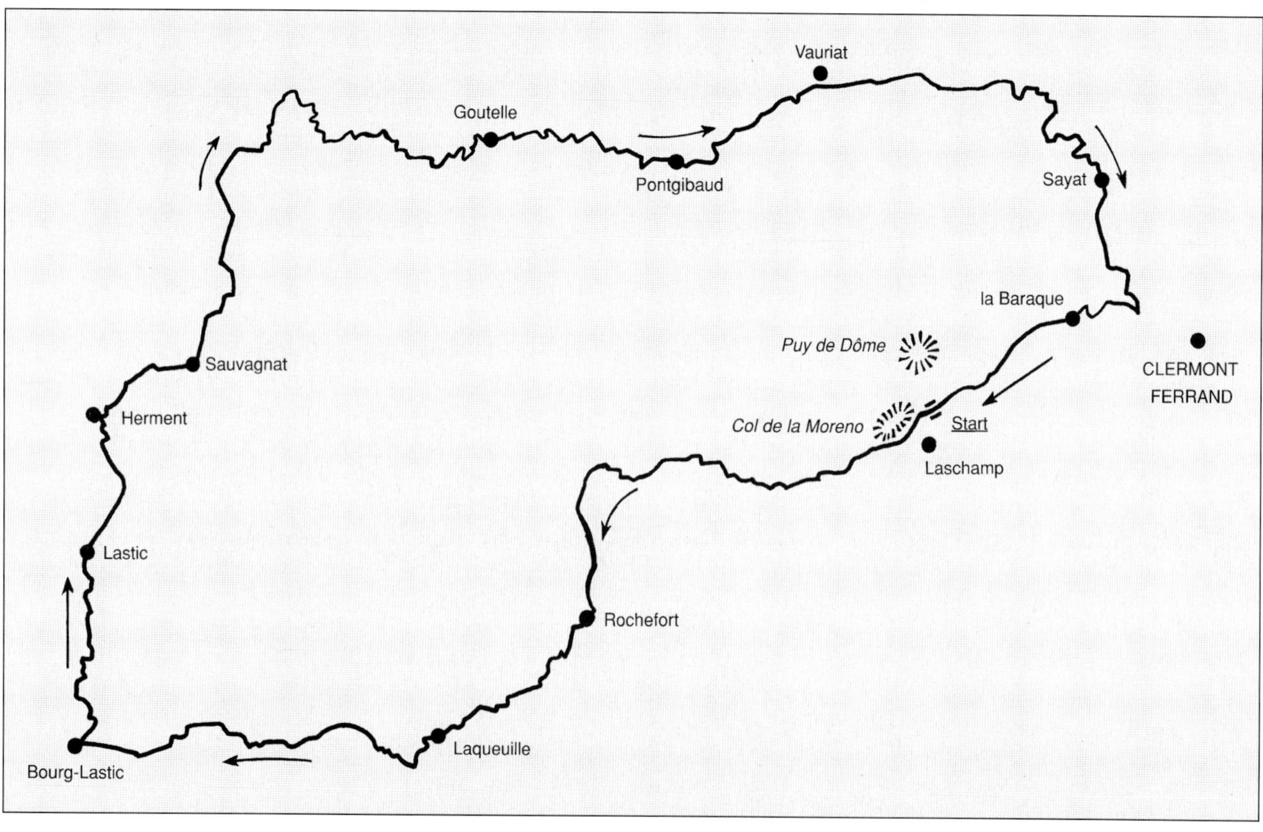

an unfair advantage, having already raced over the course. The decision was revoked and peace was restored. Earp had arrived with the L48, and Cecil Edge had brought the ex-Mayhew K5. The ACGBI had decided that Earp could use the L48 if he felt it was suitable. He decided to race the faster car, but the K5 was pressed into service as a practice vehicle. He did only four laps in each car, and by race day was not fully conversant with the circuit. He was perhaps to regret that he had not done more practice with the L48.

The cars were weighed-in on the day before the race. During the weighing, a sudden gale blew the roof off the grandstand and blew down the weighing tent, festooning the cars and the people inside. The L48 was well within the limit at 996.5kg, but the rudimentary Truffault shock-absorbers were queried, as it was suggested that these were of French manufacture. However, the scrutineers were satisfied by Edge's explanations. The 80,000

June 1905, the Gordon Bennett Trophy at Clermont-Ferrand: Clifford Earp practising with the ex-Mayhew K5 at Rochefort. (Guy Griffiths Collection)

Earp and the L48 at the weighing-in for the Gordon Bennett Trophy, 4 July 1905. (Geoffrey Goddard Collection)

spectators who had arrived in Clermont-Ferrand for the race found the local hotels were few in number, and barely adequate in quality. The crude and primitive grandstand, now re-roofed, was in marked contrast to the Imperial grandeur of Homburg. The course, which had been sprayed with Pulveranto – a cheaper form of Westrumite – was guarded by the French Army, and the course controls were manned by retired racing drivers and representatives of firms which were not participating.

On the morning of the race the cars were lined up on the road at 5.00am, and the drivers were presented to M. Clementel, the Minister for the Colonies. It was fine as the first car – Thery's Brasier – was flagged away at 6.00am. The field followed him at five minute intervals and Earp was the second away. He and his brother Arthur, who was the riding mechanic, looked suitably dramatic in their white wind caps and goggles and their white overalls. After leaving the start, the cars covered about a kilometre and then ascended the Col de Moreno, a climb of about 300 feet. The cars were timed over this section, and although it seemed that Earp, with his two-speed gearbox, had made a slow start, the timing showed that the L48 had been the fourth-fastest car. To the horror of the French, Vincenzo Lancia's Fiat led at the end of the first lap and was almost seven minutes in front of Thery. Earp was in seventh place, almost 19 minutes behind the leader and battling for his place with the three Mercedes. On the second lap Earp's troubles began. The fuel tank mountings broke and the tank leaked away its contents. Fuel had to be bought at the roadside to get the car back to the pits. The driver's seat, which was mounted with the fuel tank, now became loose and had to be fixed. Then, to compound the Napier's troubles, a rebound stop flew off a front spring and hit the carburettor, the resultant damage upset the mixture, and the engine started to cut out on sharp, cambered bends. By the end of the race, it had stopped 21 times from this cause. By the end of the second lap Earp had fallen back to 11th place, his time for the lap being 2hr 13min 29sec, a sad contrast to the 1hr 42min 1sec recorded by Lancia, who still led.

Although the Napier's problems became no worse, the stalling engine was a constant source of delay and the Earps were also suffering severely from the effects of the Pulverato, which was inflaming their eyes. Towards the end of the race the dust turned to mud, as there was light rain. Tyres had not been a problem and the Palmers on the front lasted the race, though the rears needed one change. The L48 was picking up places as the runners in front fell out, and although he was going well below his best, Earp was consistent, and the speed of his driving impressed observers. The L48 had been noted as one of the quickest cars when it passed the grandstands. At the end, however, it was another victory for France, as Thery had taken the lead when Lancia's Fiat seized on the third lap after all the cooling water leaked away. Earp finished in ninth place, just failing to be the highest placed Briton, as Rolls's Wolseley finished only 47 seconds in front of the L48 after nearly eight and a half hours' racing. After the

Clifford Earp at speed in the L48 during the 1905 Gordon Bennett Trophy. (Geoffrey Goddard Collection)

event, the Earps had to be led around with their eyes bandaged up.

The last Gordon Bennett race had been a setback for Napier, despite having one of the fastest cars in the field. That the outcome had been a particular disappointment to Selwyn Edge was evident when the race was ignored in Napier publicity. The L48 and the K5 returned home and Earp's vision was soon restored, as two weeks later he had an engagement to drive the L48 in the biggest British sprint yet held. The English seaside resorts had been vying to organise the major sprint event of the year; the crown had passed from Bexhill to Blackpool, and now it was the turn of Brighton. It was organised by the ACGBI and had the enthusiastic support of Brighton Council. The venue was Madeira Road, now Madeira Drive, which ran eastward along the seafront from the Palace Pier. The course was specially resurfaced with tarmacadam for the event and a course was marked out which incorporated a standing mile and a flying kilometre. The start line was at Black Rock, the eastern end of the front, so the cars ran west towards the Palace Pier, the opposite direction to the modern Brighton Speed Trials, and the terracing of the front provided a magnificent grandstand for the spectators. The meeting was held over four days, from Wednesday to Saturday, on 19–22 July, and there were classes for every category of touring and racing car, which were run in the usual heats and final. The racing classes were for 1,000kg, Gordon Bennett, and Unlimited cars. On the first day, Earp was victorious with the L48 in the 1,000kg class in 47.6 seconds. On the Thursday, however, he was unable to repeat his success, making a bad start in the final and being beaten by Hutton's 120hp Mercedes. Arthur Brown, who had bought the Gordon Bennett car from Edge in 1902, was entered with the 1903 K5 but was eliminated in the heats.

The Friday saw the competition begin over the flying kilometre, where the Gordon Bennett type cars were competing for the *Daily Mail* Cup. Sadly, the day was marred by an accident to Arthur Brown. While driving the K5 through Telscombe, about five miles east of Brighton, on his way to the meeting, Brown, who was accompanied by Collins, Mrs Edge's personal chauffeur, swerved off the road to avoid a tramp. The car went into a chalk pit and overturned. Brown and Collins were thrown out of the car; Brown suffering severe head injuries while the unfortunate 19-year-old Collins was killed. The K5 was badly damaged and the front axle was torn off. When news of the accident reached Brighton it cast a gloom over the competition, but racing went on, and Earp covered the kilometre at 97.25mph (156.47kmh) in the final, to win the class and establish a new British kilometre record.

On Saturday, the final day, the main event was for cars of unlimited cylinder capacity, racing for *The Autocar* cup over a flying kilometre. Once again the L48 came out, but ran into trouble when, in the first heat, the crankshaft was reported to have 'twisted' and the car finished the course on one cylinder. Earp was said to have made repairs, though this sounds a daunting task, as it must have necessitated stripping the massive engine; however, the car ran again, but did not make the final. There was one Napier success, which must have pleased Edge, as the ex-Mayhew K5 had been entered for Miss Dorothy Levitt; with her tulle frock and scarf streaming in the slipstream, she took fourth place in the *Autocar* class and then went on to win a handicap sweepstake for Gordon Bennett cars.

Dorothy Levitt had started work in Edge's office in 1902/3 as an 'emergency lady type-writer' – what is now known as a 'temp-typist'. Edge appreciated her talents and she soon became his private secretary. She was keen to drive, and Edge was the first to discover what many found in later years – that the publicity value of a woman racing driver merely competing greatly exceeded that garnered by the victory of a male driver. If she won, it was even better. The Motor Power Company held the agency for the French marque Gladiator, and Dorothy Levitt began her racing career driving one of these in the 1903 Southport Speed Trials, where she won her class. She also had a successful run with a Gladiator in the ACGBI 1903 1,000-mile Trial, and repeated this success in the 1904 Hereford 1,000-mile Trial with a De Dion. By now she seemed to be with Edge on many occasions: she had been in the Napier pit during the 1903 Gordon Bennett at Athy and was present at the weighing-in. In 1904 she accompanied him during his motor boat racing and competed at Cowes in his Napier-powered boat, being congratulated by King Edward VII for her skill. Nearly a century later it is, perhaps, permissible to speculate that the relationship was closer than employer/employee.

Only five days later, having enjoyed the seaside at Brighton, the competitors had to journey north to sample the delights of Blackpool, where the ACGBI had organised its third major sprint event of the year along the front. On the first day, Thursday the 27th, the course was a flying mile, and Earp appeared with the L48. It was in splendid form, so presumably the engine had been rebuilt in some haste at Acton after the Brighton failure. Despite problems caused by dogs roaming on the course, the L48 covered the flying mile at 96.25mph (154.86kmh) in the 1,000kg class, to beat Guinness's 100hp Darracq. Dorothy Levitt had also travelled north with the ex-Mayhew K5 and was fourth in the class, though somewhat slower, doing the distance at 69.23mph (111.39kmh). The next day Earp excelled himself. The course had a

Dorothy Levitt in the ex-Mayhew K5 at the Blackpool Speed Trials on 27 July 1905. She was fourth in the 1,000kg class. (Guy Griffiths Collection)

distinct bend where it passed the Central Pier, and many drivers were easing off for this, but Earp kept his foot down and covered the course in 22.8 seconds (98.11mph/157.85kmh). This gave him victory, but the organisers then asked him to run again and attempt to better the world kilometre time. Despite the unsuitable course he agreed to try. As the *Automotor Journal* put it, in terms which captured the spirit of the times, 'Earp is a Britisher and therefore not to be beaten'. His passage past the Central Pier was spectacular, and his courage was rewarded – he equalled the record with a speed of 104.53mph (168.19kmh). This was the last competitive outing in England for the Acton racing cars in 1905, though Cecil Edge took the L48 to Skegness on Saturday 2 September, where he did some untimed demonstration runs at the Nottingham Automobile Club sand sprint meeting.

Looking after the L48 and the K5s had not been the only task occupying the small racing department at Acton during the summer of 1905. At the beginning of the year, the ACGBI had announced that it would organise a race for standard touring cars, which would compete for the Tourist Trophy. This would be held over the Gordon Bennett Trial course on the Isle of Man on Thursday 14 September. The rules were strict. Although it was not stipulated that the cars had to be production models and little was said about engine modifications, the manufacturer had to fix a price on the chassis before the race, and then had to undertake to accept and fulfil orders for identical chassis at that price, for one month after the race. The chassis had to weigh between 1,300 and 1,600lb (591 and 727kg) and had to carry a load of not less than 950lb (432kg), of which the driver, passenger, and ballast had to be at least 600lb (273kg), the ballast being 50lb (23kg) sandbags. The body was required to have four comfortable seats and to be of a design approved by the Club scrutineer. The minimum track and wheelbase would be 4ft (122cm) and 7ft 6in (228.6cm) respectively. There was a sting in the tail: the race would be over four laps, a total of 208 miles (334km), and the entrants would be given a measured quantity of fuel, one gallon (4.54 litres) being allowed for each 25 miles (40km). Only the driver and riding mechanic would be allowed to work on the car during the race and all tools and spares had to be carried on the car. Each manufacturer would only be permitted to enter two cars.

When the regulations were published, Edge immediately realised the necessity of Napier competing in the race, and in April he began tests with an 18hp six-cylinder L49, running it from Acton to Dashwood Hill and back again, a distance of 50 miles (80km), and limiting the fuel for this run to two gallons (9.1 litres). The results were satisfactory, so the preparation of two cars for the race was put in hand. These were based on the L49, but new engines were built. Although it probably riled Edge, who was looking for every opportunity to promote the Six,

Montague Napier approved the design of a four, with a bore of 90 mm, a stroke of 108 mm, and the modest capacity of 2,748cc. In a search for fuel economy, the design had reverted to automatic inlet valves. Napier probably had doubts about the advantages of a Six in the peculiar conditions of the race, where torque on the Manx hills and fuel economy were going to be more important than power. Arthur Rowledge having left Napiers early in 1905 to join Wolseley, and his place having been taken by Thomas Barrington, it is not known who designed this engine.

Final drive was by chain and the chassis was an almost standard L49. The wheelbase was 8ft 7½in (262cm) and the track 4ft 2in (127cm). The cars were not given a type number, but had the order number D4. Chassis numbers were probably 929 and 930 and the respective engine numbers 633 and 628. Clifford Earp was the obvious choice to drive one car and the other was entered for F.G. Cundy, who worked in the Acton factory. For success in the race, careful, sensitive driving and an understanding of the car were going to be as important as sheer speed.

The race attracted a big entry and most of the leading British and Continental manufacturers planned to take part. Edge had the Napier cars and drivers in Douglas at least a week before the race, to test and practice. For Earp, the course was by now very familiar, but Cundy had to learn his way round. The weighing-in took place in the club enclosure, which was in a big field adjoining the course at Quarter Bridge. The need to weigh the chassis and body separately, using a primitive beam and weights machine, meant that it was a protracted affair, taking two days. The two D4s passed the test without problems. Earp's chassis was 1,576lb (716kg), with a body of 339lb (154kg), compared to the 1,573lb (715kg) and 346lb (157kg) of Cundy's car. Doubtless the components had been checked rigorously at Acton before departure. When the cars had been weighed, the fuel, oil, and water were added and then all the components were sealed.

The day before the race the weather was most unpleasant, with rain and a gale, but the morning of race day was fine and clear. The Isle of Man hotels had extended their season for two weeks to accommodate the event and a large crowd turned up to watch. Hot favourites were the new Rolls-Royces, and in the modern idiom, Claude Johnson, who had now joined the company, was applying heavy PR, with champagne receptions for the press and photo calls for stage celebrities. Rivalry between Rolls-Royce and Napier was beginning, and Edge must have felt that he was being beaten at his own game.

To avoid using any of their precious fuel allocation the 42 entrants were pulled to the starting line by cart horses and arranged in two

The British Gordon Bennett Eliminating Trials 1904 and 1905 and Tourist Trophy 1905, Isle of Man – a circuit of 52 miles (83.6km).

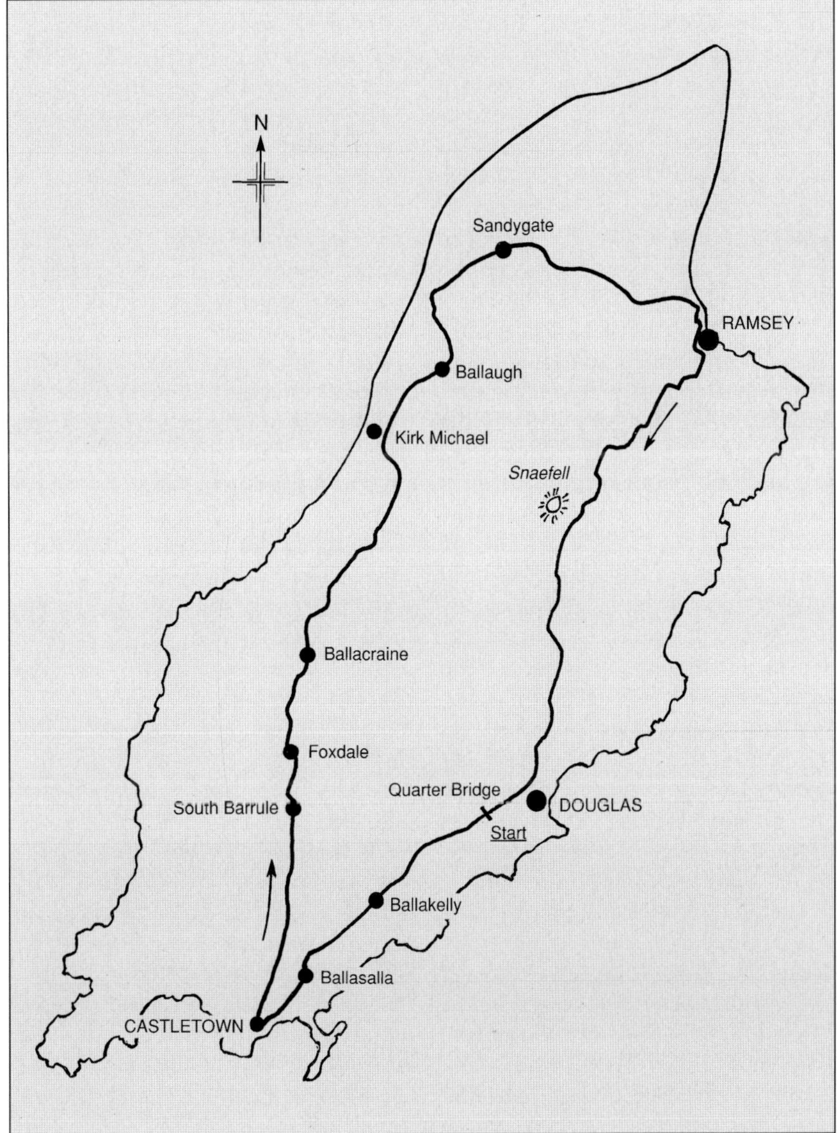

columns. The Hon Charles Rolls, driving one of his own machines, bore race number 1 at the head of one column, while Earp headed the other as No 2. The secretary of the ACGBI flagged Rolls away promptly at nine o'clock, but there was no bark of engine; instead, with the need to conserve fuel being paramount, Rolls released the brake and simply let the car roll down the hill, engaging a gear and letting in the clutch as the car gathered momentum. A minute later, Earp left the line in the same silent manner. He must have been astonished to find Rolls stranded by the roadside only a few hundred yards further on. The gears in the Rolls-Royce had been stripped by a clumsy change down to third, and the favourite was out of the race already.

Unfortunately, Rolls's failure did not improve the Napiers' chances, as the two D4s were not fast enough to challenge for the lead. The race instead became a battle between the second Rolls-Royce, driven by Percy Northey, the Vinot of Littlejohn, and the Arrol-Johnston designed and driven by John Napier, who apparently had no connections with the branch of the family which had founded the Napier company. Earp ran steadily. For the first two laps he was in 15th place, but subsequently improved his position to 12th, and finally finished tenth. His lap times had been consistent, at around 1hr 48min, apart from a slow second lap when he had lost over ten minutes, perhaps delayed by a puncture. On his final lap he went round in 1hr 46min, casting economic driving to the winds. When the tank was drained by officials at the finish, the report was of finding 'a trace only'.

The race was won by Napier's Arrol-Johnston in a time of 6hr 9min 14sec. The Rolls-Royce was just over two minutes behind, followed by the Vinot and the second Arrol-Johnston. Earp had taken 7hr 27min 44sec when he received the yellow and black chequered flag. Cundy, whose D4 had been the third car flagged away at the start, also ran a steady race, though slower than Earp. From 25th at the end of lap one, he progressed upwards as the cars in front fell out, mostly eliminated with empty fuel tanks or by minor crashes. Altogether there were 18 finishers, and Cundy came home 15th, in a time of 8hr 17min 10sec. His fastest lap had been 1hr 51min, a distinct contrast to his last lap, which took 2hr 23min, perhaps prompted by a fear of running out of fuel, though he did not need to worry as he had still had 6.4 pints (3.6 litres) in the tank at the end. He was slower than Earp not only because he lacked racing experience and a knowledge of the course, but also, perhaps, because Earp, who was one of the principal factory testers, probably had a better sense of combining speed with economy.

The result was not as good as Edge and Montague Napier would have liked, but both cars had finished without mechanical problems and had shown a fair turn of speed. The comments in the press about the Napier effort were all favourable, and reflected that the firm could not only make out-and-out racing cars, but could also make quite rapid 'production' cars. A Mors had been entered in the Tourist Trophy for Dorothy Levitt, but just before practice began it was announced that the car had been withdrawn, as her doctor would not permit her to drive. There were private and unpublished suggestions that to substitute 'Edge' for 'doctor' would probably have been more accurate, as Edge did not hold the Mors agency.

Although the English motor sporting season had now finished, Earp still had some more racing to do. The L48 had been entered in three French sprints which finished the Continental season. He drove the car down to Southampton, whence it was shipped across to Le Havre. His first destination was Château-Thierry, about 60 miles (96km) east of Paris, on the Reims road, where the annual speed trial was being held on Sunday 1 October. It was attended by all the leading French sprint exponents, running over the uphill standing start kilometre. It must have been some compensation for the failure at Clermont-Ferrand, that the L48 came out on top, with a time of 38.2 seconds, beating Stead's 120hp Mercedes and showing that in terms of sheer speed it was a match for the fastest cars in Europe.

A week later, presumably having sampled the delights of Edwardian Paris, Earp and the L48 journeyed to Dourdan, about 30 miles (56km) south-west of Paris, where the course was a standing mile followed by a flying kilometre. Once again, the Napier combination did their stuff and Earp was the fastest competitor, with times of 53.8 seconds over the mile and 25.6 seconds over the kilometre. The third leg of the French trip took the pair to Gaillon for the hill-climb on 14 October. After Macdonald's success with the car in 1904, Earp was keen to do well, so he was at the hill several days before the event and did some 30 practice runs. Using a higher gear ratio than Macdonald, Earp recorded a practice time of 28.2 seconds, 0.8 seconds better than the hill record. It was wet on the day, and the hill was slippery, and the *Automotor Journal* reported that the L48 was off-form, though the results indicate that this was relative. Earp was placed third, with a time of 32.8 seconds, behind De Caters's Mercedes (31.00 seconds) and Villemain's Clement-Bayard (32.00 seconds). As a compensation, Earp won the prize given by *L'Auto* for the best combined results of Chateau-Thierry and Gaillon. The Gaillon result was a disappointment to Earp and to Edge, and the latter suggested that the timing had been at fault.

On Wednesday 11 October, at 6.10am, Cecil Edge was driving a full touring-bodied 40hp T20 up and down Madeira Drive at Brighton.

This was the start of an ambitious test under ACGBI supervision. The car had started from the Ship Hotel in top gear and covered two miles on the Brighton front, the first at 5.8mph (9.3kmh) and the second at 45mph (72kmh). Accompanied by F. Straight of the ACGBI, H.J. Swindley of *The Autocar*, and a factory mechanic, Edge then drove to London, keeping the car in top gear all the time. The first stop was at the ACGBI headquarters at 119 Piccadilly, where the crew had breakfast. Fully refreshed they then set off for Edinburgh. In the evening, still in top gear, the car reached Doncaster, where the crew stayed at the Angel Hotel for the night. The following morning, at 6.00am, the journey resumed. The car travelled northwards without any problems, although a steep hill at Alnwick, near the Scottish border, was only just surmounted. After that the car went on, arriving at the Caledonian Hotel in Edinburgh at 7.30pm having been in top gear for the entire journey. The ACGBI issued a certificate confirming the feat and Selwyn Edge ensured that it received full publicity.

11 October 1905: Cecil Edge (centre foreground in cap) stands with the T20 outside the Royal Automobile Club at 119 Piccadilly during the Brighton to Edinburgh top gear trial. Behind Edge are (left to right): H.J. Swindley (in white coat), Selwyn Edge (in bowler hat), and Julian Orde of the RAC (with watch-chain). (Guy Griffiths Collection)

Despite the failure in the Gordon Bennett and the modest results in the Tourist Trophy, at the end of the season Edge and Montague Napier could be satisfied that they had probably the fastest racing car in Europe. Edge, however, must have been having doubts about the value of continuing to race, as he announced that all the Napier racing cars were for sale. In reality, there was more drama than substance in the announcement. Of the three K5s, the 1903 car had been badly damaged in the Brighton accident and Hargreaves's car was his personal property, which left only the ex-Mayhew car. This and the L48 were the only 'works' racing cars in running order at the end of the 1905 season apart from the two TT D4s, which had probably already been sold as production cars.

A buyer was found for the Mayhew K5, and it was shipped to the United States, where it was taken on charge by the American Napier Company of Boston, Mass. This was an independent company which was assembling Napiers under licence in a factory at Jamaica Plain, Boston. The car was to compete at Ormonde Beach in January 1906, and subsequently it was reported to have been sold to A.W. Erikson of Swampscott, Mass. There were later reports that it was raced at the Readville track near Boston, and was also prepared for an attempt on the record at the Mount Washington hill-climb. The car survived and still exists today, in the Netherlands National Motor Museum, in magnificent condition and in its original form.

It is not known if any offers were received for the L48. If any were, they must have been considered unacceptable, since in the autumn of 1905 the car was being prepared for another foray to Daytona. Despite Edge's apparent desire to abandon racing at the end of 1905, Montague Napier could reflect that the racing programme must have contributed to the evident prosperity of D. Napier & Son, which now employed nearly 600 men, fully occupied in building cars and commercial vehicles at Acton. To meet the demand, the factory had been expanded again in 1905.

Chapter 7: 1906

A Year in a Minor Key

IN the first weeks of 1906, the L48 was shipped from Liverpool to New York in the SS *Majestic* and then carried by train to Daytona. The rail journey took two days and the car arrived at Ormonde Beach in ample time for the Speed Week, which was being held between 22 and 27 January. The car had been entered for Clifford Earp, who was confronted by much stiffer opposition than Macdonald had faced a year earlier. A new Stanley Steamer had been built, the 'Rocket', driven by Fred Marriott, which was as low and shapely as the 1905 car and was expected to be quicker. The real speed of the week, however, was expected from Victor Hemery with the 200hp Darracq, who was coming fresh from setting a new world land speed record at Arles, in France, where just after Christmas he had achieved 109.65mph (176.42kmh), a figure universally accepted as the world's fastest, free of any controversy.

The L48 came out for its first event on Monday 23 January, when it ran in the flying start kilometre races, but the Napier was no match for the two special sprint racers. Hemery had a row with the organisers, so Louis Chevrolet took over the Darracq, which ran first in the flying kilometre and established a speed of 115.3mph (185.5kmh). The Stanley then came out and put the Darracq in its place with 121.57mph (195.60kmh). Earp managed to take third place in the class, but his best speed was a mere 103.4mph (166.4kmh). In the flying mile race for the Dewar Cup, the Stanley was not so quick, but still came first at 111.8mph (179.9kmh), to which the L48 had no real answer, although Earp was able to finish second by beating Young's 100hp Fiat.

Next day the competitors were running in five-mile events. The Stanley and Darracq were engaged in the Open event, while the L48 was running in the class for 'heavy petrol cars'. Here it did better, winning the class in a time of 2min 56sec to beat Downey's 90hp Mercedes by over half a minute. On Wednesday, Marriott was out again in the Stanley, shattering the opposition by covering the flying mile at 127.6mph (205.3kmh). This speed was subsequently disallowed by the International Commission in Paris, though the kilometre speed of 121.57mph (195.60kmh) was accepted as a new world land speed record.

The rest of the Speed Week was now concerned with longer races for which the Stanley ran short of steam pressure, much to the relief of the opposition. On the Friday there was a 15-mile event in which Vincenzo Lancia scored a convincing victory in the 100hp Fiat. However, in second place was the ex-Mayhew K5, now driven by Bill Hilliard, an American driver who had been engaged by the new owner, A.W. Erikson. The Fiat had been speedy and had averaged exactly 90mph (144.8kmh) for the distance, leaving the veteran K5 over a minute and a half behind. The scene was now set for the longest race of the meeting, the 100-mile (160km) Minneapolis Cup. The course was two parallel straights along the sands, with a pylon marking the hairpin bend at each end. Earp was matched against the Fiat team and led from the start. After 34 miles, the off-side rear Palmer tyre deflated, and, complying with the regulations, Earp pulled the L48 off the course. He made a quick decision and then, helped by Bater, his mechanic, the old tyre was removed from the rim and they restarted the car, to continue the race on the bare rim. This initially spun in the soft sand, but by pushing the car – in gear and with the engine running – Earp and Bater found firmer sand and scrambled aboard, Bater only just making it, and they set off again at an unabated speed. Meanwhile Cedrino, in the leading Fiat, had also stopped to change a tyre, so the L48 regained the lead and went on to complete the 100-mile course and win the cup, to the acclaim of the crowd. The L48 had averaged 79mph (127kmh) and finished nearly a minute ahead of Cedrino. It had been a good day for Napier, as Hilliard came third in the old K5, finishing about five minutes behind Cedrino. As well as a success for

On 26 January 1906, during Florida Speed Week, Bill Hilliard in the ex-Mayhew K5 gets ready for the start of the 100-mile (160km) Minneapolis Cup, in which he finished third. (Guy Griffiths Collection)

Napier, it had been a vindication of the strength and durability of Rudge wheels – a wooden wheel would have wilted and collapsed within a short distance under such treatment. When the bare rim was inspected after the race it was found that six spokes were broken on the outside of the rim, and eight on the inside.

Earp returned to England on the SS *Baltic* and received a warm reception for his drive. A few days later, on 24 February, Selwyn Edge held a dinner at the Grand Hotel in Northumberland Avenue. In his speech he announced that S.F. Edge Ltd would henceforth be giving a three-year guarantee on all Napier cars, and said that motor racing was essential to further development, 12 hours' racing being the equal of three months of ordinary road running in developing and improving a car. It was a paradox wholly typical of Edge that, despite this statement, 1906 would see no Napier participation in international races apart from Earp's American foray. Perhaps Edge had already realised that mere participation in motor racing is not enough; if a firm does not succeed, any development benefits are nullified by poor publicity. However, British sprints and hill-climbs would provide a stage on which the Napier could perform in front of an appreciative domestic audience. The results of these events were probably of greater significance to the average British motorist than success or failure in American or Continental road races.

In each year of the new century the number of sprints and hill-climbs had increased, despite the hostility of the constabulary and magistracy. The calendar for 1906 was the largest yet, and every motor club with any claim to importance was organising an event. The problem which confronted the clubs was to give every competitor a chance of success, so most events were run to complicated formulae which provided for the weight, price, and declared horsepower of the competing cars. Most manufacturers and dealers had realised the importance of the events and special cars were built to gain the maximum advantage from the regulations. Both Edge and Charles Jarrott objected vigorously to some of the practices which were developing, pointing out that the events were intended primarily for the amateur competitor, who would have little chance against specially prepared 'works' entries. Edge's stance probably caused some wry smiles when his use of the D50 and E61 engines two seasons earlier was recalled.

Early in the year Napiers granted a licence to SA Industriale San Giorgio, an Italian company based at Genoa, to make Napiers in Italy. Arthur Macdonald was sent there to supervise the manufacture of the cars. The Automobile Club of Milan announced that it would run the Coppa d'Oro reliability trial for production touring cars, classified by price, between 14–24 May. This event covered 2,405 miles (3,870km). The start was in Milan, and the route ran to Naples via Rome, before returning through Rome again to Florence, Genoa, and Turin, to finish back in Milan. Two 40hp chain-drive L76 San Giorgio Napiers were entered for Macdonald and Captain C.A. Glentworth. Both completed the course without any difficulty, but Macdonald lost 2min 22sec on the road and Glentworth lost 6min 51sec, so neither received an award. The winner was Vincenzo Lancia, driving a Fiat, who completed the course without losing any time. Subsequently the Italian venture was moderately successful and production continued until 1909, but the Coppa d'Oro seems to have been the only serious competition in which the San Giorgio machines took part.

The first 1906 home event of importance in which Napiers competed was organised by the Hereford Automobile Club at Fromes Hill on the A4103 road between Hereford and Worcester. This was held on Saturday 26 May over a 1,289-yard (1,178m) course. It was restricted to touring-bodied cars carrying the driver and three passengers, and to prevent cheating over the declared horse power, upon which the classes were based, the cylinder bore size had to be declared. To avoid the risk of prosecution no times were announced; the fastest car was declared to have established a zero time and only the deficit times of the other competitors were published. Cecil Edge ran an L76 (40hp six-cylinder) and was placed fourth on outright times. Two weeks later the hill-climb competitors went to Sussex, where the Kent Car Club organised an event at Kidd's Hill, near Crowborough. This was a one-mile course with a gradient of 1 in 6. The entry was divided into price classes and the fastest time of the day was secured by Frederic Baily. His car was described as a 50hp, and in the light of events later in the year it seems likely that it was an E61 fitted with a lightweight body. Neither Selwyn nor Cecil Edge were competing at this meeting, as they were officiating as timekeepers for the organising club.

On the following Saturday, 16 June, the Midland Automobile Club ran its second event on an improved bridle track at Court House Farm, Shelsley Walsh, in Worcestershire. Competitions could be held on this course without fear of prosecution, and the 1906 meeting was on a much grander scale than the preliminary meeting in August 1905. Much work had been done on the road surface and the bends had been eased. There were three Napier entries. In the Open class, Dorothy Levitt appeared

Arthur Macdonald sits in the San Giorgio L76 before the start of the AC Milan Coppa d'Oro trial, 14 May 1906. (Guy Griffiths Collection)

with a car described as a four-cylinder, with engine dimensions of 5 1/2 in x 5in (139.7mm x 127mm); undoubtedly an E61, this may well have been the car driven by Baily at Kidds Hill. The factory records show that an additional racing E61 was built early in 1906. This had the chassis number 1104 and engine number 729, so it is likely that it became the 'works' sprint and hill-climb car with a lightweight touring body. Frank Newton, who at that time was a factory tester, mentions this car in his personal notebooks. Without fuel or seats, it weighed 2,184lb (992kg). The engine developed 58bhp and on test it was timed at 66.1mph (106.3kmh) over a flying quarter mile with a 2.5:1 final drive.

Dorothy Levitt was joined by Cecil Edge, who had a 60hp T21 Six, which was entered by Captain Glentworth (described erroneously in some press reports as Viscount Glentworth). In the Closed class, for Midland Automobile Club members, Cecil Edge was also running an L76. Dorothy Levitt, dressed in a long white motoring coat, carried her pet Pomeranian round in the paddock, dogs not yet being banned from motor racing. There was a thunderstorm during the meeting, and on the course she had a spectacular slide entering what are now known as the Esses. One press report commented that she was lucky not to go off the edge of the track and down into the valley below. Despite this, she pressed on and recorded 92.4 seconds, the sixth fastest time. Edge was seventh in the T21 at 98.8 seconds and was also placed third in the Closed class, where the L76 climbed in 121.6 seconds.

Another hill-climb which was becoming a well-established fixture was held at South Harting, on the Sussex–Hampshire border, on 23 June. Here the ACGBI had collaborated with the Sussex County Automobile Club. As an indication of the popularity of these events, an entry of 84 was received, of which 64 turned up on the day. Napier was once again represented by Dorothy Levitt and Cecil Edge. This time Miss Levitt was entered in Baily's 50hp, probably the E61 again, running in the £500–£850 class, while Edge was out again in a T21 in the over £850 class. Competitors had to run with a full complement of passengers. Miss Levitt took second place in her class behind a Daimler, while Edge gained a third place. At the end of the event the organisers ran a match race between Miss Levitt with the Napier and Frederick Coleman's White Steamer, which had established the fastest time of the day. The cars were drawn up on the start line together, but the Napier was flagged away first and the Stanley was released ten seconds later. Miss Levitt was beaten by 1.2 seconds, but her time was 0.2 seconds quicker than the Daimler which had been the fastest car in the over £850 class, and she had the satisfaction of knowing that she had beaten every other car but the White. There were subsequently suggestions that Coleman had raised the boiler pressure of the White to danger level, to ensure that he was not beaten by 'a mere woman', a view to which many of his fellow-competitors subscribed. On the following Saturday the Levitt/Edge team were at Aston Clinton for the Hertfordshire County Automobile Club meeting. To avoid police interest, the times were given as deficits of the fastest car's time. Of the 44 entries, Miss Levitt was third overall with a time of minus 5 seconds, while Edge was sixth with minus 6.4 seconds.

During the previous week, the first Grand Prix de l'ACF, the French Grand Prix, had been held at Le Mans, on a 64-mile (103km) triangular circuit bearing no relation to the later, celebrated 24-hour circuit. There had been no Napier entry, nor had there been entries from any other British manufacturer. The British were still smarting over what was perceived to be the perfidy of the French in bringing about the demise of the Gordon Bennett Trophy, and also believed that the new race was biased in favour of the French manufacturers. With a Renault victory and French cars in the first four places, this attitude may have been felt to be justified, but a closer look at the results showed that only seven out of 23 French cars had finished and that four of the nine foreign starters had gone the distance. The race had been pronounced a great success and had met the needs of those manufacturers who wished to race, something that the Gordon Bennett had been unable to do. It is not without significance that the four makes which won the GP de l'ACF before World War One – Renault, Fiat, Peugeot, and Mercedes – are all still flourishing. With honourable exceptions, the British motor industry was meanwhile developing an insularity which was to last for over 40 years.

Since its return from Daytona, the L48 had been lying dormant at Acton, but now, with the British sprint season half-run, the car was brought out again for the Yorkshire Automobile Club meeting on Saltburn sands. This was held on 14 July and the car was entered for Cecil Edge in the 1,000kg flying kilometre class. The course ran from Saltburn Pier northwards to Marske, and the beach was in splendid condition. The L48 was off-form, however, and Edge could only manage 74mph (119kmh), so it was soundly beaten by Warwick Wright's Darracq. It was not a good day for Napier, as Dorothy Levitt, driving Baily's 50hp car, broke the differential in practice and could not compete. It seems that Napier policy was to run the L48 only in events where its performance could be used to the full. Consequently it did not come out again until Saturday 8 September, when it arrived at Skegness for the Nottinghamshire Automobile Club beach sprint. Unfortunately the course had been badly rippled by the tide and it was not suitable for the speed of the faster cars, but Edge gave a demonstration run to please the crowd, albeit at a rather reduced speed. The state of the course did not prevent the touring car classes from running, and Cecil Edge had entered a 50hp car, to be driven by Glentworth. This went well and was second to Instone's Daimler in the over £850 class. It must be wondered if this car was the same '50hp', or E61, which had been competing throughout the season, owned by Napiers and being loaned to suitable drivers.

On 29 August came a further sign of the growing prosperity of Napiers. A company was incorporated – D. Napier & Son Limited – which acquired the assets of the firm. The ordinary capital was divided into 5,000 £1 shares, and apart from seven shares which were held by directors, for qualification purposes, the entire ordinary capital was held by Montague Napier. Fresh capital was raised by the issue of £20,000 4½ per cent first mortgage debentures, which were taken up by the Law Guarantee and Trust Company. This ensured that, provided the profits kept coming in, Montague Napier would have a free hand in running the company and deciding its policy. The valuation of the assets of the firm had risen from £89,851 in 1903 to £216,373 at the time of the incorporation in 1906.

On 27 September there was another sign of change in the new company and indications of a new attitude to motor racing. The Tourist Trophy was run for a second time on the Isle of Man, but there were no Napier entries. It seems likely that Selwyn Edge looked at the regulations, which were similar in general terms to those governing the 1905 race, and decided that there was no production model which could run in the race with any prospect of victory. The fuel consumption stipulations ruled out the largest and fastest cars, and the L49, which was the most likely prospect, would probably have been too thirsty. It is evident that Napier strategy was now that no new racing cars should be built, so there would have been no incentive to make a small batch of special cars for the TT. Victory in the race went to the Rolls-Royce Light 20, driven by the Hon C.S. Rolls. Although the TT had been ignored by Napier, the Isle of Man meeting nevertheless produced a small success for the marque. On Friday the 28th, the day after the race, the competition for the *Graphic* Trophy was held. This was for cars with a chassis value of under £1,000, and was an extended sprint over a four and a quarter mile course on the Douglas–Castletown road. The event began at 10.30am and the first car to be flagged away was a 50hp Napier, entered by Frederic Baily and driven by Captain Glentworth. The Napier scored a comfortable victory and, once again, it seems that it was the much-used works E61, which bore the registration number D 2601.

The major British sprint event came at the end of the season. For this the ACGBI returned to Blackpool, where it ran a two-day meeting on Friday and Saturday 12–13 October. The course ran along the front again, and despite Earp's experiences in 1905 the kink by the Palace Pier was still there. The finishing line was beside the Tower and was overlooked by a large grandstand. The touring cars ran on the Friday in unpleasant conditions of wind, rain, and sleet. However, the sun shone on the racing car classes the following morning. Cecil Edge was entered in the L48 and his main rival was Algernon Lee-Guinness, who had bought the 22½ litre, 200hp Darracq which had taken the world land speed record the previous December and had competed at Daytona. This remarkable machine had a V-8 engine comprising two Gordon Bennett cylinder blocks mounted on a special crankcase. In the 1,000kg standing start kilometre class, the Darracq and the L48 tied in equal first place with a time of 33.6 seconds. There was then a run-off, in which the Napier managed an impressive 32.5 seconds, but the Darracq went even better and established a new world standing start kilometre record with 32.4 seconds. Edge and the L48 were also pushed into second place by the Darracq in the standing mile and flying kilometre events. In the latter the Darracq achieved 106.4mph (171.2kmh), while the L48 produced only 90.9mph (146.25kmh). Edge shared the car with Dorothy Levitt in this event, who recorded exactly the same time, showing her mettle by not easing off even when the L48's bonnet started lifting on one side. Miss Levitt ran again and did the same time, setting a British Ladies Record. She had now abandoned the tulle veil in which she had raced at Brighton in 1905, and was wearing a white leather helmet and goggles. Although the L48 had been beaten it had made a big impression, and the *Automotor Journal* commented that it 'was a delightful vehicle which runs with the smoothness of a touring car'. In the light racing car class, for cars not exceeding 650kg, a Mr Orrell Wren appeared with what press reports described as an 80hp Napier. Wren was third in the flying kilometre, at 53mph (85.2kmh), and first in the standing kilometre, with a time of 41.4 seconds. The identity of the car he was driving must remain a mystery, but it cannot have been a K5 as this would never have made the weight; nor, for that matter, would an E61 or a D50.

A week later the last hill-climb of the season was held at Kidd's Hill in Sussex, where the event was organised by the Crystal Palace Automobile Club. Hydrogen-filled balloons supplied by Dunlop held up the banner over the start-line. Captain Glentworth won his class with the hard-used 50hp, and Cecil Edge was also successful, taking second place in his class, on time, with the T21, and winning the class on handicap.

A T21 was entered by Cecil Edge for H.C. Tryon, one of the factory test drivers, who was making his competition debut and would feature prominently in Napier racing activities during the next few years. At the end of the month the L48 was taken to France for its habitual exercise at Gaillon, apparently the only time a Napier competed in continental Europe in 1906. Cecil Edge was the driver and once again he was matched against Guinness's 200hp Darracq. The outcome was to be expected. In the 1,000kg class the L48 managed 29 seconds, but the Darracq was well ahead, recording 25 seconds.

1906 had shown a definite change in Napier racing activities and the scale had been much smaller. The production cars were selling well and Montague Napier probably appreciated that developing and racing new cars would interfere with the flow of production. By the end of the year the company had 1,200 employees and the Acton factory had been expanded yet again and now covered seven acres. A new chapter in Napier's racing history was nevertheless about to open. In the autumn of 1906, a rich Surrey landowner, Mr Hugh Locke King, had commenced the construction of a two and three-quarter mile (4.42km) banked track on his Brooklands estate near Weybridge. This would be ready for racing in 1907. Among those who Locke King consulted when making his plans was Selwyn Edge. At an early meeting Edge asked if he could book the course as soon as it was opened, so that he could, unaided, attempt to drive a car for 24 hours at a speed of 60mph (96kmh).

Chapter 8: 1907

The Brooklands Champions

AT the start of 1907 activity at Acton was centred mainly on the proposed 24-hour record and the extensive calendar of events which would be run on the new Brooklands track. In January, the ACGBI (soon to become the Royal Automobile Club) announced the regulations for the 1907 Tourist Trophy. This year there were to be two races, the second of which would be the International Heavy Touring Car Race, intended to cater for the larger-engined cars. The chassis would have to carry a load of one ton (2,240lb/1,018kg), including body and ballast, and fuel would be limited to a maximum consumption of 16 miles to the gallon (or 17.7 litres per 100km). At first sight it seemed to be a race for which the T20 would be particularly well-suited, but when the entry list was published in March the Napier was conspicuous by its absence. This prompted correspondence in *The Autocar* enquiring why an entry had not been made. Selwyn Edge was unusually silent and did not leap in with a reply, as was his usual custom. More perceptive readers of *The Autocar*, however, would have realised that the reason for the Napier's absence had already appeared in the magazine's columns. Earlier in the year Arthur Brown, writing about his experiences with a T20, had said that the fuel consumption was 13 to 15 miles per gallon (18.9 to 21.7 litres per 100km) while touring. It was clear from this that if a T20 was run at racing speeds it would not be able to manage on the permitted fuel allowance, so absence from the race and a discreet silence was Edge's only option.

The season of club hill-climbs began in May with the event run by the Hereford Automobile Club at Fromes Hill on the 4th, the first in which the new Royal Autombile Club handicap formula was applied. This was based on cylinder bore and almost certainly led to the RAC horsepower rating used in subsequent motor taxation – a formula which put the engine designs of the British motor industry in a strait jacket for almost 40 years, as it ignored the stroke of the engine when assessing size for taxation purposes. As a result the British industry built cars with over-small bores and over-long strokes right up until 1947, when a flat rate of tax was finally adopted. At Fromes Hill, Cecil Edge ran a T20 (LC 6038) and won his class on handicap, being awarded a gold medal, even though he was only placed seventh on actual speed. Much interest centred on a T20 fitted with a lightweight body, in which Selwyn Edge appeared as a spectator. It was announced that this was his training car for the proposed 24-hour run.

A week later the Nottinghamshire Automobile Club held its annual sprint over the Duke of Portland's private drive in Welbeck Park. For this, Cecil Edge ran what reports described as an '80hp Napier'. It may have been that the original 1903 K5 had been repaired after the Brighton accident and dusted down for a day out in the Midlands, but there is no surviving evidence as to the identity of this car. He ran in the scratch flying kilometre class for touring cars and won with a time of 36.8 seconds. In the flying kilometre handicap class, Cecil Edge ran a 60hp T21 and was fifth on handicap, although his time of 34.8 seconds was the fastest of the day.

The sprint season continued with a two-day meeting organised by the Crystal Palace Automobile Club at Bexhill over the Whitsun weekend. However, the meeting was not a success, and *The Autocar* reported that 'the whole thing dragged wretchedly'. Its high point was an attempt on the course record by Selwyn Edge, using a 60hp T21 which had been prepared for the forthcoming Brooklands record run. Edge made runs over a flying quarter mile on both days, covering the course in both directions. On the first day he achieved 77.37mph (124.48kmh), a new course record, but on the second day he was slightly slower, which was attributed to deterioration in the condition of the track. Driving T21s, Sidney Smith and Cecil Edge took the first two places in an unusual class where both speed and slow running were tested, Cecil Edge also winning a class for Kaiserpreis cars over a standing half mile, which he achieved in 41.6 seconds. He was also successful in a scratch touring car class with an '80hp' Napier with a rudimentary four-seater body – perhaps the old K5 – recording 35.6 seconds. Henry Tryon was second in this class with a T21, recording 41.8 seconds. The '80hp' came out again on the second day and was the winner of another Kaiserpreis class, beating Smith's T21 by only a bonnet, both being timed at 37.8 seconds.

Just over a week later, on Thursday 30 May, the Tourist Trophy and Heavy Touring Car races were held in the Isle of Man, without Napier participation. Rover and Beeston Humber were the respective victors. The *Graphic* Trophy was again contested the day after the TT and in 1907 it was a hill-climb over a one and a half mile course on the Slein-Lewaigne Hill, near Ramsey. The competing cars had to comply with a formula where the cylinder diameter in inches, squared and multiplied by the number of cylinders, must not exceed 125. It was a bad day for Napiers. Two T21s had been entered for F.G. Cundy and E. Paul (chassis number 3065). Cundy's car broke down on the way to the start, while Paul's car, entered by Selwyn Edge, was excluded, as the organisers decided that the body, which had to be of a touring type, did not comply with the regulations. Before the event, 3065 was weighed at Acton and recorded at 2,625lb (1,193kg).

The motor sporting world now looked forward to the next six weeks with eager anticipation. In June, the Herkomer Trophy Trial and Kaiserpreis races were to be held in Germany, and at the beginning of July the French Grand Prix would be run, followed immediately by the opening of Brooklands. The Herkomer Trophy was a long-distance reliability trial which included a speed trial and a speed hill-climb. There were 161 starters when it began in Dresden on Wednesday 5 June, including Dorothy Levitt and Cecil Edge with 40hp T20 Napiers. The cars had to carry full four-seater bodies and be in a condition ready for delivery to a discerning customer. Several cars were rejected by the scrutineers because they were not properly painted. The first day's run of 221 miles (355km) went to Eisenach via Leipzig. At the end of the day, the cars were housed overnight in two large tents. The organisation of the first day was strongly criticised: the officials were accused of not keeping enough control on the speed of the cars, and the official car which led the field was said to have set too fast a pace. There was an early start next day and the run to Mannheim via Heidelburg began at 6.30am. It was wet and the roads were greasy, but both Napiers reached Mannheim among the early finishers without trouble, though a number of other cars had dropped out, leaving only 131 still in the running.

On the third day, with another 221 mile (355km) stage from Mannheim to Lindau through the Black Forest, Dorothy Levitt continued to keep a clean sheet, though several cars fell out on the climb over the Knerks Pass. Cecil Edge had lost two marks during the day. The itinerary of the fourth day was shorter with only 137 miles (220km) to cover, but during the afternoon, before reaching the end of the stage at Munich, the cars competed in a speed trial over a 4.3-mile (6.9km) course in the Forstenreider Park. In the speed trial, each car had to maintain a minimum qualifying speed over the course, based on its engine capacity. The Napiers were required to average 51mph (82kmh) and neither had trouble in qualifying. Dorothy Levitt was tenth overall with a time of 3min 9sec while Edge was 12th with 3min 13.8sec. Following this the competitors were allowed a rest day in Munich.

On Monday 10 June they were off again, on a 137 mile (220km) stage from Munich to Augsburg. During the morning there was a timed climb of the Kesselberg Pass, and once

Dorothy Levitt in her T20 during the Herkomer Trial, June 1907. It is interesting that, despite Edge's enthusiasm for Rudge-Whitworth wire wheels, the car has been fitted with artillery wheels for this event. (Thomas Ulrich)

again the Napiers ran well, putting up competitive times comfortably faster than the qualifying speed of 28mph (45kmh). Although it was officially a reliability trial, the press insisted on calling it a race, and to cover the stages in the time allowed the drivers could not relax. The next morning, during the last stage – a distance of 199 miles (320km) from Augsburg to Frankfurt – disaster struck Edge while he was attempting to keep up his average speed. According to *The Car Illustrated* he ran off the road soon after leaving Augsburg; a wheel was badly damaged and he had to retire from the event. *The Autocar*, however, reported that he had been eliminated by a broken connecting rod. Doubtless Selwyn Edge favoured the former reason!

Dorothy Levitt had kept out of trouble, and reached the finish in the Hanauer Landstrasse, a long tree-lined avenue about four miles from the centre of Frankfurt. Prince and Princess Henry of Prussia were among those who saw her arrive in 13th place, without any penalty marks, the highest placed woman driver. Miss Levitt's placing rather upset the expected form, as Frau Lehmann, a German competitor driving a Metallurgique, was expected to be the highest placed woman competitor. To rub it in, at the prize-giving that evening, while Frau Lehmann attended in her driving outfit, Dorothy Levitt swept in to receive her gold medal wearing a ball gown in the full height of Edwardian fashion, much to the delight of the assembly.

Two days later the second leg of the German Speed Festival began with the Kaiserpreis races, on the Homburg circuit which had been used for the 1904 Gordon Bennett race. The circuit had been reduced to 73 miles (117km), however, and the race was run in the opposite direction to the 1904 Trophy. The formula for this event was decided by the Kaiser himself and showed a refreshingly simple approach to the sport, as competing cars were merely restricted to an engine capacity of 8 litres and it was left to the ingenuity of the manufacturers how this was achieved. There were no control points on the course so the cars were racing all the way. A T21 had been entered by the Acton factory with Captain Glentworth as the driver. The race was run with two eliminating heats on the Thursday and the qualifiers went on to run in the final the following day. The heats were over two laps and Glentworth was running in the first heat, which began at 4.00am in a fine drizzle. The Kaiser had already taken his seat in the Grandstand when the cars were flagged away at two minute intervals. Napier's luck was out, however, and Glentworth pulled in at the end of the first lap. *The Car Illustrated* reported that he had 'scorched his big end bearings'. Frank Newton noted that this car developed 110/112bhp, and later in the season it lapped Brooklands at 92mph (148kmh) while he was testing it.

The English sprint season was flourishing, and Saturday 22 June produced a clash of events which demonstrated the burgeoning interest in motor sport. Some competitors travelled north to Saltburn sands, while others ran in the Leicestershire Automobile Club Inter-Club hill-climb at Kettleby, where Cecil Edge recorded the fastest time of the day at 1min 7sec. It was reported that he had used one of the 60hp Herkomer Cup cars, which is puzzling since these were 40hp T20s. Perhaps Glentworth's car had been repaired and returned to England. Meanwhile, in the south, Sidney Smith ran in the Southern Motor Club event at Toys Hill, between Westerham and Sevenoaks, with a touring-bodied T21. Smith won his class easily by a seven second margin, but, as usual, actual times were not published. *The Autocar* commented of the Napier's climb: 'For it, the steep section appeared to be non-existent.' Smith's success was offset to some extent by the failure of Frank Newton's T20, which stopped on the hill after overheating.

The new Brooklands track had meanwhile been formally opened by the Earl of Lonsdale, President of the Brooklands Automobile Racing Club, on Monday 17 June. Selwyn Edge was among those at the inaugural lunch in the new clubhouse, and with the track now ready he was making the final preparations for his 24-hour run. The declared aim was to cover a mile a minute for the 24 hours, a distance of 1,440 miles (2,317km). This would achieve the secondary target of beating the record of 1,096 miles (1,763km) established by the American drivers Merz and Clemens in 1905. The run was to start at six o'clock in the evening on Friday 29 June. The time had been chosen with care, as Edge wanted to drive during the night while he was still fresh.

Three cars were to attempt the run. Edge would drive alone, while Frank Newton and F. Draper shared the second car, and Henry Tryon and A.F. Browning the third. Like Newton and Tryon, Draper and Browning were test drivers at Acton. According to contemporary press reports the cars were production 60hp models, ie, T21s with the standard engine dimensions of 5in x 4in (127mm x 101.6mm). Newton, in a letter to Anthony Heal in 1943, confirmed that his car and the Tryon/Browning car had this engine size, but Edge's vehicle had a larger engine of 5in x 5in (127mm x 127mm). After the run, *The Autocar* commented that Edge seemed to have a more powerful engine but no admission of this was forthcoming. Napiers were sometimes rather casual in their model descriptions, and when the larger engine went into production it was often described as the '60hp'. The engines of the 24-hour record cars were not measured by either the RAC or the Brooklands Automobile Racing Club (BARC).

Selwyn Edge and Dario Resta pose with the L48 in the Paddock at the newly-completed Brooklands track in June 1907. The car is fitted with headlights for Edge to practice night-driving on the track before the 24-hour run. (Guy Griffiths Collection)

Edge's car, painted green, had a shorter chassis, though the dimensions are not known, while the other cars had the standard length frame. The touring body was removed and replaced with two buckets seats mounted in front of a large oval fuel tank. There were no mudguards, but light canvas splash guards were fitted behind the front wheels. It had Bleriot acetylene headlamps, and an odd-looking glass windshield was installed in front of the driver. It was realised that there would be many tyre changes during the 24-hour run, and much time could be lost in this, so Edge arranged with John Pugh of the Rudge-Whitworth company that the three cars would be fitted with the new centre-lock wheels that had just been introduced by the company.

Newton's car was painted red and Tryon's was white. They were built to a similar specification to Edge's, but the windshield was made of gauze, mounted on an aluminium plate. Edge's car was known as 804, allegedly because this was the chassis number, but this does not fit in the sequence of Napier chassis numbers as number 804 is recorded as being a D50, so its identity cannot be confirmed. It bore the registration number A 8977. Newton noted the chassis number of his red car as 3108, which is in the sequence of the T21. The white car, however, remains anonymous.

Edge had been practising at Brooklands in both the L48 and 804. Tests in the latter showed that after two or three fast laps the engine began to pre-ignite badly and overheat. He discussed the problem with Montague Napier, who concluded that the valve caps needed to be water-cooled. A re-design was put in hand immediately and all three cars were modified. Frank Newton noted when testing the red and white cars that these could lap the track at 86mph flat out. Edge drove round the track at night and found that the acetylene headlights were useless and only gave a misleading reflection from the white track. As he left the Byfleet banking and approached the Fork there was nothing at all to guide him, and he observed that 'I felt like the skipper of a ship at sea without a compass'. A call went forth for red lanterns; Edge had calculated that if these were placed at ten-yard (9m) intervals on the 50ft (15.2m) line of the track, he would need 352. Buyers sought out every available lantern and all the road-mending firms in the London area were approached. As an added safeguard, Wells flares were placed at intervals at the top of the banking.

Edge had gone into strict training for the physical demands of the run, relying on his Sandow regime that he had used for the Gordon Bennett races. He was also concerned about the effect of a tyre coming off a wheel rim at speed and had conducted tests at the Crystal Palace. He

Selwyn Edge just before the start of the 24-hour run at Brooklands on 29 June 1907. The makeshift windscreen collapsed during the 24th hour. (Guy Griffiths Collection)

stayed at the White Lion Hotel at Cobham, only about two miles from Brooklands. On the day of the run, the Napier team, assisted by specialists from the various accessory manufacturers, set up camp at the top end of the Finishing Straight, adjacent to the bridge across the Members' Banking. There was a tent for the drivers, and a huge pile of Rudge wheels fitted with Dunlop tyres. To these were added countless cans of Shell petrol, oil, and water. To speed up wheel changes a simple quick-lift jack was devised using beams of timber. The team managers were Cecil Edge and Sidney Smith, while Montague Napier supervised the whole venture. Cecil Edge took each car round the track for a final test lap, and shortly before 6.00pm on 28 June the three Napiers were lined up on the track just beyond the Members' Bridge. Edge's green car was on the outside, Newton's red machine was in the middle, and the white car of Tryon was on the inside. Edge was not to ride alone, as J.H. (Joe) Blackburn, one of the factory chauffeurs from Acton, was to accompany him, insisting that he, too, would go the full distance.

A.V. Ebblewhite, the official Brooklands timekeeper, indicated that he was ready; Julian Orde, secretary of the RAC, gave the starting signal; and the run was on. The start line was further along the track, as a flying start was permitted. The cars ran smoothly, and at the end of the first hour Edge, who was leading, had covered 70 miles 130 yards (112.64km). At 8.10pm he pulled into the depot, as the car was showing a tendency to boil, so water was added. Soon afterwards the task of lamp lighting began, but the three Napiers ran on without drama and after three hours pulled in for refuelling and wheel changes. Edge made his first set of tyres last for 350 miles (563km). The drivers found that their headlights were unnecessary and were able to follow the line of lanterns.

Tyres came off their rims several times, and on one occasion Edge had to run almost a full lap on the bare rim. The pit crew became deft at changing wheels, and at one stop a single wheel was changed in 24 seconds. At his final stop, Edge's wheels were changed and the car refuelled in 1min 24sec, offering an interesting comparison with a modern Formula 1 team. On Edge's car, 24 wheels were changed altogether – three left fronts, three right fronts, seven left rears, and eleven right rears. *The Autocar* calculated that the efficiency of the pit crew, and the Rudge-Whitworth hubs, saved Edge 1hr 24min during the run, when compared with the time that conventional tyre changing with detachable rims would have taken. The red car had 21 wheel changes, while the total for the white car was 16.

At midnight the white car of Tryon and Draper was leading the trio, having covered 72 miles 900 yards (116.67km) in the sixth hour, the

The three T21 Napiers line up before the start of the 24-hour run. Edge is on the left, Tryon in the centre, and Newton on the right. (Guy Griffiths Collection)

greatest distance achieved in a single hour during the run. At the end of the seventh hour Edge was back in front, and although he fell back behind the white car during the eighth hour, the green car went ahead again as dawn broke. The night had been unusually cold for mid-summer and Edge had worn thick clothes, but after sunrise he changed back into cooler wear. At the pit stops, while the drivers of the other cars changed over, Edge lay down behind the pit encampment for a short rest. He did not take food during the stops, but was fed with bananas on the move by Blackburn. Half-time, at 6.00am, found Edge just 160 yards (146m) short of 800 miles (1,287km). The white car was almost exactly a lap, or two and a three-quarter miles, behind, and the red car was five miles further back. All three cars were fitted with Castle accumulators and coils to ignite the Napier plugs, and – as a precaution – at 1,000 miles Edge switched on the first accumulator. However, the coils needed no adjustment throughout the run.

The public had been admitted to watch the record attempt, and were charged 10s for admission at the start on Friday with a reduction to 2s 6d at 2.30pm on the Saturday afternoon. During the day the crowd swelled as the news spread of the likely success, and it seems there were few who doubted that Edge and his team would do it, for his reputation was formidable.

Throughout the run, world records from one hour onwards, as well as distance records, were being established. At about 10.20am Edge broke the existing American 24-hour record, but his aim was a mile a minute, or 1,440 miles (2,316km). However, the pace was dropping, and in the 19th hour, which began at noon, the green Napier only covered 60 miles 340 yards (96.85km), the slowest hour of the run. Only one wheel was changed during that hour, so clearly – and unsurprisingly – the driver was flagging somewhat. At about 3.40pm a huge cheer went up from the rapidly growing crowd and the Napier team – Edge had covered 1,440 miles, so the goal of a mile a minute had been achieved. By now he was about 25 miles (40km) ahead of the white car and almost 50 miles (80km) in front of the red car, but as these passed the 1,440 mile target they too were cheered on. An unexpected problem troubled all three cars as the run neared its end: the newly laid concrete of the Brooklands track was breaking up along the 50ft line, where the cars were running, and the drivers were having to steer a careful course to avoid the potholes which had appeared. Workmen were dashing onto the track, to fill up the largest holes with gravel, which did not make much difference. The potholes delayed the red car, which had an extended stop to replace a broken rear spring. Rain had also begun to fall at 5.30pm, and with about five minutes to go there was alarm amongst the watching crowd. As

Edge approached the pit area there was a loud rattling noise, but it was not a mechanical disaster. The glass windscreen had shattered, showering Edge and Blackburn with broken glass, though fortunately they were not cut. The pit crew rushed onto the track and swept up the glass, and a few minutes later the three cars finished their historic run.

Edge was mobbed by the crowd, despite the very heavy rain which was now falling. He had covered 1,581 miles 1,310 yards (2,545.01km) at an average speed of 65.9mph (106.3kmh). The white and red cars had covered 1,538 and 1,521 miles (2,474 and 2,447km) respectively. For both Edge and the Napier company, the run had been a triumph. Apart from the broken spring there had been no mechanical troubles at all. The run had put Napier right back at the forefront, not only of the British motor industry, but also of the world industry. As Edge had probably shrewdly surmised, in the eyes of the average motorist such a feat was worth a lot more in terms of prestige than a quickly forgotten racing victory. Edge himself was the hero of the hour. After the run he seemed fresh and fit. He drove himself back to the White Lion, where he was examined by a doctor, at the instigation of *The Autocar*, which was curious about the effects of the single-handed run. The verdict was delivered that there were no ill-effects at all, apart from physical tiredness. At the hotel, Edge emphasised to Montague Napier that the success had been due to Napier's design and organisation, rather than his efforts at the wheel. There was a pleasant sequel on Tuesday 17 July, when a dinner was held for the employees of S.F. Edge Ltd and D. Napier & Son Ltd who had been concerned in the record run. Edge presided, and presented commemorative gold watches to Tryon, Draper, Newton, Browning, and Blackburn. Edge's friends, led by Mark Mayhew, then presented him with a gold plaque. When reports circulated afterwards about the damage to the track, humorists suggested that Brooklands should be renamed 'Edge-wear Road' – an allusion to the well-known London street.

On Tuesday 2 July the Grand Prix de l'ACF was held at Dieppe. After the success of the 1906 race there was no likelihood of a renaissance for the Gordon Bennett Trophy, and the future now lay with races between manufacturers' teams rather than national teams. Victory went to a Fiat driven by Nazzaro, and apart from two almost unknown Weigels there were no British entries. Flushed by the success of the 24-hour run, Edge and Napier were probably unconcerned about the result. The first meeting at Brooklands was to take place at the end of the week, and success there was more likely to impress the British motorist than an entry at Dieppe.

William Boddy, in his monumental *The Story of Brooklands*, summed up the first Brooklands meeting, on Saturday 6 July, in these terms: 'This first meeting . . . was not a success. It has indeed been described as a ghastly failure.' For Napier, though, it was a rather different story. Selwyn Edge had entered five cars. Tryon was the first driver to appear, driving a T20 (chassis number 2171), in the first heat of the Marcel Renault Memorial Plate, the first race to be run at Brooklands, which was for cars with cylinder bores of 85mm to 110mm, over approximately four laps of the two and three-quarter mile track, a distance of 11.4 miles (18.3km). He made a good start and gradually pulled away from the pursuing Darracq of Huntley Walker to win by several hundred yards. Tryon came out for the final of this event, and repeated the performance of the heat, winning by a good margin from Clifford Earp's Iris, and thus netting for Edge the prize of £400, referred to in the programme as 'sovereigns'. In his notes, Newton commented that the engine of Tryon's car was developing 78/79bhp. Earp, it will be noticed, had now left Napiers and joined a rival concern

Sidney Smith was the next of Edge's protégés to appear, driving a T21 (chassis number 3065) in the Gottlieb Daimler Memorial Plate, for cars with bores of 120mm to 155mm, over six laps. However, he did not cover himself with glory, as he had trouble engaging a gear at the start and then, running behind the field, the car lost water and overheated. Napier fortunes were restored by Newton. He was entered in the three and three-quarter lap Byfleet Plate, driving the 45hp T23 (chassis number 4002). As standard this had a 4in (101.6mm) bore and a 5in (127mm) stroke, but had been bored out to 4.5625in (115.9mm). Among the entry was the French ace Louis Wagner, who a week before had led the French Grand Prix until his Fiat broke down. Wagner, again driving a Fiat, led at the start, but was passed by Jarrott's Lorraine-Dietrich. Newton was in third place and passed Wagner on the Byfleet banking during the second lap. Newton closed up on Jarrott and attempted to pass as the cars ran up the Finishing Straight to the line. They crossed the line side-by side and it was adjudged a dead heat. Jarrott protested that he had won, but his protest was overruled and the £550 prize was split between them.

Newton's sudden spurt at the finish was noted and it was suggested that, like some other Brooklands competitors, he had used an oxygen cylinder, discharging directly into the carburettor inlet, as a primitive aid to extra power. Charles Jarrott wrote to *The Autocar* on 13 July condemning the use of oxygen as unsporting. This must have stung Edge, as a week later he too wrote to *The Autocar* condemning the use of oxygen, stating 'its use . . . should be absolutely prohibited in all motor competitions. In all touring competitions in which Napier cars have taken part I have expressly run the cars without the use of oxygen'. He concluded by declaring Jarrott 'most unsportsmanlike, his innuendoes uncalled for, against his more successful competitors.' Edge's use of the word 'touring' is significant, as F.R.S. Bircham, the driver of an Iris in the first race, wrote to the *Daily Mail* observing that the oxygen cylinders on the Napiers were concealed, although the regulating valves were exposed, and it was 'the greatest pity' that Edge was unwilling to admit that oxygen was being used.

The big race of the day was for the Montagu Cup, the first prize for which was £1,400 (about £80,000 in the values of the 1990s). The race was over 11 laps, and Cecil Edge had been entered in the L48, bookmakers quoting him at odds of 2 to 1 on. He led the way initially but was soon caught by Warwick Wright's Darracq, the L48 holding its place for only three laps before dropping out with a broken water-pipe. The last race of the day was the Stephenson Plate for 'standard' cars. For this Edge had entered Cundy in a car which was declared as having a four-cylinder engine with a 5½in (139.7mm) bore. The only production model which met this description was the old E61 of 1903, and it is hard to believe that Edge would have seen any purpose in entering such an outclassed vehicle. It did not run properly in the race and was unplaced; victory went to the Marquis de Mouzilly St Mars with a Darracq. All in all there was much dissatisfaction about this first Brooklands meeting. The racing, apart from Newton's race, had been dull, the spectators had difficulty in seeing, and there were serious problems in the spectators' car parks.

While the controversy raged about sportsmanship and conditions at Brooklands, the normal sporting calendar continued. The Sussex County Automobile Club ran a hill-climb at South Harting on Wednesday 10 July and Cecil Edge was the fastest with a T21, though his time failed to secure the Yellow Trophy (named in recognition of its yellow cover) presented by *The Automotor Journal*, which went to the winner on handicap. The following Saturday, 13 July, the hill-climb 'circus' had moved to Shelsley Walsh. Cecil Edge ran a T21 in the open class here, rather spoiling his chances by what *The Autocar* described as 'a dry skid' at 'the bad S bend'. This probably cost Edge the fastest time of the day, as he managed 69.4 seconds and came second to Hutton's Berliet, which achieved 67.2 seconds. Selwyn Edge must have felt that his cousin Cecil had won a moral victory at Shelsley, as S.F. Edge Ltd advertised that the Napier *had* scored the fastest time, which brought forth a storm of protests in the correspondence columns of the motoring press. A reply followed from the company, although it is not difficult to guess at the identity of the author. It explained that the advertisement referred to the Napier establishing fastest time in the closed class, although it conveniently overlooked that this time was slower than the time set up in the open class and that the closed class was decided on handicap!

Newton (T23 Napier) and Jarrott (Lorraine-Dietrich) dead-heat in the Byfleet Plate race at the Brooklands opening meeting on 6 July 1907. Newton may be crouching down to give the oxygen cylinder valve an extra turn. (John Maitland Collection)

The next weekend saw another clash of events. On the Friday, Cecil Edge took a T21 to the North-East Lancashire Automobile Club hill-climb at Rivington, north of Bolton, where, against thin opposition, he established the fastest time. The next day, Saturday 20 July, he dashed down to the Midlands and appeared in the Coventry Motor Club hill-climb at Newnham, near Daventry, where once again he took the fastest time. While Cecil Edge was raising dust on the hills of the North and the Midlands, Tryon and Newton were at the second Brooklands meeting. This was on a much smaller scale than the first, with quite modest prize money. Tryon, driving the 40hp T20 (presumably number 2171

Frank Newton poses on Ealing Common in the T23 (number 4002) which he drove in the Byfleet Plate. (Guy Griffiths Collection)

again), ran in the second race on the programme, the Hollick Plate, a sprint over three and a quarter miles (5.2km). This time there was no doubt that oxygen was being used, Tryon winning quite easily from a Daimler by 'putting on a fine oxygen sprint in the last half-mile'. Newton then brought out the over-bored T23 for the seven-lap Century Stakes. The Napier was the only car with an oxygen cylinder and it held second place behind Huntley Walker's Darracq for two laps before taking the lead and going on to win. At the finish the Darracq seemed to have brake failure, and in trying to avoid the Napier, Huntley Walker went off the track and slid about 20ft (6m) down the soft embankment at the side of the Finishing Straight, fortunately escaping without injury. *The Car Illustrated* commented: 'Indeed, it was a day of triumph for the neat Napier racers, which with their wire wheels, long torpedo-shaped bodies, and general smart finish, looked very trim and speedy, and by winning two races showed their merits in unmistakable fashion.'

The oxygen controversy still raged on. Edge challenged Jarrott to a match race, with oxygen barred, for a stake of £1,000. Edge was himself challenged, by Jarrott and others, to declare that the Napiers had not been using oxygen. He replied that cylinders had been fitted to the cars, but had not been used, as it would have given no advantage. The BARC then resolved the problem by drawing up a rule which took immediate effect: 'No fuel other than petroleum spirit shall be used in internal combustion engines, except where specially provided in the race proposition, and the use of any other ingredient shall be deemed a corrupt practice, and dealt with accordingly.'

While Edge had been breathing heavily about oxygen, he had also been engaged in a much more serious matter. On 26 July a prospectus was published inviting subscriptions for 75,000 £1 ordinary shares in S.F. Edge (1907) Ltd, a company formed to acquire the business of S.F. Edge Ltd. Edge was to be chairman and managing director and Montague Napier was a director. The main asset of the company was the exclusive agreement to take and sell the whole output of Napier cars. This agreement, which had been renewed on 23 July, was to remain in force until 1921. The sales of S.F. Edge Ltd, which had been £18,228 in 1900, had risen steadily, and were £333,117 in 1906, and £201,404 in the first half of 1907 alone. Edge was to receive a salary of £2,000 a year and 5 per cent of the net profits, at a time when the average weekly wage was about £1. The sales figures were an indication of the steadily increasing popularity and success of the Napier.

After the disappointments of the first two Brooklands meetings, better things were expected for the August Bank Holiday meeting on Monday 5 August. The no-oxygen rule was now in force and some wondered if Edge's team of Napiers would maintain their winning form. Newton was the first out in the opening race, the International Plate, which was just over three laps in distance. He was driving the enlarged T23 (chassis number 4002). Fernand Gabriel, the victor in the ill-fated Paris–

Newton in the Paddock at Brooklands with T23 number 4002 after winning the International Plate, 5 August 1907. Arthur Rowledge, wearing a pale jacket, stands beside the car. (Guy Griffiths Collection)

Madrid, led for most of the way in Jarrott's De Dietrich, but was just caught by the Napier in the dash for the line, Newton winning by about 20 yards (18m). As a result Selwyn Edge was £350 better off. Cecil Edge, who had contracted tuberculosis and came to the meeting from his sick bed, could manage no better than third when he ran one of the T21s in the Heath Stakes, which was a sprint of just under a lap. Things improved again in the Belgian Plate, for cars which complied with the regulations for the Ardennes Circuit which had taken place about a week earlier. In this race Cecil Edge appeared once more, together with Tryon, both in 5in x 4in (127mm x 101.6mm) T21s, while Glentworth ran the Kaiserpreis T21, now fitted with a 5in x 5in (127mm x 127mm) engine. Tryon and Edge ran first and second throughout, so Selwyn Edge gained another £350, but Glentworth finished last.

Brooklands was bedevilled with a horse-racing ethos, and, in the best four-legged tradition, the next event was a selling race, the Oatlands Selling Plate which was over the derisory distance of a kilometre with a first prize of £150. Edge had entered J. Hennessy with a 26hp T27 and Browning with a T20 for this, the latter winning easily. At the auction after the race, the T20 was sold to a Lieutenant-Colonel C.D. Carleton-Smith for £215, of which £100 went to Selwyn Edge, the entrant. The main race of the day was the Prix de la France over 15¾ miles (25.3km) – nearly six laps – for cars complying with the 1907 Grand Prix de l'ACF regulations. The cars had to start with full tanks and had to use not

A typical Napier advertisement.

more than 1.8 gallons (8.2 litres) during the race. For this Tryon had been entered in a T21, Newton was driving the enlarged T23, and Cecil Edge was at the wheel of the L48. Hutton and Dario Resta, both driving 80hp Mercedes, fought for the lead all the way, but Tryon kept in touch and finished a good third about 300 yards (275m) behind Hutton. Tryon must have had a good view of the drama ahead of him, as during the race Hutton's car shed its bonnet, which fell on the track, sprayed its water away, broke its accelerator pedal, and burst a tyre as it crossed the line. Newton was fifth, but the L48 had troubles and was never in the picture. At the end of the meeting, Edge, emboldened by the success of the cars, issued a challenge to any motor manufacturer in the world to race against a team of six Napiers, over distances of three, 20 and 100 miles (4.8, 32 and 160km), for a stake of £1,000.

The opening of Brooklands should have had some effect on the multiplicity of hill-climbs, but during the summer and autumn of 1907 they continued to prosper. On Saturday 24 August Sidney Smith took a T21 to the Yorkshire Automobile Club climb at Greenhow Hill, Pateley Bridge, and made an almost inevitable fastest time. He did it again, with a T21, on 11 September, in the first open hill-climb in Wales, organised at Caerphilly by the Cardiff Motor Club. The cup for fastest time of the day had been presented to the club by Selwyn Edge, who attended in person to present it. As a generous gesture, he decided that it should not go to Smith, but to the entrant of the Daimler which was in second place.

Three days later, on Saturday 14 September, the Napier team was back at Brooklands for another BARC meeting. There was a programme of short races and an innovation that was to become a major feature of Brooklands racing, the handicap race. Although one of the T20s had been bought by Lieutenant-Colonel Carleton-Smith at the previous meeting, it had not strayed far. It was entered by him in the second race – a sprint event for 40hp cars over a distance of just under a lap – with Tryon as driver. Tryon out-accelerated Hinds Howell's Iris and won by about three seconds, although no times were given. Nineteen cars had entered for the First Five-Mile Handicap, and the handicap was arranged by starting the cars at the same time, from different points around the track. Newton with one of the T21s was on scratch and Tryon with the Carleton-Smith T20 had a 738-yard (675m) start. Newton carved his way through the field and won with what *The Autocar* described as 'a lot to spare', while Tryon was second. Newton's average speed was announced as 83.5mph (134.3kmh).

In August 1907, using a T23, Napiers co-operated with the BARC in trials at Brooklands to assess wind resistance. Selwyn Edge is in the centre, with Arthur Rowledge (beard) and Henry Tryon (bareheaded) on the right. Rowledge attended the trials even though he was then with Wolseley. The variable wind resistance device can be seen on the car. (Derek Grossmark)

Edge had entered three T21s for the First 60hp race over about a lap and a half. The cars were driven by Smith, Newton, and Browning, while the Hon Dudley Piggott-Carleton had entered Glentworth with another T21. Smith was driving the Edge 24-hour car, and ran home the winner, in front of Newton with the Kaiserpreis car and Cupper's Metallurgique, with Glentworth in fourth place. Smith had lost his near side front tyre during the race and ran for the last two miles on the rim. After the race, the cars ran to the end of the Finishing Straight and then turned left onto the Members' Banking to return to the Paddock. As soon as he had turned onto the banking, Smith pulled up. However, coming up fast behind was Herman driving Moore-Brabazon's Minerva, which had won the Circuit des Ardennes in July. Swerving to miss the Napier, Herman went up to the top of the banking, where the car slid and overturned, rolling down to the foot. Herman and his mechanic were thrown out and the unfortunate driver died a few hours later from his injuries.

The accident stunned the crowd and also the BARC. Both believed that the track was wholly safe and an incident of this kind could not happen. It was accepted that the accident had not been caused by Smith, but had arisen from Herman's inexperience. Despite this first fatality at Brooklands, the last race went ahead. This was another handicap, over a lap and a half. Glentworth, driving the L48, had to give a 387-yard (354m) start to three Mercedes. He went well, but could only manage to take third place. After the meeting there was much praise from the press for the Rudge-Whitworth wire wheels fitted to the Napiers, whose strength Smith had proved so convincingly.

Although the sprint and hill-climb season had finished, the BARC still had one more meeting at Brooklands, on Saturday 12 October. Six races were run in front of a small crowd. It seemed that the novelty was already wearing off. The first race was a two-lap handicap and Tryon appeared in what was described as a 41.9hp Napier. It is not possible to identify it with any certainty, but it may have been one of the 'regulars' fitted with an overbored T20 engine. It had a start of 432 yards (395 metres) and came home in fourth place. The second event, the Second 26hp Race, produced a Napier novelty: Newton ran a four-cylinder car. This was his regular T23 (chassis number 4002) with the front cylinder block removed, thus converting it to an instant four. It had a most un-Napier like appearance, as a small radiator was set well back behind the front axle, where the missing block should have been, and recorded 2,489lb (1,131kg) on the weighbridge. This unusual contrivance went very well. The race was only over one lap, and after holding third place Newton overtook his rivals on the Byfleet Banking to finish first, beating Cupper's Metallurgique by a few yards and averaging 55.5mph (89.2kmh).

In the two-lap October Handicap which followed, Dario Resta, starting from scratch in a Mercedes, caught Smith in his T21 and Glentworth in the Kaiserpreis T21, who were both left a long way behind. The racing department at Acton had been working hard to produce a variety of engines from the components available, and in the next event, the Second 60hp Race, run over a lap and a half, Newton drove a car described as 49.9hp, which must have had a T23 engine but bored out to 4.563in.(116mm), while Smith ran one of the usual T21s. Newton took the lead on the Byfleet Banking and went on to win, while Smith battled with Cupper's Metallurgique and was just beaten into third place. Newton's average was 77.2mph (124.2kmh).

Lieutenant-Colonel Carleton-Smith had matched his T20, with Tryon at the wheel, against an Iris, driven by former Napier driver Clifford Earp, and a Dennis, entered and driven by its constructor. It was generally agreed that the trio's race over two and a half laps provided the best event of the day. The Iris led from the start, but Tryon passed it on the Byfleet Banking; the two stayed together all the way and the Napier won by a length. That was the end of the Napier season at Brooklands. The six cars which Edge had entered scored ten wins, one tie, three seconds, and four thirds. They had also collected £2,002 for their entrant. Carleton-Smith's Selling Plate T20 had also secured two firsts, a second, and a third. If the new Brooklands track had not had the expected impact on the world of motor racing, Napier had certainly made an impact on Brooklands.

The season was not quite over for the mechanics at Acton. On 20 October, three cars journeyed to France and appeared at Gaillon. Glentworth had been entered in the unlimited racing class with the L48 and was also to drive a T21 in the unlimited six-cylinder touring class, while Dorothy Levitt was driving one of the first production T23s in the 110mm bore, six-cylinder class. Glentworth was in charge of the team and it was reported that he had a furious argument with Dorothy Levitt on some point of team discipline. Both the aggrieved parties sent fierce telegrams to Acton seeking support for their cause. Tempers flared to a point where Glentworth said that if Miss Levitt did not relinquish the seat of her T23, he would drag her from it! The adrenalin generated by the row must have spurred both on, as the T21 and T23 won their classes. The L48 made fastest time of the day at 26.6 seconds, which was announced as a new course record, even though it was slower than the time recorded by the winning Darracq in 1906. Before going to Gaillon, the L48 had been tested at Brooklands by

Newton, and had lapped at 107mph.

On 6 November, Newton and Tryon were back at Brooklands. Newton brought out the abbreviated four-cylinder T23 and took the track's 26hp class flying start half-mile record at 77.92mph (125.37kmh) and the ten-lap standing start class record at 71.43mph (114.93kmh). Tryon then did the same distances in a T20, fitted with a T23 engine, with its full complement of cylinders, and took the 40hp records at 86.75mph and 80.94mph (139.58 and 130.23kmh) respectively. According to Newton the four-cylinder T23 was developing 48bhp, had a 15/46 final drive and peaked at 2,350rpm during its record runs. The full T23 developed 78bhp. On Saturday 30 November, Newton was at it again, bringing out the 60hp T21 '804' with the 5in x 5in engine. He was after the flying half mile and the ten-lap standing start records in the 60hp class. He took the short distance at 97.3mph (156.55kmh). At his first attempt on the ten-lap record the water pump chain broke after five laps, then broke again after eight laps on the second attempt. On the third attempt he succeeded, and set the record at 86.49mph (139.88kmh). On the bench the 5 x 5 engine developed about 118bhp. When testing the car on 21 November, Newton did a lap at 94mph (151kmh).

It was reported that the Kaiser, during his state visit to England in the autumn, would visit Brooklands, and that a demonstration race would be given by the Napier team to enable His Majesty to form some impression of real motor racing: nothing came of this, though. Perhaps the Emperor pointed out that he had already been the moving spirit behind the Kaiserpreis, and that, surely, was *real* motor racing! Right at the end of the year, Edge repeated his challenge for a team to race against the Napiers, and raised the stake to £10,000.

Selwyn Edge held a dinner at the Trocadero Restaurant, in Piccadilly Circus, on Tuesday 10 December to celebrate the sporting activities of Napier. The guests were those employees of S.F. Edge (1907) Ltd and D. Napier & Son Ltd who had been involved in these activities. It is reasonable to surmise that Selwyn Edge and Montague Napier may well have discussed the season over their port and would have concluded that it had been a splendid year. The opening of the Brooklands track had presented the greatest opportunities. First, there had been the remarkable 24-hour runs, and then the racing had allowed Napier to become the dominant marque. In club hill-climbs too, the car had reigned supreme. Sales of production cars were booming, and work was already well under way for most ambitious racing plans in 1908.

Chapter 9: 1908

Pseudonyms, Victories, Enigmas and an Exit

DURING the autumn of 1907, Selwyn Edge and Montague Napier made the decision that there should be a return to international motor racing in 1908. Perhaps they felt that the world of Brooklands was too parochial and success there was not making sufficient impression on the wider motoring market. The design of a Grand Prix car was entrusted to Thomas Barrington, who said many years later that the design and construction of the car took only six months. As the car was intended to run in the GP de l'ACF on 7 July 1908, the design must therefore have been started early in 1908.

The building of the Grand Prix Napier is one of the most puzzling features of this story. The rules for the 1908 race were already known in outline late in 1907 and the full regulations were published on 8 January 1908. Rule 17 forbade the use of detachable wheels of the Rudge-Whitworth type, allegedly on the grounds of safety. Less than two weeks after the regulations were published Edge announced that, although four GP cars were under construction, the provisional entry of three Napiers for the race had been withdrawn as it would not be possible for the cars to take part unless Rudge-Whitworth wheels were used.

A remarkable sequence of events then ensued, much of it conducted via the columns of *The Autocar*. Charles Weigel, who was a small manufacturer in Shepherds Bush, only about a mile from the Acton works, was also building a Grand Prix team. He said he was willing to race against Rudge-wheeled Napiers, and believed other manufacturers would take the same view. He offered to negotiate with the ACF and the participating firms to seek an amicable settlement of the dispute. Edge would have none of this, however, and it seems that he did not make any approach to the ACF about the possibility of having the rules changed. He dismissed the possibility of fitting detachable rims to the Napiers and accused the ACF of bad faith and of utilising a devious method of removing one of the French entries' biggest rivals from the field. Edge concluded a letter to *The Autocar* as follows: 'I do not intend to allow the French motor industry to trap me into a race with a device which I do not agree with, and of which a British inventor has already produced a far superior example'.

Colin Defries, the English importer of the French marque Porthos, visited the ACF in Paris and reported that the ACF members deplored Edge's attitude and considered he had 'acted in a manner which is not only extremely offensive to those true gentlemen who are at the head of the Automobile Club of France, but has caused them all to feel that British makers have not got the word "Sport" in their dictionary.'

Defries confirmed that before Edge's outburst, the ACF would have been willing to negotiate with him, and with a reasonable approach from him would probably have rescinded Rule 17. Julian Orde, the secretary of the RAC, also attempted to negotiate with the ACF on Edge's behalf, but on 20 February the ACF announced that there would be no going back; the rule would stand.

Edge persisted in his attitude and his supporters lost patience. Weigel said he wished to be dissociated from Edge's views and was obviously regretting his earlier offer of help. Charles Jarrott, who always enjoyed discomfiting Edge, derided his lack of sportsmanship. Some critics now suggested that Edge had never intended to race the GP team, but Defries went further and doubted if a Grand Prix Napier had even been built. This may have caused problems for Edge and Napier. If Barrington's narrative is correct, at the time when the wheel controversy began, the construction of the cars must have been in a very early stage. At the beginning it would probably have suited Edge to have dropped the project altogether. He had received much publicity and probably hoped to gain sympathy and support for Napier from a strong core of Francophobe Britons who suspected the French despite the Entente Cordiale.

Now, however, Defries had called his bluff and Edge's response was swift. Kenneth Brown & Co, his solicitors, informed Defries that if this allegation was not withdrawn, together with a full apology, they were instructed to commence proceedings for defamation. Defries duly apologised and Kenneth Brown & Co announced that in accepting this apology, Defries had been invited to inspect the Napier records and examine the parts already made for the cars. This did not happen until the middle of March, so if there had been a need to build the cars as a face-saving exercise, six weeks had elapsed while the work could be rushed ahead at Acton. It is not known if Defries accepted the invitation for an inspection or just accepted the assurance that work was in hand, but the interlude left Edge and Napier with the commitment to build a Grand Prix car, even though this would not race in the GP de l'ACF.

While Edge and Defries had been increasing the profits of their solicitors, the Napier team had already begun activities for the new season. On Thursday 2 January, Henry Tryon had taken a T21 to Brooklands with the aim of taking the one and two hour world records and also gaining the 50 and 100 mile records on the way. It was a fine day but with a cold, east wind. The BARC fee of ten guineas for a record attempt of up to one hour was paid, the team knowing that an additional fee of five guineas would be demanded for every record broken within the hour. Tryon began his run at noon and settled down to lap at about 85mph(136kmh). After he had covered 15 laps the offside rear tyre burst and the Napier pulled up at the depot established at the top of the Finishing Straight. The car was jacked on a trestle and the wheel was changed. Tryon let in the clutch before the car was lowered to the ground, which cost him time and the car was stationary for 1min 41sec.

On the 25th lap the offside rear burst again as the car passed under the Members' Bridge. This time the car spun three times, slid to the bottom of the banking, and crashed into the edge of the Paddock entrance tunnel, ending up on its nose at the side of the entrance road. Tryon was thrown clear and was taken at once to the Hand & Spear public house nearby, where he was examined by a doctor. Fortunately he escaped with severe bruises, but the T21 was badly damaged, with a bent front axle and buckled rear dumb irons and frame, while the radiator and oil tank had burst. Before the accident, the 50-mile record had fallen at 79.43mph (127.80kmh). Tryon believed his escape from injury was a result of divine intervention and thenceforth became a devout evangelical Christian.

Tryon's 50-mile record did not stand for long, as on Thursday 6 February, Charles Jarrott captured it in a De Dietrich. Edge's team still wanted the records which had eluded Tryon, so on Wednesday 19 February, Frank Newton, who was now the manager of the team, came to Brooklands with

2 January 1908: Henry Tryon's T21 after his crash at Brooklands. (Brooklands Museum)

'804'. This was fitted with Palmer Cord six-inch (132mm) section rear tyres, running at 65lb per square inch (4.42bar). Tryon had used a narrower section running at 95lb (6.46bar). Shortly after Newton began his run rain fell and continued intermittently, but he was not deterred, and five world records were taken. The 50-mile was taken at 85.4mph (137.40kmh), the Hour at 85.55mph (137.54kmh), the 100-mile at 85.34mph (137.31kmh), the 150-mile at 84.6mph (136.12kmh), and the Two Hours at 84.7mph (136.28kmh).

On Wednesday 1 April there was more litigious drama when a Fred Holt, who worked in the Napier drawing office, was charged in the Acton Magistrates Court with stealing drawings at the alleged request of 'three gentlemen well-known in the motor trade and in motor-racing circles'. The outcome of the case was not recorded, nor was the identity of the 'three gentlemen'.

The Brooklands season began with the two-day Easter meeting. The first day, Saturday 18 April, was cold but fine. Two Napiers ran in the three-mile Third 26hp Race of just over a lap. It is difficult to establish the identity of these cars, but it seems that one was probably the T23 (chassis number 4002) shorn of two cylinders which Newton had used at the end of 1907, and the other was a similar car, but possibly with chain drive. Edge had entered Newton, and Dorothy Levitt had entered Browning. Miss Levitt had hoped to drive herself, but the BARC had introduced a rule banning lady drivers. The drivers were required to wear registered colours so they could be identified by the spectators. Browning consequently wore a white coat with blue cuffs and cap, while Newton wore a white coat with a green cap, and a deep violet veil – an accessory probably more suitable for Miss Levitt. Browning led in this sprint race until the Finishing Straight, when he was passed by Newton, who averaged 64.5mph (103.7kmh).

The Third 40hp Race was another one-lap sprint, and in this the Marquis de Mouzilly St Mars – a keen racing motor cyclist and the prime instigator of the motor cycle TT on the Isle of Man – had entered a T20 for Newton. Edge had entered a similar car for Cundy. Newton's car seems to have been bored-out to 103mm while the other car still had the standard bore of 101.6mm. The two Napiers ran together all the way and Newton just had the verdict by a bonnet, which secured the prize of 82 1/2 sovereigns for the Marquis. For the Second Surrey Stakes, the Marquis's car was taken over by Draper, but Cundy drove the other T20 again. This too was a one-lap sprint, and once more the extra millimetre told and Draper won by half a length.

Easter Monday was cold and there were several snow showers. The Continental Stakes over two laps, for cars with a bore of less than 122mm, found the two T20s in action again driven by Draper and Cundy. On Saturday they had been weighed, the Marquis's car scaling 3,155lb

Newton in the T21 '804' after breaking five World records at Brooklands on 19 February 1908. Selwyn Edge stands beside the car. (Guy Griffiths Collection)

(1,434kg) while Edge's had recorded 2,954lb (1,342kg). On Monday they weighed 3,164lb (1,438kg) and 3,000lb (1,363kg) respectively, extra fuel presumably accounting for the difference. Cupper's Metallurgique took the lead at the start and stayed there to beat Draper by about 25 yards, while Cundy trailed in some way behind in third place. *The Autocar* noted that 'the run of Napier wins was broken'. It cannot have escaped Edge's notice that now it was news when a Napier was beaten and not when it won.

The Third 90hp Race over two and a half laps was the main event of the day and Newton brought out the rebuilt L48, now named 'Samson'. During the winter of 1907 the car had been completely reconstructed. Only the chassis side members and the casings of the gearbox and rear axle were retained. Everything else was new, and a larger engine with dimensions of 155mm x 152mm had been fitted (factory number 5019). 'Samson's' main rival was a Mercedes driven by Dario Resta. The track was wet and Resta led away, but on the second lap Newton drew level on the Railway Straight. The two cars ran onto the Byfleet banking side by side when the Napier skidded and slid down onto the Mercedes. The cars touched, the Mercedes losing two hub caps and several bolts securing the detachable wheel rims while 'Samson' lost about half the spokes from the front and rear nearside wheels. Newton held the car, however, and went on to win by about 50 yards (45.7m), skidding again when crossing the line. The Napier averaged 89.5mph (144kmh) and during the race had touched 115mph (185kmh). Resta entered a protest but this was dismissed by the stewards. The last race of the day was an almost ludicrous contrast, the Tyre Changing Plate over one and a half laps. During the race competitors had to change a wheel and tyre; as an added refinement, the tyre had to be inflated. Newton drove one of the 26hp specials and, pulling out a long lead, stopped about 100 yards (90m) before the line, changed the wheel, pumped up the tyre and went on to win.

The success of Brooklands had resulted in a marked reduction in the number of hill-climbs and sprints. It was not until Saturday 2 May that the first significant event took place. The Motor Cycling Club organised a climb on Sharpenhoe Hill four miles north-west of Luton. The course was steep but almost straight, and Selwyn Edge made a now rare competition appearance driving what the press reported as a '40hp' Napier, apparently a touring-bodied T20. He made the fastest time of the day and was placed third in his class on handicap. The results told a slightly different story, the engine dimensions being given as 102mm x 128mm, which indicate a T23 45hp model. Although the T23 had been in regular competition use since the second half of 1907, Edge made sure that publicity was given to the delivery of what was announced as the first production model in July 1908. This car, fitted with a double laundaulette body, was delivered to the Prime Minister, Herbert Asquith.

On the same day as Edge was rushing up a Bedfordshire hill, on the other side of the world, at Victoria Park, Sydney, New South Wales, the championships of the Automobile Club of Australia were being held on a cinder track just over a mile in length. In the five-mile (8km) final, a 30hp Napier driven by W. Phillips took third place behind a Talbot and a Berliet. Whether this was a new T26 which had just reached Australia, or an earlier T20A, is not known.

The next Brooklands meeting on Saturday 9 May found the Napier team out in force again. There was a report that Edge himself would appear with a Grand Prix car but the crowd, estimated at 10,000, was to be disappointed. The day began with an Allcomers' Handicap, where the scratch car had to cover three laps while the rest of the field received distance starts which must have been awkward for the starter. Edge had entered Browning with one of the 26hp cars, receiving a 2,670-yard (2,440m) start, and Cundy with the T20, departing 1,780 yards (1,627m) ahead of the scratch Mercedes. A T20 was also entered for the Marquis de Mouzilly but did not start. Neither Napier was placed, although Cundy caused some excitement when he spun twice after crossing the line as a tyre deflated. *The Autocar* commented that 'nothing but consummate skill on the part of Cundy averted an accident'.

Browning was out again immediately, as the 26hp was running in the Fourth 26hp Race. This was a fiasco: there were only two runners, and one of Browning's tyres deflated as the car went to the start, providing a hollow victory for Stocks's De Dion. For the two-lap Fourth 90hp Race a new car was produced. This was a T21 chassis with a 90hp engine, which may have had the dimensions of 155mm x 105mm and probably had much in common with the T48 90hp touring engine which was about to go into production. It looked similar to a normal T21 racer, and was entrusted to Newton, who renewed his Easter battle with Resta. This time the Mercedes won at an average of 93mph (149kmh), leading from the start, though on the second lap Newton had closed up on the Byfleet Banking and was only 30 yards behind at the finish. The longest race on the card was the Fourth 40hp Race over nearly seven laps. Edge entered both T20s, the overbored car being driven by Draper while Cundy had the standard bore model. For most of the race it was a battle between Cundy and the Humber of Tuck, but a lap before the end the Humber broke a valve spring and fell back. Draper then caught Cundy, to win by half a length at an average of 83.5mph (134.35kmh).

The T20 entered for the Marquis De Mouzilly St Mars, which did not race, is driven away from Brooklands, 9 May 1908. (Brooklands Museum)

Cundy was next engaged on a somewhat different motoring competition, as a full four-seat touring-bodied T24 65hp was entered for the Irish Automobile Club Reliability Trials. These began in Dublin on Friday 22 May. The cars then toured around Ireland, going through Belfast on the penultimate day before returning to Dublin on Wednesday the 27th. There were 63 starters, and during the run these took part in two hill-climbs and a speed trial. Marks were lost for any unscheduled stops. On the first day Cundy established fastest time in the Hollywood hill-climb – just over a mile long – recording 106.8 seconds. On Saturday the 23rd the speed trial was held on Rosbeigh Strand facing the Atlantic. Cundy was again fastest over the flying mile across the sand, at 62.92mph (101.23kmh). This did not make up for the marks which the Napier was losing on the road, though. Three minutes were lost adjusting the number plate on the first day, and worse was to come. On day three, four minutes were lost with an unscheduled refuelling stop, and then another 11 minutes were wasted replacing a coil. On the last day, after returning to Dublin, there was a timed climb of Ballinaslaughter Hill and once more the Napier disgraced itself, misfiring all the way up the hill and only going onto six cylinders as it crossed the finishing line. The lost marks meant that Cundy was not among the award winners.

While Cundy was sprinting along the Irish sands on Saturday 23 May, Newton was in Nottinghamshire for the Nottinghamshire Automobile Club speed trials, which were held on a private road at Clipstone on the Duke of Portland's estate near Mansfield. In the flying kilometre handicap for touring cars, Ross-Browne won with a T20, recording 73.6mph (118.4kmh), and was only just beaten on outright time by Instone's Daimler, which did 74.02mph (119.9kmh). Newton ran in the unlimited flying kilometre class, which he won easily with a speed of 109.4mph (176.02kmh). According to reports he drove a '60hp', and photos show an apparently normal competition T21 (registration number LN 2628), but there was more to the car than was immediately apparent. It was fitted with an engine with dimensions of 127mm x 152.4mm and was known in the Acton factory as 'Mercury'. It ran on Dunlop tyres and each front tyre tread pattern was different.

The Brooklands Whitsun meeting was a two-day event and saw the establishment of one of Brooklands's greatest legends and controversies. Saturday 6 June had the unusual feature of two match races arising from challenges issued by Selwyn Edge earlier in the year for challengers to race against Napiers in 26hp and 40hp races for a stake of £500 in each race. Oscar Cupper, the Belgian importer of Metallurgiques, had accepted the challenges. At this meeting the BARC acceded to a request of Colin Defries for entrants to be permitted to give their cars individual names, a practice which may have amused the entrants but has confused posterity, since apart from the marque the race programme failed to give any other identity, and the engine size was not shown. Before the match races there was the Second Allcomers' Handicap, where the handicap was now arranged by the normal time allowance, with all cars starting from the same line. For this race Edge had entered Ross-Browne with 'Viceroy', a 60hp T21, and Blackburn with 'Medusa', one of the 26hp specials with shaft drive. Neither was placed.

The 26hp match race was the fifth event on the card and was between Newton driving 'Firefly' – the chain-drive 26hp special – matched against Cupper's Metallurgique. The race was over five laps and Newton won easily, averaging 78.7mph, as Cupper had magneto problems. To ensure success in the event a new engine had been built. This still had the 101mm bore which kept it within the 26hp class, but the stroke was increased to 178mm (7in). The 40hp match race came next, over six laps, with Draper driving 'St George', Edge's T20 with the 103mm bore, matched against Cupper's 40hp car. The Metallurgique made a good start and pulled out a lead of about 500 yards, but the Napier got into its stride and before the end of the second lap went into the lead. After that it pulled away and won by nearly a mile. Cupper accepted defeat gracefully but said that the Metallurgique was misfiring intermittently and suspected the magneto again. Draper's average was over 85mph (136kmh).

For the 90hp Stakes over two laps Newton brought out another new car, named 'Meteor'. This was almost identical in appearance to the L48 'Samson' and used a 90hp engine, with dimensions of 155mm x 102mm. The chassis was later described by Newton as a '120' and seems to have been of the type used in the new T48 90hp, with a wheelbase of 11ft 11in (363cm). It had a three-speed gearbox and according to Newton was much too heavy. The chassis number is unknown, but the registration number was LB 4951. At the start Lane's Darracq led from Resta's Mercedes, but on the second lap Newton passed the Darracq going onto the Members' Banking, then took the Mercedes on the Railway Straight and went on to win by about 200 yards (180m). 'Meteor's' average speed was 91mph (145kmh) and during the race it was reported to have touched 116mph (186kmh). It was, as *The Autocar* reported, 'indeed a field day for Napier'.

The crowd on Whit Monday was probably the largest yet seen at Brooklands. The draw was another match race resulting from a further challenge issued by Edge. This was to be run between 'Samson', driven by Newton, and a 90hp Fiat similar to the car which had won the 1907 GP de l'ACF. It was entered by D'Arcy Baker, the Fiat importer, and was to be driven by Felice Nazzaro, the winner of the 1907 GP, who was

Frank Newton sits in the reconstructed L48 now known as 'Samson', probably just before the match race with Nazzaro in June 1908. (Guy Griffiths Collection)

then regarded as the world's leading racing driver. A new crankshaft had been fitted to 'Samson's' engine for the race. This increased the stroke from 152mm to 178mm, so the swept volume was now 20,155cc, and it developed 212bhp at 2,500rpm. After the last race on Whit Saturday, Newton had taken the car out for a test, but when leaving the Paddock first gear of the two-speed box stripped, so the car was taken back to Acton immediately so that the team mechanics could cut a new gear and rebuild the box. Work went on throughout Sunday and the car was road-tested early on race morning. The Fiat was also in trouble, and D'Arcy Baker's mechanics spent Sunday rebuilding the engine.

On the Monday morning all was well with both cars and Cecil Edge, his tuberculosis now very advanced, was in the Paddock with the Napier team to see what was expected to be the greatest Brooklands race yet. The stake was £500 and it was to be over ten laps. Newton was to wear his usual white coat with a green cap. Nazzaro wore a red and white halved coat, he also wore the 'lucky' black gloves in which he always drove. At 3.40pm the cars came out to the start on the Members' Banking, by the top of the Finishing Straight. The Brooklands bookies had the Fiat at odds-on and the Napier at evens. Using the considerable torque of the new engine, and able to achieve 70mph (112kmh) in first gear, Newton made a good start. He had a lead of 100 yards (90m) by the end of the Railway Straight then continued to pull away and had a lead of nearly eight seconds as the cars crossed the Fork at the end of lap two. As the Napier went behind the Members' Hill at the end of lap three, however, something was amiss; it slowed down abruptly and coasted to a halt. The new crankshaft had broken. The crippled car was pushed back down the Paddock road, the first mechanical failure of a Napier at Brooklands. Nazzaro eased off and completed the distance to take the stake. During the race he had been struck in the face by a bird.

Then came sensation. The race had been timed with the electrical timing gear and A.V. Ebblewhite, the chief timekeeper, announced that Nazzaro had done a fastest lap at 121.64mph (195.71kmh), a new lap record by an enormous margin. The electrical

The exhaust side of the engine fitted to 'Samson' in its final form. It developed 212bhp at 2,500rpm. (Guy Griffiths Collection)

The inlet side of 'Samson's' engine. The carburettor is seen below the chassis member. (Guy Griffiths Collection)

timing had also recorded Newton's second lap at 113.01mph (181.83kmh). There was uproar, as not only was such a high speed disbelieved, but the race had also been hand-timed and this gave the Fiat's fastest lap as 107.98mph (173.73kmh) and the Napier's as 105.08mph (169.07kmh). The Nazzaro lap record has been the subject of controversy among motoring historians ever since and the arguments for and against the speed have been evenly balanced. The BARC, despite the controversy, accepted the speed officially; it was duly recorded as a lap record and stood until 1922.

The day was not quite over, and Newton now brought out the chain-drive 'Firefly' for the Fifth 26hp Race over six laps. Waiting until the last lap, Newton passed Cupper's Metallurgique on the run to the line to win by a bonnet. Cupper misjudged the braking distance after the line and spun from the Finishing Straight onto the Members' Banking. Newton's win had partially restored Napier's fortunes and made some amends for the failure of 'Samson'. His average speed was 76.2mph (12.6kmh). When 'Samson' was stripped down at Acton, a piece of the broken crankshaft was suitably inscribed and presented to Newton by the mechanics.

The day after the Brooklands Whitsun meeting, the Prince Henry Trial began in Berlin. Dorothy Levitt was entered with a fully equipped 45hp T23, but she had no success and was unplaced. The trial was surrounded with much controversy. There were fierce allegations that many of the entries were thinly disguised racing cars and the organisers were strongly criticised for not disqualifying these cars.

One of the major motoring events in Britain in 1908 was the RAC 2,000 Mile Trial. It was declared to be the most severe open trial which had been held in the British Isles. It started in London, ran to Scotland with various tests and hill-climbs en route, and then returned, ending at Brooklands where there was a 200-mile race which would now be regarded as a high speed trial. There were entries from all the major manufacturers, a 40hp T20 and a 60hp T21 being entered by S.F. Edge (1907) Ltd. The event started on Thursday 11 June, and at the beginning of that week it was announced that both Napiers were being withdrawn. Edge said that the preparation of the cars had not been completed; he wanted the Napiers to be fastest on all the hills in the Trial, and the preparation of the cars was such that he could not be sure of this.

The Napier competition story became surprisingly complex in 1908. Not only was there the puzzle of the Grand Prix car but there were also the unusual events surrounding the Hutton. On 14 February 1908 a terse entry appeared in the minute book of the Board of Directors of D. Napier & Co Ltd: 'An agreement for the sale of cars between J.E. Hutton Ltd (1) S.F. Edge (1907) Ltd (2) and the Company (3) submitted resolved and sealed.' The minute book is silent as to the details of the agreement, which has not survived, though it has been suggested by Wilson and Reader in *Men & Machines* that it provided for the manufacture of 360 cars.

The events surrounding the manufacture of the Hutton car have never been fully resolved. Late in 1907, the RAC had announced that the regulations for the Tourist Trophy were to be changed drastically. In 1908, the event would be for racing cars built to a specific formula. An outline of

June 1908: Dorothy Levitt about to leave London for the Prince Henry Trial with a 45hp T23. (Autocar)

the proposed regulations indicated that it would be restricted to four-cylinder cars with a maximum bore of four inches. This was a race which Edge wanted to win, as it would be the year's main race in the British Isles. There was a major problem, though. For four years he had been championing the six-cylinder engine and there could be not only a loss of face – something which Edge could not countenance – but also adverse publicity, if a four-cylinder Napier was built for the TT. The problem could be solved, however, if the cars were built ostensibly for another company and raced under another name. If the cars were successful, the world would know Napier had been the constructor; if they failed, Napier were merely building the cars to the specification and instructions of another party.

The agreement sealed on 14 February gave effect to this decision. J.E. Hutton was an enthusiastic young motorist. He had the agency for Mercedes and Panhard cars, which were sold from showrooms in Shaftesbury Avenue in the West End of London, and had been an active and successful competitor at Brooklands during the 1907 season. He had already been involved in the small-scale manufacture of a belt-driven car in 1901–2, and had been the backer of a six-cylinder car for the 1904 Gordon Bennett Trials which did not appear. If Napier was to have a front man for the racing and subsequent sale of a four-cylinder sporting car, Hutton was a good choice.

The final regulations for the Tourist Trophy were published during the last week of March. The race would be over a distance of about 300 miles (480km) on the Isle of Man. The regulations governing the construction of the cars were simple:

> The race is for cars the D^2n [diameter of the cylinders in inches squared and multiplied by the number of cylinders] of whose cylinders shall not exceed sixty-four i.e., whose RAC rating is not greater than 25.6hp. Cars fitted with internal combustion engines shall not have less than four working cylinders. The minimum weight shall be 1,600lb/727kg (which shall exclude the driver, mechanic, petrol, oil and water, spare parts, spare tyres and tools). The use of auxiliaries to combustion (other than atmospheric air), such as oxygen, acetylene, etc., is prohibited.

With the final regulations to hand, the team in the Acton drawing office went to work. It is not known who played the major part in the design of the Hutton, but presumably Barrington had a considerable influence. The design which emerged was pure Napier and broke no new ground in its specification, but the designers and the Acton factory worked fast and the car was announced in the press early in June. Perhaps a more tangible indication of the speed at which they had worked was the appearance of the first Hutton at Brooklands on Whit Monday, when Hutton himself drove it in the Fifth 26hp Race. He led the field at the start and finished third after being passed by Newton's 'Firefly' and Cupper's Metallurgique. Another Hutton-type engine had already made its debut the same day, in 'Firefly' in the 26hp match race with the Metallurgique.

The Hutton engine had a bore of 4in and a stroke of 7in (101.5mm x 177.8mm), swept volume was 5,756cc, and it developed about 70bhp at 2,300rpm. The cylinders were cast in pairs, with copper water jackets formed by electrolytic deposit on wax moulds. It was a side-valve design with all the valves on the near side and bronze valve caps screwed into the cylinder head. There were two sparking plugs for each cylinder and dual ignition. The distributor for the trembler coil was shaft-driven at 45° from the rear of the crankshaft and the Bosch magneto was driven from the front of the crankshaft by a chain which also drove the water pump. A single Polyroe carburettor was fitted, which fed two 3in (7.6cm) induction pipes, each going to a common induction port on the offside of each pair of cylinders. The pistons were of malleable iron and the crankcase was aluminium. The pressure-fed crankshaft was supported in the top half of the crankcase on five plain bearings.

A multi plate clutch drove through a short shaft to a four-speed, all-indirect gearbox, the ratios of which were 3:1, 4:1, 5.5:1, and 7.25:1. There were two gear levers, one controlling the forward speeds and the other reverse. The hand brake operated 12in (30cm) contracting rear brakes, while behind the gearbox was a foot-operated transmission brake. The chassis was conventional, with semi-elliptic springs all round, and a wheelbase of 9ft 6in (289cm). The wheels were Rudge-Whitworth carrying Dunlop tyres, 870mm x 90mm at the front and 875mm x 105mm at the rear. The car was slightly crab-tracked, with a front track of 5ft 2in (155cm) and a rear of 4ft 8in (142cm). The body was simple: a one piece bonnet, two bucket seats, and a bolster fuel tank. The radiator had a strong look of Napier with the 'trademark' water tower. The Hutton design became the Napier production type T27 and this first car had a Napier chassis number 8001, the engine number being either 5025 or 6224, both numbers are given in the Napier records.

Hutton did not wait long after the Brooklands debut before bringing out the new car again. On Wednesday 17 June, a cloudy wet day, he broke the local 26hp short and long records. The short record, over half a mile, fell at 78.9mph (126.95kmh) and the long record, ten laps, fell at 76.59mph (123.23kmh). The fastest lap was 79.95mph (128.63kmh).

The sprint season, meanwhile, was well under way. On Saturday 13 June, Ross-Browne established fastest time of day at the inter-club

J.E. Hutton at Brooklands with the T27 Hutton 'Little Dorrit' on 17 June 1908, when he broke the local 26hp records. (Guy Griffiths Collection)

hill-climb at Oakamoor in Staffordshire, his T21 recording 69.4 seconds. Two weeks later came one of the major sprint events of the season, the Yorkshire Automobile Club meeting on Saltburn beach. The sand was heavy, and the meeting began at 8.30am to avoid the rising tide. In the closed class for two, three, and four-cylinder 26hp tourers, Hutton won an easy victory with the new car, though its claims to be 'touring' were perhaps tenuous. Cundy won the 65hp touring class with a T21 entered by Cecil Edge. It was in the open classes that the real competition began. Algernon Lee-Guinness had entered the 200hp Darracq and declared his intention of attempting

'Mercury' waits on the sands beside 'Meteor' during the Saltburn speed trials, 27 June 1908. 'Mercury' may have used the prototype Grand Prix engine in this event. (Guy Griffiths Collection)

Saltburn speed trials: Frank Newton waits for his run in the 90hp 'Meteor'. (Guy Griffiths Collection)

Henry Tryon (T21) takes Kennel Bend at Shelsley Walsh on his way to setting a new record for the hill, 25 July 1908. (Midland Automobile Club)

to break the world record, which was held by Marriott's Stanley at 121.57mph (195.60kmh). On his best run Guinness did 121.6mph (195.65kmh) over the flying kilometre, but he was unable to reach this speed on his return run, so Marriott's record was still just intact. However, Guinness had the satisfaction of setting a new outright British record. As opposition, Guinness had 'Meteor' and 'Mercury', both being driven by Newton. Unfortunately 'Meteor' was no match for the Darracq, and Newton's highest speed was 102.61mph (165.09kmh). In the standing start open class Guinness did 66.7mph/107.32kmh (32.5 seconds) beating 'Mercury' by an appreciable margin.

The Brooklands meeting on Saturday 4 July was billed as an amateur event. It was hot, and the last race of the day was a match race between Selwyn Edge, driving the 26hp special 'Firefly', and J.W. Stocks with a 26hp De Dion. The stake was 50 sovereigns and the distance was four laps. Before the race a broken valve had been replaced in 'Firefly's' engine. Edge made a good start but

Stocks went past, crossing the Fork at the end of lap one. Edge regained the lead, but going under the Members' Bridge on lap three the Napier was misfiring. The cars continued side by side until Stocks pulled in front just enough to win by about half a length. Afterwards it was found that the Napier's replacement valve was sticking.

Edge was out again the following Saturday, winning his class with a T21 at the Hertfordshire County Automobile Club hill-climb at Tring. Second in the class was Dorothy Levitt, while Browning with a T20 was another class winner. At the Coventry Motor Club Daventry hill-climb on Saturday 18 July, Tryon won the class for touring cars over 26hp and set fastest time of the day with the almost inevitable T21. A week later the sprint exponents were at Shelsley Walsh for the Midlands Automobile Club meeting. Tryon set fastest time once more in the T21, with 65.4 seconds, a new record for the hill. It was reported that he took the Esses 'in magnificent style' despite hitting a drain cover. This performance could only gain Tryon 14th place on formula, however, which was regarded as the more important category, whereas Browning, who had climbed in 87.4 seconds with his T20, gained a formula third. The Napier run of successes in hill-climbs continued when on Thursday 30 July, despite rain and mist, Watson set fastest time at the Lancashire Automobile Club Rivington Pike event, near Bolton, driving a T21 entered by Selwyn Edge.

On Monday 27 July, Cecil Edge died at Selwyn Edge's home at Telford, in Surrey. He was 28 years old and his death deeply affected his cousin. He had played a key part in establishing the Napier – as a riding mechanic with his cousin in the Gordon Bennett victory, as a driver in many events, and as team manager during the 24-Hour record. Selwyn Edge had not only lost a close relative and friend, but Cecil had also played an active and important part in the running of S.F. Edge (1907) Ltd, particularly in the London showroom at 14 New Burlington Street and in the competition activities.

In the middle of July, the Grand Prix Napier was proved to be a reality and it was shown to the press. Every attempt had been made to reduce weight. The engine was the usual six, with dimensions of 127mm x 152.4mm, giving a cubic capacity of 11,590cc, and was reported to develop about 120bhp. The cylinders were cast separately and each had its own copper water jacket formed by electrolytic deposit. The overhead inlet valves were operated by pushrods and had tulip heads and leaf springs. There were side exhaust valves. The light steel pistons had concave crowns and weighed 4lb 5oz (1.95kg). The cylinders were mounted on an alloy crankcase. A Napier variable choke carburettor supplied mixture through a long V-shaped inlet manifold and a Bosch magneto provided the ignition. The engine which had been used in 'Mercury' had the same dimensions, so it is possible that the car had been used as a test-bed.

A short shaft drove the three-speed gearbox on which the multi-plate clutch was mounted. Behind the gearbox was a foot-operated transmission brake. A propeller shaft drove a live rear axle on which were small contracting band brake drums operated by the hand lever. The chassis frame was unusual, being of lattice construction. The front semi-elliptic springs were mounted outside the frame, and at the rear there was a complete break with usual Napier practice. Two pairs of cantilever springs were mounted on the outside of the frame and the rear axle was suspended at the rear of these. There was a lightweight racing body and the radiator did not have the usual water-tower. The wheelbase was 9ft 8in (294cm) and the track was 4ft 8in (142cm). It seems that the first car had the chassis number 5130 and the engine number 5009, but Napier racing and experimental records do not show that it was given a type number; however, it had the factory order number R 232. According to Newton and Barrington, only three cars were built, but the records show that chassis numbers 5131, 5132, and 5133 were also allocated, and during World War Two a correspondent to *The Motor* mentioned that he had been able to identify four separate cars. On Friday 24 July, Cundy tested the car at Brooklands, and it was perhaps ironic that Baron De Zuylen, the President of the ACF, was taken round the Track for several laps as a passenger.

After the comparatively low-key amateur meeting, the August Bank Holiday Brooklands meeting was a major event and saw the running of the longest motor race in England up to that time. It was a two-day event and on Saturday 1 August the meeting was graced by the attendance of the chairman of the RAC, HSH Prince Francis of Teck, the brother of the Princess of Wales, later Queen Mary. The meeting began with two-lap heats of the Fourth Allcomers' Handicap, and in the first heat a second T27 Hutton appeared, driven by P.D. Stirling, though it was unplaced. This was given chassis number 8002 and engine number 5020. There were detail differences from the first car, principally, a three-speed gearbox. G.H. Levick brought out a four-cylinder 26hp special in the second heat, but the car was unplaced. It had been built using some parts from 'Firefly', though not the Hutton-type engine. Levick had an unpleasant experience during practice when one of the seat cushions became trapped in the driving chains, which broke; the chain then wrapped itself around his arm, leaving him bruised but otherwise unhurt. Hutton himself participated in the third heat and came home the winner, and in the final he came up

July 1908: Two views of the Grand Prix Napier. The road equipment was fitted to encourage sales. With such small rear brakes it must be wondered if the car was intended for serious road racing. (Guy Griffiths Collection)

into third place after starting near the back of the field.

The main race of the first day was the 11-lap, 30-mile Second Montagu Cup. At the start, Lane took the lead driving a 1907 GP Mercedes, and held it until half-distance, but then Newton, who had been holding second place with 'Samson', passed the Mercedes and went on to win by a margin of about 100 yards (91.4m). It was a fast race and Newton's average speed was 101.5mph (163.3kmh).

On Monday 3 August there was another large crowd. The First O'Gorman Trophy was the fourth event on the card and among the entries was GP car number 5130, driven by J.G. Reynolds, an Acton test driver participating in his first race. Also in the field were Newton, driving 'Mercury', and Hutton with the T27. It seems surprising that the GP car was entrusted to a novice on its debut, especially as Cundy had already done the track testing. Newton had considered driving it, but had decided that there was little to choose between the performance of the two cars, and felt that 'Mercury' was likely to be more reliable. The race was over 37 laps, a distance of 100 miles (160km), and would now be known as a formule libre event with no restrictions on the cars, including fuel; the only stipulation was the need for two seats.

Lane in the GP Mercedes was much fancied and he took the lead from the start, which was at the Pond by the Fork. He was followed by Reynolds, but was setting a fast pace, averaging nearly 100mph (160kmh), and was pulling away from Reynolds by over two seconds a lap. By lap nine the Napier was trailing and the gap had opened to 58 seconds; on lap 15 Reynolds was lapped; Newton had done 13 laps,

The engine of the T27 Hutton. (Motor)

while Hutton had only done 11. On lap 17 Lane pulled into the temporary pits established at the Fork, as the Mercedes was misfiring. This gave Reynolds and Newton their chance and the GP Napier went into the lead followed by the T21. By the time Lane restarted Reynolds had over a lap lead, but on lap 19 the GP car stopped to top up the radiator and Lane, who was lapping at 97mph (156kmh), cleared most of the deficit.

The Mercedes was not running quite as well now, and on lap 25, although Lane had caught Reynolds, he had only pulled about 300 yards (270m) ahead. On lap 26 the misfiring returned and Lane stopped again, so once more the GP Napier led. Two laps later Reynolds's offside rear tyre punctured as he passed the top of the Finishing Straight, and when he pulled down the banking and ran along the inside edge of the track a wheel went over the edge onto the grass verge and dropped into a small hollow, causing the Napier to overturn. Fortunately Reynolds and his riding mechanic were thrown clear and only suffered minor bruises, and the car suffered little damage beyond a bent steering arm and a slightly dented wheel rim. Newton, who had been running at a steady pace waiting his chance, now took the lead, as Lane was still in the pits.

When Newton had just three laps to go the Mercedes re-entered the race, too far behind to have any chance of winning. Despite this, Lane started to lap as fast as he had done earlier in the race. Coming under the Members' Bridge he was almost at the top of the banking, and as he approached the point where the banking crossed the River Wey he lost control. The Mercedes spun, just missing the Hutton as it slid down the banking. It struck the parapet of the bridge and crashed over the top, breaking up and catching fire as it landed on the riverbank. Lane was thrown out and landed partially in the water, while his mechanic, Burke, was thrown right across the river into the rising ground on the far side. Burke died within a few minutes, and Lane was carried to an ambulance with serious injuries.

Newton completed the distance and pulled off into a silent Paddock; Hutton, who had covered 30 laps, was the only other competitor still running. Newton had run with Palmer tyres, 35 x 5 on the front and 35 x 6 at the back. His average was 83.88mph (134.96kmh) and his fastest lap was at 90.39mph (145.43kmh). During the race Reynolds had lapped at 97.67mph (157.15kmh) and Hutton at 83.62mph (134.54kmh).

The last race of the day was to have been a match race between Selwyn Edge with a second GP Napier and Charles Jarrott driving a GP Lorraine-Dietrich. There is some uncertainty about the circumstances of this race. Edge is supposed to have informed the BARC that following Cecil Edge's death he did not wish to take part. According to one account the club agreed, but another report states that the BARC insisted that Edge drove. It was reported that both cars were weighed and waiting

J.G. Reynolds sits in the GP Napier, August 1908. This photograph must have been taken before the Brooklands crash, though the car bears its race number on the radiator. Reynolds may be wearing the green cap and white smock which were his race colours. (Guy Griffiths Collection)

to race, but other sources state that Jarrott was alone and was ready to drive over the course to take the stake. In the event, the BARC decided to cancel the race following the fatal accident, and the crowd of 7,000 drifted sadly away. If Edge's car was weighed and ready to race there must be doubts that it was a GP model, as factory records show that the second car was not ready until 9 September, while number 5130 was not race-worthy following Reynolds's accident.

The death of Burke had considerable repercussions. Just over a week later, on 14 August, *The Times* attacked motor racing in a fierce leading article. Not for nothing was *The Times* called the 'Thunderer'. Under the heading 'Motor Racing in Isle of Man', it blazed forth:

> It is difficult to imagine any more audacious flouting of public opinion than is involved in this proceeding or a better opportunity for Mr Burns [President of the Local Government Board] to show his words have a serious meaning . . . If he can find any means whatever to put down this open defiance of public opinion he will command the approval not only of the public at large, but of a great number of responsible motorists and of the manufacturers of motor cars themselves . . . Speeds of 80 or 100mph ought to be prohibited even on a private track like Brooklands. The exhibitions on the track are simply demoralising.

In the same issue of *The Times* a letter was published, signed by 'Manufacturer', which supported the editorial view. The sport was suddenly put on the defensive, and those concerned realised that another mishap could bring motoring competitions to an end in Britain.

Although a dark cloud hung over the sport, there was still competitive motoring in Ireland. On Friday 21 August the Irish Automobile Club held the Newton Mount Kennedy hill-climb near Dublin. This was a two-mile (3.2km) course and Cundy appeared with a T21, registered A 8977, entered by Edge. It was announced that Edge had been so dissatisfied with the Napier performance on Ballinaslaughter Hill during the Irish Reliability Trials in May that Cundy had been sent to show what a Napier could do. A 8977 was the registration number of the short chassis T21 driven by Edge in the 24-hour run the previous year, so it seems likely that this quicker and lighter car, fitted with a four-seater body for this event, was sent to Ireland to ensure success. Cundy obliged by setting fastest time with 2min 7.6sec. On Thursday 28 August Dorothy Levitt was in Trouville. It was the height of the summer season in the fashionable resorts of Deauville and Trouville, and, in a hill-climb which started in the centre of the town and ran up the Côte du Calvaire, she took first place in the over 110mm touring class, driving either a 60hp T21 or a 65hp T24, with a full tourer body and carrying three passengers.

Cundy sits at the wheel of T21 A8977 while his passengers clamber aboard for the Newton Mount Kennedy hill-climb, Dublin, 21 August 1908. This was almost certainly Edge's 24-hour record car, disguised as a standard T21 for the event! (Guy Griffiths Collection)

Despite pressures to cancel the race the RAC decided that the Tourist Trophy should go ahead, but Hutton's hopes received a sharp setback when a receiver was appointed for J.E. Hutton & Co Ltd on 19 August. On 8 September the receiver put the company into liquidation with debts of £16,170. At the same time it was announced that a new company, Hutton & Co Ltd, had been formed with issued capital of £10,000 to market the Hutton car and this would be unaffected by the liquidation.

Despite the financial dramas, the Hutton team was being prepared for what was now popularly known as the 'Four-Inch Race'. Hutton was having a new car built at Acton so in early August the original car, which had the Brooklands nickname 'Little Dorrit', was sold by Edge to William Watson, a motor dealer in Liverpool who had the Napier agency and had been successful in hill-climbs with a Berliet. The car was bought with an entry which Edge had made in the TT, and Watson was assured that 'Little Dorrit' was to the same specification as the car under construction. The Hutton team for the 'Four-Inch' event would be Hutton himself, Watson, and Stirling with the second Brooklands car. Hutton's own car was completed at the beginning of September. It was similar in general specification to Watson's car, but according to Watson a number of components had been made of light alloy, so it weighed less. The main change in the specification was an increase in the stroke to 8in (203.2mm). This was done to exploit the regulations, which placed no restriction on stroke dimensions. The result was a very high piston speed, and it was hoped that the extra power would be an adequate compensation for the likely unreliability. The capacity of Hutton's car was 6,577cc. It was given the chassis number 8011 and the engine number was recorded as both 5025 and 6225.

The teams arrived in the Isle of Man early in September, as practising over the course was permitted daily, from daybreak until 8.00am, from Saturday 5 September until Tuesday 22 September, two days before the race. The course was what is now known as the Mountain circuit, used for the motor cycle TT, with a $37\frac{3}{4}$ mile (60.73km) lap. It differed from the course used for earlier Tourist Trophy races as the detour through Peel had been eliminated. As the road surface was poor and much of it was unmade, an Akonia dressing was sprayed on it to lay the dust. The Hutton team stayed at the Glen Helen Hotel, about ten miles round the course, in company with the De Dion and Berliet teams. Hutton and Stirling were out practis-

24 September 1908: Stirling's Hutton after his crash at Ballacraine on the first lap of the Tourist Trophy. (Motor)

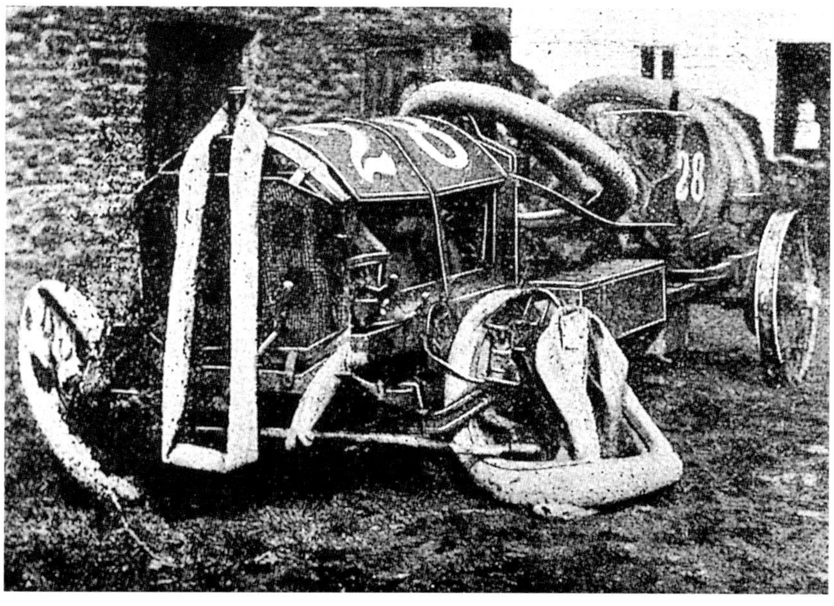

ing on the first day, and on Wednesday the 9th they were joined by Watson. George, with a Darracq, was the fastest in practice, lapping the course in 43½ minutes, and it was soon evident that the Darracqs were the favourites for the race. Stirling had a narrow escape while practising when he encountered a stray horse, and on Friday the 18th Watson went off the road approaching Sulby Bridge, damaging the radiator and the front tyres. A GP Napier had also been taken along with the team, and was tested unofficially over the course.

On the last day of practice, against the advice of the Napier engineers with the team, Hutton advanced the ignition on his long stroke car by a tooth. When the car was tried, the cylinder blocks lifted from the crankcase. A Douglas shipyard came to the rescue; the compression ratio was reduced by packing the valve caps, a piece of boiler plate was put on top of the engine, and the blocks were clamped to the crankcase by four long bolts passing through the boiler plate and under the sump.

On Tuesday the 22nd the cars were assembled in the club enclosure, a field beside the start. An RAC official had visited each factory while the cars were being built and all the main components were marked; now these marks were checked. Once this had been done the cars were weighed dry, without spare tyres or tools. The three Huttons were the heaviest team in the race – only one De Dion weighed more. Stirling's car was the lightest of the team at 2,759lb (1,254kg), Hutton's was next at 2,789lb (1,267kg), and Watson's was the heaviest, scaling 2,830lb (1,286kg). These figures perhaps add strength to Watson's comments. The cars were also weighed on the front and rear axles to ascertain weight distribution. The figures for the team were 1,474/1,285lb (670/584kg), 1,565/1,224lb (711/586kg) and 1,520/1,310lb (691/684kg) respectively.

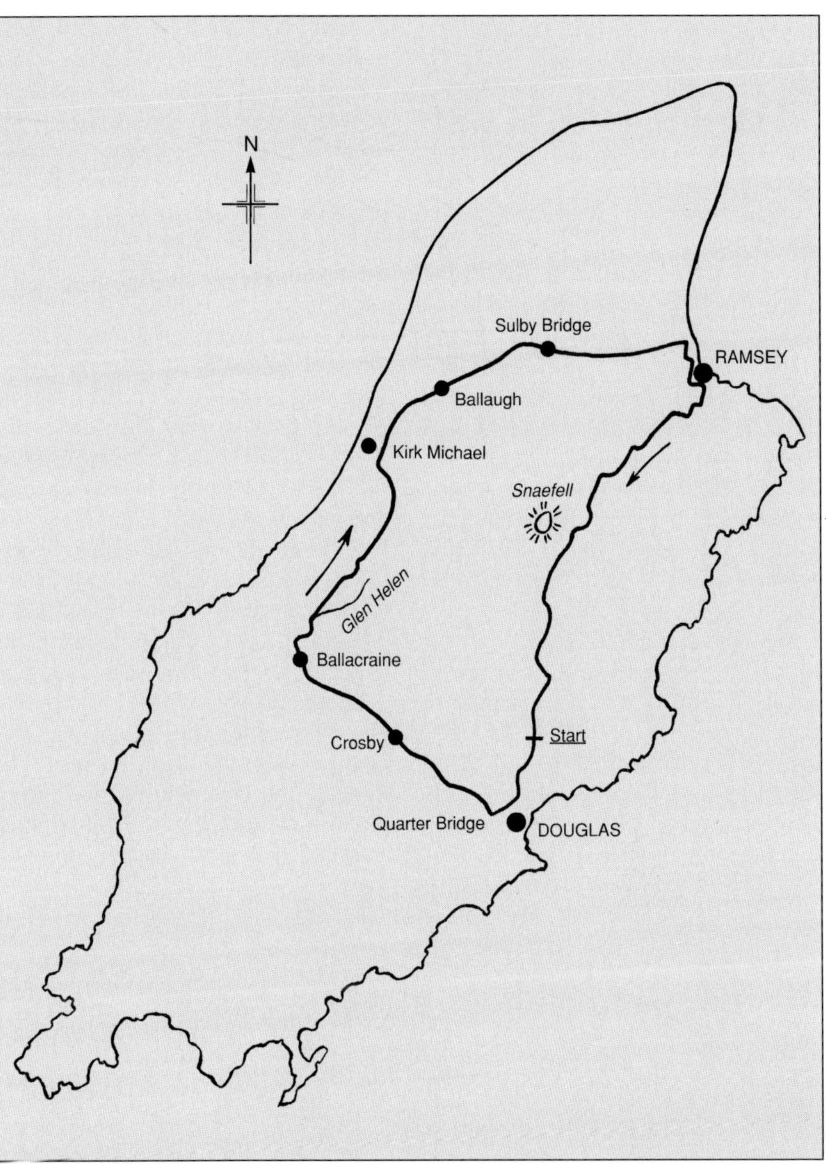

Tourist Trophy 1908, Isle of Man. The circuit measured 37.7 miles (60.7km), and the race distance 339.7 miles (546km).

Hutton's car was noticeably heavier at the front, which gives rise to speculation that the boiler plate was already in place. After the weighing the drivers were given a medical examination, including hearing and eyesight tests. All passed.

The first car to start at 9.00am on Thursday 24 September should have been a Rover driven by Browning. However, it had been so slow in practice that Browning agreed to start last of all, and the honour of being the first of the 35 entrants to go fell to Watson instead. The cars lined up in a column in starting order on the road at Hilberry. On an overcast morning, Prince Francis of Teck and Lord Raglan arrived at 8.40am. Two minutes before the start Watson started his engine, and at 30 seconds after 9.00am A.V. Ebblewhite dropped his flag. Watson was immediately away, facing nine laps totalling 341½ miles (549km). At the end of the first lap he led on the road, having lapped in 45min 45sec, but already the Hutton team was minus a car – Stirling had hit the wall of an hotel at Ballacraine, buckling the front wheels, bursting the radiator, and bending the dumb-irons. He was cut over one eye but otherwise unhurt. As more cars completed their first lap the order became clear: George (Darracq), who had passed 13 cars on the road, led from the Beeston-Humbers of Tuck and Reid, while Watson was sixth. After two laps George still led, followed by the Darracq of Guinness; Tuck was third, and Watson had moved up to fourth, though the Hutton still led on the road. Despite the makeshift repairs to his engine, Hutton was going steadily and had worked his way up from 14th to eighth.

By the end of lap three George had a lead of 1min 17sec from Tuck, while Guinness was over a minute and a half behind the Humber. Watson was still fourth, but 2min 50sec behind George. Hutton had kept his eighth place, nine minutes behind the leader; then he lost another five minutes changing tyres at Ramsey. So far there had not been the mayhem which the national press had forecast. *The Autocar* commented that 'the absence of blood-curdling news was visibly depressing the spirits of those Pressmen who had been instructed by their journals to smother the course with blood and strew the hedges with smashed-up cars and corpses'. On the fourth lap, George had a problem. Coming down the hill from Keppel Gate on the Mountain, the highest point of the course, he took the corner at Craig na Baa too fast and struck the bank, bending the front of the Darracq's frame. Taking two fence posts from the side of the road, he bent the frame straight and was away again without losing the lead.

On the fifth lap it was Hutton who was in trouble. The engine was still going well, but he took the hairpin at Ramsay too fast. The nearside front tyre burst and the car hit a wall, buckling a rear wheel and bending the front axle. The tyres of Hutton's car were also badly worn, whereas Watson's tyres were still in good order. At the end of the fifth lap the Darracqs of George and Guinness still led. George now had a lead of 4min 50sec over Watson and was catching him up on the road. A lap later the gap between the Darracq and the Hutton had opened up to over seven minutes and it seemed unlikely that Watson was going to make any impression on George, but he had done the sixth lap a minute quicker than Guinness.

On lap seven Watson again won back a minute from Guinness and moved up to second place. George, too, had lost time when he stopped at Ramsey to change all four wheels. Watson was now flying, and on his eighth lap he went round the course only 12 seconds slower than George, whose lead was now only 2min 2sec. The tension rose as the cars set off on their last lap. The crowd waited at the finish. It was announced that the Hutton had passed the Bungalow, four miles from the finish. Then a cheer went up as Watson completed the course and pulled off into the

William Watson, on his winning Tourist Trophy drive, takes the Ramsey hairpin in front of Guinness's Darracq, which finished second. (Motor)

Watson in the victorious Hutton. This was probably one of the first times that a radiator stoneguard was used. (Derek Grossmark)

club enclosure. The crowd now waited for George, but the seconds and then the minutes ticked by and the Darracq did not appear. It was realised that Watson was the winner and the crowd gathered round to offer congratulations. Only then did George come down the road, having lost six minutes at Glen Helen when he had stopped to put out a carburettor fire. Watson's time was 6hr 43min 5sec, giving an average speed of 50.3mph (80.93kmh). Guinness was second, 2min 16sec behind, and George was third, 5min 31sec behind the Hutton. If his carburettor had not ignited the finish would have been close.

That evening the prizes were presented in the Palace Hotel in Douglas, Watson receiving the Tourist Trophy from Lord Raglan, Lieutenant-Governor of the Isle of Man. All the forecasts of bloodshed had been unfounded. In the most serious accident a mechanic had received slight concussion; two spectators had been hit by some bits of a crashing car, but were unhurt, and some children had been shaken when they fell off a wall as a car hit it. After the race the outcry against motor racing vanished as quickly as it had appeared.

The Hutton story had a finale as puzzling as the rest of the saga. At the end of October, Hutton informed the motoring press that he had decided to relinquish trading on his own account and would not take over the contract with the Hutton car, with which he did not intend to be identified any longer. He was taking up an offer to join the Wolseley Tool and Motor Car Co Ltd. *The Motor* assumed that the contract would then be cancelled and the Hutton would be sold as the 26hp Napier. This appears, indeed, to have been the outcome, as a four-cylinder 26hp Napier was advertised in 1909 and factory records show that eight T27s, now presumably called Napiers, with chassis numbers from 8003 to 8010, were delivered to customers during 1909. It seems that the only Hutton T27s were the three which competed in the Tourist Trophy.

On 23 September, the day before the Tourist Trophy, a letter appeared in *The Times* which marked a major turning point in the story of Napier competition motoring:

Sir,

The views which have been so well expressed in your columns with regard to dangerous motor racing have interested and impressed me greatly.

I feel you will realise the question is a very serious one for the manufacturer. There can be no doubt the rapid development of the automobile has in the past been very largely due to racing and the public undoubtedly then took a great interest in it; but your recent utterances have developed the fact there is now an immense volume of feeling against dangerous racing and that there is a general idea that the automobile is developed and established so sufficiently that racing demonstrations of an extreme kind are no longer necessary.

As one who has been responsible for most of the racing in this country, I think it may perhaps be my duty in deference to public feeling to be the first manufacturer to publicly announce my intention of withdrawing Napier cars from all dangerous competition.

In making this announcement, I hope the public will accept my assurance that my sole object in automobile racing in the past was to demonstrate the ability of a British manufacturer to hold his own in this high type of engineering against any one in this world, notwithstanding the long start our faulty legislation gave our foreign competitors in this great industry.

I feel that object has now been achieved and that the British motor car now leads in type, design and workmanship.

As I have said, this matter is a serious one for the manufacturer; and it is possible that abstention from racing contests may, as some think, react on my firm. I must therefore qualify this declaration of my withdrawal from abnormal contests by claiming liberty to lead the way again if I have mistaken the trend of public feeling.

I would add that my decision in relation to racing will involve no relaxation in every possible scientific effort towards the refinement and development of the British motor car.

Yours truly

S.F. Edge
14 New Burlington St, London W.
September 22nd 1908.

Reaction to Edge's proclamation was remarkably subdued. It is evident that no one believed him, as he had written an escape clause in the penultimate paragraph of the letter. 'Oh dear, Edge is up to his old tricks again'. It was reported in *The Autocar* and *The Motor* as a single paragraph news item. There was no other comment and no editorial views were expressed on a matter which surely would have aroused considerable interest in the light of the uproar preceding the 'Four-Inch' race.

The motives behind the decision to withdraw from motor racing must have been complex. Edge and Montague Napier were sensitive to the campaign against motor racing led by *The Times* and realised that to be associated too closely with the sport could alienate a substantial part of their clientele. They knew the likely effect of a serious accident in the Tourist Trophy, so the timing of Edge's letter must have been deliberate. They were already looking over their shoulders at Rolls-Royce, which was steadily chipping away at the top end of the Napier market and was doing so without any serious competition programme and no racing at all. Edge had realised too what many other firms were to find in the years ahead: to climb to the motor racing pinnacle is one thing – the successes will bring customers – but the advantages are only short-term. A firm then has to go on winning, and any defeat gets excessive adverse publicity. Napier was now in that position and the opposition was getting stronger. Motor racing was expensive, and the bills which were being met and presumably shared between Edge and the Napier company would have been an appreciable part of their annual budgets. In addition there was an appreciable slump in the motor industry in 1908, so to be relieved of the cost of racing would probably have been acceptable to both Edge and Napier.

To have admitted all these points in the argument would have been alien to Edge's nature and it was in keeping with the man that the adoption of a high moral tone would have been seen as the most suitable way out. There was another factor which may also have forced the decision. Cecil Edge had been a key figure in Napier competition activities until he became ill during 1907. Once he was no longer active, it is possible to detect a decline. Without his late cousin's help it was becoming very difficult for Selwyn Edge to maintain the racing activities and conduct the complex affairs of S.F. Edge (1907) Ltd and his other business enterprises. On a personal note, it is possible, too, that without Cecil, Selwyn Edge no longer found motor racing enjoyable.

The motoring world waited, expecting that within a few weeks the withdrawal would prove to be qualified, but nothing happened, and gradually it was realised that Edge had meant what he said. The last entry that Edge had made, apart from Watson's entry in the Isle of Man, was at the Yorkshire Car Club Greenhow hill-climb at Pateley Bridge, where Cundy made fastest time with a T21 on 12 September. When the entries were published for the Autumn Brooklands meeting on Saturday 3 October there were no Napiers in the list. Meanwhile, Edge announced, almost defiantly in the face of the slump, that Napier sales for the year ending on 1 October 1908 showed an increase of 29.5 per cent over the previous year, though the mere percentage without production figures meant little.

Although racing had stopped, there was still activity with Napier racing cars. Newton brought 'Samson ' to Brooklands on Friday 30 October to take the 90hp local records. It was a clear, dry day and he covered the flying half mile on the Railway Straight at 114.98mph (185.00kmh) and went on to take the ten-lap or 'Long' record at an average of 102.21mph (164.45kmh). The 60hp local records which Newton had previously held were taken by a 1908 GP Brasier on the same day, driven by the French driver Paul Bablot who had been brought to England specially for the task by Clement Hobson, the Brasier importer. This must have rankled, so Newton was back at the track again on Wednesday 4 November. As an indication of changing times, despite all his efforts with the T21 Newton failed to retake the 60hp records. He made several attempts and his best runs over the half mile were at 107mph (172kmh); but Bablot's record of 108.34mph (174.31kmh) remained intact. 'Samson' was then brought out, and once again Newton failed to improve on his 90hp records. For these attempts the two Napiers were running on Kempshall tyres, a new make with treads which extended down the side walls. It is likely that the rolling resistance of the Kempshalls was greater than the Palmer Cords normally used, so perhaps the failure was the fault of the tyres and not the cars.

Edge's critics tried to discomfit him by saying that the continued record activity was evidence that the retirement was illusory. He refuted this by pointing out that the cars had been entered for the record runs by an 'A. Brown' with whom he had no connection, a point confirmed by the BARC, although the identity of the mysterious Mr Brown has never been established. On Wednesday 18 November, while the Motor Show was in full swing at Olympia, Newton came to Brooklands for the last time as a competition driver, to make another attempt to improve on his 90hp short record with 'Samson'. The car came out at noon and bystanders were surprised that Newton had elected to make the run over the flying half mile in the clockwise direction of the track so he would approach the distance from the Byfleet Banking. Newton explained that there was a south-west wind which would be a head wind in the normal direction. The Napier was estimated to be touching 130mph (210kmh) along the Byfleet Banking, but it gave a lurch as it left the banking. Newton held it, although there was a slight stammer from the engine as the carburation was affected. Despite this 'Samson' covered the half-mile at 119.34mph (192.01kmh).

After the record run Newton announced that he was giving up motor racing as he was to be married shortly. Following an engineering apprenticeship, he had gone to the Klondike to seek his fortune in the Gold Rush of the 1890s. He returned to England penniless and worked for the MMC (later the Motor Manufacturing Company) until he joined Napiers in 1904. After his racing retirement, he set up his own motor business in Northampton. Montague Napier backed the business, taking a £5,000 debenture in Newton's new company and matching Newton's capital with a similar sum. Newton disposed of the company in the 1920s, after which he was the Chief Engineer of the Automobile Association for many years. He died on 8 January 1961, aged 86.

The Napier team was now dispersed. The T20s and T21s were sold privately to enthusiastic owners and some would appear again. For 'Samson', though, it was a different story. Edge advertised it for £800 but it seems there were no serious enquiries. The car mouldered at Acton for some time and eventually the engine was removed. This was displayed for many years in the works foyer, but the rest of the car was dismantled, 'Sammy' Davis – the Sports Editor of *The Autocar* – reporting that he had seen pieces of it on the factory scrap-heap, a sad and ignoble end to a fine machine. The smaller engine was sold by Edge to an Australian, who used it with great success in a racing motor boat. In the 1970s this engine became the basis of a re-created 'Samson' constructed by Australian Bob Chamberlain.

The great racing years of Napier had ended. The final season had had its share of triumphs and setbacks, but at the end of 1908 Napier was still indisputably one of the great British marques, rivalled only, perhaps, by Rolls-Royce. The bitter rivalry between these two firms was to take many forms over the coming years.

Chapter 10: 1909–14

Decline and Divorce

AS an indication that the retirement from racing had not affected the company Napiers announced in February 1909 that they now had 1,200 employees, who were working day and night shifts with some Sunday shifts as well. Also in February came the news from Australia that a T21 had broken the Melbourne to Adelaide record, covering the distance in 22hr 24min. This record did not last long, though, as within a month a 35hp Talbot had reduced it by over two hours.

Edge's advertisements now included a Grand Prix model at £1,500 in the 1909 range, and at least two of these had been sold. At the opening Brooklands meeting on Easter Monday, 12 April, one of the GP cars was entered by A. Baker White for the Easter Senior Handicap. This was a two-lap race and the Napier was starting from scratch. Unfortunately, however, Baker White was riding a JAP motor cycle in an earlier race and fell off at the Fork. Despite being cut badly he still wanted to race the GP car, but after friends had persuaded him to withdraw he handed the car over to his mechanic, L. White. It was a cold, showery day and the track was wet. White started from the scratch mark with Tate's 60hp Mercedes and a GP Brasier. He led the Mercedes for a lap but it then went ahead and won; a De Dion was second and the Napier was third. Perhaps because of his inexperience, White braked too hard on the wet track after the finish and spun, but came to a stop without mishap.

Brooklands and police pressure had made considerable inroads into the sprint and hill-climb calendar. The fear of prosecution in some areas also meant that very little was disclosed about some events. The Manchester Motor Club held a hill-climb 'on the Cheshire–Yorkshire border' on Saturday 1 May. A fall of snow during the event cannot have given much encouragement, but a T20 40hp driven by Wilfred Stone won its class on formula. The weather had improved for the two-day Brooklands Whitsun meeting. On Saturday 29 May, in the two-lap second Naval & Military Cup, for serving officers, the ex-team T20 'St George' appeared, driven by Sir George Abercromby Bt, a lieutenant in the Scots Guards. 'St George' was now registered LB 9277 and the chassis frame had been lightened with lattice cutting, similar to the GP car. Abercromby started from scratch and finished third. Baker White, now recovered, ran the GP car in the four-lap May Senior Handicap, in which it received an eight second start, while Abercromby in 'St George' had a one minute allowance. Neither was placed and Baker White stopped before the finish when what press reports described as 'an ignition ball joint' fell off.

On Whit Monday, Stirling brought out his Hutton 'Dolly Varden' for the four-lap Four-Inch event. It was a scratch race and Stirling was unable to keep up with Stocks's De Dion, but came second, even though he was nearly the length of the Finishing Straight behind at the end. Abercromby ran in the four-lap Whitsun Senior Private Competitors' Handicap. He started from the minute mark, but when passed by the scratch Mercedes he stayed with it and finished third. Baker White was entered for this race but it was reported that the GP car had been driven away from the track before the race. The meeting ended with a two-lap team race and Abercromby, teamed with a Nagant-Hobson, was the winner.

The Nottinghamshire Automobile Club's Clipstone sprint was still one of the major events of the year, and being on private land was unmolested when it was held on Saturday 12 June. Baker White ran a car described as a 60hp. By now he had also bought the 60hp 'Mercury', so it is not known if he ran this or the GP, but it was fast enough for him to win the flying kilometre scratch class at 80.04mph (128.78kmh). Baker White must have been a welcome customer for Selwyn Edge, for now he also owned the 8-inch stroke Hutton. This was entered for the Brooklands meeting on Wednesday 30 June but it was a non-starter.

The machine shop and drawing office at Acton, c1907. (Guy Griffiths Collection)

It is an interesting sidelight on the social attitudes of the time that the BARC was confident that a mid-week meeting would attract sufficient spectators and competitors. Baker White had entered Cundy in the GP car in the 10-mile (16km) Grand Prix Sweepstake, which attracted only three starters. The Napier led from the start but was then passed by Stirling's Brasier, which was 18 seconds ahead at the end of the first lap. The Brasier then stopped with a broken petrol pipe, so Cundy went on to win, easing off at the finish to lead a Weigel home by 3.8 seconds, having averaged 72.5mph (116.65kmh). The main event of the day was the Montagu Cup Handicap, and a second GP car was entered in this, driven by H.J.D. Astley. The handicap did not favour the back markers and the winning Bianchi was uncatchable, but Astley chased and passed a Daimler driven by Sir Everard Pauncefort-Duncombe to take second place.

On Thursday 7 July, a few days after the Whitsun meeting, two Oxford undergraduates, Wigglesworth and Wright, appeared at Brooklands with the old K5 Napier that Hargreaves had driven in the 1905 Gordon Bennett Trials. They took the car round the track for several laps then pulled into the Finishing Straight. However, they misjudged the distance to the end of the straight and the car went up the Members' Banking and over the top. The pair were thrown clear and knocked unconscious, but escaped with severe concussion. The car was bent round a tree and had to be cut up before it could be removed.

On Thursday 29 July the 8-inch stroke Hutton was at Brooklands, where it made a successful attempt on the local 26hp half-mile record. Baker White had nominated W.E. de B. Whittaker as the driver, and the speed attained was 84.58mph (136.08kmh). Like Newton the previous autumn, Whittaker went the 'wrong' way round the track to get the advantage of a following wind. Like Newton too, he found that this gave him a difficult drive, and it was tricky getting the Hutton off the Byfleet Banking in the right position.

The August Bank Holiday Brooklands meeting was another two-day event. Saturday 31 July was fine but windy and began with heats for a two-mile (3.2km) sprint race. Abercromby ran 'St George', Astley had the GP car, and Baker White entered 'Mercury', which was only made ready the day before the meeting after an engine rebuild with a new crankshaft. Abercromby, starting with an eight second advantage, won his heat, while Astley and Baker White were third and fourth, but none of the trio was placed in the final. In the July Senior Private Competitors' Handicap, Abercromby had a nine second start and was catching Thompson's Austin on the run to the finish when an accumulator wire came adrift, but he was nevertheless able to cross the line in second place.

Monday 2 August was another fine day. To the surprise of the press the crowd was bigger than on the Saturday, though the increase was understandable. Most people then worked a six-day week. A day off on a Saturday was a luxury, but a Bank Holiday was a universal day of leisure. Brooklands on a fine day was a pleasant place and easily reached from London by train.

The August Senior Handicap was run in heats and a final, each race being run over three laps. Baker White was on scratch with 'Mercury' in the first heat, but the handicap was too much and after going well for a lap the car pulled up with a bad misfire, a wire having become detached from the distributor. The second heat found Abercromby on the 40 second mark with 'St George'. He went well and won by 300 yards (275m) at an average speed of 84mph (135kmh). However, in the final 'St. George' had to give best to Thompson's Austin again, but came a good second.

The Second Grand Prix Race, restricted to cars built for the 1908 Grand Prix, was over three and a half laps, and had a mere three runners. Baker White had not entered his GP car and sought to put in 'Mercury', which was eligible on engine size and, it could perhaps be argued, had a GP engine. The car was rejected, however, as it did not comply with the strict regulations. The press suggested that the real reason for its exclusion was that it would have been too fast for the genuine Grand Prix entrants. At the start Loder's Itala led, with Astley in close attendance. The Itala then pulled up and Astley went on to win. The only other runner was a Weigel driven by Whittaker which was not up to the pace. In this short race the Napier had pulled out the remarkable lead of almost a lap, averaging 86.25mph (138.77kmh).

After his Tourist Trophy victory Watson had sold the Hutton 'Little Dorrit', now bearing the registration number LB 6327, to Emmanuel Hoyle, a Huddersfield industrialist. Hoyle entered the car, with W. Bradwell as driver, in the Yorkshire Automobile Club hill-climb at Pateley Bridge, about 12 miles (19km) west of Ripon, on Saturday 25 September. It rained all day and *The Autocar* correspondent said the scene looking down from the top of the hill was reminiscent of 'Gustave Doré's pictures of the nether regions'. To add to the discomfort of the competitors, the Pateley Bridge cattle fair was being held on the same day and cars had to wait while sheep, cattle, and farm carts were driven by. Bradwell was perhaps less daunted by the conditions than others, as he set fastest time in the open class for both trade and amateurs, recording 85.8 seconds. Then in the closed class, restricted to amateurs, he went better still and set the fastest time of the day at 84 seconds. This was almost the end of the hill-climb season, the last major climb of the year being held on Saturday 2 October by the Wolverhampton & District Automobile Club at Harley Bank, on Wenlock Edge in Shropshire. Only one Napier ran, a two-seat T21 driven by W. Evans, which won its class

After the August Bank Holiday meeting there was no racing at

Brooklands until the beginning of October. The BARC realised that the fashionable membership were 'out of Town' during August and September. The track was still busy, though, with testing and some record attempts. On Wednesday 22 September, Whittaker brought out the Hutton again and pushed up his half-mile 26hp record to 87.99mph (141.57kmh). The circuit's closing meeting of the year was on Wednesday 6 October. In the October Senior Handicap over four laps, Baker White was on scratch with 'Mercury' while Whittaker with the Hutton was in the middle of the field. Neither was placed, but Whittaker did two laps at 84.66mph (136.21kmh). The Hutton had a water leak and it was reported that as a safeguard extra oil was added to the sump.

In the Second Sprint Race over two miles, Astley with his GP was a non-starter. The Hutton had a seven-second start from the scratch Itala and made a slow getaway. It was reported that the drag of the extra oil was slowing it down, but despite this it came third. Baker White was unplaced with 'Mercury'. The Hutton found its speed again in the Four-Inch Handicap, finishing third.

On Wednesday 13 October the Hutton was back at Brooklands again, as Whittaker was to attempt the ten-lap 26hp local record. He set off at a fast pace and his times were well inside the existing record, but after seven laps he stopped as a big-end had run. H.C. Lafone, in his gossip column in *The Autocar* entitled 'On the Track', confidently predicted that Whittaker would return in a few days with repaired big-ends to take the record. This never happened, though, as shortly afterwards Baker White sold the 8-inch Hutton to Emmanuel Hoyle, who now had a pair of these useful competition cars.

Times were changing rapidly in the competition motoring world. The handful of Napiers which were still competing were becoming outclassed by newer designs which were smaller and more lively. The new models which still emerged from Acton had few pretensions for competition. The two-cylinder 10hp T29 and the four-cylinder 15hp, which had a multitude of type numbers, were both intended for a prosperous middle class which had no interest in motoring competition and felt that motor racing was a dangerous sport. The company was still making the T21 60hp and the T24 65hp, but a young man with sporting aspirations would now go to Talbot, Sunbeam, or Vauxhall if he wanted a car to use in sprints, hill-climbs, or the occasional race at Brooklands.

It was sign of these changing times that only one Napier was entered for the 1910 Brooklands Easter meeting. This was a T21 to be driven by G.C. Colmore, but it was a non-starter. The Napier exponents of 1909 had deserted to other makes or retired. Baker White and Astley had disappeared from the sport while Abercromby was now racing a 90hp Fiat.

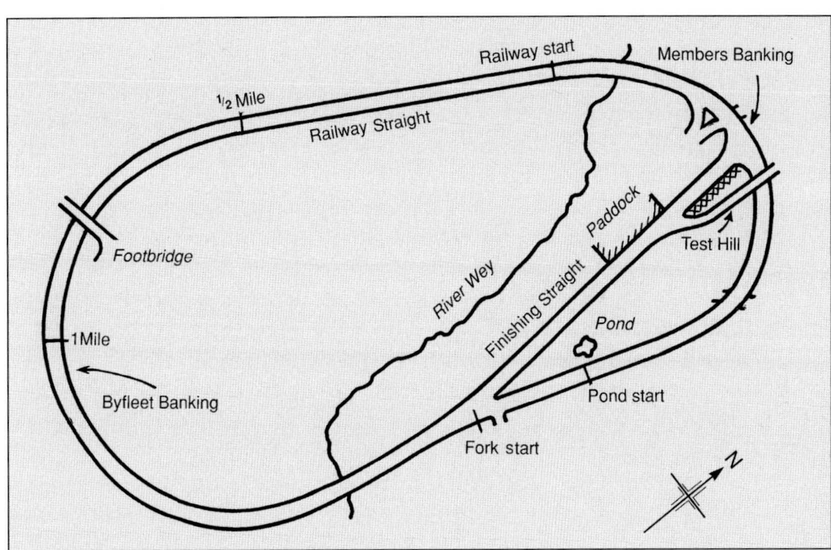

Brooklands. At a line 50ft (15.2m) from its inside edge the Outer Circuit measured 2.767 miles (4.449km).

A postcard with a hand-drawn illustration sent to Newton by A. L. Johns in February 1908. Dunlops may not have appreciated the joke! (Guy Griffiths Collection)

Strangely, the racing Napiers disappeared too. The cars must have been sold but the new owners did not race them. Even the GP cars which were newer and more advanced than the old T21 variants did not come out again.

One competition car still remained at Acton. This was a special car which in the 1960s was owned by the motoring writer Ronald Barker. He discussed the car with a then-elderly Henry Tryon, who said it had been built for the 1908 *Daily Graphic* Trophy on the Isle of Man, an extended sprint for larger cars. However, it had not competed as the event had been cancelled for lack of entries, everyone being more interested in the Four-Inch TT. This car had a T21-type chassis but with straight semi-elliptic springs at the rear, not supplemented by the usual transverse spring – known as the 'platform' spring – of the standard car. The engine had standard 65hp T24 5-inch (127mm) cylinder blocks, but a 6-inch (152.4mm) stroke crankshaft, so the capacity was 11,580cc. The chassis number was 5127. The car was bought, probably early in 1910, by Christopher Bird, who lived in Birmingham, the younger son of Alfred Bird, the MP for Wolverhampton West who had made his fortune as a manufacturing chemist. It was fitted with a four-seat body, but the rear section was detachable so it could be converted to a two-seater for competitions.

Bird's first outing with the car was on Saturday 7 May when he took it to the Sutton Coldfield Automobile Club hill-climb at Coalport, on the south bank of the River Severn at Ironbridge in Shropshire. This was a small event and Bird had little difficulty in setting fastest time with a climb of 67.8 seconds. King Edward VII had died the previous evening, just before midnight, and as a mark of respect all sporting events were cancelled or postponed while the country was in mourning. However, the news seems not to have reached Coalport in time to call a halt.

The Brooklands Whit Monday meeting on 16 May was postponed, but the Royal mourning did not stop an RAC trial at Brooklands of a 30hp T26 on Wednesday 11 May. Manufacturers submitted cars to the RAC for officially supervised and measured trials and a certificate of performance was issued, declaring what had been achieved. A certificate of good performance was useful and incontrovertible advertising material. The RAC Trials were held monthly and the T26 began with a 105 mile (169km) road test when a consumption of 19.95 miles per gallon (14.2 litres per 100km) was recorded. The car was then taken round Brooklands for several laps at an average speed of 52.90mph (85.11kmh) and the fuel consumption during the track test was recorded at 11.06 miles per gallon (25.6 litres per 100km). The car was also weighed, scaling 3,635lb (1,652kg), and the frontal area was measured at 19.6sq ft (1.82m^2). The driver is not known, though he was presumably one of the Acton testers (the RAC certificate was an anonymous document). At the end of the year this performance received further recognition by the award of an RAC gold medal for the best performance recorded during the 1910 monthly trials.

On Saturday 28 May the postponed Whitsun Meeting was held at Brooklands. Stirling had sold 'Dolly Varden' and this was run by C.L.E. Geach in the first heat of the two-mile (3.2km) Whitsun Handicap sprint. Geach was second, but was unplaced in the final. At the next Brooklands meeting three weeks later, on Saturday 18 June, Bird made his racing debut with the T21/24 special. He ran in the Brooklands Allcomers' Plate. In Brooklands terms this was a comparatively long race over seven laps. All the runners started from the 62 second mark except the scratch Fiat of Abercromby. Bird went well and at the finish was third behind Young's GP Itala and Stirling's GP Brasier. The performance of the Napier was noted by the handicappers, and Bird started from scratch in the three lap June Handicap. This was a bit too much for him and he was unplaced. The last race of the day was the two-mile June Sprint in which Bird, starting from the three second mark, retired.

The sprint season was now under way, though the calendar of events was somewhat sparse. On Saturday 11 June the South Wales & Monmouthshire Automobile Club held a hill-climb at Buttrill's Hill, Barry, near Cardiff. This was a 500-yard (457m) course and attracted some of the leading competitors. One of the class winners was Mrs W.G. Morel with a T26. Women competitors were still unusual and Dorothy Levitt had disappeared from the lists with Edge's withdrawal from racing; it is not known what subsequently became of her, it is believed that she may have taken up dog breeding, but the Kennel Club has no record of her name. The Yorkshire Automobile Club's Saltburn meeting on Saturday 25 June was one of the major events of the season. The day began at 8.30am to allow for the tides, and one of the runners was Emmanuel Hoyle who, unusually, drove one of the Huttons himself. The Hutton was beaten into second place in its class by one of the 25hp Talbots which were now becoming a powerful force in sprints and hill-climbs.

Shelsley Walsh was already one of the most important hill-climbs in the country and Bird was at the Midland Automobile Club meeting on Saturday 2 July. The Napier was fitted with the two seats at the rear and Bird was accompanied on the hill by three brave passengers. Going onto the Esses on one of his runs, it was reported that he 'skidded bodily about 4ft'. On his fastest run he recorded 77.6 seconds, which was third fastest of the day, but the run was slightly spoiled by a misfire caused by fuel starvation at the Esses. Two weeks later he took the

Christopher Bird setting fastest time of the day at Sutton Park with his T21/24, 16 July 1910. (Guy Griffiths Collection)

T21/24 Napier to the Sutton Coldfield Automobile Club sprint at Sutton Park. The one-mile course (1.6km) was rough and poorly surfaced, but Bird set the best time of the day, recording 64 seconds from a standing start. It is slightly puzzling that at Sutton Park, Bird's car was recorded as having dimensions of 127mm x 127mm, the size of a standard 65hp T24.

On 7 July another Napier was submitted to the RAC for a trial by S.F. Edge (1907) Ltd. This time it was a four-seat touring-bodied 60hp T21 and it was going to be a much greater test. The car was driven from London to Edinburgh and back again using only top gear, including starts from rest. The top gear ratio was 2.7:1. No work or adjustments were done to the car during the trial, in which it averaged 20.2mph (32.5kmh), and the fuel consumption was 19.35 miles per gallon (14.6 litres per 100km). The car was weighed before the run and was 4,105lb (1,866kg) unladen. The axle weight distribution was 2,090lb front and 2,015lb rear (950/916kg), and the load carried during the trial was 832lb (374kg). The trial finished at Brooklands on 12 July, where the T21 covered a flying half mile at 76.04mph (122.34kmh). At the end of the year this remarkable feat was recognised by the RAC, which awarded the Dewar Challenge Trophy to Selwyn Edge for the most meritorious performance during the year in certified trials held by the Club. This must have given great satisfaction to Edge, as this performance would have had much appeal for the type of customer that Napier was now pursuing.

Although the T21 made a great impression, Napier feats at Brooklands were becoming fewer. At the August Bank Holiday meeting there was no Napier or Hutton participation. Christopher Bird was still active on the hills, though, and he set fastest time in the Wolverhampton & District Automobile Club meeting at Coalport on Saturday 10 September. For this event he had only two seats and one passenger. *The Autocar* commented that 'the big Napier induced a decided thrill among the onlookers'. It was a family occasion, as Alfred Bird MP, the chairman of the organising club, announced the winners and presented the prizes. A week later the 8-inch Hutton, now with the registration number LD 8768, was entered by Hoyle for the Yorkshire Automobile Club Pateley Bridge hill-climb. As a contrast to 1909, the day was dry and sunny and W. Bradwell, who was driving again, had a successful afternoon, winning the silver cup for fastest time and also winning his class on formula.

Bird was back at Brooklands for the closing meeting on Wednesday 5 October. It was a grey day but the expected rain kept off. Bird ran in the three-lap Second 100mph Handicap and came sixth. He was out again for the last event of the day, the October Sprint, where he was joined by Bradwell driving one of the Hoyle Huttons. Bradwell, with a 14-second start, managed to come second in the two-mile dash, while Bird was eighth.

The opening Brooklands meeting in 1911 had no Napier entries, but Bird was there for the Easter Monday meeting on 17 April. He ran the T21/24 special in a match race over two laps with Louis Coatalen's 16hp, 3,217cc Sunbeam. The Napier was well beaten, finishing nearly half a mile behind, and it was an indication of how the new generation of competition cars did not need huge engines to get high performance. Bird also ran in the two-lap Easter Private Competitors' handicap. He started from the 12 second mark and battled all the way with Lacon's 80hp Mercedes. The Napier finished third, just leading the Mercedes across the line by inches. He finished the day by taking third place in the two-mile (3.2km) Easter Sprint. When Bird drove back into the Paddock after the race another chapter of Napier history was finished, as no Napier was to compete at Brooklands again before the 1914–18 war.

During the season the RAC held a 279 mile (449km) race for 16hp production cars at Brooklands. In earlier years this would certainly have been an event which would have attracted Edge, but there were no Napiers among the 24 starters. In June the Austrian Alpine Trial attracted over 100 entries for an event which was adjudged to be one of the toughest tests of touring cars yet, and once more no Napiers joined in. Even the sprint and hill-climb entries were now few. Bird ran once more at Coalport on Saturday 20 May in the Sutton Coldfield Automobile Club event and made fastest time. At Shelsley Walsh on Saturday 10 June he was second fastest, once again skidding luridly with opposite lock in the Esses and setting a time of 66.4 seconds. The fastest time was recorded by Holder's Daimler in 63.4 seconds.

Bradwell was out again at Pateley Bridge on Friday 25 September, this time in bright sunshine. He used 'Little Dorrit', but as the opposition was getting stronger and the age of the Hutton was beginning to tell he was unplaced. Bird was still in winning form, though, and in the last hill-climb of the season, the Leicestershire Automobile Club Beacon Hill event, he won the unlimited class in 65.4 seconds, and then on a second run made fastest time of the day in 64.6 seconds.

1912 saw only two recorded Napier successes. On Saturday 11 May, Emmanuel Hoyle drove one of the Huttons himself at the Lancashire and Manchester Automobile Club's combined hill-climb at Rivington Pike. For this event the car was entered as a 26hp Napier and proved itself to be still competitive, making the best time on formula in the closed classes. On 18 July Mrs Morel was in action again at the Caerphilly hill-climb, held as part of a double event with the Porthcawl speed trials by the South Wales Automobile Club and Cardiff Motor Club. She took a third place in her class and so gained what appears to be the last recorded Napier competition success before the outbreak of World War One. Two weeks after the Caerphilly event, Bird ran a Coupe de L'Auto Sunbeam at the Leicestershire Automobile Club Beacon Hill event, having realised that his Napier was no longer going to be competitive.

While the competitive decline of Napier continued, the relations between Selwyn Edge and Montague Napier had been deteriorating. The breach had been growing for some time and had been exacerbated by the increasing difficulties of selling luxury cars. Rolls-Royce had become a real threat to Napier in this profitable market. The Rolls-Royce 40/50 – the famous Silver Ghost – had also done an RAC London–Edinburgh top gear trial run early in 1911 and had improved on the Napier figures, recording 24.32 miles per gallon (11.6 litres per 100km) and covering the Brooklands half-mile at 78.26mph (125.92kmh). The Rolls-Royce was a better-looking car with more balanced proportions. Probably more important, Napier had never found a proper solution to the inherent vibration problem of a six-cylinder engine. Edge told customers that it was a 'power rattle' but it was not a desirable feature for a luxury car. Rolls-Royce, however, had solved the problem, and their sales continued to rise at Napiers' expense.

Montague Napier was incensed that while Napiers were now having a commercial struggle and profits were falling, the profits of S.F. Edge (1907) Ltd were still rising, despite the sale of fewer cars. The Edge company was showing a gross profit of 22 per cent on each sale, greatly in excess of that received by Napiers. Montague Napier wanted to expand the company's commercial vehicle market. These were already being built at Acton and he felt the growth was being restricted by the need to put all sales through the Edge company. Napier had resigned from the board of S.F. Edge (1907) Ltd during 1909, but Napiers had been buying shares in the Edge company and by 1910 held 110,000 of the ordinary shares. With the strength of this holding a new agreement was negotiated between the Napier and Edge companies during 1910. This permitted the Napier company to sell all types of commercial vehicle from the autumn of 1911, although the exclusive right to market cars still remained with the Edge company.

For his part, Edge was now unhappy about the situation within Napiers. He wrote in *My Motoring Reminiscences*:

> I saw that his [Montague Napier's] interest in Napier cars was beginning to wane; there was not the old enthusiasm, there was a certain air of indifference as regards the class of work which left his factory. Trivial complaints which I made occasionally and which were formerly taken up with the utmost energy were allowed to pass almost unnoticed. His

> thoughts wandered towards the financial side of his business to too great an extent, for he did not seem to realise that increased trading profits could only result from perfection of detail. His chief interest seem to pass from the drawing office to his own bank pass-book, which was never the case in the early days.

Montague Napier was also unhappy, and the profits being made by the Edge company continued to rankle with him. He felt that with the difficult market conditions, the Edge company should agree voluntarily to reduce its profit on each car sold. It was not possible to reach any compromise, so Napiers decided that the obduracy of the Edge company constituted a release from the 1907 agreement and started selling cars on its own account. This aroused the ire of Selwyn Edge and early in 1912 his company began proceedings in the High Court, applying for an injunction restraining Napiers from a breach of the 1907 agreement.

Wisely, the parties to the action soon appreciated that litigation would damage both companies and play into the hands of their commercial rivals. Terms were negotiated during the spring and early summer of 1912. A new public company was registered under the name of D. Napier & Son Ltd which acquired all the assets of the existing private Napier company. The share capital was £650,000, comprising £300,000 7½ per cent cumulative preference shares and £350,000 ordinary shares, with authority to issue £100,000 5½ per cent first mortgage debenture stock. Montague Napier took a personal holding of 98 per cent of the ordinary shares. The new company bought Selwyn Edge's share holding in S.F. Edge (1907) Ltd, for which it paid in excess of £160,000, and the Edge company went into voluntary liquidation on 30 September 1912. As one of the terms for the sale of his shares, Selwyn Edge agreed to leave the motor industry for a period of seven years.

So, on sad and acrimonious terms, a remarkable partnership which had achieved astonishing feats came to an end. Edge retreated into rural Sussex to start intensive pig-farming

The 30–35hp T44 pauses in the Stelvio Pass during the RAC-observed trial in September 1913, while a 1hp vehicle makes way. (Derek Grossmark)

and Montague Napier took stock of his new company. The principal need was for new designs. Thomas Barrington had left Napiers in 1911 and had joined Rolls-Royce. His post was not filled, and for two years, there does not seem to have been a chief designer at Acton. The problems of the new company were compounded when the workforce went on strike between 22 August and 20 October 1913, seeking better pay and working conditions.

The situation of Napiers was serious, and there must have been doubts in the minds of Montague Napier and his co-directors that the company would survive; there were uncomfortable parallels with the problems of James Napier at Vine Street. It is possible that a return to competitions was contemplated as a means of generating publicity. The success of Rolls-Royce in the Austrian Alpine Trials must have rankled and several RAC-observed runs took place including a London–Edinburgh–London top gear trial. Most highly publicised was an extended Alpine tour in September 1913, which was clearly intended to show that anything Rolls-Royce could do, a Napier could do equally well. The run began at the RAC in Pall Mall at 6.00am on Saturday 13 September. The car, a 30–35hp T 44 (chassis number 11625) went via Paris to Milan, crossing the Mont Cenis pass. Six Italian Alpine passes were then surmounted and the car returned over the Simplon Pass, through Geneva to Dieppe, and thence to London on 27 September. The distance covered was 2,106 miles (3,388km) and the RAC report noted that the only work needed was the tightening of a petrol tank holding bolt on the last day, which took 2min 8sec. The average speed was 20.3mph (32.5kmh) and the fuel consumption was 18.09 miles per gallon (15.6 litres per 100km). After the run the car covered a flying half mile at Brooklands at 62.61mph (100.73kmh).

In November 1913, Arthur Rowledge rejoined the company and work was put in hand for a complete redesign of the Napier range of cars. There were to be three basic engine designs – two four-cylinder engines of 16hp and 20hp and a six-cylinder of 30–35hp. The small cars at the bottom of the range and the large cars at the top were to go. It was intended to launch the new range in the autumn of 1914. The cars went into production, but the majority were bought for military use. How the new range would have been received by the motoring public will never be known, but events were about to unfold which would not only save Napiers but would launch the company into a completely new and unexpected field.

Chapter 11: 1914–26

Enter the Lion

WITH the outbreak of World War One on 4 August 1914, the comfortable Edwardian world in which the Napier motor car had grown and flourished departed forever. Montague Napier and his board of directors anticipated that the War would be a complete disaster for Napiers; the new range of cars could not be launched and there seemed little other work in prospect. As it transpired, they could not have been more wrong. The demand for luxury cars diminished immediately, although a number of the new 1914–15 range were sold to the War Office, but the Army needed lorries, and needed a lot of them quickly. Within three weeks of the commencement of hostilities the company had orders for 200 3.5-ton chassis, and by the end of the year further orders had been received for 250 30-cwt chassis. By the end of the War, in November 1918, Napiers had produced almost 2,000 commercial vehicles. However, in August 1914 the directors could not have foreseen that even making lorries would eventually become a mere sideline, and that a completely new product would not only become the company's main wartime output, but would also ensure its survival and moderate prosperity in the difficult post-war years.

In the first month of the conflict, while huge armies still moved about in fluid warfare in Eastern France, it was realised that air power could make an essential contribution to the war effort. By the time both sides had become bogged down in trench warfare – after the end of the Battle of the Marne in September 1914 – the War Office and the Admiralty had begun a search for aero engines of sufficient power to equip the next generation of aircraft already taking shape on the drawing board. It was in September that Napiers began a design study for a 200hp engine, but they were then asked to undertake the production of airframes. To do this, new assembly shops had to be built on land facing the Uxbridge Road, east of the existing works at Acton.

At the outbreak of war Parliament had passed the Defence of the Realm Act, which gave the Government sweeping powers which would not have been out of place in a totalitarian state. One of its provisions empowered the Government to control the supply of machinery and labour to firms. This was followed by the Munitions of War Act 1915, which gave the Ministry of Munitions the power to direct what firms should produce, and took away from them the right to make their own decisions on such matters. On 2 August 1915 the Ministry declared that the Acton factory was a 'controlled' establishment, under the powers contained in the Act, and it was immediately decreed that the production of all vehicles should stop and that the Acton factory should be devoted solely to the production of aero engines.

Vehicle production did eventually start again, but in the meantime Napiers found that the company was to be an 'out-station', manufacturing aero engines from the designs of other establishments under Government direction. Two such designs were imposed upon them. The first was a V-12 air-cooled device, designed by the Royal Aircraft Factory at Farnborough and known as the 3a. This was based on a Renault design and developed about 140hp, but it was inherently unsound, as the rear cylinders of an air-cooled Vee engine had a very hot and uncomfortable time, and the engine was always prone to terminal overheating. The RAF engine was soon followed by the Sunbeam Arab, a V-8, and in a burst of official enthusiasm 3,000 were ordered off the drawing board, and production began before the prototype was tested. The Arab turned out to be a disaster, and Napiers among others had, almost literally, to pick up the pieces.

Montague Napier realised there had to be a better way of doing things, and at the end of 1915, suggested to his Board that Napiers should start work on their own design. The Board, perhaps with reasonable caution, were reluctant to proceed. After all, the firm had remunerative Government contracts which could be fulfilled without any risk, so it seemed foolhardy to go into the expensive and hazardous field of aero engine design when the rewards could be chancy, or perhaps non-existent. A compromise was reached, and Napier agreed to fund the preliminary design studies himself. If these were successful, he would receive a royalty on each engine built. As they were not being asked to put up any money, the War Office and Admiralty were much more enthusiastic, and agreed to make available to Napier all the materials he needed.

Napier turned to Arthur Rowledge, who set to work with a will, and within a few months he produced one of the truly great piston aero engine designs, the Napier Lion. This was a 12-cylinder, laid out in three banks of four to make a broad arrow of 60°, with two overhead camshafts on each cylinder bank. It was a very compact engine, with a bore and stroke of 139.7mm x 130.2mm. and a swept volume of 23,970cc. Thus Rowledge had achieved an 'over-square' design more than 40 years before it became a motoring necessity. Not only was the Lion compact, at 915lb (416kg) it was also light, and in its original form it developed 450hp at 2,000rpm. The compression ratio was quite high, at 5.8:1.

This engine went into production towards the end of 1918, and the first examples were fitted to the Airco (De Haviland) DH 9, though too late to see active service before the Armistice. Even though all military contracts were slashed as soon as the War ended, the Air Ministry recognised the quality of the Lion, and the decision was taken that it should be one of the principal power units for the Royal Air Force. Napier therefore received new production contracts, which meant that the company could look forward to the uncertain post-war period with some assurance that it still had a future.

Montague Napier had been forced to relax his control of the company as his health, which had never been robust, steadily declined. Like his rival engineer-manufacturer, Henry Royce, he took up residence in the South of France, where he lived at the Villa des Cistes, Cannes. He felt that the future of Napier now lay in aero engines and was reluctant to see the company go back into car manufacture, though he accepted that it could be a gradual disengagement over a short period rather than a complete withdrawal.

The Board had rather different views, feeling that post-war Britain would have enough rich buyers to provide a comfortable niche for a new Napier. Rowledge was therefore instructed to evolve a new luxury car, and came up with an overhead camshaft, six-cylinder engine of aluminium construction with a capacity of 6,177cc. This was to go into a chassis which was almost pure Edwardian, and rather let down the excellence of the engine. It may be argued that the kind of customer which Napier was seeking would care very little for the refinements of the chassis; luxury would be the

The Acton factory in 1919. The racing and experimental department was at the top left-hand corner. (Napier Power Heritage Trust)

watchword. However, the T75, which was the basic type number of the new car, seemed to be doomed from the start.

It was intended to lay down an initial batch of 500, but there were production delays, compounded by labour disputes in the factory. Napier had acquired the Cunard Motor & Carriage Co with the intention of marketing the car as a complete vehicle, fitted with Cunard coachwork, but this arrangement had unforeseen repercussions. First, there were numerous labour disputes at Cunard; and secondly, carriage trade customers preferred to stipulate their own coach-builders and went to those manufacturers who catered for this practice. The delays meant that the immediate post-war car boom was missed, and by the time the T75 was marketed a slump was setting in. Only 187 examples of the 40/50, as it became known, were eventually sold before production stopped in 1924.

If Napier still had any motor sporting pretensions, the debacle of the T75 must have killed them. Blamed by Montague Napier for the

Publicity photographs of 1920. The first shows a Lion head being machined, while the other displays the engine's components. (Napier Power Heritage Trust)

car's lack of success, Rowledge resigned in June 1921 and followed Thomas Barrington to Rolls-Royce, where he became Chief of Design and played a key part in the design and development of the Kestrel, the R, and the Merlin. Rowledge has never received the recognition due to him as the man responsible for the initial design of the engine which won the Battle of Britain. He was replaced as Chief Designer at Napiers by George S. Wilkinson, who lacked Rowledge's innovative flair. No masterly designs came from his drawing board, but he was a patient and reliable development engineer, a desirable quality which was to serve Napiers well in the future.

It was a great pity that the T75 was a failure, as the engine deserved a better fate. With proper development it could have become a good sporting unit, possibly comparable with the Speed Six Bentley. As it was, no more cars of any kind were to come from the Acton works. However, the name of Napier was not to die in the motor sporting world and there were great glories yet to come.

Brooklands reopened in 1920, and the pattern of races continued much as it had done before being interrupted in August 1914. The Outer Circuit was the only course in use, and the formula for success was substantial power and a chassis able to take the hammering meted out by the circuit's worn and uneven concrete surface. There seemed to be no place for Napiers. The new T75 had no racing aspirations, and the few survivors of the earlier era were now too slow and too old. However, at the end of the War quantities of surplus aero engines had come on to the market at astonishingly low prices: for as little as £30 (£1,500 in 1990s values) a new 160hp Mercedes could be bought from the Aircraft Disposals Board, while £75 (£3,750) was the price for a new Wolseley Viper. Very soon these engines began to find their way into Edwardian car chassis, and the result of these unlikely marriages were cheap, powerful, and comparatively reliable outer-circuit racing cars.

One of the exponents of this new mongrel breed of racers was Captain Alastair Miller, and it was through his efforts that a Napier found itself racing at Brooklands again, albeit somewhat disguised. Miller was competitions manager of Wolseley Motors Ltd, and there is a story – perhaps apocryphal – that, while at a dinner party, he mentioned to the Prince of Wales (later King Edward VIII) that he was looking for a suitable chassis as the basis of a Brooklands special. The Prince said there was an abandoned 60hp Napier chassis on the Sandringham estate which had previously sported a shooting-brake body, and arranged for this to be given to Miller. Whatever the truth of the story, Miller had a Napier chassis, allegedly with the number 2482 (though this does not fit into the sequence of factory numbers). This was overhauled, given a new set of gears, a multi-plate clutch, and a new, stronger crown-wheel and pinion of KE 805 steel. The clutch came from Count Zborowski, whose father was to have been a member of the Napier team for the 1901 Gordon Bennett race.

Into this revitalised chassis Miller fitted a V-8 Hispano-Suiza Type 34 aero engine with a bore and stroke of 120mm x 130mm and a capacity of 11,762cc, capable of developing about 180hp at 2,000rpm. The car was assembled by the Line brothers in London and fitted with a smooth-contoured, two-seater body made by a firm in Hammersmith. With this machine, still painted in primer, Miller entered for the 1921 Autumn meeting. The Napier chassis was probably rather discomfited by the undignified things it was now expected to do, and developed a reputation for uncertain and sometimes dangerous handling in its new Viper form. It retired from both the handicaps in which it ran, and only managed a best lap of 86.62mph (139.37kmh).

While the Viper had been rumbling around Brooklands, there had been remarkable happenings in Yorkshire. Emmanuel Hoyle, now Lieutenant-Colonel Hoyle and soon to become a baronet, had sold the TT-winning Hutton 'Little Dorrit' in 1919, but he had retained the 8-inch stroke car, which now had an unpainted four-seat aluminium body and a bow-fronted radiator. He entered this for the Bradford & Huddersfield Automobile Club hill-climb at Holme Moss, near Holmfirth, a course which is now part of the A6024 road. The event was held on Saturday 4 June 1921 and the car was driven by C.H. Mitchell. During some unofficial practice Mitchell was trying hard, as it was reported that he cornered on two wheels and pulled out some spokes from the rear wheels. On the big day he was up against some of the major sprint exponents, including Malcolm Campbell in a 1914 2.6 litre Talbot, Henry Segrave – already selected as a member of the Sunbeam team for the forthcoming French Grand Prix – in a 1914 TT Sunbeam, and Humphrey Cook, later to be one of the progenitors of the ERA, in a special E-type 30-98 Vauxhall. It was a glorious summer day and Mitchell climbed the hill in 92 seconds. Try as they could, his rivals could not match his time. Segrave managed only 93.2 seconds, while Cook was slower still, so the ancient Hutton left the stage after a superb finale. It is not recorded that it competed again, or that Hoyle sold it.

Miller brought the Viper out again (now painted blue) for the 1922 season, but while testing in March the Hispano engine broke a valve and was replaced with a Wolseley Viper W4A, an engine identical to the Hispano made under licence by Wolseleys during the War, when they had been fitted to the SE5A fighter. At the opening meeting it was unplaced. Miller changed the

Alastair Miller at Brooklands with the Wolseley Viper in 1922. (William Boddy)

colour for the May meeting and this time the Viper was in luck. It came second in the 100mph Short Handicap with a fastest lap of 100.61mph (161.88kmh), and then it won the 100mph Long Handicap at an average of 102.03mph (164.16kmh), lapping at 107.34mph (172.71kmh). Record-breaking was a useful way of making some money from the bonuses paid by the oil and accessory companies, so on 9 June, Miller brought out the Viper on a very hot day with the aim of taking the Brooklands Class H (7,784cc to 13,929cc) flying mile and kilometre records. After some initial problems the Viper took the kilometre record at 118.91mph (191.32kmh), but the mile eluded it as the tyres threw their treads, perhaps because of the heat.

On 5 and 6 July, Miller felt the Viper needed a change of air and took it to the Westcliff speed trials in Essex. It was a miserable wet weekend, but the journey was worthwhile as Miller established the fastest time of 34.8 seconds. Back at Brooklands again, Kaye Don appeared at the wheel of the Viper at the August Bank Holiday meeting, where, perhaps in his honour, the nose and tail were picked out in red. Don had a rapport with the car, and after starting from the scratch mark in the 100mph Short Handicap he won at an average of 101mph (162.5kmh), lapping at 112.68mph (181.3kmh). Three weeks later Miller tried another speed trial, this time at the Southsea 'Speed Carnival', a charity event run under the patronage of the Duke of York (later King George VI). The course was a standing mile followed by a flying kilometre and the Viper did not shine, as the pull-up area was too short, obliging Miller to ease off before reaching the end of the run.

At the end of the season Miller sold a part-share in the Viper to an actor, Percy Cory, and the car ran at the Easter meeting in 1923 driven by Don with Cory as passenger. Don lapped at 108.98mph (175.34kmh) in the Lightning Short Handicap. On their last lap, cars racing at Brooklands had to turn into the Finishing Straight, where the finishing line was sited. However, as the speed of cars steadily increased, it was becoming increasingly difficult for some drivers to stop before the end of the Finishing Straight was reached, relying as they did on two-wheel Edwardian brakes. At the August Bank Holiday meeting in 1922, Duff's Benz had not pulled up in time and went over the top of the Members' Banking which ran past the top end of the Straight. Don now found he had the same problem; he changed down through the gears, which stripped, and the Viper was only stopped by scraping it along the soft earth bank which lined the top end of the Straight. By the beginning of the 1924 season the Viper had found a new entrant and, presumably, a new gearbox, and it was entered by D. Fitzgerald for F.C. Norris to drive in the Easter Lightning Long Handicap. Norris must have gritted his teeth and pressed on to come second, lapping at 109.94mph (176.89kmh). He then decided to turn his hand to some record-breaking, and on 29 May he brought out the Viper – which was weighed-in at nearly 35cwt (1,780kg) – and trundled round to take the Class H 250 kilometre and three-hour records at 53.01mph (85.37kmh) and 53.08mph

(85.41kmh) respectively.

These records did not last long, as they were soon raised by Barnato's Hispano-Suiza. At the end of the 1924 season the odd class capacities were rationalised and given international status, so Miller's old Class H flying kilometre record stands for all time. With its Edwardian Napier chassis, the Viper was now getting rather long in the tooth, but this did not stop Kaye Don coming out with it – now painted red and black – at the 1925 Easter meeting, though it did not race, as rain caused the cancellation of its events.

At the Whitsun meeting on 1 June there was to be a new twist to the Napier story. J.S. Spencer entered an 11,440cc Napier with a bore and stroke of 126.2mm x 152.4mm which was none other than one of the 1908 GP cars, number 5131, fitted with a grey two-seater body. In his splendid Brooklands history, William Boddy suggests that it now had a single Polyroe carburettor. The GP Napier non-started at the Whitsun meeting but it turned up and ran at the August Bank Holiday meeting on Monday 3 August. Spencer drove the car in two races, the 75mph Short Handicap and the 75mph Long Handicap, but was unplaced. Spencer was also racing a Brooklands-model Austin Seven, built by E.C. Gordon England in a factory at Putney in South-West London, and Gordon England also worked on the GP Napier. The old car was out again at the Brooklands Autumn meeting on Saturday 12 September, where Spencer ran it in the 75mph Short handicap, in which it was unplaced, and the 75mph Long Handicap, where, lapping at 82.04mph (132.00kmh), he came third. It was a good day for elderly Napiers, as Don came second in the Lightning Short Handicap with the Viper.

The old Viper was still not done, and Don brought it out again at the 1926 Whitsun meeting, where it ran in the 100mph Short Handicap for the Gold Vase. The big excitement for the crowd in this race was the appearance of Parry Thomas's 'Babs', which had just returned from Pendine Sands, where it had broken the world land speed record at 171.09mph (275.28kmh) for the flying kilometre. Thomas did not drive the car himself in this race, the wheel being instead taken by John Cobb, whose links with Napier were yet to be forged. The Viper went splendidly in the race, coming second and lap-

2 April 1923: The Viper is pushed back into the Paddock at Brooklands after Kaye Don has stopped it at the end of the Lightning Short Handicap by sliding it along the earth bank lining the Finishing Straight. Co-owner Percy Cory, in the passenger seat, is slightly stunned and has cut his face. (William Boddy)

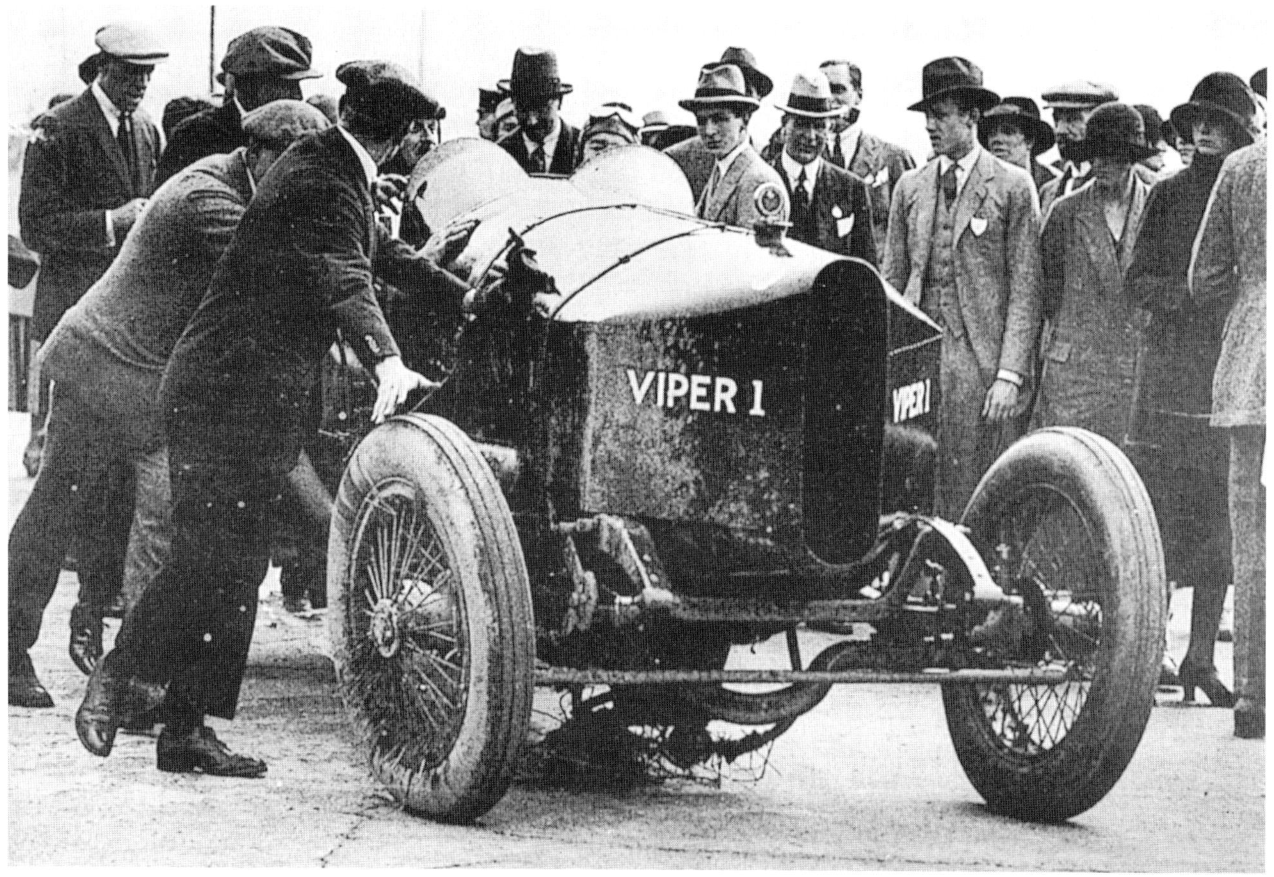

Cyril Bone in the Paddock at Brooklands on 1 July 1926 with the ill-fated Napier-Sunbeam. (William Boddy)

ping at 110.43mph (177.68kmh). Don had a good day, as he also won the 100mph Long Handicap, lapping at 111.92mph (180.07kmh).

The 1926 Summer Brooklands meeting saw another Napier chassis appear. This was an old T26 with a red and white two-seater body, powered by a 1914 V-12 Sunbeam engine with a bore and stroke of 90mm x 150mm and a capacity of 11,451cc. Entered by Cyril Bone, it did not shine at the meeting, coming to a halt only 300 yards after the start of the Lightning Short Handicap, as in the excitement of the moment Bone had let the clutch in too quickly and the prop shaft had declined to co-operate. However, Don's Viper had another a good day out, being beaten into second place by only half a length in the 100mph Long Handicap, where it lapped at 111.42mph (179.27kmh).

Tragedy struck at the August Bank Holiday meeting. Bone had brought out the Napier-Sunbeam again, and during practice, while doing about 100mph on the Byfleet Banking, the car swerved down the banking when a front axle U-bolt broke. It overturned and caught fire, and a Miss Norris, who was a passenger, was thrown out and killed. The Napier-Sunbeam, which had been officially timed lapping at 100.61mph (161.88kmh), was broken up. Don ran the Viper at this meeting but was unplaced, and also had no success at the Autumn meeting. On this unhappy note, the racing exploits of the Edwardian Napiers at Brooklands seem to have ended, though the Viper was used later by Avon for tyre testing. It was probably broken up during World War Two.

Chapter 12: 1926–31

The Fastest in the World

IN the 1920s, the great majority of people in Britain were not motor-car conscious, and certainly had little or no interest in motor racing. The exception to this was the world land speed record. The holder was always a household name and received the sort of attention and adulation which is now reserved for the motor racing World Champion. To hold this coveted record became the aim of many drivers, who realised that if they could amass the resources to build a successful contender, this would be an immediate passport to fame and, most probably, fortune. Among those drivers who set off along the road in search of this Holy Grail was Malcolm Campbell.

Born in 1885, Campbell had become a successful insurance broker. He had started his racing career riding a motor cycle at Brooklands in 1908, and during the same season participated in his first car event there, driving a 1903 Paris–Madrid Renault. He then turned to two Darracqs, the 1908 TT car – which had finished second behind the victorious Hutton – and the 1906 59.5hp car with which Victor Hemery had won the Vanderbilt Cup. He raced both cars at Brooklands in 1911 and 1912. He had a spectacular crash in the ex-Hemery car in the Finishing Straight at the 1912 August Bank Holiday meeting, knocking off both offside wheels, but still finished in fifth place. He then turned his attentions to a Coupe de L'Auto Sunbeam, and by the outbreak of war in August 1914 had become a regular and successful Brooklands driver. He joined the Royal Flying Corps and flew throughout the War, though he did not fly in action. When Brooklands reopened in 1920, Campbell had the distinction of winning the very first race, at the Essex Motor Club meeting on 11 April, when he drove a 1914 2.6 litre Talbot, the car in which he was to be defeated by C.H. Mitchell's Hutton at Holme Moss the following year.

During the 1920 season the Sunbeam company produced a new car which was intended primarily to take records, with the ultimate aim of securing the world land speed record. This car became known as the 350hp Sunbeam. It had a V-12 engine based on the 'Manitou', an aero engine produced and developed by Sunbeam during the War. One cylinder block had bore and stroke dimensions of 110mm x 142mm, while the other was 110mm x 135mm. The outcome of this combination was 18.3 litres. This splendid car captured the imagination of a lot of drivers, Campbell among them. On 17 May 1922, Kenelm Lee Guinness took the Sunbeam to Brooklands with the aim of establishing new short distance records over the half-mile, kilometre, and mile. The rules required that the two runs needed to establish a record had to be done in opposite directions, so Guinness did his runs along the Railway Straight, making his approaches from the Members' and Byfleet bankings. New world records were established for the kilometre and mile at 136.06mph (218.82kmh) and 127.88mph (205.75kmh) respectively, and the kilometre figure was accepted as the new land speed record.

Campbell was among those watching Guinness's feat, and he concluded that he could do better with the same car at a more suitable venue. Campbell had already established strong links with the Sunbeam company, having raced Sunbeams at Brooklands and in hill-climbs during the first post-war seasons. He approached Louis Coatalen, Sunbeam's Managing Director, and asked if he could be loaned the 350hp car for the Saltburn Speed Trials which were to be held on the beach of the Yorkshire seaside resort on 17 June, a month after Guinness's record runs. Campbell did a run at Saltburn at 138mph (222 Kph), but the timing was unofficial and there was no prospect of a record. During the winter the negotiations between Campbell and Coatalen continued, and in March 1923 a deal was finally struck and Campbell bought the 350hp car.

In April he took it to the international speed trials at Fanoe in Denmark, where he was timed at 137.72mph (221.59kmh), a new record, but this was not recognised by the Alliance Internationale des Automobile Clubs Reconnus (AIACR), as the timing apparatus was not of the approved type. Campbell took the Sunbeam back to England and began a programme of modifications to get more speed, having resolved to return to Fanoe in 1924 to capture the record. Meanwhile interest in the world land speed record was increasing and on 6 July 1924 a meeting was held at Arpajon, on the N20 between Paris and Orleans, when the record was broken twice. The first success went to the French driver René Thomas, who drove a specially designed sprint and hill-climb Delage which had a V-12 10.6 litre engine and covered the measured mile at 143.31mph (230.38kmh).

Thomas had only held the record for a few minutes when an English driver, Ernest Eldridge, who was a regular Brooklands competitor with aero-engined cars, brought out the Fiat 'Mephistopheles', which had taken part in the memorable and controversial duel at Brooklands with Newton's Napier in 1908. The Fiat's engine had been destroyed in a spectacular 'blow-up' at Brooklands in 1922 and had been replaced with a Fiat A-12 six-cylinder aero engine with a capacity of 21,714cc. With this fearsome device, Eldridge covered the Arpajon kilometre at 146.8mph (236.20kmh), but his record was disallowed as the car did not have a reverse gear, which was a requirement of the international regulations. Eldridge took the Fiat back to Paris and made up a simple reversing mechanism. A week later, on 12 July, he was back at Arpajon and this time, supervised by Count De Knyff, President of the Sporting Commission of the ACF, he took the record, with the mile at 145.89mph (234.73kmh) and the kilometre at 146.01mph (234.93kmh). The thought of travelling along the narrow, poplar tree-lined, indifferently-surfaced N20 at almost 150mph (240kmh), on the tyres and suspension possessed by the Fiat, is a daunting one!

This left Campbell with a much more difficult target to reach as it was getting near the Sunbeam's limits, but he rose to the challenge and took the car back to Fanoe in August 1924. This time, to avoid misunderstandings, he was accompanied by Colonel Lindsay Lloyd, the RAC timekeeper, but once again his efforts were dogged by misfortune. During its timed run, one of the Sunbeam's tyres left the rim as the car was approaching 150mph (240kmh). The tyre struck and fatally injured a boy spectator and tore through the timing box, just missing Colonel Lloyd. The record attempt was consequently abandoned.

Campbell did not want to go back to Fanoe, with its unhappy memories, but was still eager to win the land speed record. He decided to make some more modifications to the Sunbeam and sought the advice of Amherst Villiers, who was just establishing a reputation as an engineer and designer of racing engines. Campbell had encountered him while competing in hill-climbs, where Villiers had been working on the Brescia Bugattis 'Cordon Bleu' and 'Cordon Rouge', with which Raymond Mays was starting to make his name. Villiers suggested fitting modified camshafts to the Sunbeam, and during the course of their discussions Campbell and he agreed that the right way to take the record was to build a car specially for the purpose, with the target of raising the record to 180mph (290kmh). They therefore began to formulate the plans for a new car. Meanwhile, Campbell had been told of a beach at Pendine in South Wales, where conditions seemed to be suitable for a record run. In September 1924 the Sunbeam was taken there, and despite a water-logged course Campbell established a new record at 146.16mph (235.17kmh).

With his sights firmly set on making a special car, Campbell felt he had no more need of the Sunbeam, which was offered for sale in November 1924. However, there were no serious offers, and since the new car was progressing very slowly he decided to take the Sunbeam out again in 1925, in the hope of being the first to achieve 150mph (240kmh). This time the beach at Pendine was in an ideal condition, and, on 21 July, Campbell broke his own record, achieving 150.86mph (242.73kmh) over the kilometre, and 150.76mph (242.57kmh) over the mile.

Villiers and Campbell realised that the key to the performance of the new car lay in the engine. With the exception of the Delage, all the successful record breakers since the end of the War had been powered by war-surplus aero engines, but in technical terms these were becoming dated and did not have the power output which would be needed to make an appreciable improvement to the record. Campbell knew that the most powerful engine available in Britain was the Napier Lion, which had won the 1922 Schneider Trophy in the Supermarine Sea Lion. The possibility of obtaining a Lion seemed unlikely, but according to Leo Villa – his chief mechanic throughout his record-breaking years – Campbell approached the Air Ministry with a request for an engine. To the surprise of everyone, it was agreed that an engine would be released for the new car. Presumably the initial approach had to be made to the Air Ministry rather than Napiers because all the engines were being manufactured for the Air Ministry, and Napiers did not own any engines themselves. However, Campbell was a member of the Royal Thames Yacht Club and one of his particular friends in the Club was Wilkinson, the Chief Designer at Napiers, so the loan of the engine may well have been discussed, and facilitated, over a drink in the club premises in Knightsbridge. The engine supplied was a Series VA in its standard form, developing an output of 502hp at 2,200rpm with a compression ratio of 5.8:1.

Villiers began to design the car and made the drawings for the chassis frame, which was to be a conventional channel section with very deep side members and four machine-forged tubular cross-members. The frame, made from 3% nickel steel, was manufactured for Campbell by Vickers Ltd at the Don River Works. At that critical point in the car's production, however, there was a disagreement between Campbell and Villiers and their partnership came to an abrupt end. This was perhaps to be expected, as Campbell was a demanding, almost pernickety man, and Villiers had prima donna qualities of his own. The departure of Villiers slowed the project down, but Villa suggested to Campbell that he knew of an engineer who had the abilities to finish the job. This was an Italian, Joseph Maina, whose principal skill lay in the design and development of an epicyclic gearbox which was to be marketed by an entrepreneur, Foster Brown. Campbell agreed with Maina that he should complete the design of the car, and as part of the deal a Foster Brown–Maina gearbox would be used.

Maina produced a design which had a tubular two-piece front axle carried on Woodhead springs 3ft 1in (95cm) long. A torque tube connected the gearbox with the rear axle, which was underslung and also carried on Woodhead springs 4ft 2in long (127cm) long. The gearbox was made by Beard & Fitch Ltd at their works at Clerkenwell, in the centre of London. It had three speeds with ratios of .333, .666, and 1:1, and had a system of conical friction wheels which slowed down the layshaft pinions. The ratio of the final drive was 1.27:1. The Lion engine drove the gearbox through a dry multi-plate clutch with sixteen 11-inch plates. This was operated by a hand-lever as well as a pedal, and was intended to overcome the inherent drag of an epicyclic gearbox. The car was fitted with Alford & Alder brakes on four wheels, using Perrot shafts at the front, and the steel drums were turned from the solid. A Dewandre vacuum servo could be brought into operation if needed. The steering column operated a cross shaft, working two Marles steering boxes, with a separate drop arm for each front wheel. To avoid excessively long drag-links which could flex, Maina divided each link with a bell-crank, attached to the side of the frame. The car had a 12ft 1in (368cm) wheelbase, a front track of 4ft 9in (144cm), and a rear track of 5ft 5in (165cm). Rudge-Whitworth wheels were fitted, and Dunlop made special tyres after an initial proposal to run the car with solid wheels was abandoned.

The chassis frame, engine, and gearbox were delivered to the Robin Hood Engineering Works at Kingston Vale, owned by Kenelm Lee Guinness, where KLG sparkplugs were made. Guinness had loaned Campbell a workshop for the construction of the car, which proceeded slowly. Much delay was caused by manufacturing problems with the gearbox and rear axle, and parts had to be scrapped frequently. In the autumn of 1926 Campbell moved the car to his house at Povey Cross, which was near the present Gatwick airport site, and engaged more mechanics to work on it. He knew that time was running out and that there was the nightmare possibility the car would be outclassed before it was even finished. Parry Thomas had already taken the world land speed record with the Liberty-engined 'Babs' in April, doing 171.02mph (275.17kmh) at Pendine, and intended to attack the record again; while Sunbeam were building a new car for Segrave, which had two 500hp 'Matabele' aero engines.

By November, 11 mechanics were working on the car; Elsons of Epsom had been engaged to make the body to Maina's designs, and two panel-beaters from that firm now joined the team. Work stopped on Christmas Eve 1926 but was resumed again on Boxing Day, and the car was finished on 30 December. The blue-painted body was a neat, slim, single-seater, but little thought had been given to the problems of drag,

A side-elevation drawing of the 1927 Napier-Campbell 'Bluebird' chassis.

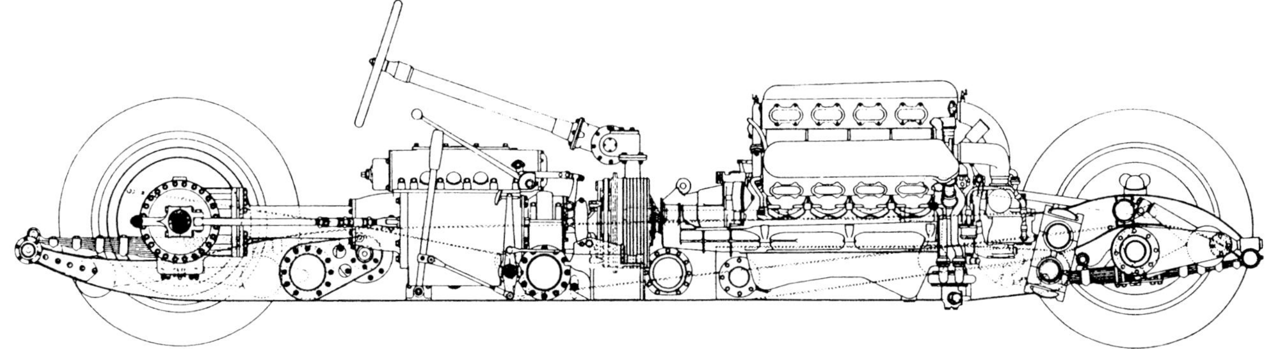

as the gear and brake levers were outside, the steering was exposed, and the front brakes were an unnecessary addition on a record car. It was estimated that the car had cost Campbell £9,500, which was a very large sum in 1926, and this did not include the cost of the engine loaned by Napiers. It was called the Napier-Campbell, but was always known as 'Bluebird', a name which Campbell had given to all his racing cars since 1912.

On New Year's Day 1927, the Napier-Campbell was taken to Pendine Sands and Campbell decided he should attempt a record run without delay. The very next day the car was towed out from its shed in Pendine village by a Crossley tender. There had been a drizzle the previous night and the beach was shrouded in mist. This cleared at about nine o'clock and the course was marked out with flags, but then it began to rain, and this continued until about 11 o'clock. The sands were wet and soggy, and Campbell decided to roll 'Bluebird' onto boards to prevent it sinking into the sand. When the engine was started, however, the car moved forward for about two feet and then stalled. A second attempt was made with the same result, as there was a gearbox fault. Adjustments were made which took about an hour, and then Campbell tried a third time. The car stalled again, and by now had begun to sink into the sand. A lorry tried to tow it free, but it had sunk up to the frame, only being freed and pushed back onto the planks with the help of about 60 bystanders, just in time to escape the tide which was coming in rapidly. The attempt was abandoned for that day and further work was done on the gearbox.

At noon next day 'Bluebird' was towed out again; this time the car started and ran along the beach. Campbell reached about 135mph (217kmh), but found that it was very difficult to change gear. In addition he was sitting out in the slipstream and the aerodynamics were spraying the cockpit with sand and water, and at the end of the run the brakes were almost ineffective. He realised that without considerable further work there was no prospect of breaking the record; furthermore, the beach was not then in a suitable condition for record-breaking. Having returned to the starting point he decided to do another test run, but the car stalled and again had to be rescued from the sand.

Elsons's panel-beaters with the half-finished tail of the Napier-Campbell 'Bluebird' in December 1926. (Angela Pugh)

'Bluebird' was loaded on its lorry, and that afternoon set out on its journey back to Povey Cross. Campbell turned on Maina and vented his anger, while the rest of the team prepared for some hard work, as Pendine had been provisionally booked for another record attempt two weeks later. The Elson panel-beaters modified the cockpit, while Maina stripped down and altered the gearbox. The brake drums were found to be flexing, so these were scrapped and thicker drums were made, using different linings. Campbell then went to Acton and complained that the engine was giving insufficient power. Napiers, and Joe Coe in particular, who had prepared the engine, were not convinced. They believed that their calculations of the power needed were correct, but to be fair to Campbell, their calculations had probably not taken into account the conditions at Pendine and the drag of the wet sand. In his autobiography *My Thirty Years of Speed*, Campbell states that the engine was immediately fitted with higher compression pistons, but there would have been no need to strip and rebuild the engine in the short time available. Napiers had a continuous policy of improvement and development, and had already produced a racing version of the Series VA. In this, the compression ratio had been raised to 8:1, which increased the power output to 585hp. Campbell states that 'Bluebird's' engine was returned to him developing 635hp, so it seems likely that he was given a racing Series VA that had been tuned on the test bed for his purposes.

After two weeks' work, the Napier-Campbell returned to Pendine on Sunday 16 January, and on Tuesday the 18th the car was taken out. Campbell did two runs at about 140mph (225kmh) and was satisfied with the way the car went. He did two more runs at 160mph (257kmh), but as the beach was waterlogged

The Napier-Campbell 'Bluebird' is pushed out for its first test run at Pendine, 2 January 1927. (Guy Griffiths Collection)

A strained-looking Campbell sits in the cockpit of 'Bluebird' at Pendine. Parry Thomas, in a leather coat, leans on the side and glances at the gauges. (Guy Griffiths Collection)

and there was a strong cross-wind there was no hope of a record that day and it was arranged to make an attempt two days later, on the 20th. Conditions were little better then. There were hail and snow showers during the morning, but a thin sun shone through at midday, when the car was rolled out once again. Campbell made two runs and could feel the car being slowed by the drag of the wet sand, but despite this his average speed for the runs was 166.38mph (267.70kmh), while with a following wind he had been timed at 171.3mph (275.62kmh). This was better than Thomas's record, which spurred Campbell to try again. This time disaster was only just avoided when a tyre was cut by a shell and burst. 'Bluebird' swerved off the marked course and cut down one of the marker posts, which dented the bonnet, but Campbell was able to pull up without any further mishap. It was now clear that the car was capable of capturing the record when conditions were suitable, so Campbell reluctantly decided to abandon the attempt and wait for another two weeks, when tide conditions on the beach would be better.

The Campbell team returned to Pendine again on Sunday 30 January to find that conditions were even worse. The next day was spent preparing the car, but that night a storm strewed the beach with sea shells and debris. A team of helpers walked the beach next morning, sweeping it clear and picking up detritus, which included a 40-foot wire hawser, two dead sheep, and many baulks of timber. The sand was so soft, that the cars laying out the course marker flags had to keep moving, to avoid becoming bogged down. Campbell tried a practice run, but once again a tyre burst when it was cut by a shell. Before he could make another run it began to rain heavily, so the team packed up and waited for the morrow.

Next morning the cars set out once more with the marker flags, but the beach was too wet for a run. However, Campbell noticed that the ruts left in the sand by the cars had formed drainage channels leaving the adjoining sand comparatively dry. He concluded that if a furrow was ploughed on each side of the marked course, this would leave a dry track down the middle, on which he could run. The following morning, as soon as the tide had receded, two ploughs were towed along the beach, making parallel six-mile (9.6 km) furrows. One of the tractors broke down, so the driver of the other was told to return back along the beach to make the other furrow. As soon as Campbell saw that the ploughing was effective, he could wait no longer, as he suspected that the weather was going to turn against him once more. The Napier-Campbell was timed at 175mph (281kmh) on the first run, but as he entered the measured mile on the return Campbell realised that the plough was still on the course, so he had to ease off, and the record still eluded him.

On the next morning, Friday 4 February, the weather held and the sun shone, even though the wind was still strong. The plough set off again, but with less work to do since it had been realised that just one furrow, on the landward side of the beach, was sufficient. Though the beach was clear by two o'clock, the engine would not fire at first, and when it was running Campbell missed the change into second gear and had to stop. The car was push-started on the firm beach and Campbell tried again. He was timed on the first run at 179.158mph (288.26kmh) through the kilometre, but on the return run the car hit a bump and Campbell was thrown up into the slipstream, his goggles being torn off. He kept his foot down in spite of this, and although his kilometre time was down to 170.608mph (274.50kmh) for the second run, the record was his, as his average for both runs was 174.883mph (281.38kmh) for the kilometre and 174.223mph (280.32kmh) for the mile. Still hoping for the three-miles-a-minute record, Campbell tried again, but this time both runs were slower and it seemed that the engine had gone slightly off-tune.

Campbell realised that the Napier-Campbell was unlikely to go much faster in its present form, but before he could make any plans for the future there were two dramatic developments in the world of land speed records. On Thursday 3 March, Parry Thomas was killed at Pendine when 'Babs' overturned during his record attempt. Just over three weeks later, on Tuesday 29 March, Henry Segrave, who had taken the twin-engined 1,000hp Sunbeam to Daytona Beach in Florida, shattered Campbell's record by covering the measured mile at 203.792mph (327.901kmh). Campbell had calculated that the Napier-Campbell, with more power, could perhaps exceed 200mph (320kmh), but the speed established by Segrave was beyond its reach. A new design was therefore required, and Campbell made the decision to rebuild his car while sitting at a London dinner held in honour of Segrave on his return from America. The Daytona Chamber of Commerce issued an invitation to Campbell to make his record attempt there in February or March 1928, so his team had little time to spare in designing and building the new car.

Campbell went to Napiers again, and with the approval of the Air Ministry it was agreed that he should have a Series VIIA Lion, which was being prepared for one of the Supermarine S5s which were to compete in the Schneider Trophy at Venice in September 1927. Much secrecy surrounded the Series VIIA, which developed 900hp at 3,300rpm, with a 10:1 compression ratio. The weight had been pared down to 850lb, and more importantly the cylinder blocks and connecting-rods had been redesigned to reduce the overall height of the engine and thus reduce the frontal area. The Series VII had an overall height of 39in (99.06cm) but the height of the Series VIIA was 34.1in (86.67cm).

Napiers also agreed that the car should be assembled at the Acton factory, but whether this was to safeguard the security of the engine, or merely a benefit of Campbell's friendship with Wilkinson, is not known. Agreement was reached about the engine in the week after Easter, and soon afterwards Leo Villa, Campbell's chief mechanic, moved into Acton Vale with another mechanic, George Miller, and work started on the car. Joseph Maina had been retained by Campbell to supervise the re-design. The original body was scrapped, and the back axle, transmission and engine were removed. The only components which were to be unchanged were the frame, front axle, and steering. The FMB epicyclic gearbox went back to the makers, Beard & Fitch, for modification, as changing gear was always a problem, and the bottom gear ratio was lowered to assist acceleration, while the clutch was redesigned.

A growing appreciation of aerodynamics had impinged upon Campbell's team, and Rex Pierson (later Sir Rex Pierson), the Chief Designer of Vickers, was commissioned to design a new body, which was tested in model form in Vickers's wind-tunnel at Brooklands. The tests showed that the exposed wheels were responsible for about 60 per cent of the drag, so rudimentary fairings and wheel discs were fitted, to reduce the drag caused by the turbulence of the spokes. To assist lateral stability, a fin was built into the tail of the car. The nose of the body had no apertures, as a surface radiator was mounted on each side of the tail. These were made by another aircraft company, Fairey Aviation, at a cost of £400, which was a very high figure in contemporary terms. Unfortunately, despite the cost, the radiators were not a success, as they ran in a partial vacuum when the car was at speed. This problem was not evident in the wind-tunnel tests, as radiators were not fitted to the model. Campbell would once again sit high in the car, as he was astride the prop shaft and gearbox. The engine was not fitted into the car until the Schneider Trophy had taken place, and Campbell wrote that some parts – probably the cam boxes – were sealed. When the chassis was finished, and the engine installed, the car was towed to the works of coach-builders H.J. Mulliner Ltd, in Bath Road, Chiswick, who were to make the body.

Hopes had been considerably boosted by the result of the Schneider Trophy, which had been won by Flight-Lieutenant S.N. Webster, flying a Supermarine S5 using a Series VIIA Lion, at an average speed of 281.66mph (453.17kmh). Campbell and his small team – comprising Leo Villa, George Miller, Joe Coe, and David MacDonald of Dunlop (the legendary 'Dunlop Mac') and his brother Steve – sailed for New York at the end of January 1928 in the SS *Berengaria*. The car was carried from New York on the 'Dixie Flyer' train, and arrived at Daytona with the team at just after midnight on Sunday 12 February. In addition to the car there were 18 cases of spares and equipment, including a spare engine. Early in the morning, Campbell studied the beach. He wrote: 'My first impression was one of disappointment; the weather was cold, the sea was rough and the sand was very uneven'.

Daytona Beach is a narrow spit joined to the mainland by four bridges. Although 24 miles long, only the southern ten miles was available for record-breaking, as a pier crossed it in the middle. The surface of hard, white sand was in a poor state because a south wind had been blowing, which had left it rippled. A north wind was necessary for record-breaking conditions, so

January 1928: 'Bluebird' is crated for the trip to Daytona. (Ronald Barker)

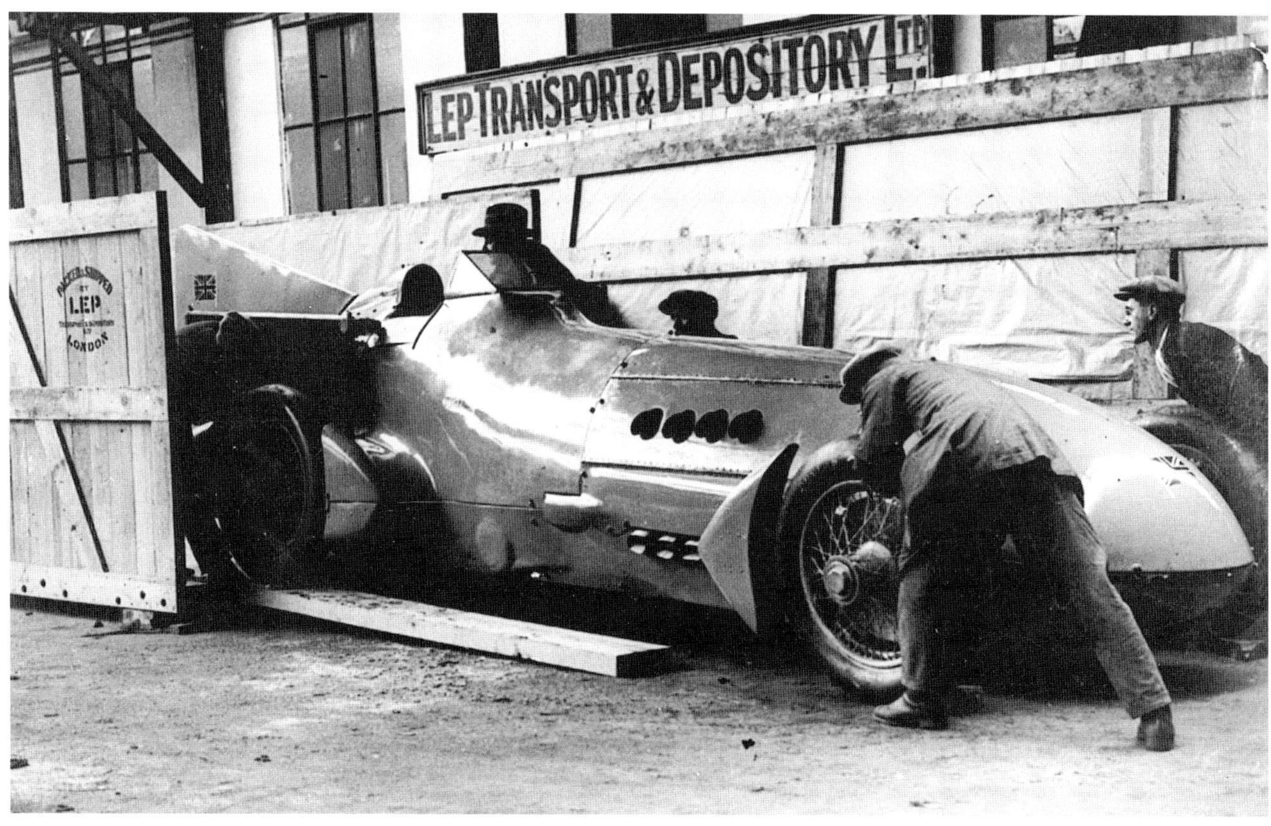

the team had to wait, even though Campbell was impatient to try the car under its own power for the first time. Prohibition was at its height, but the hospitable Americans welcomed the Campbell team and invitations to parties flowed in, at which the liquor flowed out. Leo Villa comments that the quality and purity of some of the alcohol offered were questionable; he was particularly intrigued when some spilt in the boot of a car taking him to a beach barbecue acted as a very quick and efficient paint stripper.

The car was ready on Tuesday morning, but the time of the tide made a run impracticable. Next day the wind had changed again and the beach was uneven, but by Thursday morning Campbell could wait no longer and decided to take the car out despite the condition of the sand. The beach was closed, but marker flags were not put out as he told the organisers he would only do a test run. He agreed with Coe that he would not exceed 2,200rpm and set off along the beach. While doing about 180mph (290kmh) the Napier-Campbell hit a ridge in the sand and the car jumped about 30ft (9.1m) and skidded. Hearing a loud clattering, Campbell slowed down, and when he reached the far end of the beach where Villa was waiting the undertray was found to have been ripped off and doubled back under the tail. In addition the rear shock absorber mountings had broken and the driver's seat had collapsed. A somewhat chastened team towed the car back to its garage, where the rear springs were replaced, new shock absorber mounts were made up, and a local panel-beater was instructed to make a new undertray and repair other body damage. Fortunately for Campbell's patience, while the repairs were being done the weather was unsuitable for any record attempts. The car was ready again by Saturday 18 February, but there was heavy rain and a high wind.

Campbell was under additional pressure, as he was not the only contender for Segrave's record: there were two American challengers who were also waiting for conditions to improve. The contrast between the two American cars could not have been greater. The White Triplex Special was a massive machine which relied on sheer brute force to get results. It had three Liberty aero engines with a total capacity of 81 litres, one in front of the driver and two behind him, packed into a converted truck chassis; there was no attempt at streamlining. The driver of this fearsome contrivance was a board track driver, Ray Keech. The other machine, the Black Hawk Stutz, was a pointer to the future. This had a supercharged 16-cylinder 3-litre engine based on two Miller 91 engines with their crankshafts geared together. This remarkable engine was mounted in a small, slim, and superbly streamlined chassis. This was being driven by Frank Lockhart, the undisputed champion of American board track racing. The resultant three-cornered struggle for the world land speed record delighted the American press and public alike, and huge crowds were in Daytona waiting for the expected drama to unfold.

The rain stopped on Sunday morning and Campbell decided to take the car out again for a test. This time he asked for the course to be marked. Although he had no intention of trying for the record, he wanted to be in a position to take advantage of any change in the conditions. The marking of the course could only be done as the tide receded. Telephone lines were laid out, and the timing apparatus was set up and linked to the tapes marking the start and finish lines of the measured distance. Marker flags lined the course and posts were erected at each end carrying a large coloured banner at which the driver would aim. The MacDonald brothers were sent to the southern end of the beach to establish a tyre depot. The beach itself was not in perfect condition. In addition heavy clouds were building up, and a strong cross-wind was blowing from the north. However, Campbell was making his first run from north to south, and therefore had a following wind.

Although it was announced that it was only a test run, a huge crowd had gathered in anticipation of a possible record. Villa and Coe fired up the Lion with the gas starter engine and Campbell made a clean getaway along the beach, although he had trouble with gear changes as the top gear dogs would not engage and had to be rammed home by brute force. The state of the sand made the car hard to hold in a straight line, but as Campbell approached the measured distance he could see that the rev counter was indicating a speed of about 210mph (338kmh) so he decided that a record attempt could be made. At the end of the mile the revs indicated about 220mph (355kmh), but as the car cleared the finishing banner it struck a bump, and Campbell was thrown up into the slipstream and once again lost his goggles. He wrote that 'the wind seemed as if it would lift me from the car; I believe I should have gone, but for the tenacious grip that I had on the rim of the steering wheel.' Campbell's foot was simultaneously jerked off the throttle, and on the sudden over-run the car swerved sideways, hitting a patch of soft sand. It took nearly a mile before he had recovered control, and as he approached the waiting MacDonalds he decided that he would not stop, but would turn the car round and go through the distance again on the same tyres.

Campbell realised that the bump and the ensuing skid had sapped his nerve and strength; the rev counter readings indicated that he had broken the record, but if he stopped, he knew he would lose the resolve to drive the car. Swinging it round, he waved the MacDonalds away and set off along the course for his second run. Campbell found how much his strength had been sapped when he tried to change into top gear. He had to let go of the steering wheel and tug the gear-lever with both hands before he could engage top. On this run the car missed the bump and the soft sand, and covered the measured mile without mishap. When he pulled up beside Villa and Coe, Campbell had to be helped out of the car. He said nothing would make him attempt another run with the sand in that condition and was abusive about the gearbox, but none of these things mattered. His speed on the first run had been 214.7mph (345.45kmh) and on the return it was 199.9mph (321.63kmh), which gave him an average of 206.956mph (332.99kmh) and a new world land speed record.

Campbell realised there was a good chance that Keech or Lockhart could break his new record, so, knowing that the Napier-Campbell had the potential to do at least 220mph (355kmh), he decided to remain at Daytona for a few days, hoping for an improvement in the weather and the beach conditions. The very next day both Lockhart and Keech took their cars out for test runs, but, despite conditions being better, Campbell decided to wait until his rivals made actual record attempts. On 22 February, Lockhart brought out the Black Hawk Stutz for an attempt, and Campbell had 'Bluebird' towed to the beach and warmed up ready for a record run if it was necessary. A warm rain had started to fall when Lockhart set off on his run. As the car approached the measured mile at about 200mph (320kmh) it swerved to the left, then to the right, and somersaulted into the sea. Bouncing across the water like a skimming stone, it came to a halt in about four feet of water with Lockhart still in the cockpit. A human chain of bystanders dragged the car out of the sea and rescued Lockhart, whose injuries were surprisingly slight – a badly cut wrist, shock, and bruises. Campbell, who was considering a run, was stopped by a motor cycle policeman, and he drove along the beach in another car to see if he could give any help to the unfortunate Lockhart. There was no possibility of any more runs that day, so 'Bluebird' was taken back to its garage, which it had been sharing with the Black Hawk Stutz.

Next afternoon, Keech brought out the Triplex for his record attempt. Once more Campbell held a watching brief, with the car warmed up and waiting to go should Keech establish a new record. When Triplex was approaching 200mph (320kmh) on his first run, going north, a water hose burst on the front engine, badly scalding Keech's thigh. He was able to pull the car up without any further mishap, but he had to abandon his record attempt as his burns needed hospital treatment. After a discussion with his team, Campbell decided not to make an attempt to improve on his record – the beach conditions were still not ideal, and memories of the problems encountered on his earlier runs were still too fresh in his mind.

The team were duly fêted and were the guests of honour at a banquet held by the Daytona police department to celebrate the new record. It was the opinion of the team that the genuine Scotch served to them by the police was probably the only decent liquor they had received during the whole American trip! The team returned to England on the *Berengaria* and were fêted once more, while the car was exhibited at Gamages department store in High Holborn in the centre of London, where it attracted large crowds. Campbell's new record was not to stand for long, however. On 22 April, Ray Keech, now recovered from his burns, took Triplex out again. He was clocked at 203.97mph (328.18kmh) on his first run, but then the timing apparatus failed and he had to do it all over again. He tried once more, and recorded 201.56mph (324.31kmh) running into a strong headwind, despite burning his arm when the front engine backfired and hitting a bump in the sand which made the heavy car jump 50ft (15m). On the return journey he recorded 213.9mph (344.16kmh), which gave him an average of 207.552mph (333.95kmh), thereby breaking Campbell's record, albeit by the narrowest of margins.

Three days later, Lockhart too came out again with the repaired Black Hawk Stutz. Daytona Beach was in a poor condition, with ridges left by the tide. On his first run he recorded 203.45mph (327.35kmh), but on the return, while travelling at an estimated 220mph (355kmh), a tyre burst and the car somersaulted three times. Lockhart was thrown out and killed instantly. Just over a year later, on 15 June 1929, the courageous Keech was also killed, in a six-car crash while leading a race at the Altoona board track in Pennsylvania. By a strange irony, he was driving a Miller 91 that had previously been owned by Frank Lockhart.

Henry Segrave had been watching the record attempts at Daytona with a close professional interest. Understandably, he wanted to regain the record, but he had severed his links with the Sunbeam company when he decided to retire as an active racing driver, and he was now in much the same position as Campbell, a 'privateer' who would have to find sponsorship and organise the building of his own car. Finding sponsorship was nothing new to Segrave. Although the 1,000hp Sunbeam had been built at the Wolverhampton works, and the company had met the cost of its manufacture, all the other expenses of the 203mph record had been paid for by Segrave, with funds from a variety of sources. Once he knew that his record was broken he wasted little time. On 19 April 1928 a report appeared in the *Wolverhampton Express & Star* announcing that Segrave was to have a new land speed record car,

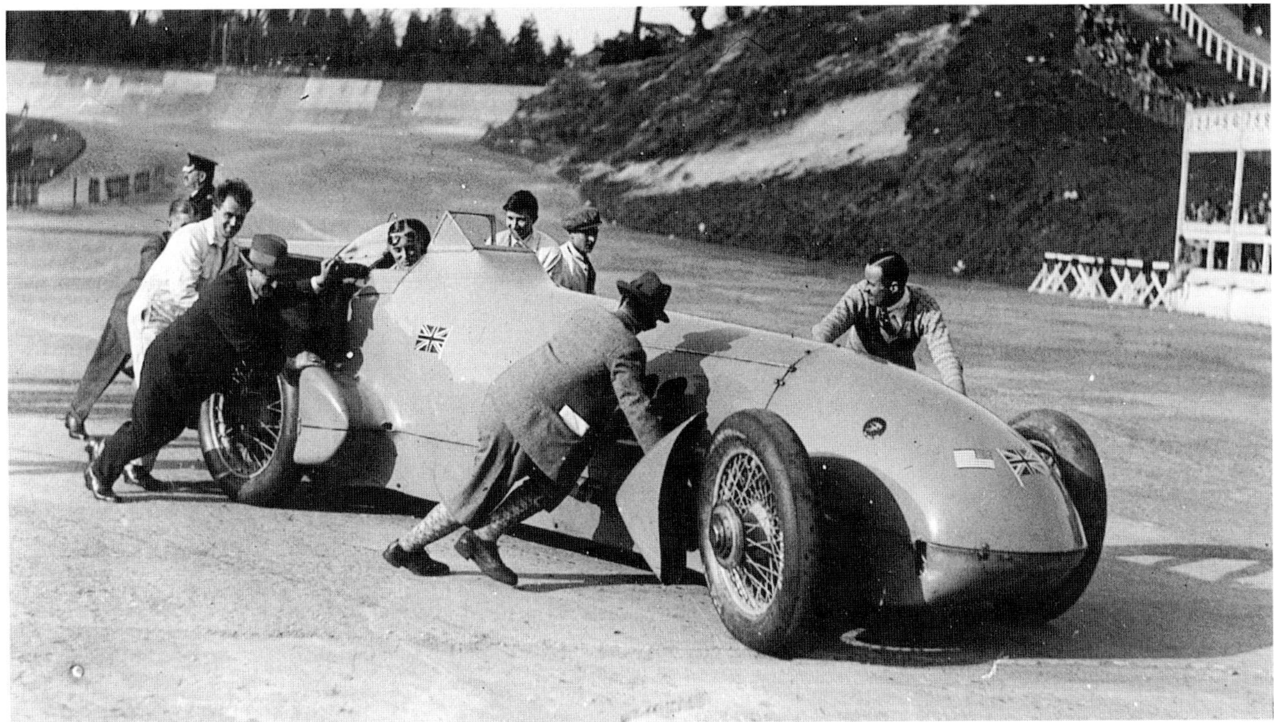

'Bluebird' is demonstrated to the Easter Monday crowd at Brooklands on 9 April 1928. Leo Villa, in white overalls, pushes on a back wheel. (Ronald Barker)

which was to be designed by Captain J.S. Irving and would be powered by a Napier Lion engine.

Irving had been the Chief of the Experimental Department at Sunbeam. He had done much work on the Sunbeam racing cars and had also been responsible for the 1,000hp record breaker. He had left Sunbeams at the same time as Segrave and had gone to work for the Humfrey-Sandberg Company, which was a transmission manufacturer and specialist in free-wheels. Segrave was now a director of the Portland Cement Company and he turned to two of his fellow directors, Henry Horne and Oliver Pepper, for financial help with the new car. More funds came from C.C. Wakefield (the makers of 'Castrol' oil), British Petroleum, Dunlop, KLG, and William (later Lord) Rootes.

If he was to have an all-British car, Segrave had little option but to seek an engine from Napiers. There was no other British aero engine available with a power output that was adequate for record purposes, and the cost of building a special engine for the task would probably have scared his backers away. Segrave would have readily appreciated that Campbell, despite his other difficulties, had found no problems with the Lion, which had done all that was asked of it, and Napiers, presumably with Air Ministry approval, agreed to the sale of a Series VIIA Lion. During the two years since Campbell had used it the Series VIIA had profited from more development. In factory trim, with a compression ratio of 10:1 and using a fuel mixture of 75 per cent petrol and 25 per cent benzole, with tetra-ethyl-lead additives, the maximum output was now 931bhp at 3,600rpm. Irving decided to use BP alcohol fuel. This reduced the maximum output to 912bhp, but gave the advantages of better low-speed acceleration and cleaner plugs. Lion development was proceeding apace, and the Series VIIA was not now surrounded by such an aura of secrecy. To obtain the engine, Segrave's backers paid Napiers £3,078.

Irving was making progress with the design of the car, which was to be an Irving-Napier, although it was always called the 'Golden Arrow'. W.U. Snell was the chief draughtsman, while Irving's brother supervised the building of the car and his daughter looked after the clerical work and the accounts. The car was to be built in the KLG factory at Putney Vale, and the keynote of the design was to keep frontal area and drag to a minimum. The outcome was probably one of the most elegant land speed record cars ever built. The body fitted tightly round the Lion engine, which had modified cam boxes to assist the body air-flow. There was a compact three-speed gearbox with ratios of 1:1, 1.54:1 and 3:1, and a multi-plate Dewandre servo assisted clutch. The driver sat low in the car, between divided Hardy Spicer prop shafts. These contra-rotated and fed the power to twin bevel final drives, without differentials. The chassis frame was of heavy channel section, 13in by 5in (33cm x 12.7cm), and was construct-

Autumn 1928: Three views of the Irving-Napier 'Golden Arrow' being built at the KLG factory. The take-offs for the two propshafts can be seen, and the close fit of the engine cover is apparent. (Chas K. Bowers & Son)

ed by John Thompsons Motor Pressings without charge. A three-piece beam tubular front axle was mounted on semi-elliptic springs, sliding in trunnions, and the axle was located by two radius arms linked to a crossmember. The rear axle was mounted on four quarter-elliptic springs, each pair being clamped on the axle to make, in effect, a semi-elliptic. Twin Marles steering boxes controlled a drag link to each front wheel. The car was fitted with built-in screw jacks, covered by streamlined fairings, to speed up the wheel changes after the first run. As there would be no opportunity to run-in or bed-in the car, the gearbox, steering, brakes, and transmission were assembled with the clearances that would normally be caused by the wear of 5,000 miles' running.

In designing the body, Irving admitted that he had looked carefully at the Supermarine S5 fuselage, and in the process he had started along the aerodynamics road which has lead to the modern racing car. The narrow, contoured body ended in a tail fin, but between the front and rear wheels were sponsons which reduced the drag of the wheels and also contained surface radiators which had been made by the Gloster Aircraft Company. These radiator sponsons were attached to the body by long aerofoils, which were angled with the intention of obtaining downforce when the car was at speed. Irving had doubts about the effectiveness of the Gloster radiators, so he also provided what was described as a 'eutectic' cooling system. This consisted of an ultracold chemical cooling agent, contained in a tank, past which the cooling water could circulate, controlled by a thermostat. The cockpit was fitted with a gunsight to help Segrave aim at the course.

While the construction of the car continued in the KLG factory the advanced body, which had a frontal area of only 11.8sq ft (1.1m^2), was built in ten days at the Cricklewood works of Thrupp & Maberley, on wooden bucks, using 500sq ft (46.5m^2) of aluminium. Thrupp & Maberley had become part of the emerging Rootes Group, so it must be assumed that the cost of making the body, which was supplied without charge, was William Rootes's contribution to the venture. Thrupp & Maberley did a good job, as the panels fitted with very little alteration when offered up to the car. All the forward panels overlapped the rear panels to prevent the slipstream lifting them and tearing them away. On completion the body was given a gold finish. The 'Golden Arrow' was a big car, being 27ft 8in (843cm) long and 3ft 1in (94cm) high, with a wheelbase of 13ft 4in (406cm). It weighed 3.6 tons (7,935kg), including 5cwt (550kg) of lead ballast carried at the rear to equalise weight distribution. Rudge-Whitworth wheels carried 37 x 7 Dunlop tyres, which were inflated to 125psi (8.5bar) for the record runs. The car would be doing a theoretical 241mph (388kmh) at 3,400rpm, Dunlop having stated that the safe maximum for the tyres was 250mph (400kmh).

The Irving-Napier had cost £10,059. When it was finished it was exhibited in the Rootes showroom at Devonshire House in Piccadilly. Segrave had his eye on the water speed record too, and his boat *Miss England*, which had a Lion engine, was also on show. A celebration party was attended by the Prince of Wales, Prime Minister Stanley Baldwin, Home Secretary Joynson Hicks, and the American Ambassador. With the best wishes of his illustrious guests, Segrave and his team departed for New York on 30 January 1929 aboard the White Star liner *Olympic*. The party included Mrs Segrave, Lord Brecknock, Colonel Warwick Wright, head of the large London motor dealers, William Rootes, Captain Irving, and six mechanics, among whom was the ubiquitous Joe Coe, with his usual task of looking after the needs of the Lion. The whole enterprise was on a much grander scale than Campbell's venture had been 12 months earlier, but Segrave had a strong commercial instinct and his sponsors wanted the publicity.

The party arrived in Daytona on 9 February to find that there was another land speed record contender in town. The White Triplex was being brought out again by its owner, J.M. White, who declared that it would defend its record if the 'Golden Arrow' was successful. This time Triplex would be driven by Lee Bible, who had been one of the car's mechanics on its previous record attempts. Ray Keech had decided that he wanted no more to do with the car, which he regarded as excessively dangerous.

Segrave took 'Golden Arrow' out for a test run as soon as it had been checked over. The purpose was merely to ascertain that everything was functioning properly. Not exceeding 3,200rpm, he changed into second gear at about 80mph (128kmh), and into top at 170mph (274kmh), but did not push the car past 180mph (290kmh). He decided to remove the gunsight, which had been rendered unnecessary as the measured distance was clearly marked by powerful red arc lights mounted on 50ft poles at each end of the course. When the test run was over, the car was driven off the beach on two planks, across the Promenade, and through the main street of Daytona to the garage.

Like Campbell, Segrave then had

The 'Golden Arrow' on the beach at Daytona for a test run in February 1929. The 'gunsight' was removed for the record runs. (Chas K. Bowers & Son)

the frustration of waiting for the tide and weather to co-operate. He passed the time by testing *Miss England* off the beach. On Monday 11 March conditions were better, though not ideal, so it was decided to make an attempt, and a crowd estimated at 120,000 turned up to watch. The mechanics brought the car to the beach, and Segrave appeared in a touring car, attired in immaculate white overalls. The Lion was started with a compressed air starter and warmed up. With no further ado, Segrave set off for the southernmost point of the beach, which gave him a four-mile (7.5km) run into the measured course. The sand was bumpy, there were patches of surface water, and visibility was poor, with patches of mist. Just after entering the measured mile the car hit a bump which made it leave the ground for about 30 feet, but it continued to run straight. Segrave maintained 3,250rpm through the mile and this gave him a speed of 231.51mph (372.49kmh). He pulled up at the northern end of the beach, where it was found that a pipe had broken away on the cooling system, so while the wheels were changed and the fuel topped-up, the 'eutectic' system was switched on. The 'pit-stop' took only six minutes to ready Segrave for the return run, which went without mishap but was marginally slower at 231.213mph (372.02kmh). Segrave turned the car round and stopped at the timekeepers' base, and as he climbed out he was mobbed by the crowd. His average speed was 231.446mph (372.39kmh), he had broken the Triplex record by almost 24mph (38kmh). The land speed record had never been broken with so little drama and with such apparent ease.

However, Segrave's triumph was soon to be overshadowed by tragedy. The next day, Lee Bible brought out the White Triplex. He did a first run at about 180mph (290kmh), and when leaving the mile at the end of his second run, having recorded 202mph (324kmh), he closed the throttle too soon and lost control as the huge car swerved on the over-run. It charged into the sand dunes lining the landward side of the course, knocking down and killing a photographer, and as the car rolled Bible was thrown out with fatal results. Following this accident the beach was closed for further record attempts, so Segrave's hopes of trying again, and raising the record to 240mph (385kmh), were frustrated.

Before he returned to England, Segrave raced *Miss England* at Miami, with notable success. He then went to Washington, where he was presented to President Hoover at the White House, and on the steps of the Capitol received a huge trophy given by the city of Daytona to mark his exploits. Segrave and his wife left New York in the *Olympic* on 6 April. When the ship put into Cherbourg, Segrave received a telegram which

Daytona, 11 March 1929: The 'Golden Arrow' is jacked up while the wheels are changed after the first record run at 231.51mph (372.49kmh). There are covers on the radiators. (Guy Griffiths Collection)

announced that King George V had conferred a knighthood on him in recognition of his achievements. The *Olympic* docked at Southampton on the evening of 12 April, and the reception was overwhelming. Sir Henry Segrave was the nation's hero. A special train carried him to London, where he was met at Waterloo Station by the Lord Mayor of London, the Mayor of Westminster, and Sir Charles Wakefield. He was carried in a motor cavalcade to the Houses of Parliament, where a Government reception awaited him in Palace Yard. The cavalcade then carried him in triumph through the West End to another reception in the Mayfair Hotel, given by the Society of Motor Manufacturers and Traders. Three days later Segrave was the guest of honour at a dinner at the RAC, where the Prince of Wales was the principal speaker. Among the thousands of congratulatory telegrams he received was one which said, tersely, 'Damn good show – Campbell'.

Segrave's new record had been a bitter pill for Campbell to swallow. When his own record had been broken by Ray Keech, Campbell had resolved to regain it, but after his experiences at Daytona he was reluctant to return there, and decided to seek a new location for a fresh record attempt. He considered a venue in Syria, and had a narrow escape when the DH Gipsy Moth in which he was flying to inspect a Saharan site crashed in Spanish Morocco. He eventually decided that he would take 'Bluebird' to South Africa. The motoring correspondent of the *Cape Times* had persuaded him that a dried-up lake known as Verneuk Pan, which was about 450 miles (724km) north of Cape Town, was suitable for record breaking. Campbell sent a friend, Waters, to inspect the lake, and he returned with enthusiastic reports.

Henry Segrave. (Guy Griffiths Collection)

Meanwhile, work was being done to the Napier-Campbell. The car had been fitted with a new body which had a similarity to the previous version, but the side-mounted radiators had been abandoned. Instead a conventional ducted radiator had been fitted to the front of the car. The bonnet line was lowered, the cockpit sides were raised, and the fin was now an integral part of the tail. Apart from further attempts by Beard & Fitch Ltd to make the gearbox more usable, the car's mechanical specification was unchanged. The body was built by Arrol-Johnston & Aster Engineering Co Ltd at their Heathall works in Dumfries. This firm, which had been making cars since 1897, was now in difficulties, and it was probably hoped that the publicity from a successful record attempt would be commercially beneficial. The firm's chief engineer was the John Napier who had driven the victorious Arrol-Johnston in the 1905 Tourist Trophy. Campbell dispatched the faithful Leo Villa to Dumfries to oversee the body building.

The rebodied Napier-Campbell, now known as the Napier-Campbell-Arrol-Aster, was taken, by lorry straight from the Dumfries works to Southampton, where it was loaded on to the SS *Caernarvon Castle*. This sailed for Cape Town with Campbell and his party in the middle of January 1929, about two weeks before the Segrave team departed for Daytona.

The South African venture was ill-fated from the start. Verneuk Pan was about 20 miles (32km) long and about ten miles (16km) wide, and had a surface of dried mud which was completely smooth. Unfortunately, however, the entire surface was embedded with small, sharp splinters of shale. Waters had gone ahead of the main party to prepare the course. He came up with a plan to employ local labourers to scrape the top surface off the 12-mile measured distance, sieve it, mix it with water, and roll it back to make a shale-free surface. He enlisted the help of the Provincial Roads Department of Cape Province. The Department loaned an engineer named Nesbitt to look at the problems. There were just two snags: there was no water and no labour. The water had to be carried by lorry from a well 12 miles away, and the labourers had to be transported from Cape Town. Instead of the 400 that Nesbitt estimated would be needed, it was possible to recruit only 100.

Campbell was desperate to make a record attempt before Segrave could push it out of his reach and work went ahead as quickly as possible. The Government of South Africa and the corporations of Cape Town and Johannesburg made contributions to the cost of the work, and the Germiston Town Council loaned a steam-roller and driver free of charge. This had to be driven over a hundred miles under its own steam to reach the lake. After five weeks work the course was almost completed when there was another major setback. It had not rained at Verneuk Pan for over five years, but now the drought was suddenly broken by a torrential storm which lasted all night. In the morning the course was found to have been washed away and the lake bed was partially flooded. The tented encampment which had been set up for Campbell's team and the labourers was blown down. While the course was being relaid, Campbell flew down to Cape Town in his

'Bluebird's' body being remodelled in the Arrol-Aster works in autumn 1928 prior to the unsuccessful record attempt at Verneuk Pan. (Guy Griffiths Collection)

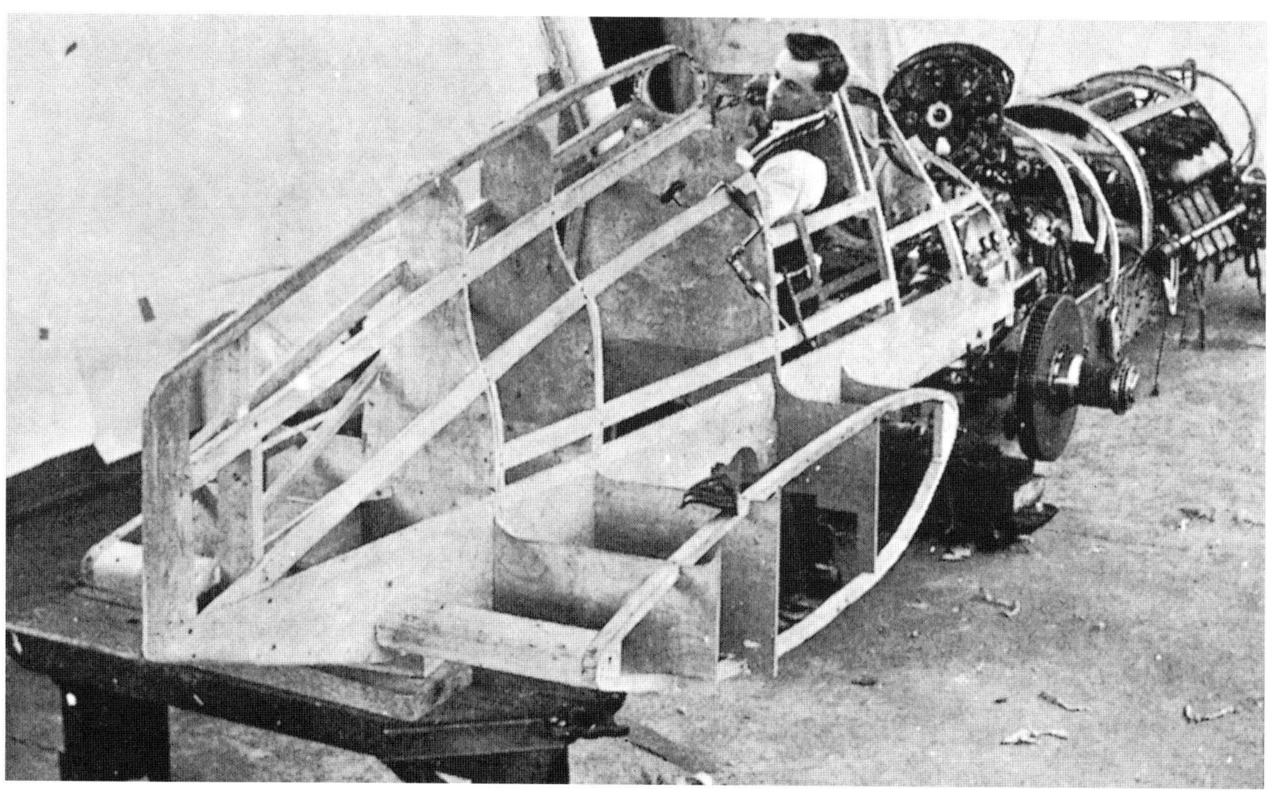

Gipsy Moth on 11 March to celebrate his 45th birthday. It was during the party that he was called to the telephone to be told of Segrave's new record by Reuters.

For Campbell, the news was a cruel blow indeed. The theoretical maximum of 'Bluebird' at peak revolutions was 231.8mph (373kmh). He knew that Segrave had pushed the record almost out of the car's reach even in optimum conditions. At Verneuk Pan, however, the conditions were anything but ideal. The Lion would be at least ten per cent down on power at the altitude of the lake, and the dry hot atmosphere would also take a toll.

At the Pan, a dyke was built around the course to prevent further flooding, and after a month the course was almost ready. The track was only 50 feet wide, and a white line was painted along the centre of the course to help Campbell keep the car straight. The troubles of the small team continued. While the course had been being prepared 'Bluebird' had remained in Cape Town, still in its crate. A local firm had been contracted to take the car to the lake on a specially prepared lorry, but during the enforced delay the firm had converted the lorry to a bus and another lorry had to be found. In its crate 'Bluebird' was too much for this lorry to cope with, so the car was removed from the crate and travelled lashed down, protected by a tarpaulin.

The lorry reached the lake on Thursday 18 April, and there was a need for urgency, as more rain was expected. There were no ramps, so a pit was dug into which the lorry was backed so that the car could be rolled off. When it was tested over the course the following day the next blow hit the ill-fated expedition; it was found that the weight of the car was breaking up the prepared surface and exposing the sharp shale underneath, which was cutting the tyres badly. However, the car had gone well and the rev counter had

Leo Villa changing the axle ratio of 'Bluebird' at Verneuk Pan on 18 April 1929, in preparation for the record attempt. (Guy Griffiths Collection)

indicated a speed of approximately 215mph (345kmh). Campbell intended to make a record attempt on Saturday, but a strong cross-wind persuaded him to postpone the attempt for a day. The wind did not ease until Sunday afternoon, when Campbell was told that the conditions indicated that rain was likely. He decided immediately to make an attempt.

The car ran straight and true along the course, despite some bumps, and Campbell found that the white line was an excellent guide. The revs indicated that the speed had been rather more than 230mph (370kmh), so hopes were high until the time came through: 225.5mph (362.8kmh) – not quick enough. The return run was slower, 212.5mph (341.9kmh), and Campbell had felt the car being held back by the deteriorating surface. Bitterly, he accepted that the

Campbell sits in 'Bluebird' as it is rolled out ready for its record attempt on 21 April 1929. (Guy Griffiths Collection)

conditions and power loss from the altitude had beaten him. He was not going to break Segrave's new record. To salvage something from the debacle, he decided to make an attempt on the world's five-mile and five-kilometre records – perhaps not much, but at least something to bring home. Dunlop Mac had gone to Daytona with Segrave, but Steve Macdonald, who had come to the Pan, warned that the tyres were not likely to stand a five-mile run over the shale. Once more troubles beset the little team, as before the timing equipment could be moved and the measured distance could be changed the wind blew again, and for five days no attempt was practicable.

Campbell found that the wind was still during the night and did not start to blow until about half an hour after dawn. Consequently he had the car readied in the dark, and as the first glimmer of daylight appeared he made ready for the attempt. Leo Vila says in his book *The Record Breakers* that when Campbell climbed into the cockpit, he muttered, 'You know, Leo, I'm getting too old for this sort of thing.' The engine was fired up with a gas starter, and the Lion fired, ran, spluttered and then stalled. Once again it was started, and the team pushed the car to save the clutch. Once more it stalled, and the team went through the starting procedure for a third time. The car ran through the five-mile course without mishap, but at the far end it was found that the tyres were badly torn. All four wheels were changed, but as Campbell accelerated back onto the course wheelspin tore the tread from one of the rear tyres and the run had to be done on the canvas. The average speed over the five kilometres was 216.03mph (347.59kmh), and the five-mile speed was just over 212mph (341kmh). Both records had been broken by a handsome margin but it was little consolation; the only prize worth having had eluded the Campbell team. A small but bitter crumb of comfort may have been the knowledge that the car had covered the mile at 217.52mph (349.98kmh), which was a substantial improvement on Keech's land speed record, which had stood when they disembarked at Cape Town.

The team packed up for the return

to England. For Campbell, the homecoming was not that which he had hoped for. There was no hero's welcome and his efforts had passed almost unnoticed. In financial terms it had also been a disaster; he estimated that the cost had been over £7,000. In the values of the 1990s this represents almost a third of a million pounds. 'Bluebird' remained in South Africa for six weeks, being exhibited. It then came back to England by cargo ship, and Villa towed it from the Lep Transport depot in Chiswick to Brooklands, where it was pushed away into a corner of Campbell's shed and seemingly abandoned. As a final postscript to the sad South African adventure, a few months later Arrol-Aster went into receivership.

Campbell now devoted his time to his motor racing and business interests. Segrave, meanwhile, had announced that he would make no more land speed record bids; he would now turn his attention to similar exploits on the water. Reports were circulating that the Napier-Irving 'Golden Arrow' was to be bought by Henry Birkin, one of the leading British drivers who was coming to the apogee of his career. It is improbable that Birkin would have contemplated buying the car himself. His finances were chronically unstable and it is more likely that he tried to persuade the Hon Dorothy Paget, who was sponsoring his racing, to buy it. Birkin probably hoped that the rewards from a successful record run would give him not only glory, but also more financial security. Birkin knew there was great potential in the 'Golden Arrow', as Irving had designed it to have a maximum speed of 270mph. Nothing more was heard of the proposal, so presumably Miss Paget was not persuaded.

Others, though, were making more positive efforts to take the record from Segrave. The Sunbeam company had built a huge car, the Silver Bullet, with two supercharged V-12 engines coupled in tandem. Each engine had a capacity of 24 litres and the crankshafts alone were five feet long. This monster was entrusted to successful racing driver Kaye Don, who had been much in the public eye after his victory in the 1928 Ulster Tourist Trophy with a Lea Francis. The Sunbeam team went to Daytona early in 1930, but they were plagued with mechanical troubles and internal tensions within the team; conditions on the beach were poor too. The best speed recorded, when runs were attempted in March, was 186.046mph (299.34kmh). In Britain, where the land speed record had become something of a national totem, the failure of the Sunbeam Silver Bullet was regarded as a national humiliation that had to be redeemed. Kaye Don's personal reputation probably never recovered.

Campbell was a complex man. While he wanted, more than anything else, to make another attempt on the record, he needed an excuse to justify it to himself before starting out again on the expensive, wearying, dangerous, and often heartbreaking quest. The Silver Bullet failure was just the spur he needed, and he saw himself as being entrusted with the task of saving the nation's pride. Campbell looked at 'Bluebird', languishing in the corner of the Brooklands shed, and realised that it needed a radical redesign if there was to be any chance of success. There was no question of going back to Joseph Maina. As Leo Villa put it in *The Record Breakers*: 'Maina had been a very clever designer . . . but he always solved every problem in the most complicated way possible. He would never use a straightforward shaft or lever if he could dream up an elaborate hydraulic arrangement, all valves and connections, to do the same task.' The solution lay less than a mile away, on the Byfleet side of the track.

Working closely with Thomson & Taylor, the leading Brooklands tuners, whose workshop was alongside the edge of the Byfleet Banking, was a young engineer and designer, Reid Railton. He had already gained a considerable reputation, specialising in chassis design. He had worked at Leyland Motors, as Parry Thomas's assistant, helping with the design of the Leyland Eight, a car aimed at the same market as the T75 Napier. After leaving Leylands, he had designed the Arab sports car, which had been greatly admired for its advanced features, even though it was not a commercial success. The Riley company had commissioned Railton to design the chassis of the Brooklands Riley, which by 1930 was the leading British 1,100cc sports cars and already gaining many racing successes. The Napier-Campbell was towed across Brooklands to the Thomson & Taylor sheds, where it was stripped. Railton examined it and began his preliminary designs. After a month, he approached Campbell and said that to achieve the target of 240mph (385kmh) the key would be an engine with an output of 1,500hp.

The only choice could be the latest version of the Lion. Much work had been done on the Lion at Acton by George Wilkinson and his team. A supercharger expert, A.J. (Alfred) Penn had joined the company and had developed a gear-driven centrifugal installation which was fitted to the rear of the engine. To take advantage of the improvement in fuels, the compression ratio was raised. A figure of 10:1 has been stated by a number of authorities, but for a supercharged engine this would have been astonishingly high and disaster would have been almost inevitable. A figure of 6:1 has also been mentioned for the VIID, and this seems much more likely, as it would have been similar to that of supercharged racing engines of the late '20s and the '30s. The magnetos were now driven from the front of the engine. The reliable and dependable Lion took all this in its stride. The power output had gone up from the 468bhp of the Mark I to the 1,320hp of this new variant, the VIID.

The VIID was only being produced for the Air Ministry, with the intention that it should be used in the Schneider Trophy, so there was a reluctance to divulge details of its specification. Campbell had some difficulty in persuading the Air Ministry to let him have a VIID, but after some negotiation – perhaps supported by the argument that the land speed record would bring as much national prestige as the Schneider Trophy – it was agreed that he should have two engines. With the engines available, Railton now began the detail design work on the car.

It was at this time that the whole nation was shocked at the news of the death of Sir Henry Segrave. He had been attempting to break the world water speed record on Lake Windermere on 13 June 1930, when the boat struck some floating debris and sank. Segrave died of his injuries two hours after the accident. Aged 34, he had been an international hero and universally admired for his courage and modest charm.

By a strange quirk, as a result of Segrave's death fortune now smiled upon Campbell from another source. He was given £10,000 backing by Marion ('Joe') Carstairs. Miss Carstairs, who, with her masculine appearance and demeanour, would probably have felt much happier in the world of the 1990s than that of the 1930s, was the granddaughter of one of the founders of the Standard Oil Corporation. She had become a leading competitor in motor boat racing during the 1920s, and had intended to make an attempt on the world water speed record herself. At Segrave's death, however, she abandoned her plans and decided to sponsor Campbell's new record bid instead. With an attitude a world apart from a modern sponsor, and perhaps fearing a stream of supplicants at her door, Miss Carstairs insisted that her generosity should remain a complete secret.

The rebuilt 'Bluebird' in Thomson & Taylor's workshop, autumn 1930. Standing behind it are, from left to right, Ken Thomson, Malcolm Campbell, Reid Railton, Ken Taylor, and Leo Villa. The chassis is a reflection of contemporary racing design practice, but on a larger scale. The jacking points can be seen behind the rear wheels. (Chas K. Bowers & Son)

Railton had made a radical redesign. His first action had been to throw away the FBM epicyclic gearbox. This was replaced by a dry multi plate clutch and a three-speed constant mesh box built by KLG, with ratios of 1.58, 2.27 and 4.01. The box was off-set to the nearside by a gear train, and Campbell would now sit beside the propeller shaft. To accommodate the new transmission line, a new rear axle was built with the final drive unit off-set by seven inches. The final drive ratio was 1.58:1. The old chassis frame, suspension, and steering were retained, but to reduce wheelspin nearly three-quarters of a ton (750kg) of lead was bolted over the rear axle, filling the rear tubular cross-member. An additional lead ingot was placed under the driver's seat. Each rear spring was set up with a different camber, so that when the full torque of the engine was applied the car would ride on an even keel. A 24-gallon (110-litre) fuel tank, which would contain Pratts 'Ethyl', was placed behind the driver. It was not a large tankage, but the car was not going on a very long journey. A second rev counter, in a fairing, was mounted on the bonnet so that Campbell could note the revs without taking his eyes off the course. The old spoked centre-lock wheels were replaced by pressed steel wheels, covered by Ace discs, which were considered essential to with-

December 1930: Campbell sits in the completed 'Bluebird' in the workshops of Gurney Nutting, the coachbuilders. (Chas K. Bowers & Son)

stand the extra speed and power. The radiator was out-rigged on the nose of the car, in a ducted housing.

The work was done on the car at Thomson & Taylor, and Joe Coe came from Acton to fit the engine and test it in the frame. Railton threw away the old body and designed a new one. A wood and plasticine one-tenth scale model was tested in Vickers's wind tunnel, and when Railton was satisfied with the drag coefficient the car was taken by Villa to Gurney Nutting, the coachbuilders in Chelsea, where the body was built. It was formed over a tubular steel frame, and the rear comprised a large fixed fin which was set slightly to the off side. The body used 600sq ft (55.8m^2) of aluminium and was finished in six weeks. It was given ten coats of cellulose, the final coat being given a high polish to reduce surface friction.

When it was finished the car was exhibited in the Rootes showroom in Piccadilly, and then taken to Southampton, where it was loaded on to the SS *Homeric*, which sailed for New York on 14 January 1931. The small Campbell team followed shortly afterwards in the *Aquitania*. Campbell was accompanied by Villa, 'Dunlop Mac' and his brother Steve, Joe Coe, and Harry Leech. Leech had been with Campbell during his Sunbeam days and had now rejoined the team, having been one of the few survivors of the R101 airship disaster the previous year. The press reported that to aid his fitness for the record attempt, Campbell had given up smoking and reduced his alcohol consumption. He had decided to return to Daytona again despite his previous problems with the course. He had considered going back to Verneuk Pan, and had contemplated courses on a dried salt lake at Cordoba in Argentina and on Ninety Mile Beach at Auckland in New Zealand, but the relative accessibility of Daytona and the facilities there had ultimately decided him in favour of the American venue. At the start of the voyage Campbell was warned that there had been a local political dispute at Daytona and there was a possibility that the beach would not be available for him. He decided to depart in any event, and planned to go on to New Zealand if the need arose. During the voyage he received cables informing him that the dispute had been resolved and that he would be most welcome at Daytona.

The Napier-Campbell and its 21 cases of parts and equipment were unloaded at New York and arrived at Daytona on 29 January. By Saturday the 31st the car had been made ready and Campbell asked for the beach to be cleared so he could make a test run. This was a tense time, as the car in its new form had not yet run under its own power. A big crowd gathered behind the team as the car was started up and Campbell set off along the beach, going up to about 120mph (195kmh). He turned the car and ran back, this time increasing the speed to about 200mph (320kmh). He then realised to his horror that he was driving straight towards the crowd. He braked, but the linings faded, and he had to stop the car by changing gear down through the box, ending up only 50 yards short of the spectators. He had been prepared to swerve the car into the sea as a last desperate resort.

The car had gone well, and after some minor adjustments another test run was made on Monday 2 February. This time it was extended to about 240mph (385kmh). Campbell told the officials he would make a record attempt next morning. A gale blew up overnight and the beach was not in its best condition, but the wind abated during the morning and Campbell decided to make the attempt anyway. The new wheels fitted to the car weighed two hundredweight (102kg) each, and it needed two men to change each wheel. The small team would have had difficulty in changing the wheels in the half hour allowed between each run, so Campbell would turn and make his second run on the same tyres. Campbell felt the acceleration was greater than he had ever experienced before. The course had been lengthened by taking some of the supports out of the pier, so that the car began its approach to the measured distance by passing under the pier. He commented afterwards that at 150mph (240kmh) the gap looked 'bloody small'. As he approached the start of the mile, Campbell looked at the rev counter and was amazed that it indicated a speed of about 260mph (420kmh). The car was still accelerating and he realised that he could over-rev the engine so he lifted his foot. The car jumped out of gear and the revs went right round the dial. Fearful that the engine was damaged, Campbell coasted the distance, turned round, and came back at a touring speed. The car was taken back to its garage and Coe spent that night and the whole of the next day checking the engine over, but could find nothing wrong. Leech made a catch for the gear gate to prevent it jumping out of mesh again. Campbell told the officials that the car would be ready for another attempt on Thursday 5 February.

'Bluebird' was brought out at about three o'clock in the afternoon. The sand was smooth but with some wet patches. Just before four o'clock the car was started and pushed off for the run. Campbell realised immediately that the fierce acceleration was now missing, so the edge had gone from the engine. The car made its south-bound run through the marked course without problems and it turned round to make the return run. Campbell had been followed up the course by a motor cycle policeman, who was now confronted with 'Bluebird' coming straight at him. He swerved away into the dunes and fell off. Campbell could not see the marker for the start of the measured distance until,

The Wakefield Trophy, presented by Sir Charles Wakefield of Castrol to the current holder of the world land speed record during the 1920s and 1930s. It is now displayed in the RAC clubhouse at Pall Mall, London. (Royal Automobile Club)

seeing it almost too late, he found he was not on the course and swerved back just in time. The second run passed without any more problems.

He stopped at the northern depot where the team waited, and was told that he made the first run at 246.575mph (396.73kmh), and come back at 244.897mph (394.01kmh), so his average was 245.736mph ((395.39kmh); he had broken Segrave's record by 14mph (22kmh). The team considered fitting the spare engine and trying to raise the record again, but the Daytona Speed Trials would be over and the course closed before the job could be finished, so the idea was abandoned.

The team set off for home. Campbell went to Washington on the way, where he was presented to President Hoover and joined the rest of the party to sail from New York on the *Mauretania*. Among his fellow passengers was Charlie Chaplin, who decided to leave the ship when it put into Plymouth as he felt that if he stayed with it until it docked at Southampton his presence might detract from Campbell's welcome. A tug met the ship in Southampton Water and an official came on board with a message from Prime Minister Ramsay MacDonald: 'I am glad to inform you that His Majesty has been pleased to approve that the honour of a knighthood be conferred on you.' A private train, 'The Bluebird Special', carried the team from Southampton to Waterloo, for a Government reception at Westminster Hall, and Sir Malcolm Campbell now found that he was a national hero, just as Sir Henry Segrave had been two years earlier.

'Bluebird' did not come back to England with the team but was sent to the British Empire Exhibition at Buenos Aires, where it was displayed for three weeks. Campbell was soon restless; he wanted to be the first man to exceed 250mph (400kmh) and he knew that the Napier-Campbell could do it without any modification if the engine was in perfect tune. There was also another threat. A car of which great things were expected, the 'Enterprise', was being built in Australia, sponsored by Fred H. Stewart, a rich Sydney businessman. It was to be driven by Norman 'Wizard' Smith on Ninety Mile Beach on the North Island of New Zealand. The car, was in many respects, similar to the Napier-Irving 'Golden Arrow', and Campbell realised it had to be taken seriously as it was using a Lion VIID. The aim of its designer, Don J. Harkness was to exceed 300mph (480kmh). When 'Bluebird' returned to England, therefore, it was taken back to Thomson & Taylor and Railton was given instructions to do all that was necessary to deal with the Australian threat. Railton fitted a new nose cowling of better aerodynamic form, the gear gate was changed, and the spare Lion, which was still unused, was installed. With this done, the car was put to one side.

The 'Enterprise' project, meanwhile, was progressing more slowly than its sponsor had hoped and it was unlikely to be ready before the beginning of 1932. Campbell was becoming restless: 250mph (400kmh) beckoned and so also did the financial rewards of another successful record attempt. Furthermore, if he was able to push up the record speed again it would make the task of the 'Enterprise' harder still. He was still considering the matter, when, just after New Year's Day 1932, he received a telegram from the Mayor of Daytona, inviting him to return in February for another record bid. This was the stimulus he needed, and the team made preparations, which were now becoming almost routine. With the exception of 'Dunlop Mac', the team was the same as the previous year. They and the car sailed from Southampton on the *Aquitania* on 26 January and Campbell followed them a few days later on the *Berengaria*. Campbell arrived in New York on 9 February, and travelled on to Daytona on the 'Dixie Flyer'. Although it was midnight when he arrived he was greeted by a huge crowd at the station.

Beach conditions were bad, and until there was a change in the weather any record runs were out of the question. The team had to wait until Saturday 20 February before the first test runs could be made, and the beach was still unsuitable for record breaking. Campbell went over the measured course at about 140mph (225kmh) and returned shaken and bruised. The weather and the beach were improving, however, and on the morning of Wednesday 24 February conditions were good enough to bring the car out for another test. Campbell had already decided that if all went well he would try for the record.

The extension of the course through the pier meant that he could attempt records for the kilometre, the mile, five kilometres, five miles and ten kilometres. The car hit a wet patch just before entering the mile and Campbell was blinded by spray, but he kept his foot down and noticed that in the middle of the measured mile the rev counter was showing 3,800rpm, equivalent to 273mph (440kmh). He ran on to the end of the measured ten kilometres and then turned the car and set off on the return journey without stopping. The car felt slower on the second run as it was running into a strong headwind, but when Campbell pulled up he was greeted with the news that he had broken the record with an average of 253.97mph (408.63kmh). His speed on the southern run had been 267.45mph (430.32kmh) but the headwind had reduced the north-bound run to 241.70mph (388.89kmh). The five-kilometre record had also been collected at 241.5mph (388.57kmh), but to Campbell's frustration the timing equipment for the five-mile and ten-kilometre distances had failed. Campbell wanted the two additional records, not only for the satisfaction of completing the job, but also because the extra records were worth substantial sums in bonuses from the fuel, oil, and accessory manufacturers. The car was brought out next day, but it was raining and the Mayor of Daytona intervened and would not permit a run. On Saturday 26 February the weather had improved again and the sun was shining, although the beach was rippled. Campbell had a bumpy ride, but saw a reading of 4,000rpm during the runs, the equivalent of 287mph (462kmh). The bumps prevented any improvement on the mile and kilometre figures established two days earlier, but the longer distance records were taken, the five kilometres at 247.94mph (398.93kmh), the five miles at 242.75mph (390.58kmh), and the ten kilometres at 238.66mph (384.00kmh).

Once more, the Campbell team returned to England and received the praise that was their due. But already Campbell was thinking of new records, and 300mph (480kmh) beckoned to him seductively. With this target in mind, Campbell decided to abandon the faithful Lion, which had never failed him, and went to talk to Rolls-Royce. No more would 'Bluebird' be a Napier-Campbell.

While Lion-engined cars had been pushing the land speed record ever higher, there had been a small and almost unnoticed Napier reappearance at Brooklands. Captain Alastair Miller had entered a car at the 1929 August Bank Holiday meeting which was called an Auto-Speed-Special. It had a six-cylinder engine with dimensions of 101.6mm x 127mm, with a declared capacity of 6,226cc. It was fitted with a navy-blue two-seater body and closer inspection revealed that it was a T75 Napier. The car's first owner had been Sir Otto Beit and the original body was a landaulette. There is a story, probably apocryphal, that Napiers insisted that Miller should rename the car, threatening litigation if it raced under the Napier name, though it is difficult to recognise any cause of action. The Auto-Speed-Special ran in the 90mph Short Handicap but was unplaced.

Two years later, on Saturday 17 October at the 1931 Autumn meeting, the car reappeared. This time it was called a Napier-Miller-Special and was entered by G.M. Denny with Miller as the driver. It was now painted grey and although the bore and stroke were unchanged the capacity was now announced as 6,178cc. Running in the Cumberland Junior Short Handicap it was unplaced, an inauspicious result for the very last Napier car raced at Brooklands.

The 'Enterprise' had been finished at the end of 1931 and was taken to Ninety Mile Beach. It had a three-speed gearbox, twin propeller shafts,

'Enterprise' at Sydney, New South Wales, on 12 January 1932, ready to be shipped to New Zealand for its unsuccessful record attempt. (Ronald Barker)

and final drives. Harkness, the designer, had aircraft experience, and had not made a clone of Irving's 'Golden Arrow' design. Instead of sponsons between the wheels, carrying surface radiators, it had ice radiators, and there were fairings behind the rear wheels, which were extended to form two stabilising fins. The first trials showed the ice radiators were not providing adequate cooling. Ninety Mile Beach was an isolated place, and the 'Enterprise' team had logistical problems of the kind that beset the Campbell team at Verneuk Pan. It may be wondered if one of the problems was obtaining a sufficient supply of ice. A large and poorly cowled front radiator was then fitted. Its appearance was surprising on a car designed by an aerodynamicist.

Not only was the car a problem, so was the course. The heavy tides made the beach very wet and it drained slowly, while the sand contained razor-sharp toheroa shells which cut up the tyres. On 1 May 1932, 'Wizard' Smith made his attempt, but sea-water entered the air intake, a magneto cut out when it was swamped, and the carburettor caught fire. The attempt was abandoned, and Smith did not try again. He had one consolation: he took the ten-mile record at 164.084mph (264.01kmh), during an earlier run. This record had escaped Campbell as Daytona Beach had not been long enough to measure out the distance. It seemed that the days of the Napier Lion as a record-breaking engine were now over, but it had had a marvellous run. Since 1927 it had taken the world land speed record five times, and had raised it from 174mph (280kmh) to 253mph (407kmh). However, contrary to most expectations, the roar of the Lion was not yet muted.

It is likely that the success of the Lion in gaining and holding the land speed record probably produced no more than a satisfied smile at Acton. The performance of the engine would have been of little surprise. It would have been more of a surprise if the records had not been gained, or if there had been any problems or anxieties concerning the engine. However, when Sir Malcolm Campbell had his final triumph with the Lion at Daytona in February 1932 it may well be that the feat went almost unnoticed in the confines of D. Napier & Son Ltd. The previous 12 months had been a time of drama and trauma for the firm. On 22 January 1931, Montague Napier had died at the Ville des Cistes. His health had been failing since the end of World War One and he had become very frail, but his death at the age of just 61 was a great shock to the company. He had taken the firm into motor manufacturing and had transformed it, in less than a decade, from a small concern making specialist equipment, into the maker of one of the finest cars built in Britain. It had also made him a very rich man. His estate was sworn at £1,267,662, equivalent to about £50 million in the values of the 1990s. It was his foresight that had resulted in the design and construction of the Lion, which had undoubtedly saved the company in the 1920s and was now pulling it through the Depression. With his death there was no longer a member of the Napier family directly concerned with the management of the company. An era had ended. The comfortable paternalism that had imbued the firm, despite the distance of the chairman from its daily doings, would now fade away.

H.T. Vane now became chairman of the board of directors. He had joined the company from S.F. Edge (1907) Ltd in 1913, and in Montague Napier's absence had been de facto chairman since 1919, although the final word on policy had always rested with Napier himself. The board realised that the company was facing a major problem. The Lion was now an obsolete design and Air Ministry orders for it were drying up. There were new aero engines on the drawing board, but these would need Government contracts if they were to ensure a prosperous future for the company. The country was in the grip of a massive depression and Government spending was being cut back to a bare minimum. Furthermore, the Air Ministry policy was still governed by the 'Ten Year Rule', that there would be ten years' warning of a possible war in Europe. Quite soon this rule would be abandoned, but the Napier board could not have foreseen this in the spring of 1931. The effect of the rule was harsh for aero engine manufacturers, though, and the prospect of any profitable new Government contracts was unlikely. The company would survive, as during the 1920s, when maximum profits had been received from the Lion, the board had prudently saved nearly a million pounds, which had been used in the purchase of Government stock. The dividends from this stock were now keeping the company afloat. Napiers needed a new source of business and the board, after many discussions, believed they had the answer.

If, in the first decade of the century, Napiers had 'worn the green', and this honour had fallen to Sunbeam in the first few years of the 1920s, in the mind of the man in the street the green mantle was firmly round the shoulders of Bentley in 1930. Four consecutive victories at Le Mans and countless other successes, together with the image of 'The Bentley Boys' and the aura of the car itself, had made Bentley the epitome of the sports car, not only for the British public but also for many people all over the world. Sadly, though, the image belied the truth. Since its inception in 1919 Bentley Motors had been grossly under-capitalised. Throughout the 1920s the company staggered from one financial crisis to another. This situation was compounded by the unwillingness of founder W.O. Bentley to cut the company coat according to the cloth, and, undoubtedly, by the expense of its racing programme. To be fair, the racing had probably kept the firm alive, maintaining the sporting image; if it had merely become a maker of luxury cars the final crisis would probably have come several years sooner.

All the assets of the company had been mortgaged since its earliest days. By the beginning of 1931 its finances were clearly beyond repair, and the mortgagees had had enough. London Life Association Ltd was the principal mortgagee and creditor, and on 10 July 1931 it applied in the Chancery Division of the High Court for the appointment of a receiver. The receiver was Patrick Raper Frere, and the Napier board wasted little time in approaching him. Napiers had looked at many possible ventures. A merger with the Gloster Aircraft Company was negotiated, but fell through. The company had started to make 'mechanical horses' to pull railway freight, but this was not going to be enough, and after much deliberation the decision had been made to go back into car manufacture. To Napiers, the Bentley crash was a godsend. If a price could be agreed with the receiver it could take over the Bentley firm, with the name, all the expertise, and above all W.O. Bentley himself, who had a service agreement with his company which he would be willing to honour. Most of the pain and problems of going back to making cars would be solved merely by the signing of a cheque. The under-capitalisation which had plagued Bentleys would be a problem no longer. Frere, the receiver, was happy to negotiate, since having a ready and willing buyer made his task much easier.

The negotiations continued throughout the summer and into the autumn. Meanwhile, W.O. Bentley had started work at Acton under conditions of the greatest secrecy, designing the new Napier-Bentley. There have been many conflicting rumours about the form that the car would have taken. Bentley himself, in his autobiography, is somewhat vague, but it seems likely that some preliminary work was done. By the end of October it had been agreed that Napier would pay £103,675 to buy Bentley Motors Ltd and all that remained was to have the deal approved by the Court. All concerned were so confident the Court would approve the arrangement that the receiver gave permission for the unsold 8-litre Bentley chassis to be moved from Cricklewood to Acton.

And so it came to pass that the little pigs played in their house with the new car they were going to build, and although the big, bad wolf did not exactly range up and down outside their door, he was doing accounts furiously in a rival boardroom.

The courtrooms and corridors of the Royal Courts of Justice in the Strand are not of themselves dramatic places, but they have seen great dramas. On a grey November morning, the solicitors and counsel for the receiver and for Napiers gathered in the corridor outside one of the Chancery courts for a last minute discussion, certain that the deal would have judicial approval. The matter had not been 'listed', as, being unopposed, it just needed a short mention to the judge and a request for an order approving the settlement, which would only take a few minutes. Their dismay can be imagined, when, just before the start of the hearing, a confident barrister accompanied by his solicitor and clerks, strode along the corridor and announced that he had been instructed to intervene in the matter on behalf of undisclosed clients. An urgent discussion took place between the three counsel on how the application would be made now that there was a third party.

The parties went into Court before Mr Justice Maugham and counsel for the receiver presented the details of the Napier offer, which counsel for Napier then confirmed. At that point the mysterious newcomer stood up and stated he was acting for the British Central Equitable Trust and had been instructed to offer a sum slightly larger than the Napier offer, on behalf of his clients. Napier's counsel asked for a short adjournment and there were then frantic telephone calls to Acton. Who made the decision is not known, but shortly afterwards, the parties returned to Court where a new offer was presented to the judge on Napiers' behalf. Counsel for the British Central Equitable Trust rose to his feet, but before he could speak the judge intervened. The Chancery judges of that era were not renowned for their affability or equanimity, and with typical testiness Mr Justice Maugham said he was not conducting an auction. He would adjourn until 4.30pm and then would accept sealed bids from the interested parties.

At the appointed time the parties trooped back into court. The two envelopes were handed up to the judge by the usher, and on opening them he declared that Napiers' bid was £104,775 and the Trust's was £125,256 and that the Trust was therefore the new owner of Bentley Motors Ltd. In fact the new owners were Rolls-Royce Ltd, the Trust had only been acting as a nominee. It may be contended that Mr Justice Maugham erred in law. It was the duty of the Receiver to obtain the highest possible price for the benefit of the creditors. When the judge knew that there were rival bids, the proper course would have been for the application to have been adjourned, and the receiver directed to resolve the matter of the bids and return to the Court when he was satisfied that the highest bid had been secured. The judge's directions for the sealed bids could perhaps have been grounds for an appeal by Napiers and the receiver, but such speculation is pointless.

Rolls-Royce had done the better homework. In his book *Bentley –*

Cricklewood to Crewe, Michael Frostick gives the details of the preliminary studies that had been made. Arthur Sidgreaves, the Rolls-Royce director entrusted with the task, had calculated that Bentley was worth £148,015, and said that an offer of £109,500 should be made. Rolls-Royce were determined to have Bentley, and it is likely that the solicitor acting for the Trust was able to get full instructions from Sidgreaves to push up the offer to a level where the purchase would be certain. Napier, on the other hand, had not expected any opposition and there would probably have been difficulty in getting full instructions from the Napier board during the short time available.

Rolls-Royce feared a Napier-Bentley, and the fear probably went beyond the car itself. With the additional resources that car manufacture would bring, it would make Napier a much bigger rival in the lucrative aero engine market. Defeated, Napier made no more attempts to enter the car market and aero engines became, once more, their sole product. What-might-have-beens are a fruitless exercise, but if Bentley had been secured, any car he designed would surely have been a formidable machine. W.O. Bentley could not keep away from motor racing and it is certain that he would have persuaded Napier that the car should be developed in competition. Such speculation is fascinating, but has no place here.

Chapter 13: 1933

The Lion Roars Again

JOHN Cobb was born in 1899. His parents were landowners at Esher, between London and Brooklands, where they owned a farm and were well-placed to develop their estate in the rapid expansion of the outer London suburbs after the end of World War One. He was educated at Eton and went into the City, where he became a fur broker. Between the Wars the ambition of most women was to own a fur coat, the more expensive the better. The fur trade was large and prosperous, despite the economic troubles of the times, and since fur brokers shared in that prosperity Cobb did not lack funds for his motor racing activities.

Physically, he was a big man, though his size contrasted with his shy and modest demeanour. As befitted his size, he liked big racing cars. He had started his Brooklands racing career in 1925, driving a 1910 10-litre Tipo S61 Fiat, a production version of the 1910 Grand Prix car. He had also driven the legendary 'Babs'. In 1929 he bought the V-12 Delage with which René Thomas had broken the land speed record at Arpajon in 1924 at 143.31mph (230.58kmh). It was in the Delage that Cobb became one of the great exponents of Outer Circuit racing at Brooklands. He won many races with the car, took British Class A records and by 1932 had achieved a fastest lap of 133.88mph (215.41kmh). Throughout his ownership, though, Cobb knew that the Delage was not quite fast enough. However hard he tried, and despite the intensive work of Thomson & Taylor, the car could not beat the 4-litre V-12 Sunbeam of Kaye Don or Miss Dorothy Paget's supercharged 4½ litre single-seater Bentley, driven by Sir Henry Birkin. At the beginning of the 1932 season the BARC scrutineers found creeping cracks in the aluminium crankcase of the V-12 engine, so the car was barred from races exceeding 150 miles (240km). Despite this restriction, Cobb won the British Empire Trophy after a breath-taking duel with George Eyston driving an 8-litre Panhard. Cobb knew that the days of the Delage were numbered and he was also mindful of the BARC reluctance to permit cars which were more than ten years old to race at Brooklands. The Delage would reach its tenth birthday in 1933.

To succeed on the Outer Circuit a car had to be fast, tough, and stable. At the end of 1932 Cobb had discussions with Reid Railton about the possibility of building a car not only for Brooklands, but also to attempt the world 24-hour record. The qualities needed would be equally desirable for both purposes. The decision about the engine was soon settled. When working with Malcolm Campbell on the Napier-Campbell 'Bluebird', Railton had been very impressed with the strength and reliability of the Lion. The engine had always done everything asked of it and had never let Campbell down. There would be no need for one of the supercharged racing Lions to get the results Cobb wanted – an unsupercharged unit would give the required power output.

The Air Ministry placed no restraint on the sale of the standard production Lion units, so Railton and Cobb negotiated the purchase of a Mark XIA from the Acton factory. This had the triple Napier carburettors and BTH magnetos mounted at the rear of the engine. With a 6:1 compression ratio it developed 530/540hp at 2,350rpm, with a maximum of 570hp at 2,585rpm. It seems that some slight improvements were made to the engine at Acton before it was delivered, as the factory bench test report showed that it developed 564hp at 2,350rpm, giving a maximum of 590hp at 2,700rpm, running on standard 80-octane National Benzole. In aviation trim the engine weighed 995lb (452kg). A second engine in the same tune was bought as a spare.

Construction of the car to Railton's designs had begun in Thomson & Taylor's workshops beside the Byfleet Banking at Brooklands at the end of 1932. Railton had drawn up the main specification, but much of the detail design was done by Ralph Beauchamp, a draughtsman in the

Cobb (third from left) stands with the Thomson & Taylor team beside the partially finished Napier-Railton in spring 1933. (Ronald Barker)

Thomson & Taylor drawing office who had done a five-year apprenticeship with Napier between 1919 and 1924. A massive channel-section frame was built, using side members supplied by John Thompson Ltd. The side-members tapered at the front and rear and passed underneath the axles. These were joined by a tubular cross-member at the front and a channel-section at the rear, while another channel-section cross-member and two tubes linked the middle of the frame. There was a straight three-piece front axle, carried on semi-elliptic leaf springs and shackled at the front. The axle was located by short radius arms. The steering box – an adapted Bentley component – was mounted to the frame and connected to the steering arm by a very long drag link, while the steering arm was fixed to the stub axle below axle level and the axle was damped by two pairs of Hartfords. There were no front brakes.

Two Woodhead cantilever springs on each side carried the fully-floating rear axle, which was made of three high tensile steel forgings, with an electron sump to cool the lubricant of the final drive. This was made by ENV and the ratio was 1.66:1. The rear axle carried conventional brake drums with expanding shoes, and was damped by two pairs of twin Hartfords. By hinging the axle at the rear end of the springs, these took all the driving and braking stresses. To fit the Lion engine to the car Railton had reversed it, so the carburettors and magnetos were at the front, and it was mounted on a three point sub-frame. A large diameter flywheel was fitted to the nose of the crankshaft and carried a single-plate Borg & Beck clutch which drove a separate three-speed Moss gearbox, mounted on a sub-frame, with a neat remote control. Immediately behind the gearbox was a transmission hand-brake and the driver sat alongside the Hardy Spicer propeller shaft. The milling of the banjo casing for the rear axle was contracted to Gay Bros of Kingston-upon-Thames. Reid Railton was so concerned that this should be done properly, that he sat beside the machinist in Gay Bros' workshop throughout the operation. The car ran on Rudge-Whitworth centre-lock wire wheels, initially with Dunlop 35in x 6in track racing tyres. A 65-gallon (295-litre) fuel tank was mounted in the tail, and the 15-gallon (68-litre) oil tank sat on the nearside of the propeller shaft, beside the driver. The wheelbase was 10ft 10in (330cm), track was 5ft (152cm), overall length was 15ft 6in (472cm), and the car weighed 3,360lb (1,527kg). When the chassis was completed, it went to Gurney Nutting Ltd, who made an aluminium single-seater body. As an acknowledgement of the car's constructors, a very small, enamelled 'T&T' badge was fixed to the radiator cowling.

It had been hoped to have the car ready for the 1933 Brooklands Whitsun meeting, but delays in the building prevented this deadline being

Two photographs taken of the Napier-Railton during assembly. (Geoffrey Goddard Collection)

met. Left in bare aluminium, with black wheels, the car was wheeled out of the Thomson & Taylor workshop and shown to the press on Tuesday 6 June, the day after the Whitsun meeting. The high quality of the workmanship attracted favourable reports. Cobb began testing in July, first doing many laps at

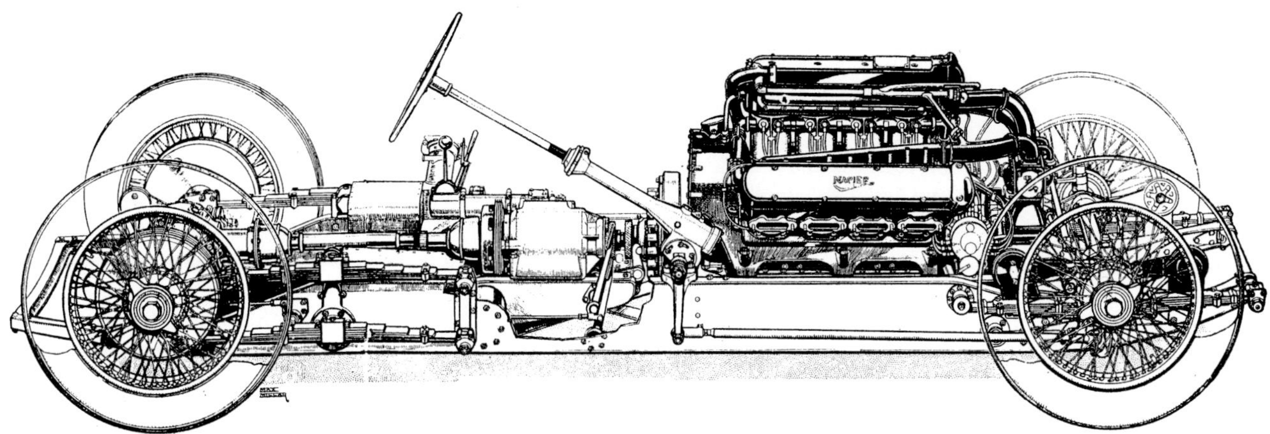

A drawing of the Napier-Railton chassis published in The Autocar *on 9 June 1933.*

about 100mph (160kmh) to bed the car in. Cobb entrusted some of this work to friends, and one of the drivers was Dr Neville Whitehurst, a general practitioner in Weybridge who attended the Cobb family. When the car was adjudged to be ready, Cobb opened it out and found that it handled perfectly and lapped at 130mph (210kmh) with ease.

The car made its racing debut at the Brooklands August Bank Holiday meeting on Monday 7 August. Cobb must have been satisfied with the car, as he restricted himself to two practice laps. Race day was intensely hot, which was probably why the crowd was smaller than usual, and the bars ran out of soft drinks early in the afternoon. The Napier-Railton was the principal object of attention in the Paddock and was surrounded by a large crowd. Cobb's first race was the Byfleet Lightning Short Handicap over about 6½ miles (10.5km) on the Outer Circuit. The Napier-Railton was on scratch, while Oliver Bertram, a barrister, with Cobb's old V-12 Delage, and Kaye Don with his 4.9-litre T54 Bugatti, started three seconds in front. Leaving the start, the car astounded onlookers with its acceleration, and it passed the Delage and Bugatti in less than half a lap. Coming onto the Members' Banking after the start of the second lap, Cobb then came up to pass Bouts, who was driving the Leyland-Thomas. Bouts obviously did not expect to be caught so soon and drifted up the Banking into Cobb's path. Cobb braked hard, there was a large cloud of dust, and some eye-witnesses said the cars touched. Gathering the Napier-Railton together, Cobb swept past the Leyland-Thomas on the Railway Straight and went on to win by 2.4 seconds from Bertram. His race average was 122.23mph (196.66kmh) and he had set a new standing lap record at 120.59mph (194.02kmh).

Such an impressive debut did not go unnoticed by A.V. Ebblewhite, the Brooklands handicapper, and when the Napier-Railton came out for the nine mile (14.5km) Byfleet Lightning Long Handicap it had been given an additional handicap of 13 seconds.

The Napier-Railton, making its debut at Brooklands on 7 August 1933, is about to collide with Bouts's Leyland-Thomas on the Members' Banking before going on to win the Byfleet Lightning Short Handicap. (Burmah-Castrol Ltd)

Despite lapping at 137.20mph (220.75kmh), a new Class A (over 8,000cc) lap record, the extra handicap was too much and Cobb finished fifth. Throughout the '20s and the early '30s, racing on the Outer Circuit had usually been dominated by one car that was faster than the others. The crowd at Brooklands that Bank Holiday afternoon realised that another car had come to take the place of such machines as Parry-Thomas's Leyland-Thomas and Birkin's 'Blower' Bentley. For Cobb, the meeting had shown that the work and expense had been worthwhile. He not only had a car that was the fastest at Brooklands, but it would also fulfil its other purpose and contend for international class and world records.

Cobb decided to abandon Brooklands competition for the rest of the season and instructed Thomson & Taylor to prepare the car for an attempt on the world 24-hour record. As Selwyn Edge could have confirmed, this would not be easy. The existing record of 113.4mph (182.46kmh), which had stood for six years, had been established at Montlhéry by Morel, Marchand, and Kiritoff in 1927, with an 8-litre sleeve valve Voisin. This was a comparatively modest speed, but the length of time for which the record had stood indicated the size of the task. Cobb's attempt could not be made at Brooklands. Apart from the inherent limitations of the track, night running was not permitted, so Montlhéry, south-west of Paris, was chosen as the venue. This had been opened in 1924 and comprised both a banked track and an artificial road circuit, on which the GP de l'ACF (the French Grand Prix) had been run several times. The 2.5km (1$^{1}/_{2}$ mile) banked track had two parallel straights joined by steep constant curve bankings, and was used regularly for record attempts. In 1932 there had been a major fire in a garage under the banking, which had buckled the concrete track and damaged the supports, and the track had only been reopened in the summer of 1933 after extensive repairs.

Thomson & Taylor did not have much to do to the Napier-Railton. Presumably the Lion was checked over, but was probably not returned to Acton, as it had done little work since its installation in the car. When it was built, the car had been wired and fitted with Rotax switchgear, so a bracket was made up with three Lucas headlights and fitted to the front of the car. The Brooklands silencers were removed and the manifolds replaced with stub exhausts, the nearside of the cockpit being shielded to prevent the glare from the exhaust flame distracting the driver at night. The Lion revved at such low speeds that it was difficult to gauge any increase in speed accurately. To overcome this problem, a vernier throttle stop was installed which, when turned, allowed the accelerator pedal to be depressed a bit further. Brooklands had shown that the rear axle could become very hot with extended running, so separate gauges showed the temperature of this component.

Cobb had picked his team of drivers carefully. There was Cyril Paul, who had shared the V-12 Sunbeam with Cobb in the 1929 500-Mile Race, coming third, and had won the '500' in 1931, sharing a Bentley with Jack Dunfee. Paul had also done much sports car racing and made his living dealing in sports cars. Accompanying him were Tim Rose-Richards, a stockbroker, and the Hon Brian Lewis, who was the heir to a shipping fortune. This pair had also had much Brooklands and sports car experience, both having been with Cobb in the Talbot sports car team in 1931 and 1932, and there were those who considered that Lewis was perhaps the best British driver racing at that time. Probably more important, all three co-drivers had the reputation of being in sympathy with the cars they drove. Cobb had also picked the best people available as the team personnel. As manager, there was the legendary S.C.H. ('Sammy') Davis, the sports editor of *The Autocar* and the winner of Le Mans in 1927. Davis's knowledge of motor racing and record breaking and his organisational skills in the pit would be essential; he was also responsible for all the preliminary paperwork and travel arrangements. The timekeeper was Roland King-Farlow, who was also an expert in his field, while to look after any casualties Dr Whitehurst was in attendance. The technical side was in the hands of two Thomson & Taylor mechanics, while Joe Coe had come from Acton to tend to the needs of the Lion. Tyres were going to be a crucial issue and were the responsibility of 'Dunlop Mac' with his assistant, Walter 'Fiddle' Hicks. Lucas and National Benzole, the fuel company, also sent technicians. Not wanting to miss the searching test of his brainchild, Reid Railton came along too.

The Napier-Railton and the technical staff left Brooklands bound for Paris late in September. Cobb and the drivers, together with the 'managerial' team, flew from Croydon to Le Bourget in an Imperial Airways Handley Page HP 42. At the time of their departure they heard that the 24-hour record had been broken by a Pierce-Arrow driven by the American Ab Jenkins on Lake Muroc in California, at 117.82mph (189.57kmh). Although Jenkins's record had not yet received official confirmation from the AIACR, it meant that King-Farlow had to recalculate the times and speeds that the Napier-Railton would need to maintain, and the task was going to be harder. Pitwork was the key. Time lost while the car was standing still would negate all the efforts of the driver at the wheel. Tyre wear was the greatest problem. Sammy Davis explained the difficulty facing the team in his biography of Cobb, *The John Cobb Story*:

If the tyres lasted 200 miles at the rear and 400 at the front, there were fifteen stops to arrange and the schedule could be 126mph. If the rear treads only lasted 160 miles it meant nineteen stops, so the more tyre wear the higher speed the car would have to run – though the higher the speed the more wear one would expect.

A vicious circle indeed. The team were drilled in pit-work, as described in *Motor Sport*:

The heavy wheels were far from easy to handle with speed, and all four were changed, and forty gallons of petrol, and oil and water were taken on in less than a minute. There was an army of helpers; two on the petrol, one on each wheel, one on each jack (later going on to help the wheel men) and one on oil.

The Brooklands experience of 'Dunlop Mac' ensured that the centre lock wheel nuts were only tightened just over finger tight. The nuts tightened up with high speed running and if hammered right up, they would have been almost immovable when the wheels were changed, and much time would have been lost. Refuelling practice showed that if any fuel was spilt on the track the stub exhausts of the Lion ignited it when the engine was restarted. This problem was solved by dropping a large metal sheet over the spilt fuel. The drivers also had to ensure that they stopped in exactly the right place, as the fuel came from a gravity feed tank which could not be moved.

The car lapped the Montlhéry circuit at 138mph (222kmh) when tested, and all the drivers familiarised themselves with the car and the track, including night practice. This showed that the headlights fitted to the Napier-Railton were inadequate at speeds over 120mph (190kmh), so, like Edge at Brooklands in 1907, Cobb found he needed red hurricane lamps to line the inside of the track. George Eyston spent much of his time taking records at the track, an activity which he found was very profitable. He had his own lamps stored at Montlhéry and these were hired to Cobb. The upper edge of the track was marked with red electric bulbs. As a diversion, the veteran driver Jean Chassagne, who had driven with Davis in the Sunbeam and Bentley teams, took Cobb's team on tours of the gastronomic delights of Paris.

The run was to start at 7.00am on Monday 2 October, but when the team assembled in the early morning Montlhéry was heavily befogged. It was not until 1.00pm that visibility was sufficient for Cobb to start the attempt. He settled down immediately to lap at 130mph (210kmh). After 96 minutes he was flagged in, having already taken six Class A records and the first world record for 200 miles at 126.44mph (203.44kmh). The team had one unexpected problem, caused by the many friends and well-wishers who had come from England to watch and had crowded round the pit, including a youthful Lord Forbes in bizarre tartan overalls, and some firm methods were needed to clear the pit for this first stop. Although all four wheels were changed and it was refuelled and had its radiator topped up, the car was only stationary for 52 seconds; then Cyril Paul was on his way. He had not been running for long when the engine note was heard to cut out on the back straight. Paul came round slowly to the pit with the offside rear tyre in shreds. 'Mac' and 'Fiddle' changed both rear tyres in 32 seconds and the car was away again.

Paul was having serious problems, however. The surface of the track was breaking up, especially at the place where the fire damage had been repaired, and a pronounced ridge had developed which pounded the tyres at each lap. He came in again, all the wheels were changed, the car was refuelled once more, and Paul handed the wheel over to Rose-Richards. King-Farlow recalculated the schedule to make up for the lost time, and the car was speeded up. The three-hour record fell at 124.33mph (200.04kmh), but soon afterwards Rose-Richards passed the pit pointing to both front wheels, on which the breaker strips were showing, thus necessitating another unscheduled stop. Next, the offside rear tyre burst again, but 'Mac' and 'Fiddle' had the car away in 40 seconds. At the next scheduled stop, as daylight was beginning to fade, the headlight bar was fitted, but it was noticed by Railton that the radiator was taking more water than was expected. Meanwhile, the Montlhéry Model-T Ford tender 'Valentin' plodded steadily round the track, dropping off the red lamps on the inside verge. It was now evident that the pounding of the track had damaged the radiator, and as darkness fell Railton and Cobb discussed the situation. The radiator was a lesser problem, but Cobb was concerned about the safety of the drivers if tyres burst in the darkness. Reluctantly it was decided to abandon the attempt. At 7.00pm the car was called in. The last record to fall was the six-hour, at 122.62mph (197.29kmh).

Although the team was very disappointed, the attempt had not been fruitless. The Napier-Railton had taken six Class A records from 50km to one hour, the hour at 126.83mph (204.06kmh). More important, six world records had fallen: the 200 miles (125.64mph/202.15kmh), the 500km (123.63mph/198.92kmh), the 500 miles (123.27mph/198.34kmh), the 1,000km (122.05mph/196.37kmh), the three-hour (124.33mph/ 200.04kmh), and the six-hour (122.62mph/197.29kmh). There was an anomaly with the 500km, 500 miles and six-hour records, as Ab Jenkins had already gone faster over these distances, but his claim had not been formally submitted to the AIACR. Cobb's claim was submitted and accepted, though, so for the time being at least, the Napier-Railton held these records. Ironically, sometime later the AIACR declined to ratify Jenkins's records, so there had been no need for the Napier-Railton to set such a fast pace. Perhaps, at a lower average, the pounding of the track would have taken a lighter toll and the tyres would have lasted.

On returning to England the Napier-Railton was checked over at Thomson & Taylor and minor repairs were made. The car had not quite finished its efforts for 1933, though. On 26 October the Swiss driver Hans Ruesch took a 3-litre 8CM Maserati to Montlhéry and raised the world standing start kilometre record to 88.33mph (142.12kmh). This was a comparatively easy record to capture as it had been set by Parry Thomas in 'Babs' back in 1926. Five days later, Cobb brought out the Napier-Railton at Brooklands, with the intention of taking Thomas's record, unaware that Ruesch had already raised it. The kilometre course was marked out on the Railway Straight, but this was too short for the distance so the course began at the end of the Members' Banking and finished as it ran onto the Byfleet Banking. The rules for a standing start sprint record were similar to those for the short flying start records: the course had to be covered in both directions and an average taken of the two times. Cobb did the kilometre at 88.14mph (141.81kmh) and the standing start mile at 102.5mph (164.92kmh). The kilometre time was not fast enough, as he realised when he heard of Ruesch's record, but the mile time was a new world record.

To take these records at Brooklands was not easy. The Napier-Railton would probably have been doing well over 140mph (225kmh) as it finished the distance, and on the return run this meant entering the Members' Banking at that speed, and almost immediately hitting the notorious 'bump' where the track crossed the River Wey. Normally cars hit the 'bump' from the other direction, so from the reverse direction it was almost certainly sharper and more abrupt. Cobb wanted both records, so to get the best gearing smaller rear tyres were fitted and on Friday 4 November the car came out again. This time it was successful; the standing start kilometre time was 88.52mph/142.42kmh (25.28 seconds) and the world record was Cobb's. During the attempt he also established a local Brooklands record, being timed over the flying kilometre at 143.67mph (231.16kmh).

Chapter 14: 1934

Thwarted in France

THE Napier-Railton was put away for the winter. Dunlop worked on some larger tyres and an alternative 2:1 final drive was made up. The car was tested by Cobb, Cyril Paul, and Brian Lewis on 10 March in preparation for the 1934 season. It covered 75 miles (120km) on the Outer Circuit, putting in a best lap of 134mph (214kmh) and averaging about 130mph (208kmh). There had been an opening meeting in March, which was restricted, as the winter track repairs had not been finished, so the proper Brooklands season began with the meeting on Easter Monday. This brought in a crowd larger than usual, as they were promised the spectacle of John Cobb making an attempt on the lap record, currently held by the late Sir Henry Birkin in his single seater 'blower' Bentley at 137.96mph (221.97kmh). The expected rain held off, but there was a gusting wind which could make things difficult for Cobb. In the Paddock there was a small exhibition of Veteran and Edwardian racing cars, arranged by William Boddy, then the assistant editor of *Brooklands-Road & Track*. Among the exhibits was the 1903 E61 Gordon Bennett Napier that had suffered at the hands of Jarrott and Earp. It was still in good fettle and running well, doing a lap of the track during practice, with the enthusiastic Boddy as a passenger, when it touched 70mph (112kmh).

The Napier-Railton was greatly admired in the Paddock. It now had a mottled aluminium finish with a green frame, and won the Appearance Prize awarded for the best-presented competing car. Cobb made his attempt after the end of the fifth race. The car came out of the Paddock and did two warm-up laps; then came the fast one. On the Byfleet Banking the car seemed to be in a four-wheel drift, the tail riding higher than the nose. Cobb pulled it off the banking early so that he would have a straighter run across the reverse curve at the Fork. As it approached the Fork, Cobb eased the throttle slightly and the wind, gusting off the side of the Vickers works, caught the car, which swerved out and then back again, raising a cloud of dust as Cobb corrected the slide. It was full throttle again as he went onto the Members' Banking higher and earlier than was the usual practice. Passing under the Members' Bridge, the car snaked badly as the wind caught it again. Then, on the Railway Straight, just before entering the Byfleet Banking, the Napier-Railton touched 165mph. Cobb came round at the end of the lap and was signalled that he had a new record, so he slowed, drove slowly up the Finishing Straight, and turned into the Paddock gates to be greeted by a huge ovation and the congratulations of countless friends and well-wishers.

To the shy, modest Cobb, the terrors of his reception were probably much worse than anything he had experienced during the record lap. The physical and nervous tensions of the attempt were such that helpers had to ease his fingers from the wheel and massage his arms. But it had all been worthwhile; the Napier-Railton held a new lap record at 139.71mph (224.79kmh). Cobb had shown, once again, the difficulties of driving a truly fast car on the Outer Circuit. It could not be kept flat out all the way round, the peculiarities of the track forcing drivers to treat it like a road course, and at some points there was a need for considerable skill and courage. Cobb's comment afterwards on taking the lap record was that it was somewhat like 'seeing how far one could lean out of a window without falling out, and therefore somewhat risky.'

His day was not yet over, however, as less than an hour later the Napier-Railton came out of the Paddock again to take part in the nine-mile Ripley Lightning Long Handicap. It was on the scratch mark, and Cobb did his standing lap at 113.19mph (181.12kmh), and on the next lap he went round at 133.52mph (214.83kmh). He realised that the handicap was going to be too much, even for the Napier-Railton, and he would not catch the cars in front, so he eased off and the last lap was at 129.7mph (208.68kmh). As he drove

2 April 1934: John Cobb is surrounded by the crowd as he brings the Napier-Railton back to the Paddock at Brooklands after setting a new lap record at 139.71mph (224.79kmh). (William Boddy)

back to Esher that evening Cobb must have been very content with his afternoon's work. One of his aims for the car had been achieved, but there remained some unfinished business in the field of record-breaking.

Montlhéry had been booked already, and just over a week after Brooklands the Napier-Railton was on its way back to France. For this new attempt on the 24-hour record there was a change in the team of drivers. Cyril Paul was able to join the party, but Brian Lewis had business commitments and Tim Rose-Richards was engaged in long-running litigation in the High Court. As replacements, Cobb chose Charles Brackenbury and Freddie Dixon. Brackenbury was a flamboyant Brooklands regular, who in the past two seasons had raced there frequently, while Dixon was already on his way to becoming a motor racing legend. He had been a motor cycle racer in the 1920s, winning the Sidecar and Junior TTs in the Isle of Man. In 1932, at the age of 40, when most were thinking of giving up the sport, he had begun racing cars, specialising in Rileys. He had no experience of large racing cars at that time though, all his racing had been with 1,100cc Rileys. Although the drivers had changed, Cobb was accompanied by the same pit staff and supporting team as in the previous attempt, with the addition of Norman Freeman, the Dunlop racing manager. He was evidently concerned that the tyres should not fail again.

Once again, the drivers flew to Paris in an Imperial Airways HP 42, and the team stayed at the Hotel L'Escargot near the track. Testing was uneventful, but Dixon was some 12 inches shorter than Cobb and the team had difficulty in packing the seat of the Napier-Railton so that he could drive the car comfortably. The pit stops were rehearsed and a large shed beside the track made a greatly improved pit.

The run began at 12.14pm on Monday 16 April and Cobb took the wheel for the first stint. After much prevarication, the AIACR had eventually ratified Ab Jenkins's 24-hour record, which stood at 117.82mph (189.57kmh), so the attempt was not going to be easy and there was little in hand if there was any trouble. Cobb came in after 1hr 50min; during his run he had switched off the dynamo when the battery was sufficiently charged. The car stopped for only 54 seconds and then, refuelled and with four new tyres, it set off again with Paul at the wheel. The tyres seemed to be standing up to the stresses, although one deflated with a slow puncture after it had been removed from the car. Cobb reported that the track was as bumpy as it had been during the previous attempt.

It had been arranged that if the driver cut the engine as he passed the pit it was a signal that he was coming in. The engine cut and Paul pulled in, the stop was unscheduled and he was clearly in great pain. He was helped from the car and Brackenbury took over. Like most Brooklands drivers, Paul was wearing a body belt which supported and protected the back and the abdomen from the pounding of the track. It appeared that the belt had been too loose and Dr Whitehurst took him away and strapped him up, but had to report to the team that he might be unfit to drive again.

Brackenbury had a trouble-free run and came in at the appointed time to hand over to Dixon after a 62-second stop. All seemed to be going well, but any complacency was dispelled when the engine cut and Dixon limped into the pit, the offside front tyre having been shredded when it had thrown a tread. This was changed quickly and the car went off again. The first world record to fall was the 1,000km at 122.82mph (197.61kmh). Cobb took over again from Dixon, but it was evident that the cockpit was too large for Dixon and he had been thrown around in the seat and badly pounded. Cyril Paul declared himself fit enough to try another spell, so he relieved Cobb at the next stop, keeping up the pace for a while helped by an illuminated semaphore which indicated to the driver that the correct speed was being held. Before his stint was completed Paul stopped again, in agony, and was replaced by Cobb. Dr Whitehurst reported that Paul was probably suffering from appendicitis and would not be fit to drive again. Shortly before Paul came in, the six-hour record had fallen at 123.01mph (197.92kmh).

The attempt was now threatened by a driver shortage. With Paul out of action and Dixon badly bruised, the onus was going to fall on Cobb and Brackenbury. There were discussions in the pit about additional drivers. Tommy Wisdom, the motoring journalist, who was reporting the run for various papers, was an experienced competition driver and expressed his willingness to participate. Sammy Davis, too, was prepared to abandon management for driving. At dusk, the ancient Model-T Ford deposited the red lanterns around the course and the headlights were fitted to the Napier-Railton. Cobb handed over to Brackenbury after a stop of 51 seconds, during which 'Dunlop Mac' changed one of the wheels single-handed in 23.8 seconds. Brackenbury came in when a tyre threw a tread and reported that the track was breaking up and he was being badly shaken. Dixon succeeded Brackenbury and another tread was thrown. Dr Whitehurst was now concerned about Dixon, who had become exhausted by the pounding he had received in the cockpit; Brackenbury was also badly in need of a rest, so there seemed little alternative to Cobb driving yet again. At this point Paul staggered into the pit, insisting that he felt better, and said he would try to carry on. Despite universal protests, he climbed into the car and set off. He managed to cover another 103 miles (165km) before coming back into the pit in agony and handing over to Cobb, his courage having enabled the other drivers to get some essential rest.

The 12-hour record fell soon after midnight at 121.19mph (194.99kmh), but a little later rain began to fall, which made the drivers' task much harder, particularly as a large hole had appeared in the banking. At the next stop, when Brackenbury handed over to Cobb, the team slowed the refuelling down to give two workmen time to attempt repairs to the hole. The 2,000 and 3,000km records both fell at 120.71mph (194.22kmh), a tribute to the drivers' consistency. The track was now slippery and the Napier-Railton was snaking as it left the bankings, but as the sky lightened spirits lifted, and it seemed that the full 24-hours would be completed. Cobb came in and handed over to Dixon, but it was agreed that after Dixon's run Wisdom and Davis would take a turn at the wheel, as the rain and the pounding of the disintegrating track had exhausted the team.

At 7.35am disaster struck. The Napier-Railton came unusually low off the western banking, then slid sideways and just missed the timekeeper's hut and the pit. Sliding the full length of the straight at 120mph (190kmh) as Dixon struggled to regain control, it ran up the eastern banking, spun, and smashed through the retaining fence at the top. The front wheels went over the edge and hung over the 40-foot (12m) drop while the car slid along the lip of the banking on its belly, with the frame scraping along the track. It then spun again and slid down the banking and onto the infield, ending up on its side in a ditch. Cobb and Dr Whitehurst were the first there, and found Dixon already out of the cockpit, very shaken but unhurt, and already with a glass in his hand!

The attempt was over. Apart from buckled front wheels and a dented and scraped frame, the car seemed undamaged, but it was stuck in the ditch. With the combined efforts of the team and all the available helpers at the track, and with a tow from a car as well, it was eventually hauled clear. Cobb was much relieved, as it had to be produced to the AIACR officials and verified before the records it had taken could be ratified.

Cobb was universally liked and respected, not least for his thoughtfulness and concern for others, and these qualities were to the fore in his anxieties for Dixon's well-being. Although the 24-hour record had almost been in the bag there was no word of reproach for Dixon, even though the tyres had been intact when the accident started, and there

The Napier-Railton after Freddie Dixon's skid at Montlhéry on 16 April 1934. (Guy Griffiths Collection)

were suggestions that Dixon had dozed off at the wheel.

The party returned to England and the Napier-Railton went back to Thomson & Taylor, where it was stripped and inspected. The damage was found to be more extensive than had first been thought. The frame was dented, the engine sub-frame was twisted, all the wheels were beyond repair, the spring shackles were damaged, and the crankcase and sump of the Lion were cracked. While the chassis was rebuilt, the Lion went back to Acton. It is not known if the engine was repaired or a new unit was sent back to Brooklands. It is possible that the spare engine went into the car at this time. While the repairs continued, Cobb kept his hand in by racing his 2.3 litre 'Monza' Alfa Romeo in the Junior Car Club International Trophy and the British Empire Trophy, over artificial road circuits at Brooklands. He finished seventh and fourth respectively in these races.

The Brooklands August Bank Holiday meeting, on Monday 6 August, saw a fully repaired Napier-Railton back in action. It was an overcast day and there was only an average crowd. The Napier-Railton was to run in the main event, the 1934 Brooklands Championship, which – almost unheard of at Brooklands – was to be a scratch race over four laps of the Outer Circuit. This was the sixth race on the card and Cobb showed he was in good form by taking second place in his Monza Alfa in the Esher Lightning Short Handicap, being beaten by only half a length by his old V-12 Delage, driven by Oliver Bertram.

There were only four starters in the Championship: the Napier-Railton, Bertram's Delage, the T54 4.9 litre Bugatti of Dudley Froy, and the T51 Bugatti of Tom Fothringham. Cobb had the initial advantage, but was passed by Bertram as the cars ran onto the Members' Banking. Cobb was back in front when the cars came off the Banking and onto the Railway Straight, and he stayed there for the rest of the race. Froy and Bertram battled for second place, but Cobb swept away into the distance. His standing lap speed was 118.30mph (190.34kmh), but on the second lap, with a clear track in front of him and no wind to contend with, he set a new lap record at 140.93mph (226.75kmh), the first 140mph (225kmh) lap at Brooklands. Cobb now eased off and the Napier-Railton did the two remaining laps at 138.34mph (222.58kmh) and 134.60mph (216.57kmh). The race average was 131.53mph (211.63kmh), the fastest race speed recorded at Brooklands. Froy and Bertram battled to the finish, separated by only a length at the line.

The Napier-Railton was out again for the nine-mile (14.5km) Esher Lightning Long Handicap. Cobb was on the scratch mark and the combination of the handicap and the difficulty of passing fast cars in front on the bankings gave him an impossible task, so he finished in the middle of the field. His fastest lap was at 134.60mph (134.60kmh). The Napier-Railton was evidently fully restored to health and Cobb had shown that with the right conditions it could go faster. Perhaps, too, Archie Frazer-Nash, the progenitor of GN and Frazer Nash cars, was right when he said a car always went better after it had been crashed, as this relieved the stresses!

The Napier-Railton still had one more engagement before the end of the 1934 season. In 1929, the British Racing Drivers' Club (BRDC) had established the 500-Mile Race on the Outer Circuit. Regarded as the finale of the British season, it was a flat out event, albeit a handicap, and had already become a classic race. As his co-driver for the '500' Cobb had chosen Tim Rose-Richards. Neither had any illusions about the task ahead of them. The Napier-Railton would start from scratch, and to win it would have to average almost 130mph (210kmh). This alone would be difficult, but there would also be the problems of having to pass the other 30 cars in the race continuously. Practice during the previous week showed it would be run at a very high speed. Whitney Straight, with his ex-Scuderia Ferrari Duesenberg, lapped at 138mph (220kmh); Froy in the Bentley-based Barnato Hassan lapped at 130mph (210kmh); while Freddie Dixon in a 2-litre unsupercharged Riley had gone round at 125mph (200kmh).

The cars were started in capacity class groups. The smallest cars were flagged away at noon, while the largest capacity class, which included the Napier-Railton, was released at 12.24pm. Cobb quickly settled down to lap at 126mph (202kmh), and when the first announcement was made of the race order on handicap he was in second place, behind George Eyston's K3 MG and in front of Dixon's Riley. At about 1.00pm it began to rain; this soon changed from a drizzle to a downpour, and the whole pattern of the race changed. Cobb now dropped his speed and was lapping at only 112mph (180kmh); on the bankings he was no faster than the 750cc machines and could only use the power and speed of the Napier-Railton on the Railway Straight. At 1.30pm Cobb still held second place on handicap, having averaged 122.82mph (197.60kmh), but by 2.00pm his average had fallen to 116.73mph (187.81kmh) and he was making little impression on the cars which were ahead of him. Soon afterwards the Napier-Railton pulled into the pits, Cobb had a discussion with Reid Railton and Rose-Richards, and then climbed out of the car. They had decided that in the prevailing conditions the risks were too great and the possibility of success had gone, so the Napier-Railton was withdrawn. Only seven cars reached the end of the 500-mile race, the winner being Freddie Dixon, at an average speed of 104.8mph (168.62kmh).

Chapter 15: 1935

Records on Salt

LIKE 1933, 1934 had been a mixture of triumph and frustration for Cobb. The goal of the 24-hour record had been tantalisingly close at Montlhéry, and the failure had been no fault of the Napier-Railton, which had proved to be a model of speed and reliability. Cobb realised that there was little likelihood of breaking the record at Montlhéry; the track was not sufficiently durable for such a heavy, powerful car, which was also too quick for the track. Any further attempts there could end in another failure, or worse.

The obvious place to go was the Bonneville Salt Flats in Utah. Here there was a perfect, smooth surface and unlimited space, which had already been used for record attempts by Ab Jenkins and others. The only problems were the distance and the cost. Cobb was a comparatively rich man, but such a venture would need outside support, so he began negotiations with the trade suppliers who had backed his previous record attempts. While the backing was being secured, Thomson & Taylor made some minor modifications to the car. A 100-gallon (450-litre) fuel tank was fitted, which slightly extended the tail, and Luvax hydraulic dampers were added to assist the existing Hartford friction shock absorbers. The 1:1.66 final drive was used and Dunlop supplied 7.50-20 tyres. When the Napier Railton was built, the radiator cowl had a central vertical dividing strip. While the car was being prepared for the American trip, George Bulman, the Hawker test pilot, was looking at it in Thomson & Taylor's workshops. Much to Ken Taylor's annoyance, he prodded the strip with his thumb and it snapped off. It was not replaced, and shortly afterwards the lower half of the cowl was reshaped.

For his drivers, Cobb engaged Tim Rose-Richards again, and also recruited Charles (Charlie) Dodson. Dodson was a motor cycle racer who had won the Senior TT twice before turning to motor racing. He had been equally successful with cars, and had won the 1934 Ulster Tourist Trophy with an MG Magnette. Like Dixon, he was small in stature, but with the smooth surface expected in Utah he was unlikely to be pounded the way Dixon had been at Montlhéry. It seems that there were no financial arrangements between Cobb and his co-drivers on the record-breaking attempts; they drove for the satisfaction of doing it. However, at Cobb's expense they were always given the most luxurious facilities available during the trips.

The Bonneville Salt Flats were the surviving part of Lake Bonneville, which had dried out in prehistoric times leaving a vast, level plain of hard salt. In winter the Flats would flood, maintaining the smooth surface, but at other times it was a dry, hot, inhospitable place. The nearest town was Wendover, which had originally been a watering place for a railway which ran round the edge of the Flats. The nearest large settlement was Salt Lake City. The Flats were 4,200ft (1,280m) above sea level, so engines suffered an 18 per cent power loss, though this was compensated by a 14 per cent reduction in wind resistance. Cobb was going to use the same course as Ab Jenkins. This was a circle ten miles (16km) in circumference, laid out on the best area of salt. The measurement of the course and the timekeeping was entrusted to the American Automobile Association. Graders went over the course to eliminate any bumps and the inside of the measured track was lined with a post and wire fence. (Iron posts had to be used, as the salt was too hard for wooden ones.) As a safeguard, an alternative $12^1/_2$-mile (20km) circle was marked out, using the same depot area, to which the drivers could switch during the run if the ten-mile course broke up.

The Napier-Railton, accompanied by three mechanics, was loaded onto a New York-bound freighter in the middle of June. Two weeks later, on 26 June, Cobb, his two drivers, and Reid Railton sailed from Southampton on the *Berengeria*. When both parties had arrived in New York, they set off on a 2,300-mile (3,700km) rail journey which took them through the Rocky Mountains to Salt Lake City.

The Napier-Railton, along with its fuel, oil, and spares (including the spare engine and 50 tyres), were unloaded and then carried by lorry to the salt flats. There was much concern among the party, particularly 'Dunlop Mac', about the effect of the salt on tyres. It had been suggested that the sharp salt crystals would shred the tyres very quickly, but tests with a touring car, braking hard with locked wheels, showed that the crystals were flattened by the tyres, which showed no damage at all.

The altitude had posed no problems for Napiers when preparing the engine for the attempt, as the Lion's carburettors had been prepared on aviation settings, as for a flight at 4,000ft (1,220m). As soon as the Napier-Railton was checked over, Cobb began tests on the ten-mile circle and soon went round at a speed exceeding anything done before, setting a new 'lap record'. After this the Lucas lights were fitted and tested. The car was in excellent fettle, so Cobb decided to make an attempt on the world one-hour record as a preliminary.

During the day the temperature on the salt flats rose to 50°C, so the hour attempt was made when the day was still relatively cool. On Monday 15 July the team gathered at dawn, and at 6.00am Cobb set off on what was, in relative terms, a sprint dash. The run was uneventful. The Napier-Railton rumbled round, leaving a plume of salt dust behind it. The car was not difficult to hold on the circle, there were no bumps, and at the end of the hour the tyres showed little wear. The one-hour record was taken at 152.70mph (245.69kmh), which was a considerable advance on the previous record of 134.90mph (217.05kmh) set by Hans Stuck's Auto-Union at the Avus track outside Berlin. On the way Cobb had also taken a bag-full of world records – the 50km record at 154.46mph (248.52kmh), the 100km at 153.1mph (246.33kmh), the 200km at 153.24mph (246.56kmh), the 50 miles at 153.60mph (247.14kmh), and the 100 miles at 152.95mph (246.09kmh). During the hour record the car had used 25 gallons (112 litres), which meant the team could plan – provided the tyres permitted – on making refuelling stops every four hours during the 24-hour run.

The Hour run gave the team great encouragement, as none of the expected problems had arisen. The decision was therefore made to go for the 24-hour record the next day, Tuesday 16 July. Two large tents had been erected, of which one served as the refuelling depot and sheltered the team from the hot sun, while the other was provided for the timekeepers. The run was to start at 2.00am. Although the drivers were starting in the dark, the reflection of the three headlights from the white salt provided adequate light and the car would be well into the run before it was subjected to the full heat of the day.

Cobb took the first turn at the wheel and settled into a 150mph (240kmh) pace immediately. The first record to fall was the 200 miles at 146.50mph (235.71kmh), followed by the 500km at 146.89mph (236.34kmh). At 500 miles, when the record fell at 147.66mph (237.58kmh), Cobb came in to refuel. He then carried on and completed his four and a half hour spell before stopping again to hand over to Rose-Richards. While Rose-Richards was at the wheel the 1,000km and 1,000 miles records fell at 145.00mph (245.05kmh) and 144.93mph (233.19kmh). At the 1,000 mile point Dodson took over. By now spectators were starting to gather. Some pitched tents close to the course and wandered dangerously near the Napier-Railton as it swept steadily on at 150mph (240kmh). After eight hours the wheels were changed, the stop only taking 90 seconds. By now the drivers were suffering from the heat of the blazing sun and also from salt being blown into their faces. The surface was beginning to break up in places, so at one of the refuelling stops the decision was taken to switch to the 12 1/2-mile (20km) course.

The drivers continued to change at four and a half hour intervals and records continued to fall. At one stop Dodson misjudged his speed as he braked to stop and the car slid sideways, damaging a tyre and overshooting the depot. The team rushed forward to push the car back, only to be commanded to desist by a frantic Ken Taylor, as only the driver could touch the car until it was in the designated area at the depot – any outside help would have meant instant disqualification. The team had to stand and watch as the small driver pushed on a wheel and gradually eased the car back to the refuelling point.

At 6.00pm the car came in for its second wheel change. Just after 10.00pm, when Rose-Richards was at the wheel, the team heard the engine cut and rushed out into the darkness, expecting the worst. The Napier-Railton came crawling in. A rear tyre had burst about two miles short of the depot, and while the car crawled along the tyre had caught fire. The wheel was changed without difficulty and Rose-Richards set off again, increasing the lap speed to compensate for the lost time, though a strong wind blowing across the course made driving difficult. The drivers also found that the continuous passage of the car on the salt had polished the surface, making it very slippery. At 2.00am the Napier-Railton came in for the last time, having taken the 24-hour record at 134.85mph (216.97kmh) along with 20 other records. It now held every world record from the 50km to the 24-hour.

It was a happy and satisfied team which packed up and loaded the car and equipment for the journey home. The 24-hour run had aroused a surprising amount of interest in the

Cobb demonstrates the Napier-Railton at the JCC race meeting at Donington Park, 31 August 1935. The 24-hour record lights are still in place. (Geoffrey Goddard Collection)

American press, though the shy, modest Cobb seemed the very antithesis of a hero. The team returned to an enthusiastic welcome in England, Cobb and his co-drivers being the guests of honour at a luncheon held by the RAC in the Great Gallery of the Pall Mall clubhouse on Friday 2 August. The motoring press carried many advertisements from the firms which had supplied parts or materials for the Napier-Railton, announcing their association with the record successes. Thomson & Taylor were quick to advertise that the Railton car, for which they were distributors, came from the drawing board of the same designer as the Napier-Railton!

Cobb had entered the Napier-Railton for the BRDC 500-mile Race on Saturday 21 September, no doubt hoping for better weather than in 1934. The Bonneville Salt Flats or the Brooklands Outer Circuit were the natural setting for the car, so it was a matter of some surprise to find Cobb in the entry list for the Brighton Speed Trials a week before the big Brooklands race. The surprise probably abated when the regulations for the half-mile sprint showed that the prize for the fastest time along Madeira Drive was £100. This was a huge sum for such a relatively minor event and the equivalent in the 1990s would be nearly £5,000. Cobb was not the only one drawn to Brighton and the entry contained the fastest Grand Prix cars in England at that time.

Although it had held the world standing start kilometre record in 1933, the Napier-Railton was not particularly quick off the mark. At Brighton, Cobb's technique was to change into second gear about a car's length after leaving the line and let the torque of the Lion do the rest. The battle for fastest time of day became a four-cornered contest between Cobb, Richard Shuttleworth (2.9 litre Tipo B Alfa Romeo), Lindsay Eccles (3.3 litre T59 Bugatti), and Raymond Mays (2-litre ERA). At the end of the afternoon, the Napier-Railton took second place in the unlimited racing class behind Eccles's Bugatti, recording a speed of 76.27mph /122.71kmh (23.6 seconds) and was also second in a 'Top Six' run-off for the fastest time, behind Shuttleworth's Alfa, at a speed of 78.44mph/126.14kmh (22.9 seconds).

Cobb shared the Napier-Railton with Tim Rose-Richards again in the BRDC '500'. The car was on scratch, and as in 1934 would have to find its way through the field of 32 other cars to win. As the first group of cars – the blown 750s and unblown 1,100s – were flagged away at noon there was a brief shower, raising fears that the race would be run in the wet again, but the rain then held off, even though it remained dull and overcast.

At 12.24pm Cobb rumbled away and settled down to lap at about 126mph. Soon afterwards the timekeepers released the first race order which showed the Napier-Railton was lying second on handicap, four seconds behind the 8-litre Barnato-Hassan being driven by Oliver Bertram. At the August Bank Holiday meeting, Bertram had taken the lap record from Cobb, going round in the Barnato-Hassan at 142.60mph (229.44kmh), so the two cars were very evenly matched. Just after 1.00pm Bertram's front tyres were through to the breaker strip, so he came in for a wheel change and lost the lead to Cobb, who was averaging 125.90mph (202.57kmh).

By 1.30pm Cobb had pushed his average up to 126.89mph (204.16kmh) and had a two-minute lead over Bertram. Just before 2.00pm Cobb came in for his first stop. In contrast to the 24-hour record runs, only three mechanics were permitted to work on the car and they had to change all four wheels and pump in 50 gallons (225 litres) of National Benzole. On this occasion the stop took ten minutes, as it was very difficult to take off the the rear wheels from the hubs. Bertram stopped at the same time and was stationary for 11 minutes while there was a long inspection of the fuel tank. The next announcement of the race order showed that Cobb still led, but only by four seconds, as Bertram had speeded up and had been lapping at over 130mph (208kmh) before his stop. Within a few minutes, however, the Barnato-Hassan came into the pits again and retired, as the fuel tank had split. This left Rose-Richards, who had taken the wheel at the stop, with a comfortable lead on handicap; at 2.30pm he was over three minutes in front of the T59 Bugatti being shared by Earl Howe and Brian Lewis.

The Napier-Railton stopped again and Cobb took over. At 3.0pm it still led at 122.75mph (197.50kmh) and was now four and a half minutes in front of the Bugatti. The track surface was breaking up, particularly on the Members' Banking, and Cobb was hit by a sizeable fragment of concrete, which cut his face badly. At 3.30pm he came in again. This time the stop took only 90 seconds and Rose-Richards set off on the final stint. The average had now dropped to 121.49mph (195.47kmh) but the lead had been extended to over six minutes. Freddie Dixon then began to challenge with his 2-litre Riley, which was lapping at over 130mph (208kmh), well over his handicap speed. It was going to be a close thing. But as the race ran out, the Riley threw a con-rod while Dixon's co-driver, Walter Handley, was at the wheel, and at 4.28pm Rose-Richard crossed the line to win. Edgar Maclure and von der Becke were second in another Riley and the Bugatti was third. The Napier-Railton had averaged 121.28mph (195.13kmh) and had now proved it could be everything from a sprint car to a 24-hour record holder. The Lion engine had run perfectly all the way,

The Napier-Railton makes a pit stop on its way to victory in the BRDC '500' at Brooklands on 21 September 1935. 'Dunlop Mac' brings up a wheel, 'Fiddle' Hicks wields a clouter, and Ken Taylor adjusts Cobb's seat. (Guy Griffiths Collection)

A Hawker Hart loops over Brooklands in October 1935. This aerial view emphasises the pronounced reverse curve at the Fork which made Cobb's record laps so perilous. (Guy Griffiths Collection)

as it had done at Bonneville; combined with Reid Railton's superb chassis, it made a truly formidable car. After the race Cobb gave each member of the pit crew a bonus of £5, probably rather more than a week's wages.

Cobb's season had not quite finished. Although the Napier-Railton had come out on top in the '500', the Barnato-Hassan still held the Brooklands record. It would add the final touch to a season of success to regain it, so on Monday 7 October the track was booked by Cobb for an attempt on the record. This time there was no excited crowd of spectators, but most of the usual Brooklands regulars, working in their sheds and in the small firms inside the track, came out to watch. They all appreciated the risks inherent in the attempt and admired the courage that was needed. There was no wind, but it had been raining and the track was still damp. Cobb did some warming-up laps and then did the two quick ones. The Napier-Railton slid around on the bankings and when crossing the Fork, but despite this Cobb's best lap was at 143.44mph (230.79kmh), a speed which would never be exceeded at Brooklands and a lap record which was to stand for all time. During his run Cobb was timed over the measured kilometre on the Railway Straight at 151.97mph (244.51kmh), the fastest speed ever officially recorded at Brooklands. At the end of the two fast laps the tyres were worn out. The small crowd which gathered around Cobb in the Paddock afterwards offered their congratulations with complete sincerity, for they knew what had been involved.

Many years later, in the *BRDC Silver Jubilee Book*, Cobb made some observations about taking the lap record:

> The key to a fast lap at Brooklands consisted of a good entry on to the Home [Members'] Banking. If it was taken too slowly time was lost; if taken too fast the resultant skid towards the top of the Banking caused one to have to slow down – to say nothing of scaring one stiff. Down the Railway Straight I could reach 160mph and then ease a little to enter the Byfleet Banking. After that, full chat as far as the one-mile post and then about three-quarter throttle until reaching the Fork. This could be taken on full power provided there was no wind but could be very awkward if the car was not placed right.

On Saturday 19 October, Cobb brought the Napier-Railton out again for the Autumn meeting which closed the season at Brooklands. The car was entered for only one race, the Second October Handicap. Inevitably it was on scratch, and in a nine-mile (14.5km) race was expected to give the limit 750cc MG a start of more than a lap. Once again the handicap beat the car and Cobb, whose best lap was at 133.52mph (214.83kmh), was unplaced.

During the autumn of 1935 John Cobb could look back on his season with the Napier-Railton with some satisfaction. It had taken 21 world records, had won the longest and fastest British race, and held the Brooklands lap record. Despite these triumphs, however, it must have niggled him that almost all the records which his team had taken at Bonneville had since been captured by George Eyston and his Rolls-Royce Kestrel-engined 'Speed of the Wind'. Already Cobb was making plans for another foray to the United States.

Final Glory on Salt and Track

THE Napier-Railton did not compete at Brooklands during 1936. The new lap record meant that the handicappers would not give it any chance at all and Cobb would need to take even greater risks with little prospect of success. Instead he used another famous car in his stable, the 4-litre V-12 Sunbeam. This was the car with which Segrave had taken the land speed record in 1926. It had been bought by Sir Malcolm Campbell in 1932 and was extensively rebuilt by Thomson & Taylor, with a new frame and front axle, hydraulic brakes, and a pre-selector gearbox. Not much of the original car remained except the engine. The Sunbeam gave Cobb quite a successful Brooklands season with a number of places.

The Napier-Railton remained in the Thomson & Taylor workshop and was prepared for another 24-hour attempt. The only major change made to the car was the fitting of an electric starter-motor. A matter of some anxiety during the previous visit to Utah had been how the engine would be restarted if it stopped in the middle of the ten-mile lap. AIACR rules decreed that only the driver could push-start the car if it stopped away from the pit or depot, and the weight of the Napier-Railton would have made this almost impossible. A Lucas lorry starter was used, bolted to the outside of the frame beside the cockpit. It drove a roller against the offside rear tyre, being engaged by a lever. The starter also relieved the pit-crew of the strenuous push after each stop. To give its drivers some help in holding the car on a constant circle, a vertical aerofoil was fitted at the front and was slightly angled.

The team left Southampton on the *Queen Mary* in August. The car had gone earlier on a freighter, with the mechanics. For this attempt Cobb had chosen Rose-Richards and Brackenbury again; the new driver was Johnny Hindmarsh, a Hawker test-pilot who had been a member of the Talbot team and had won the Le Mans 24-Hour race with a Lagonda the previous year. Ken Taylor was the team manager. It seemed a good omen that on the voyage the *Queen Mary* broke the record for the Atlantic crossing. On arriving at Bonneville the team found that the course was in rather poor condition, as it had been used for a number of record runs earlier in the year and would only regain its true surface after the winter floods. This time a 12 1/2-mile (20km) circle was marked out.

As soon as the Napier-Railton had been checked over, the depot and timekeeping tents had been pitched, and the drivers had familiarised themselves with the track, the record attempts began. On Thursday 10 September, Cobb set out for the hour record at 7.30am. Taylor had suggested beforehand that there was insufficient fuel in the tank to complete the run, but Cobb was confident that the car would go the distance. After a short run, however, the pit-crew heard the Lion spluttering, and Cobb was towed in, out of fuel! After fuel was added he set off again, and this time there were no problems, four world records falling in the next 60 minutes. The 10km was taken at 167.61mph (269.68kmh), the 100 miles at 168.59mph (271.26kmh), the 200km at 168.26mph (270.73kmh), and finally the hour at 167.69mph (269.81kmh).

Taylor and the mechanics now checked the car over for the big effort. The team were out early next day, and at 7.30am Cobb started the 24-hour run. The atmosphere was damp and the hydrotropic quality of the salt attracted the moisture, which made the surface unusually slippery so the car had a continuous tendency to slide. During Hindmarsh's first spell at the wheel he spun the car twice; the team heard the engine cut and immediately dashed across the centre of the course in a car, expecting to find a crisis. Hindmarsh was able to restart the engine, which completely justified the fitting of the starter, but unfortunately in regaining control of the car he pulled a shoulder muscle and at the end of his spell was declared by Dr Whitehurst to be unfit for further motoring. When Brackenbury took his turn he too lost control, and the car went

Bonneville, 10 September 1936: Cobb gets a thumbs-up from Art Pillsbury, the AAA timekeeper, as he begins the run which took the hour record at 167.69mph (269.81kmh). The starter roller can be seen in front of the rear wheel. (Guy Griffiths Collection)

off the course for a short distance.

The drivers were doing approximately three and a half hour turns, so Cobb was back at the wheel at nightfall. By now the driving conditions had changed and a strong wind was blowing across the course. While this dried out the surface, the gusts were affecting the car, which was also being thrown about by ridges which had formed on the salt. Soon after dark Cobb too had a 'moment', which damaged a wheel. The tyre then burst, and by the time the car had reached the depot the remains of the tyre were smouldering, and Taylor was burned in removing the wheel. The wheels were difficult to remove at every stop, as the hub nuts had become very stiff, perhaps clogged by the salt, and when loosened had to be driven off rather than spun off. Despite these difficulties the Napier-Railton thundered on, and at 7.30am the following morning it came into the depot with the 24-hour record secured again, at 150.16mph (241.60kmh). En route it had taken the 1,000, 2,000 and 3,000 miles, the 3,000 and 5,000km, and the 12-hour records.

The success once again attracted the interest of the American press, and an embarrassed Cobb was interviewed on US radio networks. The team returned home on the *Queen Mary*, but on docking at Southampton, to Cobb's evident annoyance and to general disappointment, they received the news that Ab Jenkins had wasted no time, and on 23–24 September had set a new 24-hour record at 153.76mph (247.39kmh) in his 'Mormon Meteor'. This machine had a production Duesenberg SJ chassis, using a Curtiss Conqueror aero engine and a body with faired-in wheels. Not content with spending one whole day record-breaking at Bonneville, Jenkins and his co-driver, Babe Stapp, had gone on for another 24 hours and had set a new world 48-hour record at 148.62mph (239.12kmh). On hearing this news Cobb felt that enough was enough. The Napier-Railton had reached its limit in the record-breaking field, and there would be no point in trying for the 24-hour record again. He had already started on a more exciting and demanding project.

When the Napier-Railton returned to Thomson & Taylor's workshops it was stripped down to individual nuts and bolts, as the fine salt had pervaded every part of the car. The Lion went back to Acton, where apparently little more than routine maintenance was needed. Cobb decided that with the passing of a year, perhaps the Brooklands' handicappers would have forgotten quite how fast the car was, so it was made ready for a limited final season at the Track.

The car's first outing in 1937 was the Brooklands Easter Meeting on 29 March. The main race of the day, for which the Napier-Railton was entered, was a ten-lap Outer Circuit handicap for the BBC Trophy and a cash prize of £100. A live commentary on the race was transmitted on BBC Radio. It was a bright but very cold day and Ken Taylor, who was looking after the car, kept the bonnet and radiator covered until it left the Paddock. As he climbed into the car, Cobb commented to Tommy Wisdom, 'I think I have a chance, don't you?' He started from scratch and worked his way steadily through the field of ten cars. There was little wind, so the Napier-Railton was steadier than it had been in the past. At half-distance he was second and just caught A.P. Hamilton's Monza Alfa on the last lap to win by 4.4 seconds. Cobb's average was 136.03mph (218.87kmh), the fastest race-winning speed at Brooklands, and he did three laps at 139.90mph (225.09kmh).

In 1937 there were considerable changes at Brooklands. The owners realised that motor racing had moved away from pure track racing. If Brooklands was to have any future, the promotion of road racing was essential. As a result, during the winter of 1936 an artificial road circuit was constructed within the confines of the Outer Circuit. This was known as the Campbell Circuit and it was formally opened on Thursday 22 April 1937. After Dame Ethel Locke-King had cut a ribbon, Selwyn Edge, driving the 1903 Gordon Bennett E61 and accompanied by his daughter, led a procession of cars round the new circuit. The old E61 was described in a press release as being identical to the 1907 24-hour record T21; a statement which must have amused Edge.

At the Brooklands Whit Monday Meeting on 17 May, the Napier-Railton was entered for the 20-mile (32km) Coronation Gold Trophy, so-named in honour of King George VI's coronation, which had taken place the previous week. Another entrant for this race was the Bimotore Alfa Romeo, which many expected to take the lap record, though the instability of this car made the possibility unlikely. On the day the Bimotore was a non-starter, and in the Paddock the Napier-Railton was surrounded by the usual crowd of admirers. Cobb was on scratch and had to catch a field of 12 cars. The task was too much. His speed on the fourth lap was 141.89mph (228.30kmh), but there were several cars in the field capable of lapping at 130mph and these needed the top of the banking, so when Cobb came up to pass them he had great difficulty in getting by. His speed on the last lap was only 129.36mph (208.14kmh), as he was slowed by a duel between Hamilton's Monza Alfa and Duller in the ex-Straight Duesenberg. Getting past this pair in the run to the flag, he came up to take third place.

Brooklands policy had changed. The July meeting was held entirely on the Campbell Circuit and instead of the August Bank Holiday meeting there was a long distance race, the Junior Car Club International Trophy. The next race for which the Napier-Railton was suitable was the BRDC '500' on Saturday 18 September. Realising that the race had a reputation as a car-breaker, and was not attracting entries, the club decided to reduce the distance and made it 500km. As an additional improvement, all the classes were given credit laps and only the Napier-Railton, on scratch, would go the whole distance. This change meant that the whole field could be released at once, in a massed start, which would have much more spectator appeal.

Practice was marred by a serious accident when the 'works' 750 Austin of Kay Petre, at that time the leading British woman driver, collided with Reg Parnell's K3 MG on the Byfleet Banking and Mrs Petre was badly hurt. Non-starters reduced the field to 20 which, however, still included the Bimotore Alfa, receiving a one lap start from the Napier-Railton. The quality of the field and

A National Benzole advertisement in Speed, *October 1936.*

Oliver Bertram on the Byfleet Banking at Brooklands on 18 September 1937, as the Napier-Railton goes on to win the BRDC '500'. (Motor)

the handicap meant it was going to be hard work for Cobb again. This time he had enlisted Oliver Bertram as his co-driver.

It had been bright earlier, but the sky had clouded over as the field lined up in rows at the Fork. There was also a gusting wind which would make a difficult race for the faster cars. The Napier-Railton was on the outside of the front row, beside the Vickers sheds. It was push-started by the Thomson & Taylor mechanics and took its place next to the V-12 Sunbeam which Cobb had loaned to Brackenbury for the race. At 2.30pm Sir Malcolm Campbell, who was the starter, dropped the flag. Cobb surged away and took the lead as the field went onto the Members' Banking. He settled down to lap at 130mph and led easily on the road, or more accurately the track, followed by the Bimotore which was lapping at about 122mph (195kmh). It was a different story on handicap, though. At 3.00pm the 'works' 1½ litre Rileys of Arthur Dobson and Cyril Paul were first and second with Cobb running third.

Ken Thomson was running Cobb's pit and had done his calculations carefully, realising that the pit stops could be crucial. The pace of the Napier-Railton began to tell and at 3.30pm it led on handicap at 129.4mph (208.2kmh), while Charlie Dodson, with Dixon's 2-litre Riley, was up into second place. Shortly afterwards the offside rear tyre of the Napier-Railton threw a tread and Cobb came into the pits. Walter Hassan, the builder of the Barnato-Hassan, who had joined Thomson & Taylor, changed the damaged wheel while the other mechanics changed the nearside rear and the offside front. The tank was filled, Bertram received the order 'Forward driver!', and in three minutes the car was away. At 4.00pm Bertram was still in the lead on handicap at 127.4mph (204.98kmh), pursued by various Rileys whose order changed continuously. At about 4.15pm Bertram came into the pits, all four wheels were changed in 90 seconds, and Cobb took over again. He now pushed the pace up, lapping at 135mph (215kmh) and just keeping ahead of Dodson's Riley on handicap; this, too, had speeded up and was averaging 119.9mph (192.91kmh). On his 112th and last lap, Cobb lapped at 136.45mph (219.54kmh), the fastest of the day, and coming up to the line the offside rear tyre threw a tread. Cobb and Bertram had won at an average of 127.05mph (204.42kmh) and finished three minutes in front of Dodson. If the tyre had gone a lap earlier, the result might have been different!

The car was towed into the Paddock with a very happy Ken Taylor at the wheel, while Cobb and Bertram received their victors' plaques from Earl Howe at a ceremony in the Finishing Straight. Cobb also received the winner's cheque for £250 and an additional £100 for the first British car to finish. That was the Napier-Railton's last major race, though it was to run in vintage events in the 1960s. The combination of Napier engineering, Reid Railton's design, and Thomson & Taylor's workmanship had produced a car which always did everything required of it. It never retired from a race, and its small setbacks while record-breaking were the result of driver error and track failure. It was one of the finest cars ever to race at Brooklands and one of the great racing cars of the 1930s. It has been estimated that it covered more than 12,000 miles (19,000km) at racing speeds, a record which probably no other racing car can rival. Although the Lion's roar would not be heard in that car again, further glory still lay ahead.

Chapter 17: 1938–9

Speed with Science

FROM 1931 until 1935 the world land speed record had been the exclusive prerogative of Sir Malcolm Campbell. Having abandoned the Napier Lion after setting the record at 253.97mph (408.63kmh) in February 1932, Campbell had fitted 'Bluebird' with a Rolls-Royce R engine similar to that which powered the Supermarine S6B and had won the Schneider Trophy outright in 1931. Ironically the R had received much attention from A.J. Rowledge, who was in the midst of aero engine design with Rolls-Royce and was already engaged in work on the Merlin which was later to have great influence in an even more demanding sphere of aviation activity.

With the aid of the R, Campbell raised the record to 272.46mph (438.38kmh) at Daytona in February 1933. The Campbell-Rolls-Royce, as it had now become, was then returned to Thomson & Taylor where it was rebuilt and modernised, with the wheels almost enveloped within the bodywork. In this new form the car was taken back to Daytona in March 1935 and, despite bad conditions, the record was raised again to 276.82mph (445.40kmh). Campbell knew the car was capable of 300mph, so in September 1935 he went to Bonneville. Here he achieved his lifetime ambition and set a new record of 301.129mph (484.51kmh). Campbell was now 50 years old, and on his return to England he announced his retirement from motor sport and record breaking.

Campbell's announcement indicated that the field was now wide open for a new contender. John Cobb enjoyed the satisfaction of record-breaking and had nursed a secret ambition of seeking the land speed record. In October 1935 he had discussions with Ken Taylor and Reid Railton, who agreed that it was feasible to build a new car with the aim of taking the record to over 350mph. When working on 'Bluebird', Railton had been constrained by Campbell's budget and the limitations imposed by the original Villiers/Maina design. Now Cobb had offered him a clean sheet of paper. There was little discussion on which engines should be used. The three agreed that the Lion was the obvious choice. It had given no trouble in the Napier-Railton and the supercharged version would give a reliable 1,400hp. For some years a racing boat – the *Estelle*, once owned by Marion Carstairs – had been lying in the factory at Acton. This had two supercharged VIID Lions which Napiers were happy to sell to Cobb. The engines were rebuilt and the compression ratio was raised from the standard 6:1 to 6.6:1, and when bench-tested they developed 1,480hp at 3,600rpm. The altitude at Bonneville would bring this output down to 1,250hp, but Railton was satisfied that this would be adequate.

Railton's aim was to make as small a car as possible, with suspension which worked properly and transmitted the power without wheel-spin, so he evolved a revolutionary design. The frame was a cranked back-bone and the engines were hung on each side, one ahead of the other, at 10° to the centre line of the car. The front engine drove the rear wheels and the other drove the front. The driver was seated ahead of the front wheels. Railton sketched out the basic design and then handed his ideas to Ralph Beauchamp, the chief draughtsman at Thomson & Taylor, who, since working on the Napier-Railton, had played an important part in the design of the ERA chassis. Beauchamp was left to deal with all the detail and such essential matters as the stress calculations. Five scale models were built, including a three-wheeler, to establish the optimum shape which would cover the mechanical components and offer the least frontal area. These were tested in the wind-tunnel at the National Physical Laboratory. The shape known by Beauchamp as the 'Bun' was chosen as the most efficient. Meanwhile Wally Hassan had joined Thomson & Taylor to become the progress chaser and trouble-shooter for the project. Hassan himself gave his job the more dignified title of sub-contracts manager!

In the centre of Thomson & Taylor's small works was an old

The Railton with Cobb at the wheel, spring 1938. (Guy Griffiths Collection)

building which had been a non-conformist chapel before Brooklands was built. Known, unsurprisingly, as 'The Chapel', it was used as a storage for the derelict chassis and spares from the Leyland-Thomas project which had been abandoned when Parry Thomas was killed. To make space for the construction of the new car the Leyland-Thomas spares and chassis were put up for sale, but when no offers were received they were cleared out and sold for scrap.

John Thompson Ltd made the frame up in four sections, which were hot riveted together. There were no radiators, the engines being cooled by tanks filled with ice cubes. Clutches and flywheels were also omitted. Each engine drove a separate three-speed gearbox, built by David Brown, containing a free-wheel device to enable gear changes to be made. The final drive ratio was 1.35:1. The front drive was taken through exposed half shafts and double universal joints and the front suspension was independent, with long tubular wishbones and coil springs in traction. The design and proportions of the front suspension would not have looked out of place on a Formula One racing car of the 1990s. The rear axle was live and suspended on two coil springs with parallel fabricated trailing links. All the coil springs contained rubber damping. The car had a pronounced crab track, the front track being 5ft 6in (167cm) and the rear 3ft 6in (106cm). Dunlop made tyres with a safe maximum speed of 380mph (612kmh), which were carried on 44in (111cm) wheels. The wheelbase was 13ft 6in (411cm) and the overall length was 28ft 8in (873cm). The car was 8ft (244cm) wide and stood 4ft 3in (129cm) tall. When finished, the dry weight was approximately 7,000lb (3,180kg).

The body was made of 18swg aluminium supplied by the Northern Aluminium Company. Plywood formers were made up and the body shell was beaten out at Brooklands by George and Jack Grey, who were considered to be the leading builders of competition bodies at that time. The completed shell weighed 700lb (318kg). It was located on the car by eight pegs, and when finished and fitted for the first time it dropped into place without any alterations. The Greys had taken great care to ensure that the cockpit area was properly sealed, this being fully enclosed with a removable cover. As an extra safeguard the panels around the cover were made of doped aircraft fabric, which could be torn out in an emergency.

The completed car was known simply as the Railton, which must have pleased Noel Macklin, who was manufacturing the Railton touring car; it is not known if Macklin helped to fund the project in return for the extraordinary publicity for the Railton name. The Railton was a wholly new concept in the history of land speed record cars. With the exception of Lockhart's ill-fated project, science rather than brute force was being applied for the first time, and a study of the Railton 60 years after it was built shows a design which still does not seem outdated or archaic.

John Cobb was not the only man who wanted to hold the land speed record. While the Railton was being built in the shadow of the Byfleet Banking, George Eyston was also being industrious. At the beginning of 1937 he had worked out the layout of a car. He had the plans drawn up by an engineer working for Peugeot, and the body designed by a French aerodynamicist, Jean Andreau. The manufacture of the components was sub-contracted, and the car was assembled at the Bean works in Staffordshire. Only seven months elapsed from inception to completion. The resultant car, named 'Thunderbolt', was a halfway house between the old brute-force record-breakers and the science of the Railton.

'Thunderbolt' used two Rolls-Royce R engines – one had come from the 1931 Schneider Trophy winner and the other from the Supermarine S6B which had taken the world air speed record – and had eight wheels. The front four were independently suspended on transverse leaf springs and wishbones and steered the car. The driver sat just behind them in front of the two engines, mounted side by side. These drove through separate clutches and a gear train to a three-speed gearbox. There was a bevel final drive and the pair of twin rear wheels were also independently suspended with a huge transverse leaf spring. There was no attempt to save weight; the car was built on a massive scale, with the intention that the weight would inhibit wheelspin. Eyston took 'Thunderbolt' to Bonneville in the autumn of 1937. After dealing with clutch problems and waiting for the salt to dry out, on 19 November he set a new land speed record of 312.00mph (502.00kmh). This was not a big advance on Campbell's speed, but 'Thunderbolt' had the potential to go much faster.

The Railton, spring 1938. (Guy Griffiths Collection)

The Railton did not run under its own power in England before the record attempt, although the engines were run up. There was a moment of drama at the start of this short test, as there was no oil pressure; then it was realised that the long pipe to the oil gauge needed priming. On Easter Monday 1938 it was displayed to the public in the Brooklands Paddock. At that time the bodywork was not quite finished and the wheels protruded through the main shell, as the covering fairings were not fitted. As soon as it was finished it was shown to the press outside Thomson & Taylor's workshop. Shortly after this the press blazed a headline 'Cobb's Railton Stolen', but the story lost most of its impact when it was revealed that John Cobb's touring Railton was the object of the crime.

In July the new car was loaded into a special crate by Lep Transport. When 'Bluebird' had been shipped to Bonneville it had shifted inside the crate and the steering had been damaged. To prevent this, Jimmy Rands, one of the Thomson & Taylor mechanics, climbed into the confined space when the Railton was inside the crate and bolted steel angle plates around the wheels and disconnected the track rod. The crated car was then taken to Southampton, where it was loaded onto the German liner *Bremen* as deck cargo.

The party on the *Bremen* was quite small. Ken Taylor was in charge, accompanied by Ralph Beauchamp, with mechanics Jimmy Rands and Bob Reading. Joe Coe was also there again. From Dunlop came Harry Fletcher, the manager responsible for record attempts, with the inevitable 'Dunlop Mac' and Syd West. The voyage took four and a half days and on arriving in New York, Taylor and Beauchamp flew to Salt Lake City in a Boeing 247 while the rest of the team travelled on by rail with the car. Cobb, who was already in the United States combining the record attempt with business, flew down from Boston to Salt Lake City to join the team.

Railton touring cars were built from Hudson components, so when the team arrived at Salt Lake City it was provided with a selection of Hudson Sixes and Eights as transport during the stay. The team made its base at Wendover and set up camp in a garage on the south side of the main street. Eyston and his team were also in town with 'Thunderbolt', installed in a garage on the north side of the street, so the scene was set for a shoot-out in the best Western tradition, though the weapons were going to be British aero engines rather than American Colts. When the Railton arrived it was found that there was no crane in Wendover capable of lifting the crate off the rail truck, so the team had to manhandle the crate off with sleepers and rollers. When it was unloaded from the crate, the car was towed through the town to the garage on slave wheels and tyres, with Jimmy Rands in the cockpit.

As soon as the Railton had been checked over Cobb tested it, the first time it had run under its own power. It was started by a push from a Dodge truck whose front bumper was fitted with a tube and bar prong which connected with an attachment at the rear of the Railton. The Dodge also had a gang plank at the rear so Cobb could step off it and into the cockpit when the body was fitted. The starting procedure was unusual. The car was rocked into first gear, the freewheel was locked, and the Dodge truck then pushed the car up to about 15mph (25kmh). Cobb then switched on the engines, which fired, and the car went away locked into first gear. To unlock the freewheel Cobb depressed the equivalent of the clutch pedal. To change into second and top gear he would ease the throttle pedal as gently as possible to enable the freewheel to operate, move the gear lever, and accelerate. Provided the drive took up all was well, but without a flywheel the revs fell immediately and an engine could stall. The gearchange did not help, as the lever was pushed forward from first to second then back and 'round the corner' for top.

The first test run was made without the body and to the delight of the team everything functioned as intended. A lot of black smoke indicated the need for Joe Coe to make adjustments to the altitude control and to change jets and plugs. Surprisingly, the cork floats in the carburettors were affected by the aviation fuel. It was found that the inboard banks of cylinders were rather inaccessible. To alleviate the problem of the engines cutting out during gearchanges the throttles were set for the engines to tick over at 1,000rpm. One of the Lions was running too hot, but this was cured by altering the dual thermostats and separating the flow from the ice-tanks, another task that was made difficult by inaccessibility.

With these minor problems sorted out, Cobb made some test runs at speeds of up to 250mph (400kmh) over the measured and prepared course. To help Cobb and Eyston keep a straight course on the featureless white expanse of the lake, a straight black line over ten miles long was painted with oil on the salt. To Railton's satisfaction, dents appeared in the top and underside of the rear of the car, indicating equal high pressure zones in the airflow. The dents were eased out, and the panels were reinforced from inside with wooden strips. It was also found that the air pressure was holding the exhaust flames down on the body, so steel and asbestos plates were made up to prevent the aluminium burning. While Cobb tested, Eyston was getting down to serious business. The weather had prevented any earlier attempt, but on Wednesday 24 August 'Thunderbolt' covered the measured distance on its first northwards run at 347.155mph (558.57kmh). To Eyston's frustration and the dismay of Art Pillsbury, the American Automobile Association timekeeper, no time was recorded for the return southbound trip. It seemed that the timing had not malfunctioned, but the silver finish of the car had failed to provide a sufficient reflection for the light beam. Eyston returned to the north side garage, checked 'Thunderbolt' over, and painted the sides black. On the other side of the road, black paint was also applied to the Railton.

'Thunderbolt' came out again the following Saturday, and this time there were no snags. His average for the two runs was 345.49mph (555.89kmh), an increase of 33mph (53kmh) on his former record. Eyston knew that the Railton probably had the speed to beat his new record, so while Cobb's team continued their own preparations frantic work began on 'Thunderbolt' in the north side garage. The tail fin and radiator were removed and a tank cooling system was fitted. A new aluminium nose was made up without an aperture for the radiator. Railton offered the Eyston team a set of blueprints to save them the trouble of designing a new nose!

Cobb had been testing at speeds of over 300mph (480kmh). The gearchange still gave trouble and on some runs an engine cut out as the revs dropped. He had a disconcerting experience when the treads lifted on the offside front and nearside rear tyres at high speed. He held the car but described the vibration as being 'like a terrier shaking a rat'. On Monday 12 September, Cobb made his first attempt. On both runs he missed a gearchange and the speed was not quite enough, his average being 342.50mph (551.08kmh). After discussions with Railton it was decided that next time he would start in second gear. Three days later, on Thursday 15 September, the team was called at 3.00am, the Railton was made ready, and at 6.00am Cobb made his first northward run, the speed being recorded as 353.30mph (568.45kmh). The body was removed, the car was serviced, and the wheels changed within the time limit. Cobb then set off on the southbound return run. Beauchamp, who had driven one of the Hudsons to the end of the measured mile, recalled that 'with a whoosh, the Railton sped past with a really shaking bow wave of air rocking the Hudson.' As the speed came through, Eyston, who was watching with intense interest, shouted, 'John has got it!' On the second run the speed was 347.2mph (558.64kmh), giving Cobb an average of 350.20mph (563.47kmh) and the world land speed record.

Eyston declared his intention of regaining the record on the morrow, but that evening the teams joined together for a celebration dinner jointly chaired by Cobb and Eyston. Referring to Eyston's proposed attempt the next morning, Cobb said 'I hope it rains like Hell!' Cobb handed round dollar bills to the mechanics for extra beer money, commenting, 'If anyone tells you a man can become rich out of the land speed record, he is a liar.' Next morning, despite Cobb's hopes, it did not rain. Three weeks' hard work had paid off. Eyston went north at 356.4mph (573.44kmh) and came back again at 358.6mph (576.98kmh), an average of 357.50mph (575.21kmh). Cobb did not try again. He had used almost all his tyres, he needed to return to London to meet business commitments, and perhaps most important of all, Railton considered the car needed some modifications to take it over 360mph (575kmh). Eyston stayed on at Bonneville, though, and brought 'Thunderbolt' out again. As an example of the sporting relationship between the pair, Cobb had given him the Railton's unused tyres. This time there was nearly a disaster when a body panel shifted and became entangled in the back wheels, damaging the rear suspension. Eyston held the car, but 'Thunderbolt' was too badly damaged to make another run.

The Railton was crated-up and railed back to New York, accompanied by Jimmy Rands and Bob Reading, while Ken Taylor and Ralph Beauchamp went sightseeing at the Grand Canyon. The team met up in New York, where Taylor made arrangements for them to return to England on the *Olympic*. The Munich crisis was coming to a climax and it was felt that to travel on the *Bremen* could be hazardous. If war began, English passengers on a German liner would probably be interned and the Railton impounded. Cobb must have felt he had done it all before. Just as in 1936, when he had

Bonneville, 15 September 1938: Cobb takes the world land speed record in the black-painted Railton at 350.20mph (563.47kmh). (Motor)

gone to Bonneville, he had set a new world record and lost it almost immediately. However, this time there would be a second chance, as Railton was confident that the car was capable of 400mph (640kmh), so a new attempt would almost certainly bring success. Cobb's return to England was marred by the news that Johnnie Hindmarsh, a member of the 1936 team, had been killed on 6 September when a Hawker Hurricane he was testing crashed at St George's Hill, Weybridge.

During the winter of 1938–9 the Railton was stripped down in the Thomson & Taylor workshops and Reid Railton did what was needed to find extra speed. The frame was subjected to twisting tests, as Railton suspected that the tyre trouble was caused by torque distorting the frame. To cure this, one side of the suspension was pre-loaded and the back axle was restricted to vertical movements only. To speed up the superchargers and increase the boost, the driving gears were changed at Acton; the two Lions, still being in perfect condition, were not stripped. The work on the car was done in the shadow of worsening international relations. At Brooklands, Hawkers and Vickers were now working at full stretch to build Hurricane fighters and Wellington bombers respectively, and the small engineering firms inside the track were all being given arms-related contracts. Thomson & Taylor were negotiating for work on tank transmission design.

In 1938 Cobb had used National Benzole fuel and Shell-BP oil and had received the usual bonuses and sponsorship. For 1939 he signed a fuel and oil contract with an American firm instead, the Gilmore Oil Corporation. The details are not known, nor is it known who made the first approach, but it seems certain that the Gilmore deal must have offered much better terms. From the care and hospitality given to the team by the Gilmore Corporation it certainly seems likely that the latter picked up most, if not all of the bills in the United States.

The Railton was crated up by Lep Transport once more and sent by cargo freighter to New York at the beginning of July 1939. The team personnel were almost the same, although the Dunlop representation was now Harry Fletcher, who looked after the technical aspects of the tyres, with a promoted 'Fiddle' Hicks going in the place of 'Dunlop Mac', helped by Syd Cooper. The 'executive' members of the team met at Euston railway station in London early on Saturday 29 July to join the boat train to Liverpool. George Eyston came to the station to see the party off and wish Cobb good luck. They embarked on the Cunard liner *Samaria* and arrived in Boston after a seven-day voyage, stopping at Cork and Galway. At Boston they disembarked and flew down to New York. The following evening, Monday 7 August, the party went to Newark airfield where they met Ken Taylor and Reggie Tongue, who was a Thomson & Taylor director and a well-known ERA driver. A Boeing 247 took them to Chicago, where they changed planes and joined the 12.30am 'Sky-Sleeper' to Salt Lake City. Although the plane landed at 5.30am the record attempt was already news, and the party was greeted by a crowd of photographers and journalists and also by Earl P. Gilmore, the President of the Gilmore Oil Corporation.

When the Railton arrived at Wendover on the freight train from Salt Lake City, it was unloaded with the same manual exertions as before. The team then began to make it ready for its test runs. As this was to take several days, Cobb flew down to Los Angeles in a Douglas DC-3 with Gilmore and his wife. By Friday 18 August the car was ready for the first test runs and the team spent the evening making final checks. By 3.00am next morning the Dunlop crew was checking tyre pressures while the mechanics were chopping up ice to pour into the cooling tanks and warming the oil. At 4.45am the engines were started by compressed air and warmed up. Cobb arrived in a Hudson at 5.00am and posed for the newsreel cameramen. As soon as the body was fitted and Cobb had climbed into the cockpit, the car was started by the Dodge truck and went straight onto the record course. The AAA had improved their timing gear so the car had been restored to its silver finish. In the middle of the measured mile one engine spat back, which ballooned out the air intake of the front engine. Despite this, the speed for this first test run was 352.94mph (567.88kmh). The tread of one tyre had lifted, and as the intake was damaged the car did not make the return run but was towed back.

Railton was concerned that there was a possibility of overheating, so the header tanks were removed from the car and taken into Salt Lake City for modifications to the baffles. Meanwhile, on the Saturday evening the Salt Lake City Chamber of Commerce gave a dinner in honour of Cobb and his team. One of the hosts was Ab Jenkins. The header tanks were replaced, and just after midnight on Tuesday 22 August the team began to make the car ready again. The only test run had been so satisfactory that Cobb decided to go for the record without any more testing. At 5.30am he was push started and began the run, but before he reached the measured distance the car slowed and circled round, returning to the starting point. An engine had stalled when Cobb changed into third gear, so the body had to be removed. The Railton was serviced with fuel and ice and the wheels were changed. John Dugdale, who was covering the attempt for *The Autocar*, noted that while the team worked a radio was turned on, and they heard the news that Germany and Russia had signed a non-aggression pact; Germany was moving troops to the Polish frontier

The Dodge push-truck waits as the team fit the Railton's body at Bonneville on 19 August 1939. Taylor supervises on the left, while Cobb is on the right. (Motor Sport)

and the British Cabinet had been recalled for an emergency meeting. The knowledge that Europe was now on the brink of war added to the tension, but also put the record attempt in a rather different light.

By now a crowd of about 3,000 had gathered. Cobb was push-started again, the gearchanges went as intended, and the car made a faultless run through the measured distance. As the Railton slowed down, approaching the replenishing depot, Art Pillsbury, the AAA timekeeper, announced the speed: 369.23mph (594.09kmh) for the mile and 365.57mph (588.20kmh) for the kilometre. If this speed could be matched on the return run, the record was Cobb's. The wheels were changed, the fuel topped up, and at 7.30am the car was push-started once more. It accelerated towards the measured course and then, to the dismay of the team, it slowed and came to a stop. An engine had spat back and stalled. The car was towed in, but too much time had elapsed, and it was not possible to make another run in the one hour allowed.

The carburettors were adjusted and the Railton came out again for another test run late that afternoon. This time it was started in top gear and ran through the measured mile at about 350mph (560kmh). Time was running out, the international situation was deteriorating rapidly, and the team's supply of tyres was also dwindling. Of the 48 brought from England, only 20 were left. The crew were also tiring; to add to their problems, 'Fiddle' Hicks had been recalled to England that morning as his wife was ill. Cobb arranged and paid for 'Fiddle' to fly back by the new Pan American Clipper flying boat service

The Railton was not taken back to Wendover, but was left out on the salt and at midnight preparations began to make it ready for another, and perhaps final, attempt. The dawn was cold and there was a strong cool breeze which dispersed a slight haze. The sun came up and the breeze dropped, but there were probably less than 300 spectators, as apart from a brief comment at 11.00pm on the local radio there had been no announcement that Cobb was to try again. The Railton was pushed away and began to run towards the measured course, shadowed by the Gilmore Lockheed Electra flying about 100ft (30m) above it. The car left the 'plane behind, and with a following plume of black smoke passed through the speed traps and began to slow down and coast towards the replenishing depot. The team removed the body, changed the wheels and refuelled the car in a routine that had become almost automatic. The time was telephoned through to the depot: Cobb had done 370.75mph (596.53kmh) for the mile and 367.92mph (591.98kmh) for the kilometre.

The Railton was stationary for only 25 minutes. Then it was push-started for the return southbound run. Again the Electra flew along the course and was passed by the Railton as if it stood still. Trailing its plume of black smoke, the car passed through the measured distance obviously flat out and with no hesitation. Art Pillsbury, with a sense of the dramatic, made no announce-

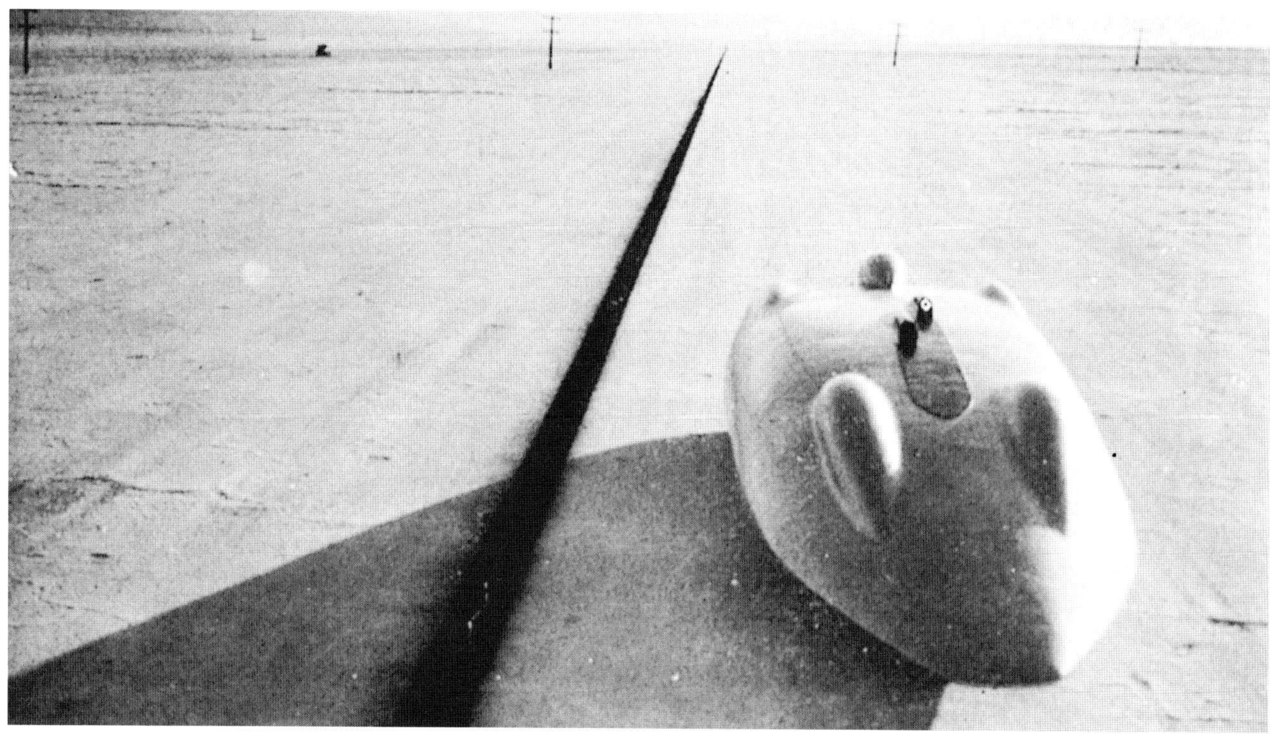

The Railton sets off into the early morning sun on 23 August 1939 to take the world record at 369.75mph (594.92kmh). (Guy Griffiths Collection)

ment of the speed. He waited while the Railton coasted up to the timing base and stopped, being pushed by the crew for the last few yards. Cobb was helped out of the cockpit and Pillsbury then announced the speed. It was 366.97mph (590.45kmh) for the mile and 371.59mph (597.88kmh) for the kilometre; the mean speeds were 368.85mph (593.47kmh) and 369.75mph (594.92kmh) for the mile and kilometre respectively. The world land speed record was Cobb's

The small crowd gathered round Cobb and showered him with congratulations. The team then returned to Salt Lake City, where a round of parties began. In the midst of these, Reggie Tongue disappeared and left a message that he was on his way back to England; as an officer in the RAF Volunteer Reserve he knew that it would only be a matter of days before he was mobilised. Despite the prospect of an imminent war, Cobb still had some unfinished business, so on Friday 25 August the team returned to Wendover. At 5.30am next morning, the Railton was ready and Cobb set off to take the world records for the five and ten miles and kilometres. Both runs went without any problems at all and were almost a canter after the high speeds of the previous Wednesday. The five and ten kilometres were taken at 326.66mph (525.59kmh) and 283.01mph (455.36kmh) respectively and the ten miles at 270.35mph (434.99kmh). The five mile did not fall as the timing gear had failed. In the light of the international situation it was perhaps ironic that these records had previously been held by Bernd Rosemeyer's Auto Union.

Once the records had been taken the team wasted no time in packing up. Ken Taylor and Cobb decided that there would be no time left to take the Railton to New York and load it onto a ship, so it was loaded onto a rail wagon and despatched to Canada. If war began they did not want the car to be in the United States, a neutral country where there might be a possibility of it being impounded. The team flew to New York, where there was a mildly diverting interlude as Cobb dodged process servers trying to serve a writ on him from a spurious publicity-seeking claimant. On Wednesday 30 August the team sailed from New York at 7.00pm on the *Aquitania*. On Friday 1 September the captain announced that Germany had invaded Poland and on the Sunday morning it was announced that Britain had declared war on Germany. Within a few hours of the outbreak of war, the liner *Athenia* was torpedoed by a German U-boat while outward bound from Liverpool to New York, so the passengers on the *Aquitania* knew that the latter part of their voyage could be hazardous. However, the liner docked safely at Southampton early in the morning on Wednesday 6 September. There was no welcome or recognition in any form for Cobb and his team. His records had almost been forgotten already, and now seemed almost trivial in the light of what had happened in the few short days since the triumphs in Utah.

Chapter 18: 1939–45

Savage Interlude

THE Railton was shipped back to England from Canada in the autumn of 1939, during that short period before all east-bound transatlantic shipping would only be permitted to carry fighting men and war materials. It was taken to Thomson & Taylor's workshops, where it was partly dismantled and, with a number of other competition cars in the care of the firm, including the Napier-Railton, was moved to a barn at Horsell, about five miles (8km) from Brooklands. As the home of two major aircraft factories, Brooklands was unlikely to be a safe place for storing racing cars in time of war, and every square foot of space was needed for wartime engineering purposes.

For the firm of D. Napier & Son Ltd and for those who had been concerned with racing and record-breaking in Napier and Napier-powered cars, much was to happen in the next six years. On 12 February 1940 Selwyn Edge died at Eastbourne. He was 71 years old. After his split with Napier, he had been bound by the condition that he would not work in the motor industry for seven years. During the 1914–18 War he had devoted himself to breeding and farming pigs at Ditchling in Sussex and was also engaged by the British Government to advise on the development of farming machinery. In October 1919 he returned to the motor industry, at first in the manufacture of the Cubitt, a light car built from proprietary components. The Cubitt did not succeed, however, and in 1921 Edge bought a controlling interest in AC. At first his forceful approach saw the firm flourish, but the slump in the motor industry in the mid-'20s took its toll of AC. Edge, too, seemed to have lost his old flair. The company was liquidated and reformed. It survived until 1929 and then went into voluntary liquidation. Edge lost almost all his assets in the AC failure and lived through the 1930s in increasing penury. When he died his estate was sworn for probate at only £480. His death went almost unnoticed in the motoring press and in the industry in which he had played such a great part.

D. Napier & Son Ltd had prospered again with the rearmament programmes initiated in the mid-1930s. The company had been manufacturing an air-cooled engine, the Dagger, but with the prospect of war a new design – the Sabre – was drawn up by Frank Halford, which would become the ultimate piston aero engine and probably the most powerful ever to be mass-produced. The old Lion was still being made in small numbers as a high speed marine engine; one of its users was the Italian Navy, which had no access to spares after June 1940 when Italy entered the War. By 1942 the company was fully stretched in trying to get the Sabre into production. Satellite factories had been opened at Luton, Liverpool, and Park Royal in West London. With this expansion the company now had a workforce of over 10,000, and the capital involved was beyond its resources. In November 1942, with full government approval, the Napier board recommended that the shareholders should accept an offer by the English Electric Company of one £1 English Electric share for every five 5s ordinary Napier shares. Thus Napier became a subsidiary of the English Electric Group and the old family company ceased to exist.

John Cobb was too old to join the RAF as he had hoped, but as a qualified pilot he joined the Air Transport Auxiliary, the organisation entrusted with ferrying aircraft from factories to service units. Cobb remained in the ATA throughout the War, mostly serving under the command of his former medical adviser, Neville Whitehurst. Tim Rose-Richards did not survive the War. He had joined the RAF and was killed in 1942 when his Supermarine Walrus was shot down in the English Channel while attempting to rescue an aircrew which had crashed in the sea. Thomas Barrington, who had remained with Rolls-Royce, died in the United States on 30 June 1943. He had been leading a technical mission to the Packard Corporation in Detroit to assist in the development of the Packard-Merlin aero engine.

Brooklands was another war casualty. The needs of Vickers and Hawkers for space to build aircraft resulted in great sections of the track being broken-up and partly built over. When the War ended in 1945 it was clear that cars would never race there again, and early in 1946 it was sold to Vickers and became an industrial site. Thomson & Taylor were still permitted to stay in their small workshop site beside the Byfleet Banking.

Chapter 19: 1947

Successful Finale and Sudden Tragedy

REID Railton had intended the Railton to be capable of 400mph (640kmh) and this knowledge had been niggling at John Cobb throughout the War. In 1946 he decided that he would make an attempt to improve on his 1939 record with the aim of achieving the goal of 400mph. Railton was now living in the United States but he looked over his designs and made some improvements which would make Cobb's task easier. The main problem had been the stalled engines and the impossibility of restarting them with the freewheel engaged. Railton designed a twin belt-drive from each propshaft which, through additional freewheels, turned the engines if they cut out. Thomson & Taylor began work on the car. New brake drums with additional stiffening were fitted. The ball and roller bearings in the gearbox were plated and reground to ensure a better fit. The engines were taken out of the car and checked over at Acton. There were no longer any facilities at Acton for bench testing so this was done by Thorneycroft, the marine and commercial vehicle engineers at Caversham, near Reading. A higher octane fuel was used and the supercharger boost was increased, so the engines now ran at a maximum of 4,000rpm, a figure which caused concern at Acton. The top gear ratio was raised. Dunlop reconditioned the original wheels and developed some new tyres which would withstand the stresses of speeds up to 420mph (670kmh).

Cobb's circumstances had changed considerably. The Labour Government elected in 1945 had a declared antipathy to the rich. Taxation of the highest incomes was at the rate of 95% and furs were regarded as the baubles of the rich and taxed accordingly. Not only was Cobb's income reduced, but taxation left him with little surplus for another record attempt. There were also difficulties in obtaining parts and material for the Railton, as all manufacturing industry was directed to produce only those goods which could be exported for hard foreign currency. During the War the Gilmore Oil Corporation had been taken over by the Socony-Vacuum Oil Corporation, which marketed its products under the name of Mobil. They agreed to sponsor a new record attempt at Bonnevile and provided substantial funds for the venture. In return, Cobb now called the car the Railton-Mobil Special, although he still drew heavily on his own resources.

By July 1947 the Railton was ready; it was crated and loaded by Adams of New Malden, and sent to the United States by freighter. In the changed world of 1947 even this had its problems. All the spare components had to be listed in triplicate and the lists submitted to the Customs before departure. An Export Licence had to be obtained from the Board of Trade for the 48 tyres which accompanied the Railton. Shortly afterwards Cobb and his team embarked on the *Queen Elizabeth* at Southampton. The Thomson & Taylor party comprised Ken Taylor, with Jimmy Rands and John Norris, while from Dunlop came 'Fiddle' Hicks and Syd Cooper.

The car was railed to Utah and the team flew from New York to Salt Lake City, where they were joined by Reid Railton. During the war years the USAAF had installed a large crane at Wendover, so unloading the Railton from its rail wagon was considerably easier. As soon as the car was uncrated testing began and the troubles of the team began too. The lake was in poor condition, with a bad surface pocked with deep holes. The holes had to be filled and the course rolled flat, but there were still bad patches on the approach to the measured distance. When the car made its first test run the engines ran roughly, with clouds of black smoke and an evident lack of power. On previous attempts problems of this kind had been the province of Joe Coe, but he was not there and now Ken Taylor had to seek the cause. At first the fuel was suspected, but tests showed that this was correct. However, the mixture was much too rich and the levels in the six carburettor float chambers all differed. Unfortunately Taylor had no means of ascertaining

Spring 1947: Now with the Mobil insignia, the Railton stands outside Thomson & Taylor's Brooklands workshops. (Geoffrey Goddard Collection)

the correct level. Fuel surge was then diagnosed, but fitting overflow drainage tubes to the float chambers did not help. At last the cause was ascertained as the warping of the cork floats where the protective varnish had dissolved. To cure this smaller jets were needed, but the team had none, so Taylor and the mechanics solved the problem by soldering up the jets and drilling them out. All this necessitated many test runs and the supply of tyres was dwindling fast.

The Railton is unloaded at Wendover, August 1947. (Guy Griffiths Collection)

At last the car began to show its proper performance, but then Cobb pulled up after an early morning test run and complained that there was a lack of power. There were signs of a small fire by one of the air intakes. The car was towed back to Wendover and further examination showed that a camshaft had seized in its bearing, locked the vertical shaft drive, and sprung the driving bevel out of position. In all the mileage that Lion engines had done in racing and record breaking this was the first time that there had been a mechanical failure. The cause was old age and probably inadequate preparation; the work at Acton had been done with makeshift facilities as the special Lion tools and jigs were no longer there, and to Thorneycrofts it was merely a testing job.

The team now had a real problem. There was no spare engine and there were suggestions that the whole attempt should be abandoned. Having come so far and already beaten so many difficulties Cobb was not to be deterred, and with Taylor's full support he decided to go on. There were urgent telephone calls and telegrams to Brooklands, seeking a new camshaft and drive. These were flown to the United States while the team waited. The new camshaft was fitted and the car was tested again. This time the lake itself was the problem. As the car was towed out and turned round for a run it began to sink into a patch of soft salt. A plank was slid under the car just before the undertray bottomed on the salt. The car was gradually raised by using jacks on the wheel rims until boards could be put under the front wheels. The same process was then applied at the rear. All this time there was a fear that the rims could be damaged, but the car was safely rolled onto planks and thence to hard salt.

The car was given an early morning test once more and this time returned with a leaking ice tank. When it had been filled with ice before the run a piece had been dropped behind the tank. During the run, the ice was thrown up by a drive shaft and punctured the tank. To repair the tank involved a major strip down so the car was towed back to Wendover and the team began a task which took 48 hours. The Railton was brought out again at dawn on Sunday 14 September. The timekeepers were advised that this was to be a full attempt for the first time. Cobb made a northbound run without any apparent problems and the speed came through: 375.32mph (603.88kmh). However, as the mechanics lifted the body off to replenish the car it became apparent that a second run was impossible as the bumpy course had caused the body to split. Once more the car was towed back to the garage in Wendover, where the body was welded.

The weather now took a hand as a gale force wind blew across the lake. The team waited for a day, and then took the car onto the lake again at dawn on Tuesday 16 September. The wind was still blowing stronger than was desirable, but Cobb must have felt that it was now or never. The course was bumpy and Cobb had a difficult drive on his first, northbound run, having to cope with a lot of wheelspin. As the car was replenished, the speed was telephoned through, 385.645mph (620.50kmh). The Railton had never gone so fast before, and all now depended on the return run. This time the speed was compensation for all the trials of the previous weeks. It was 403.135mph (648.64kmh), so the aim of 400mph (640kmh) had been achieved. The average of the runs, and the new land speed record, was 394.196mph (634.26kmh). Shortly after Cobb had climbed out of the car he was found sitting behind one of the depot tents weeping. The team had never seen the placid and imperturbable Cobb show any great emotion before, but the relief of success after the weeks of frustration had been too much for him.

Although the tyre supply was now low, the team still hoped to set the record at over 400mph and the speedograph showed that the Railton-Mobil had been accelerating all the way through the measured distance, so there was every hope of raising the record again now that the car was running properly. However, the following morning it was raining hard and continued to do so for several days. The lake was flooded, and the locals told Cobb that the salt would not be fit for more record attempts until the spring.

The team packed up and returned to England. Cobb received general praise and congratulations for his courage and his achievement, though in an austere and war-tired Britain the reception he received was muted compared with that given to Segrave and Campbell 20 years earlier. The RAC awarded Cobb the Segrave Trophy for the most meritorious achievement on land in 1947, but no other awards were given to him and there was no governmental recognition of what he had done, or for the prestige that he had gained for Britain or for British industry in the United States, the largest market for British products.

The Railton-Mobil did not go back to Utah, and only ran once more under its own power, when, two years later, John Cobb demonstrated it at the *Daily Express* International Trophy at Silverstone on 20 August 1949 and it rumbled slowly round the course to the rather muted admiration of the enormous crowd. Soon after that, Cobb, realising that he had no further use for the car, sold it to Dunlop, which still owned the tyres fitted to it and did not wish these to pass into the hands of commercial rivals. The car was put into the Museum of Science and Industry, Birmingham, where it still remains. The Railton never had the recognition it deserved as a landmark in design. When Cobb broke the record in 1938 the feat was overshadowed by 'Thunderbolt' the very next day;

Bonneville, 14 September 1947: Cobb waits while Reid Railton times the refuelling after the first run. John Norris jumps down and Ken Taylor looks at an engine. This time the record was raised to 394.196mph (634.26kmh). (Motor Sport)

in 1939 all interest evaporated with the outbreak of war; and in 1947, as a design already more than ten years old, it received scant attention.

John Cobb, like Segrave and Campbell before him, still had the desire to win more records. To hold the double of the land and water speed records was now his aim. During 1951 work started on a boat, the *Crusader*, with a De Haviland Ghost jet engine. The *Crusader* was finished in the summer of 1952 and was taken to Loch Ness. Cobb had to beat a record of 178.49mph (287.19kmh) set by an American, Stanley Sayers, in June 1952, but he was confident he could do it as his boat was designed to exceed 200mph (320kmh). On Monday 29 September, Cobb made his attempt. On its first run the *Crusader* covered the measured mile at 206.89mph (332.88kmh), but just after it cleared the end of the course it began to pitch badly. It hit some ripples made by the timekeepers' launch and broke up. Cobb was thrown from the cockpit, and when boats reached him, still floating in the water, he was dead.

Despite his death, Cobb still held the land speed record. With the ever-increasing speed of technical advances in the 1950s it seemed likely that his record would soon fall, but no-one seemed anxious to make the attempt. It was evident that the problems of exceeding 400mph (640kmh) were considerable, and as time went by the magnitude of Cobb's achievement became clear. In 1960 there were several challenges at Bonneville. Athol Graham, a resident of Salt Lake City, used a car with an Allison aero engine and was killed when the car overturned at 300mph (480kmh). Another American, Mickey Thompson, managed a run of 406.60mph (654.21kmh) in his 'Challenger', which used four Pontiac car engines, but the transmission broke up on his return run. Donald Campbell, the son of Malcolm Campbell, had built a new 'Bluebird' which looked, superficially, like the Railton-Mobil, but used a Bristol-Siddeley Proteus gas-turbine. Campbell made his attempt in August 1960 at Bonneville and the car overturned at 300mph (480kmh). Campbell escaped, determined to try again.

During the next three years there were several attempts which ended in spectacular crashes but without loss of life. Then, in 1963, Craig Breedlove appeared at Bonneville with a three-wheeled machine which looked like a jet fighter without wings. The 'Spirit of America' was powered by a General Electric J47 jet unit and with this vehicle Breedlove did two runs on 5 August. The first was at 388.47mph (625.04kmh), but on the return his speed was 428.37mph (689.24kmh), which gave him a world record at 407.45mph (655.26kmh). Cobb's record had been broken, but by a machine that was recognised as a motor cycle, not a motor car. Donald Campbell then took the rebuilt Bluebird-Proteus to Australia and on 16 July 1964, at Lake Eyre, did 403.10mph (648.58kmh) on both runs to break Cobb's record with a car.

With this the name of Napier finally disappeared from international motor racing and record breaking. The heroic efforts of Selwyn Edge and his fellow drivers had made Napier a power to be reckoned with in international motor racing. The Lion engine was the driving force which broke the land speed record eight times and in one car had held the record continuously for 23 years – surely the greatest engine ever to break records on land, and establishing a record of its own which is never likely to be rivalled. The Napier racing and record-breaking story is one of courage and great endeavour and above all of outstanding engineering integrity and workmanship, in which all those concerned could have the utmost pride. The prestige which Napier secured for Britain over nearly 60 years must never be forgotten.

Appendix 1

Outline Specifications of Napier Cars

ALL models were water-cooled. Cars made before 1914 were fitted with Napier carburettors. Those made after 1914 were fitted with Napier-SU carburettors.

Type	**G20**	**H70**	**Gordon-Bennett**
Makers' hp	8	16	50
Years	1900	1900–3	1901
Cylinders	2	4	4
Bore	4in (101.6mm)	4in (101.6mm)	6½in (165.1mm)
Stroke	6in (152.4mm)	6in (152.4mm)	7½in (190.5mm)
Capacity	2,471cc	4,942cc	16,315cc
Valves	Auto OH inlet Side exhaust	Auto OH inlet Side exhaust	Auto OH inlet Side exhaust
Wheelbase	7ft 3¾in (215cm)	7ft 8in (234cm)	8ft 9in (267cm)
Track	4ft 1½in (126cm)	4ft 1½in (126cm)	4ft 9in (145cm)
Front suspension	½ elliptic	½ elliptic	½ elliptic
Rear suspension	Full elliptic	Full elliptic	½ elliptic
Weight	2,520lb (1,145kg)	Unknown	3,960lb (1,800kg)
Tyre size	Unknown	Unknown	Unknown
Final drive	Chain	Chain	Chain
Number made	5+	5	2

Type	**D45/H8**	**L49**	**D50**
Makers' hp	12	18	20
Years	1902–4	1903–7	1902
Cylinders	4	6	4
Bore	3½in (88.9mm)	4in (101.6mm)	5in (127mm)
Stroke	4in (101.6mm)	4in (101.6mm)	5in (127mm)
Capacity	2,523cc	5,161cc	6,436cc
Valves	Auto OH inlet (later mechanical) Side exhaust	Side	Auto OH inlet Side exhaust
Wheelbase	7ft 7½in (232cm)	8ft 7½in (262cm)	7ft 8in (234cm)
Track	4ft 2in (127cm)	4ft 2in (127cm)	4ft 8½in (143.5cm)
Front suspension	½ elliptic	½ elliptic	½ elliptic
Rear suspension	½ elliptic	½ elliptic	½ elliptic
Weight	2,128lb (967kg) (chassis)	Unknown	2052lb (933kg)
Tyre size	870 x 90	870 x 90	920 x 120
Final drive	Chain	Chain	Bevel
Number made	182	67	2

Type	**L49B/T20A**	**D & L**	**D50/H70**
Makers' hp	30	45	45
Years	1904–8	1904–7	1904–6
Cylinders	6	4	4
Bore	4in (101.6mm)	5in (D) (127mm) 4in (L) (101.6mm)	5in (127mm)
Stroke	4in (101.6mm)	4in (101.6mm)	4in (101.6mm)
Capacity	5,161cc	5,149cc (D) 3441cc (L)	5,149cc
Valves	Side	Side	Auto OH inlet Side exhaust
Wheelbase	Unknown	9ft 1in (277cm)	9ft 10in (299 cm)
Track	Unknown	4ft 6in (137cm)	4ft 10½in (148cm)
Front suspension	½ elliptic	½ elliptic	½ elliptic
Rear suspension	½ elliptic	½ elliptic	½ elliptic
Weight	1,904lb (865kg) (chassis)	Unknown	2,464lb (1,120kg)
Tyre size	Unknown	Unknown	920 x 120
Final drive	Chain (L49) Bevel (T20a)	Bevel	Chain
Number made	67 (L49) 82 (T20a)	8 (D) 12 (L)	5

Type	**L76/T20**	**E61***	**T21**
Makers' hp	40	50	60
Years	1905–10	1903	1905–10
Cylinders	6	4	6
Bore	4in (101.6mm)	5½in (139.7mm)	5in (127mm)
Stroke	4in (101.6mm)	5in (127mm)	4in (101.6mm)
Capacity	5,161cc	7,708cc	7,723cc
Valves	Side	Auto OH inlet Side exhaust	Side
Wheelbase	11ft 4in (345cm)	8ft 6in (259cm)	10ft 9in (328cm) 11ft 2in (340cm)
Track	4ft 8in (142cm)	4ft 6in (137cm)	4ft 8in (142cm)
Front suspension	½ elliptic	½ elliptic	½ elliptic
Rear suspension	½ elliptic	½ elliptic	Cantilever
Weight	2,576lb (1,170kg) (chassis)	2,178lb (990kg)	2,912lb (1,323 kg) (chassis)
Tyre size	880 x 120	880 x 120	895 x 135
Final drive	Chain (L76) Bevel (T20)	Bevel	Bevel
Number made	99 (L76) 190 (T20)	10 (production) 3 (GB team)	103

*Although called here a type, E61 was the order number. No type number was allocated to this model.

Type	**T23**	**T24**	**R232(Grand Prix)***
Makers' hp	45	65	80
Years	1908–12	1908–12	1908
Cylinders	6	6	6
Bore	4in (101.6mm)	5in (127mm)	4$^{31}/_{32}$in (126.2mm)
Stroke	5in (127mm)	5in (127mm)	6in (152.4mm)
Capacity	6,178cc	9,654cc	11,590cc
Valves	Side	Side	OH inlet Side exhaust
Wheelbase	11ft 2in (341cm)	11ft 2in (142cm)	9ft 8in (294cm)
Track	4ft 8in (142cm)	4ft 8in (142cm)	4ft 8in (142cm)
Front suspension	$^1/_2$ elliptic	$^1/_2$ elliptic	$^1/_2$ elliptic
Rear suspension	Cantilever	Cantilever	Double cantilever
Weight	Unknown	Unknown	2,660lb (1,209 kg)
Tyre size	880 x 120	895 x 135	880 x 120
Final drive	Bevel	Bevel	Bevel
Number made	203	79	3 (4?)

*R232 was the order number. No type number was given to this model.

Type	**T48**	**T27 (Hutton)**	**T29**
Makers' hp	90	26	10
Years	1908–10	1908	1908–10
Cylinders	6	4	2
Bore	6$^1/_8$in (155.5mm)	4in (101.6mm)	3$^1/_4$in (82.5mm)
Stroke	5in (127mm)	7in (177.8mm) 8in (203.2mm)	5in (127mm)
Capacity	14,485cc	5,756cc/6,590cc	1,358cc
Valves	OH inlet Side exhaust	Side	Side
Wheelbase	11ft 11in (363cm)	9ft 6in (289cm)	8ft 0in (244cm)
Track	4ft 8in (142cm)	5ft 2in (155cm) front 4ft 8in (142cm) rear	4ft 6in (137cm)
Front suspension	$^1/_2$ elliptic	$^1/_2$ elliptic	$^1/_2$ elliptic
Rear suspension	$^1/_2$ elliptic	$^1/_2$ elliptic	$^1/_2$ elliptic
Weight	3,136lb (1,425kg) (chassis)	2,800lb (1,272kg)	1,568lb (712kg)
Tyre size	935 x 135	870 x 90 front 875 x 105 rear	810 x 90
Final drive	Bevel	Bevel	Bevel
Number made	25	3 Huttons 7 sold as Napiers	100

Type	**T26/36**	**T28***	**T51**
Makers' hp	30	15	45
Years	1908–12	1909–14	1912–14
Cylinders	6	4	6
Bore	3$^1/_4$in (82.5mm)	3$^1/_4$in (82.5mm)	4in (101.6mm)
Stroke	5in (127mm)	5in (127mm)	5in (127mm)
Capacity	4,074cc	2,716cc	6,178cc
Valves	Side	Side	Side
Wheelbase	10ft 0in (305cm) 10ft 4in (315cm)	8ft 10in (269cm) 9ft 10in (300cm)	11ft 2in (340cm) 11ft 6$^1/_2$in (352cm)
Track	4ft 8in (142cm) 4ft 11in (150cm)	4ft 8$^1/_2$in (143.5cm)	4ft 8in (142cm)
Front suspension	$^1/_2$ elliptic	$^1/_2$ elliptic	$^1/_2$ elliptic
Rear suspension	$^1/_2$ elliptic	$^1/_2$ elliptic	$^1/_2$ elliptic
Weight	2,408lb (1,094kg)	2,016lb (916kg) (chassis)	2,688lb (1,221kg) (chassis)
Tyre size	880 x 120	815 x 105	895 x 135
Final drive	Bevel	Bevel/Worm	Bevel
Number made	201 (T26) 49 (T36)	3,274	40

*The 15hp was the Napier model produced in the largest numbers. Between 1909 and 1914, the specification remained much the same. It appeared first as the T28, but it subsequently had the following type numbers: T31, T38, T39, T40, T41, T42, T43, T45, T46, T47, T53, T54, and T55.

Type	**T44**	**T57***	**T67a/T71a**
Makers' hp	30/35	16/22	30/35
Years	1913–14	1914–16	1914–16
Cylinders	6	4	6
Bore	3$^1/_2$in (88.9mm)	3$^1/_2$in (88.9mm)	3$^1/_2$in (88.9mm)
Stroke	5in (127mm)	5in (127mm)	5in (127mm)
Capacity	4,730cc	3,153cc	4,730cc
Valves	Side	Side	Side
Wheelbase	10ft 4in (314cm)	10ft 4in (314cm) 10ft 10in (330cm)	10ft 8in (325cm) 11ft 8in (355cm)
Track	4ft 8in (142cm)	4ft 8in (142cm)	4ft 8in (142cm)
Front suspension	$^1/_2$ elliptic	$^1/_2$ elliptic	$^1/_2$ elliptic
Rear suspension	$^1/_2$ elliptic	$^1/_2$ elliptic	$^1/_2$ elliptic
Weight	4,186lb (1,902kg)	Unknown	Unknown
Tyre size	895 x 105	820 x 120	895 x 135
Final drive	Bevel	Worm	Worm
Number made	150	959	92

*The 16/22hp Napier had several type numbers. These were T57, T64, T66, T68, T69a, T70, and T70a.

Type	**T69b**	**T75/T77/T79/T80**
Makers' hp	16/22	40/50
Years	1919	1919–24
Cylinders	4	6
Bore	3$^1/_2$in (88.9mm)	4in (101.6mm)
Stroke	5in (127mm)	5in (127mm)
Capacity	3,153cc	6,177cc
Valves	Side	OH camshaft
Wheelbase	10ft 4in (314cm)	11ft 5in (348cm) 12ft 0in (365cm) (T79)
Track	4ft 8in (142cm)	4ft 8in (142cm)
Front suspension	$^1/_2$ elliptic	$^1/_2$ elliptic
Rear suspension	$^1/_2$ elliptic	Cantilever
Weight	Unknown	2,800lb (1,272kg) (chassis)
Tyre size	820 x 120	895 x 135
Final drive	Worm	Bevel
Number made	12	119 (T75) 17 (T77) 45 (T79) 5 (T80)

Type	**L1**	**K5**
Makers' hp	20	70
Years	1903	1903–5
Cylinders	4	4
Bore	5in (127mm)	6$^1/_2$in (165.1mm)
Stroke	5in (127mm)	6in (152.4mm)
Capacity	6,436cc	13,726cc
Valves	Auto OH inlet Side exhaust	Auto OH inlet (later mechanical) Side exhaust
Wheelbase	8ft 6in (259cm)	9ft 0in (274cm) 8ft 10in (269cm)
Track	4ft 6in (137cm)	4ft 8in (142cm)
Front suspension	$^1/_2$ elliptic	$^1/_2$ elliptic
Rear suspension	$^1/_2$ elliptic	$^1/_2$ elliptic
Weight	2,178lb (990kg)	2,171lb (987 kg)
Tyre size	880 x 120	34 x 3$^1/_2$ (1903) 810 x 90 front, 820 x 120 rear (1904) 870 x 90 front, 850 x 120 rear (1905)
Final drive	Bevel	Bevel
Number made	2	3

Appendix 2

Napier Lion Series XIA Specification

THIS specification is copied from the 1929 catalogue of D. Napier & Son Ltd. Some material has been added, and this is bracketed [ ]. The Series XIA is typical of the Lion specifications and was used by John Cobb in the Napier-Railton between 1933 and 1937. (When fitted to the Napier-Railton the engine was turned round, so where this description refers to the rear of the engine, this would have been at the front of the car, and vice versa.)

Number of cylinders: Twelve.
Arrangement: Three blocks of four each, one vertical, two at 60°.
Bore: 5 1/2in [139.7mm].
Stroke: 5 1/8in [130.175mm].
[*Capacity*: 23,970cc.]
Horse power rated: Compression ratio 6.0:1, 530bhp at 2,350rpm.
Horse power at maximum speed: 570bhp at 2,585rpm.
Direction of rotation of airscrew shaft: Clockwise viewed from airscrew end.
Speed of ditto: Reduction ratio of 1:1.885 of crankshaft. [The reduction gears were removed on the Napier-Railton.]
Ignition: Two [BTH] magnetos giving dual ignition. Anti-clockwise rotation.
Starter: Napier petrol priming system and hand turning gear. [The priming system was retained but the hand turning gear was removed on the Napier-Railton].
Weight of engine: Complete with airscrew boss, reduction gear, and hand starter, 995lb [452.3kg].
Weight per hp: On rated power 1.879lb [0.854kg]. On average power at maximum speed 1.745lb [0.793kg].
Length overall to centre of airscrew: 5ft 1in approximately [154.9cm].
Width overall: 3ft 6in approximately [106.6cm].
Height overall: 3ft 3in approximately [99.0cm].
Oil consumption: The oil consumption taken on the Air Ministry 2 hour endurance test must lie between 6 pints [3.4 litres] and 12 pints [6.8 litres] per hour. This consumption may also be stated as a maximum of .030lb [.0135kg] per bhp hour on the Air Ministry endurance test. Average oil consumption .0235lb [.0106kg] bhp hour.
Fuel consumption: Will not exceed .55 pint [0.312 litres] per bhp hour at full load and normal speed. This consumption is equal to .53lb [0.24kg] per bhp hour with fuel of

The reduced height VIID Lion developed for the Schneider Trophy. (Napier Power Heritage Trust)

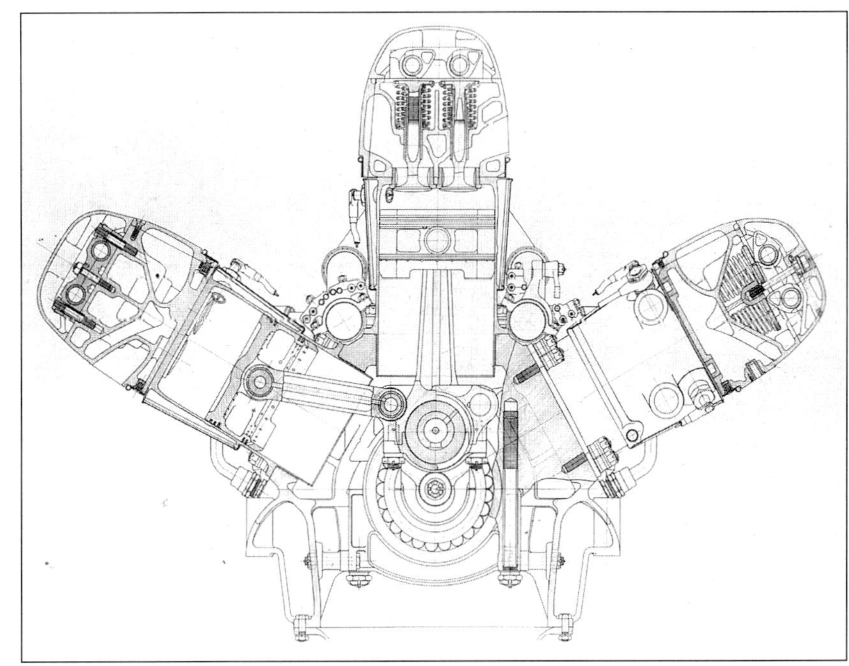

The rear of the VIID Lion, showing the supercharger. (Napier Power Heritage Trust)

specific gravity of .775. Average fuel consumption at full load as above is .50lb [0.227kg] per bhp hour.

Cylinders: Steel forgings machined all over. Water jackets of steel. Detachable aluminium cylinder head containing inlet and exhaust passages, valves and valve actuating mechanism. [Each cylinder head was placed on its bank of four cylinders and attached by screwing into it the valve seats from within the cylinders. The spigoted barrels were flange-bolted to the crankcase. An adaptor was screwed between the head and barrel for each spark plug. The water jacket was made in two parts and welded to the cylinder barrel.]

Pistons: Of aluminium alloy, fitted with two gas and two scraper rings and hollow [floating] gudgeon pins of large diameter [with bronze end-pads].

Valves: Two inlet and two exhaust valves per cylinder, each fitted with two coil springs and operated direct by overhead camshafts [two per bank of cylinders] driven through bevel gears by vertical shafts from the crankshaft. [One camshaft was driven by the bevel gears and through an extension drove its companion through equal pinions]. The whole of the valve mechanism enclosed within a detachable aluminium case. [A vernier adjustable tappet head was screwed into each hollow valve stem and locked by a spring clip.]

Connecting rods: [H-section] Machined from special high grade steel. The master rod, coupled to the pistons of the vertical block of cylinders, is formed with [two] lugs on either side, to which are attached the short auxiliary rods for the pistons of the right and left groups of cylinders. [Dowelled and tapered wrist pins are carried in the two lugs, each pin being tightened by a plug bolt screwed into its tapered end.] The [four stud] big ends are white metal lined, anchor pins and other parts work in [bronze] bushes of ample size.

Crankshaft: Machined from a solid

The front of an un-supercharged VIIA Lion. (Napier Power Heritage Trust)

steel forging. The four throws are in one plane and all journal bearings and crank pins are of large diameter and bored out. The shaft is carried in five substantial roller bearings and a large plain bearing at the forward end.

Crankcase and oil sump: Of aluminium suitably stiffened at all necessary points and having arms at either side for attachment to the aircraft. The crankcase front end encloses the reduction gear for the airscrew shaft together with the shaft and bearings. The rear end cover contains the two scavenge oil pumps, the pressure oil pump and the drive for the camshafts, magnetos, water and oil pumps. [A dog-coupling extension shaft from the rear of the crankshaft carries two bevels back to back. The forward bevel drives the drive-shafts to the camshafts. A vertical down-shaft from the forward bevel drives the water pump direct and the three oil pumps through worm gears. The rear bevel drives transverse horizontal shafts for the magnetos.]

Water pump: Centrifugal type, mounted to rear end of engine and running at crankshaft speed. The spindle is fitted with a gland and a screw-down greaser. Water is delivered through a separate outlet to each of the three cylinder blocks.

Oil pumps: Two suction and one pressure [gear] type pump driven at half engine speed through gears. The suction pump connected to the sump and the pressure pump taking oil from the supply tank through a suitable filter.

Magnetos and ignition: Two special twelve cylinder magnetos, rotating anti-clockwise, mounted on platforms at the rear end of engine. Special distributors fitted to facilitate starting by hand. Metal braided ignition cables carried in aluminium supports. Advance and retard links inter-connected with the throttle control.

Carburettors: A triple carburettor, Napier-Claudel system is fitted. The carburettor is water-jacketed and the body, which is of aluminium, is carried on a bracket on the rear end cover. The gas inlet pipes to the induction on the cylinder heads are of steel and are water-jacketed.

Lubrication: By pressure throughout to big ends, gudgeon pins, bearings of camshaft and forward bearings of crankshaft. The reduction gears are lubricated by oil ejected on to the teeth from a pipe connected to the crankshaft lubrication system. [Piston and cylinder walls splash lubricated.] Valve tappets and cams are lubricated by the oil escaping from the camshaft bearings, which drains into the sump and is delivered thence to the supply tank by suction pumps. An adjustable pressure release valve is incorporated in the system.

Bibliography

Bentley, W.O., *W.O. The Autobiography* (Hutchinson, 1958).

Bird, Anthony, and Hallows, Ian, *The Rolls-Royce Motor Car* (Batsford, 1964).

Boddy, William, *The Story of Brooklands* (Grenville, 1950).

—, *The World's Land Speed Record* (Motor Racing Publications, 1951).

—, *Montlhéry* (Cassell, 1961).

—, *Aero-Engined Racing Cars at Brooklands* (Haynes, 1992).

British Racing Drivers' Club, *Silver Jubilee Book* (1952).

Campbell, Sir Malcolm, *My Thirty Years of Speed* (Hutchinson, 1935).

Davis, S.C.H., *The John Cobb Story* (G.T. Foulis & Co, 1953).

Dugdale, John, *Great Motor Sport of the Thirties* (Two Continents/ Wilton House Gentry, 1977).

Duncan, H.O., *The World on Wheels* (Author, 1926).

Edge, S.F., *My Motoring Reminiscences* (G.T. Foulis & Co, 1933).

Frostick, Michael, *Bentley: Cricklewood to Crewe* (Osprey, 1980).

Graham White, Montague, *At the Wheel Ashore and Afloat* (G.T. Foulis & Co, 1935).

Hassan, Walter, *Climax in Coventry* (Motor Racing Publications, 1975).

Jarrott, Charles, *Ten Years of Motors and Motor Racing* (Radclyffe & Hutchings, 1906).

Lumsden, Alec, *British Piston Aero-engines and their Aircraft* (Airlife, 1994).

Lynch, Brendan, *Green Dust* (Portobello, 1988).

Montagu of Beaulieu, Lord, *The Gordon Bennett Races* (Cassell, 1963).

Morton, C.W., *A History of Rolls-Royce Motor Cars* (G.T. Foulis & Co, 1964).

Nicholson, T.R., *Sprint* (David & Charles, 1969).

Posthumus, Cyril, and Tremayne, David, *Land Speed Record* (Osprey, 1985).

Rose, Gerald, *A Record of Motor Racing 1894–1908* (RAC, 1909).

Villa, Leo, *The Record Breakers* (Hamlyn, 1969).

Wilson, C.H., and Reader, W.J., *Men and Machines* (Weidenfeld & Nicholson, 1958).

Newspapers and Periodicals

The Aeroplane

Allgemeine Automobil-Zeitung

The Autocar

The Automobile

Automotor Journal

Brooklands Society Gazette

Car Illustrated

Car Magazine

Classic & Sports Car

Flight

Journal of the Institution of Automobile Engineers

La Vie Automobile

The Motor

The Motor-Car Journal

Motor Sport

Old Motor

Omnia

Shell Aviation News

Speed

The Times

Veteran and Vintage

Veteran Car (Veteran Car Club)

The Vintage Sports Car Club Bulletin

Index